The

MAP
CATALOG

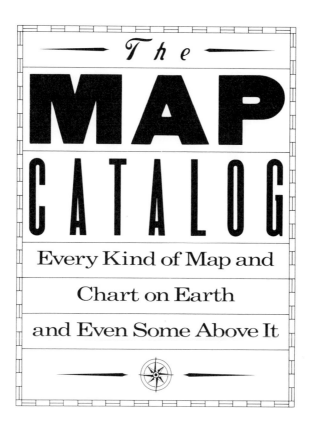

The MAP CATALOG

Every Kind of Map and Chart on Earth and Even Some Above It

Joel Makower, Editor
Laura Bergheim, Associate Editor

A Tilden Press Book

VINTAGE BOOKS

A Division of Random House   New York

A Vintage Original,
  3456789

LIBRARY OF CONGRESS CATALOGING-IN-PUBLICATION DATA

The Map catalog

  "A Vintage original" — T.p. verso.
  Includes index.
1. Maps — Catalogs. I. Makower, Joel, 1952-
II. Bergheim, Laura, 1962- .
Z6028.M23   1986   [GA105.3]   912'.029'4   86-40143
ISBN 0-394-74614-7

Manufactured in the United States of America

Book design by Tyler Feather
Typography by Chronicle Type & Design, Washington, D.C.

About This Book

A book containing a list of every map published, or even every map presently available, should such a book be possible to compile, would be of little use to most people. In this book, we have attempted to provide information about the many types of maps available, the major sources of each map type, and descriptions or examples of the map products available from each source.

Much like a map itself, *The Map Catalog* is a reference tool, a portrait of the cartographic landscape. Like a map, it shows you possible destinations, but not always the exact directions by which to reach them. Ultimately, it is up to the reader to determine how the tool may best be used. Like a map, this book may be browsed and enjoyed for the pure pursuit of knowledge; or it may serve as a source for acquiring specific maps for specific needs.

We have divided the maps and charts in this book into "Land Maps," "Sky Maps," "Water Maps," and "Map Products," with each section itself divided into several subsections. The delineations are, admittedly, arbitrary at times. A map of U.S. forests could reasonably be listed under "Ag-ricultural Maps," "Energy Maps," "Land Use Maps," "Natural Resource Maps," "Recreation Maps," "Tourism Maps," "U.S. Maps," or "Wildlife Maps"; we have chosen to list them under "Park and Forest Maps." To minimize confusion, there are cross-references within each subsection and a thorough index at the end of the book.

Most addresses of map sources appear within each section. Addresses of most map-producing government agencies, however, are listed in the book's appendixes, to avoid repeating the same addresses many times throughout the book. The appendixes, moreover, contain addresses of map sources not necessarily referred to in the text—of selected map stores, for example, and major map libraries.

We hope you find enjoyment and enlighten-ment in the pages that follow. We also welcome your comments and contributions, which we hope to incorporate in future updated editions of *The Map Catalog*. You may send them to The Map Catalog, c/o Tilden Press Inc., 1001 Connecticut Avenue NW, Suite 310, Washington, DC 20036.

Contents

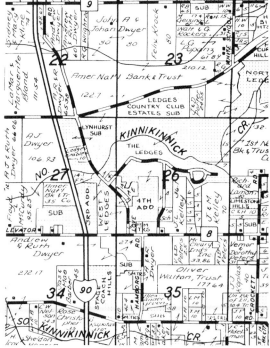

Introduction

Land Maps

Sky Maps

Water Maps

Appendix

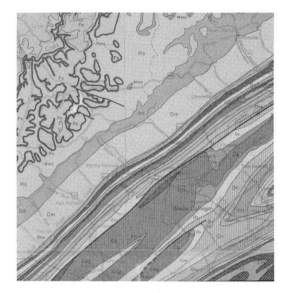

Map Products

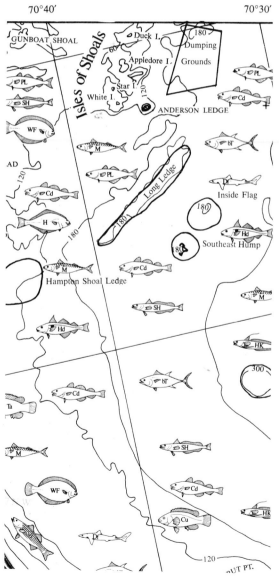

Acknowledgments

The editors would like to thank the following individuals and organizations who provided support—informational, editorial, technical, or moral—to this project:

Ruth Freytag and others at the Library of Congress, particularly the staff of the Geography and Map Division.

Robert Richardson and his staff at the National Archives Cartographic and Architectural Branch.

The public information officers, media liasons, and other helpful people at countless federal and state government agencies and map publishers, particularly the staff of the U.S. Geological Survey's National Cartographic Information Center in Reston, Va.

The staff of The Map Store, in Washington, D.C., for providing ongoing counsel; and Barbara Jackson, manager of The Map Center, in Berkeley, Calif., for providing resource material for the "Map Aids" section of this book.

Leonard Dinder and the North American Cartographic Information Society.

A variety of individuals provided editorial, photographic, and administrative assistance, including Marilyn P. Fenichel, Anita Jenkins, Nora Kengle, Joan Marcus, John May, and Melanie Wells.

Steve Smith and the staff of Chronicle Type & Design, especially Richard Muringer.

Derek Johns, Rebecca Saletan, Roseann Ward Dawson, and others at Vintage Books.

The Bergheim family, Beth and David Stephens, and Jim Medwid, for their support, guidance, handwringing, and understanding.

INTRODUCTION

State of the Art

We have become a world awash in maps.

For more than five centuries, we have measured and documented virtually every square foot of our planet, not to mention the oceans and the heavens. And we have recorded our findings with astounding accuracy in graphic representations—in black and white and in glorious color—called "maps." We have maps of everything from airports to zip codes, from highways to hurricanes to hidden treasures.

Maps are so much a part of our everyday lives that we may think of them as being more real than the "real world" itself. Consider Huck Finn and Tom Sawyer, soaring high above the Mid-west in a balloon in Mark Twain's *Tom Sawyer Abroad*. Estimating their present location, Huck claims they're still over Illinois; Tom thinks they've floated into Indiana. "I know by the color," says Huck. "And you can see for yourself that Indiana ain't in sight."

"What's color got to do with it?" asks Tom.

"It's got everything to do with it," explains Huck. "Illinois is green, Indiana is pink. You show me any pink down here, if you can."

"Indiana *pink*? Why, what a lie!"

"It ain't no lie; I've seen it on the map, and it's pink."

This is a sentiment that's been expressed by others even more worldly than Messrs. Sawyer and Finn. Astronaut John Glenn, approaching splashdown near the end of his historic 1962 Mercury space flight, informed Mission Control, "I can see the whole state of Florida, just laid out like on a map."

Maps have become a way of life.

How many maps are there? No one knows for sure, but some data from the federal government, the world's most skilled and prolific cartographer, are revealing. According to Uncle Sam, there are some 39 federal agencies involved in map making. Together, they have produced nearly a quarter-million separate maps. In a typical year, the twelve largest map-making agencies alone distribute more than 161 million copies of their maps at a cost of just over a half-billion dollars. All 39 agencies expend about 13,000 worker-years of effort annually carrying out their map-making responsibilities. That's just the tip of the cartographic iceberg. Each year, Rand McNally, the world's largest nongovernment map-maker, sells about 400 million maps, through its 2,500 or so sheet maps, atlases, and globes. The 26-million-member American Automobile Association distributes about 35 million sheet maps a year, along with another 215 million "Trip Tiks." There are road maps galore from oil companies, state and local tourism offices, foreign embassies, and other sources. And there are countless other map makers around the world, producing anywhere from a handful to several hundred different maps each year for general or highly specific audiences. Some of these maps end up in collections. While literally hundreds of private and public libraries have map collections, the seventy largest collections contain nearly twenty million maps and about 22 million aerial photographs.

It's safe to say that the output of maps, globes, atlases, and related products is well over a half-billion copies a year in this country alone.

There's good reason for this veritable map mania. In our information society, maps play an important role. A mere three-foot-square map can contain thousands of pieces of information on an endless number of topics, making maps highly efficient information storage devices. But it is more than just data for which we turn to maps. For some, maps make fascinating reading. It's not unreasonable to curl up with a good map to try to put things into perspective, to determine where you are, where you're going (or would like to go), or where you've been. For many, maps are works of art, worthy of display on a wall, perhaps even framed. Indeed, some antique maps truly *are* works of art, with price tags to match, ascending into the thousands of dollars.

The pages that follow reveal the vast and varied world of maps, atlases, and globes—who makes them, how they're compiled, how they're used, and where they can be found. All told, this information represents something more than a mere celebration of maps. Understanding the nature of, say, a topographic map, can provide insight into our planet's structure and beauty. Even a colorless census map can speak volumes about the myriad forces that shape society. From the earliest sketches to the latest in digital imaging, maps tell the story of our world and our lives in ways words can't even begin to describe.

Anybody need a map?

The Map Unfolds

The history of the map dates back to man's first realization that a picture truly is worth a thousand words. Archaeologists and other social scientists have often marveled at early man's almost instinctive ability to produce rough but amazingly accurate sketches of his surroundings. Throughout the world's civilizations—from African tribesmen to Arctic Eskimos—there are examples of these early maps, drawn in the earth or on stones or animal skins, showing the relative positions and distances of landmarks and localities. The Babylonians, more than two thousand years before Christ, surveyed individual land holdings on clay tablets. Known as cadastral maps, they represent one of the earliest forms of graphic expression. Those ancient surveys later became the basis for map making in Europe during the Middle Ages and, four millennia later, for land plats produced by the U.S. government.

The modern-day craft of making maps can be traced to western Europe in the 13th century. The regional and local maps of the day represented radical changes from the drawings that preceded them: rather than being derived from literary sources and mythology, they were based on observation and measurements, the first maps intended for practical use by travelers on land or sea. The second half of the thirteenth century produced the earliest surviving nautical charts and post-Roman road maps.

It was in the waters of the Mediterranean and the Black Sea that map making made great strides. The development of the mariner's compass permitted angular measurement, enabling a level of accuracy in nautical charts that wouldn't be seen in land maps for several hundred years. Among those first efforts were the Italian portolan charts, which were sets of sailing instructions created on parchment around 1250 by a community of Italian draftsmen just becoming familiar with mathematics and measurement. Many of the early European cartographers were recruited from the ranks of painters, miniaturists, and other artists, whose introduction to the profession consisted largely of copying and decorating existing maps. Later, they were able to compile their own. Italy,

and especially Florence, was a center of cartographic activity for several centuries. Here, a succession of explorers, artists, and mathematicians created new pictures that expressed an expanding world view.

The era of Christopher Columbus was another time of great map-making advances. The year 1492, in fact, saw creation of the first modern terrestial globe, the work of Germans Martin Behaim, a cosmographer, and Georg Holzschuher, a miniaturist. The 20-inch-wide globe showed the Equator, the two tropics, and the Arctic and Antarctic circles; the Equator was divided into 360 degrees. Another key innovation was the copperplate, which proved a far more effective medium for map reproduction than the woodcut and helped launch a booming map trade throughout Europe. By the early 1600s, the governments of Spain, Portugal, and England were among those recognizing the importance of maps, using them for property assessment, taxation, military planning, and to inventory national resources.

Mapping underwent radical changes in seventeenth-century France, due largely to an unquenchable thirst for maps and nautical charts. Such innovations as the telescope, the pendulum clock, and logarithm tables permitted accurate astronomical observations and the measurement of arcs on the earth's surface. Both contributed to major advances in cartography. New standards of precision, in turn, led to other advancements, such as the creation of the bubble level, the aneroid barometer, and the theodolite, all of which resulted in great leaps forward in plotting topographic measurements and absolute altitudes. The eighteenth century brought advancements in printing, not the least of which was the introduction of chromolithography—the ability to print several colors at once—which enabled map makers to enhance their works with color detail. All of these things aided the creation of such early cartographic masterpieces as Jacques Cassini's remarkable *Description geometrique de la France*. Published in 1783, this volume consisted of 182 engraved maps showing an entire nation in unprecedented detail—everything from canyons to

Turnabout Is Fair Play

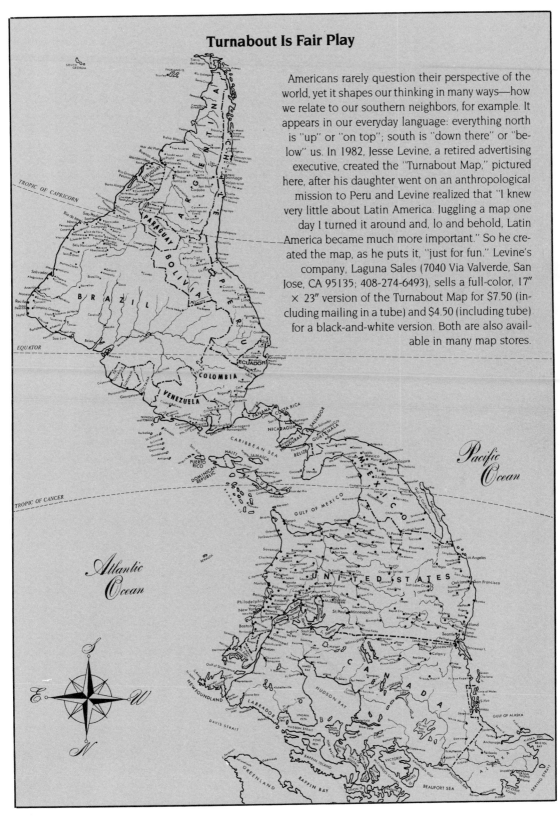

Americans rarely question their perspective of the world, yet it shapes our thinking in many ways—how we relate to our southern neighbors, for example. It appears in our everyday language: everything north is "up" or "on top"; south is "down there" or "below" us. In 1982, Jesse Levine, a retired advertising executive, created the "Turnabout Map," pictured here, after his daughter went on an anthropological mission to Peru and Levine realized that "I knew very little about Latin America. Juggling a map one day I turned it around and, lo and behold, Latin America became much more important." So he created the map, as he puts it, "just for fun." Levine's company, Laguna Sales (7040 Via Valverde, San Jose, CA 95135; 408-274-6493), sells a full-color, 17″ × 23″ version of the Turnabout Map for $7.50 (including mailing in a tube) and $4.50 (including tube) for a black-and-white version. Both are also available in many map stores.

A New World View

For centuries, map makers have grappled with the problem of how to depict a round world on a flat surface. Despite advancements in geometry and the creation of complex mathematical models, there has been little agreement on the optimum method of producing maps of the world without distorting one or more sections of the Earth's surface.

For more than 400 years, the traditional view of the world was based on models produced by Gerhardus Mercator, considered the leading cartographer of the sixteenth century. His grid system of cartography—revealed in his 1569 map of the world—became the classic expression of cartography and has dictated our geographical world concept ever since. His map was revolutionary; among other things, the spherical nature of the globe, proved by Ferdinand Magellan's circumnavigation of the world, was clearly expressed in it.

But Mercator's perspective reflected the "Europeanization" of the world. For one thing, the map placed the Equator deep in the bottom half of the map, giving about two thirds of the map's surface to the Northern Hemisphere. This allowed Germany (Mercator's chosen domicile after being exiled from his Flemish homeland by religious persecuters) to appear in the center of the map, although it actually lies in the northernmost quarter of the globe. Moreover, the white colonist nations appeared relatively larger on the map than they actually were; the colonies, inhabited primarily by people of color, appeared smaller than in reality. Thus, say critics, Mercator's map reinforced the European sense of superiority.

The results of such distortions are astonishing. Compare Europe and South America on the above maps, for example. In Mercator's world, the two continents appear to be of relatively equal size, even though South America actually has nearly twice the land mass of Europe. Similarly, Africa appears smaller than North America, although it is really about 50 percent larger.

Only recently has a new perspective emerged. A map created in 1974 by German historian Arno Peters attempts to correct Mercator's distortions in world geographic perception. The Peters map, say its proponents, shows all countries, conti-

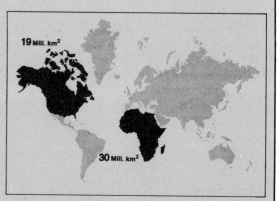

The traditional Mercator projection map (above) distorts the shape of continents to overemphasize Causcasian countries in temperate regions. Below, the Peters projection, designed to provide a more accurate view. Note that in the Mercator map, North America (19 million square kilometers) appears almost twice the size of Africa (30 million square kilometers). The Peters version draws the continents in more realistic proportions.

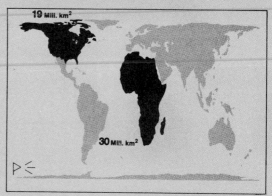

nents, and oceans according to their actual size, making accurate comparisons possible. On Peters' map, for example, South America is twice as large as Europe, and Africa appears half again as large as North America.

Peters' innovative notions, while not generally accepted by geographers and cartographers, are intriguing. Among others, they have caught the fancy of the United Nations, which helped fund the development of a detailed 51″ × 35″ color world map based on the "Peters Projection." Copies are available for $6.95 plus $1 postage and handling from Friendship Press, P.O. Box 37844, Cincinnati, OH 45237; 513-761-2100. For a more detailed interpretation of Arno Peters' work, see *The New Cartography* (New York: Friendship Press, 1983; $20).

channels to churches.

Meanwhile, in the newly formed United States of America, efforts were being made to take inventory of the burgeoning nation. As early as 1777 George Washington appointed a geographer and surveyor to the Continental Army to "take sketches of the country." This marked the first time that the U.S. government became involved in cartography. The first official large-scale U.S. surveying and mapping program was proposed by Thomas Jefferson and his congressional Committee on Public Land in 1784. This led to creation of the General Land Office, which produced a mountain of township plats and accompanying field notes. As President, Jefferson was deeply concerned with the lack of geographical information available about the newly acquired land west of the Mississippi River. During the War of 1812, his concerns led to the creation by the War Department of an elite Bureau of Topographical Engineers, later the Army Corps of Engineers, which played a vital role in surveying and documenting the nation's lands and waters. Jefferson is further credited with the creation of the Survey of the Coast, later called the Coast and Geodetic Survey.

During the nineteenth century, while General Land Office surveyors measured and subdivided regions that were relatively well known, the War Department sent exploring parties into largely unmapped territory. Many of the documents that emerged were vital in building the roads, canals, and railroads needed to accommodate a prospering populace. The topographic surveying and mapping programs conducted by the U.S. Geological Survey (USGS) from its inception in 1879 were based on a complex system set up by the Coast and Geodetic Survey, the leading scientific agency in the federal government during that century.

Prior to the Civil War, government surveys were limited to the vast hinterland of the Midwest. The westward migration that followed the war created an urgent need for detailed information about the resources and natural features of the western United States. By the beginning of the twentieth century, the USGS was undertaking a twenty-year program to map nearly every inch of the nation in rigorous scientific detail.

Map making reached new heights during World War I, when many USGS topographers were commissioned for duty with the Army Corps of Engineers. Some topographers played key roles in developing aerial photography techniques used for military intelligence. Returning to USGS after the war, these topographers applied their new aerial photography skills to cartography. Throughout the 1920s, experimenting with the new science of photogrammetry—the ability to take measurements from photographs—they succeeded in making maps from aerial photos. This development would change map making forever.

A great surge in the application of photogrammetry came with the establishment in 1933 of the Tennessee Valley Authority. One of TVA's first needs was map coverage of the entire valley. Working with USGS, surveyors prepared planimetric maps of the area using state-of-the-art, five-lens aerial photographs and innovative radial-line plotting techniques. Their efforts began a revolutionary swing away from field methods as the basis of map making, establishing aerial photos as the basis for all the maps that would follow.

After World War II, map-making innovations were rampant. Combining a variety of sophisticated measuring instruments with emerging computer systems, cartographers produced a treasure trove of new map types and products. The advent of space imagery and electronic imaging, along with the digitization of map data in computers, produced yet another revolution in map making. And there would be more revolutions to come.

Mapping the Future

There are many who predict the demise of the map as we know it, the elimination of those familiar, hard-to-refold sheets of paper upon which we depend for so many things. Along with other technofuturistic predictions—that the computer will replace the printed book, for example, or that newspapers will someday appear only on video screens—this will never be completely true. Which is not to say that maps, and map making, are not changing in dramatic ways. Or that the map of tomorrow won't appear in some rather innovative forms. But there will always be paper maps, although maybe not as many of them.

As it has with so many other things, the computer has revolutionized the world of mapping in myriad ways. Computerization has introduced an impressive list of new cartographic tools and techniques, such as electronic distance-measuring, inertial navigation, remote sensing, digital imaging, space science, and data base storage and retrieval. We are just beginning to learn how to use these tools. A new generation of cartographers is using computers' digital technology to make and modify maps. In the new high-tech car-

tography, map data are no longer entered by skilled draftsmen working on light tables but are created using satellite images by cartographers at keyboards. Map data are entered on computer tapes, which in turn generate visual displays for editing, or which can be printed out to use in producing conventional paper maps.

With map data in a computer, cartographers can easily modify maps, enlarge them, change their scale, isolate segments for use with other maps, and make them, or any part of them, instantly available to other cartographers and map users who can call up digital information on their computer screens around the world. Among the many benefits of computerization is speed: combined with other map-making techniques, computers can shorten considerably the four to five years it once took to produce a printed map from an aerial photograph or satellite image.

Map storage and production by computers is just the beginning of the new cartographic technology. Computerized map data can also be analyzed for an endless number of uses. The federal government, long a leader in developing map-

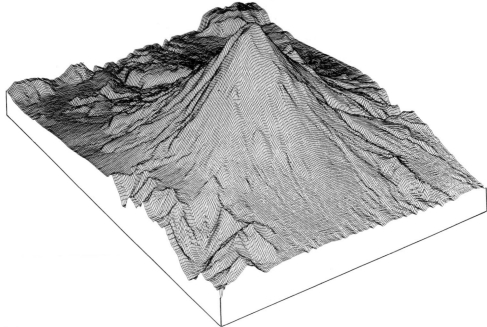

A digital elevation model (above) created by USGS shows Mount St. Helens before its eruption in May 1980. Right: the same computer-generated, three-dimensional perspective, after the eruption.

making technology, already uses computer-based map information for many things. For example:

■ The U.S. Forest Service uses terrain data in digital form for predicting likely paths of forest fires.
■ The Federal Aviation Administration uses digital information to determine possible obstructions near airports, integrating the data into obstacle-avoidance landing systems on board airliners.
■ The Fish and Wildlife Service uses map data in computer form to help locate wildlife habitats that need protection.
■ The Census Bureau is using computer-generated boundary maps to organize information gathering for the 1990 census.

Much of the technology for such projects was developed originally by the U.S. Geological Service. In 1982, USGS completed its first digital cartographic data base, a set of computer tapes that contains the outlines of boundaries, highways, railroads, rivers, and other features for the entire United States. Dubbed "GeoData," USGS has divided the fifty states into 21 sections (fifteen for the 48 contiguous states, five for Alaska, and one for Hawaii), with three computer tapes (one each containing boundaries, major transportation

routes, and bodies of water) available for each section. The entire set of 63 tapes sells for $6,300. Rand McNally, the big commercial map publisher, is similarly computerizing its vast inventory of maps.

Other digital mapping technology comes from the Defense Mapping Agency, which uses map data to guide "smart" missile systems. The process involves loading data about routes to potential targets into a missile, then instructing that missile, before launching, which route to take. DMA hopes eventually to reduce the entire world map to digits. One problem, though, is storage space: magnetic tapes containing digital information for the entire globe would require a building a half-mile cubed just to hold the tapes. Optical disks, which can hold vast amounts of data more compactly, may help.

(There are other computerized mapping programs, some available for personal computers; see the section on "Map Software" elsewhere in this book.)

Ultimately, all this high-tech wizardry is expected to become available to individuals through what may well be standard equipment on the cars of the 1990s. With dashboard navigation systems—simplified, inexpensive versions of the

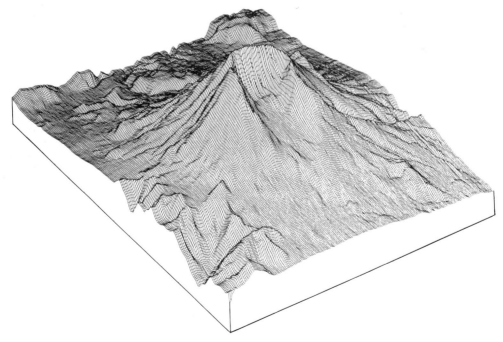

systems that allow airline pilots and ship captains to know exactly where they are even in cloudy weather—drivers of the not-too-distant future may be able to choose the best route to a destination, even taking into account an accident or construction project, or more easily negotiate unfamiliar territory. On one such system, the Electro Gyrocator, developed by Honda Motor Company and already available in Japan, a computer is linked to a magnetic sensor attached to the main drive axle. After the driver indicates the car's starting point by turning knobs on a small screen, the car's movement "tells" the computer how fast and in what direction the car is traveling, with the current position and course constantly displayed on the screen. No more awkward map folding at highway speeds! Most car makers, including the three major U.S. companies, have some kind of navigation system in the works.

Eventually, say cartographic futurists, instead of stopping at a service station for directions, we'll be able to punch in our destinations into the service station's computer, obtaining (for a fee) a made-to-order map, complete with a detailed list of restaurants, motels, and attractions along the way.

The possibilities, thanks to computers, are endless. From car driving to city planning to coastal management, digital mapping techniques are increasingly finding their way into our lives, making the world a bit more manageable and, perhaps, a little easier to understand.

But no less magnificent.

LAND MAPS

Aerial Photographs

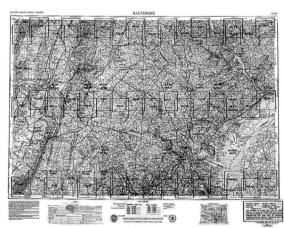

Photoindex from EROS *showing government aerial photography available for the northern Chesapeake Bay region.*

Ever since humans have been able to fly and hold a camera at the same time, aerial photographs have been an important part of the mapping process, as well as a means of preserving images of the earth and its development. Images of the land taken from above are valuable tools, suitable for use as finished products, but they are also the starting points for creating most types of land maps. Cartographers often use stereoscopic aerial photos—two aerial photos of the same site taken from two different aerial camera positions—to create the three-dimensional perspective needed for some map-making. Aerial photos are also used in such fields as aeronautics, agriculture, engineering, and land planning and development.

Cameras in airplanes photograph land section by section. The resulting photographs must first be corrected to eliminate distortion, camera-tilt, and optical effects created by the land itself. Through a series of enhancements or overlays, the photos are then transformed into a variety of map types. Cartographers often use aerial photographs to create or update planimetric or topographic maps, for example. The addition of mapping symbols (such as major roads, borders, and selected place names) to photographs results in photoimage maps. Orthophotoquads and orthophotomaps result from further enhancements, such as adding color and enhanced definition of coastlines, rivers, mountains, and other land forms.

Government Sources

Nearly every federal agency involved with land preservation, planning, or management maintains collections of aerial photographs that span the nation from picture-perfect coast to picture-perfect coast. (See Appendix A for addresses.)

■ **U.S. Geologic Survey.** The USGS's Aerial Photography Summary System, established in 1976 as part of the National Cartographic Information Center, catalogs the planned, in-progress, and completed aerial photographs for the United States to assist in locating a desired photograph. A pamphlet, *Finding an Aerial Photograph*, available from USGS, also may be helpful.

■ **National Archives.** The Archives has a large stockpile of older aerial photographs of the U.S., which may be located through queries to Archives staff. (See "Uncle Sam's Treasure Chest.")

■ **Earth Resources Observation Systems (EROS).** The EROS Data Center, near Sioux Falls, S.D., operated by the Department of the Interior, provides access to Landsat and Skylab imagery and assorted government-produced aerial photographs produced, all of which are available for sale. (See "Space Imagery.")

■ **U.S. Department of Agriculture.** USDA's Aerial Photography Field Office in Salt Lake City, part of the Agricultural Stabilization and Conservation Service, has thousands of aerial photographs covering most of the nation's major cropland. USDA's National Forest Service has aerial photographs of the nation's forests. Its Fish and Wildlife Service has aerial photographs of wildlife refuges and sanctuaries.

■ **Department of the Interior.** Interior's Bureau of Land Management has aerial photographs of most federally maintained land, available through its offices or through the EROS Data Center.

■ **Defense Mapping Agency.** DMA has aerial photographs of military installations and other defense-related areas.

■ **Department of Commerce.** Commerce's National Ocean Survey has aerial photographs of the nation's coastlines.

Aerial photograph of the rapidly growing Tysons Corner, Va., area. Courtesy Air Photographics Inc., Wheaton, Md.

Commercial Sources

Aerial maps are also available from the following sources and reference libraries:

■ Aerial Photo Company, 11807 Ohio Avenue, Los Angeles, CA 90053.
■ Aerial Surveys, 107 Church Street, N.W., Marietta, GA 30060.
■ Aerial Surveys Inc., 4616 Prospect Avenue, Cleveland, OH 44115.
■ Aerial Topographic Map & Abstract Company, Inc., One Kings Highway, Tappan, NY 10983.

■ Air Photographics, Inc., 11510 Georgia Ave., Suite 130, Wheaton, MD 20902.
■ Atlantic Aerial Surveys Inc., 803 Franklin Street, Huntsville, AL 35804.
■ International Aerial Mapping Company, 8927 International Drive, San Antonio, TX 78205.
■ Pace Aerial Surveys Inc., 11 S. Royal Street, York, PA 17405.
■ Photomaps Inc., 412 O'Keefe Avenue, New Orleans, LA 70130.

▶ **See also: "Aeronautical Maps," "Agriculture Maps," and "Military Maps."**

Agricultural Maps

Silicon Valley may be America's gold mine, but corn fields and cow pastures are still its heartland.

The history of American farmers is the history of America itself: the Indians who taught white settlers how to grow corn; the gentlemen planters who led the American Revolution and formed the federal government; the Ante Bellum plantation owners, brought to their knees in the Civil War; the sharecroppers, cowboys, and immigrant farmers who helped tame the West. These are a few of the people who created America's agricultural legacy.

A century ago, farming in the United States was an enormous industry. New technology increased productivity, creating a need for greater knowledge of the land and its resources. In 1899, the U.S. Department of Agriculture began its soil survey program. At the time, little was known about the quality or content of the nation's soil. But the methodological survey created a fund of knowledge that has grown over the years to encompass a complex system of soil testing, categorization, treatment, and usage.

The surveys contain soil maps as well as general information about soil quality and use. Since the turn of the century, USDA has published 3,586 surveys, 1,908 of which are still available. Surveys published since 1957 include a number of different interpretations for the various soils mapped in each area. Among these are interpretations of estimated yields of common crops, land capability, rangeland, soil-woodland, and soil suitability for community or recreational use. The maps in these later surveys are printed on a photomosaic base, usually at scales of 1:24,000, 1:20,000, or 1:15,840.

Older surveys are useful to agricultural or land-use historians, but the maps are more general and the interpretations out of date. More up-to-date soil surveys and other agricultural maps are used by farmers, engineers, land planners, developers, geologists, and agricultural scientists.

Through its Agricultural Stabilization and Conservation Service (ASCS), USDA also produces and maintains a large collection of aerial photographs of agricultural lands. The aerial photography program began in 1935 as a result of a congressional law passed to alleviate the farm crisis brought on by the Depression. The law, designed to establish and maintain a balance between agricultural consumption and production, required the extensive and accurate measurement of the nation's farmlands. But the standard method of mapping since George Washington's time—the surveyor's chain—was too slow for USDA's purposes, so in the mid 1930s, the agency began using "rectified-to-scale" aerial photomaps. With the use of aerial photomaps and a measuring device called a planimeter, it was possible to make land measurements that were 99 percent accurate. Today, the ASCS has aerial photomaps covering all major U.S. agricultural areas.

USDA's soil survey and aerial photomap programs are two parts of an extensive federal agriculture mapping effort. The USDA's Forest Service creates maps that indicate the use of forest resources (see "Park and Forest Maps"). Other agriculture map-producing agencies include the Central Intelligence Agency, which produces maps of foreign agriculture (see "CIA Maps"), and the Army Corps of Engineers and National Oceanic and Atmospheric Administration, both of which create agriculture-related maps about water sources (see "River, Lake, and Waterway Maps").

State, county, and local agricultural and conservation departments are good resources for agricultural maps of specific local areas. A few commercial cartographers create maps for classroom use.

Government Sources

Agricultural Stabilization and Conservation Service (2222 West, 2300 South, P.O. Box 30010, Salt Lake City, UT 84130; 801-524-5856), part of the Agriculture Department, produces aerial photographs of U.S. agricultural land. Products available include Landsat images, photographs taken as part of the National High Altitude Program, and photos taken by the Forest Service and Soil Conservation Service. Prices for copies of aerial photographs range from $3 for a 10" × 10" black-and-white paper contact print to $50 for a 38" × 38" paper print made from a color positive. A price

sheet (ASCS-441A) and order form (ASCS-441) are available upon request from ASCS, as is an explanatory pamphlet, ASCS *Aerial Photography.*

Forest Service. The U.S. Forest Service produces several forestry maps and atlases, many of them available from the Government Printing Office. (See "Park and Forest Maps.")

Government Printing Office. The following GPO publications contain agricultural maps or surveys and related text:

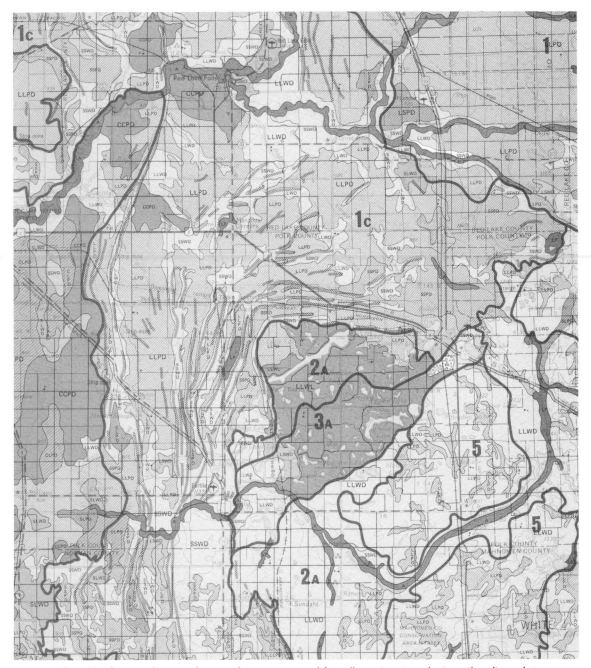

Portion of a soil landscape and geomorphic map of Minnesota created by Williams & Heintz, showing soil quality and type. Courtesy University of Minnesota, Department of Soil Science.

■ *Census of Publication*, 1980, *Vol. 2, Subject Reports, Characteristics of the Rural and Farm-Related Population* (S/N 003-024-06333-6; 241 pages, $8.50) includes maps, charts, and statistics on the social, economic, and housing characteristics of the United States agricultural population.

■ *Handbook of Agricultural Charts*: 1982 (S/N 001-000-04305-6, $5.50) and *Handbook of Agricultural Charts*: 1984 (S/N 001-019-00368-5, $3.75) both contain lists, illustrations, and many agricultural maps and charts.

■ *Heat Capacity Mapping Mission Anthology* (S/N 033-000-00890-2; $24) includes maps from and text about the National Aeronautic and Space Administration's mission that demonstrated the potential for orbital infrared surveys in monitoring soil moisture and detecting stress in natural and cultivated vegetation.

■ *National Soils Handbook* (S/N 001-007-00908-1; 644 pages, $8.50) sets forth authority, scope, and procedures of the National Cooperative Soil Survey Program. The loose-leaf handbook includes chapters on soil survey operations management, soil classification, application of soil information, soil survey investigation, information and display systems, and soil data files.

■ *Soil Survey Manual* (S/N 001-000-00688-6; 503 pages, $17), provides guidelines on survey techniques.

■ *USSR Agricultural Atlas* (S/N 041-015-00073-0, $4.75), prepared by the Central Intellegence Agency, has text, maps, and charts covering the Soviet Union's production of various agricultural products.

Soil Conservation Service (Room 5105 South Building, Washington, DC 20250; 202-447-4525), engaged in surveying the nation's soils, has soil surveys for almost all of America's farmland. There are 1,908 available surveys, although many are out of date; 1,678 are out of print. The surveys can be obtained at no charge by land users and by representatives of state and local offices of the Soil Conservation Survey, county agents, and congressional representatives. Many libraries have surveys on file for study and reproduction; they are good places to start the search for one of the out-of-print surveys. SCS publishes a free *List of Published Soil Surveys*, the most recent edition of which is available upon request.

Tennessee Valley Authority. "Soils in the Tennessee Valley" ($2.50 plus $2 for mailing tube), compiled by TVA's Soils and Fertilizer Branch in cooperation with USDA's Soil and Conservation Service, is a colorful map describing in detail a variety of aspects of Tennessee Valley soils.

Commercial Sources

Although most agricultural maps are created by federal, state, or local government cartographers, there are a few commercial maps created as classroom tools that depict the development of agriculture in America, including the following publishers:

The George F. Cram Co. (P.O. Box 426, Indianapolis, IN 46206; 317-635-5564) produces two vibrant agricultural maps as part of its American History Series, "Agricultural Regions of the United States" (No. 524; $59-$63) and "Agricultural Products of the United States" (No. 525; $59-$63). Both maps measure 52" × 40".

Nystrom (3333 Elston Avenue, Chicago, IL 60618; 800-621-8086) publishes a 50" × 38" brightly colored teaching map titled "Patterns of Agriculture in the United States" (No. QJ29; $37-$57), which depicts the products of America's major agricultural regions.

Rand McNally (P.O. Box 7600, Chicago, IL 60680; 800-323-1887, 312-673-9100 in Ill.) publishes agricultural maps in two of its classroom series. The "American History Maps" series for intermediate grades includes "Grain Growers on the Great Plains—Western North America" (No. 114-12584-8; $57), illustrating farming development in the West around 1912. Its "American Studies" Series includes "Farm, Factory, and Forest (1900)" (No. 112-12521-2; $42), showing the impact agricultural and industrial development have on the land. Both measure 50" × 50".

▶ **See also: "Aerial Photographs," "Atlases," "Land Use Maps," "Natural Resource Maps," "Park and Forest Maps," and "Weather Maps."**

Antique Maps

Old maps are beautiful and thought-provoking windows into our past, rich with the history of generations that have been outlived by the diagrams they drew of their world. Short of stumbling across finds at auctions or on a store's dusty shelves, the best places to find antique maps are through the numerous collections of map libraries (see Appendix D). historical societies, or museums. Reproductions usually can be made from the originals. There also are a number of publishers that create reproductions of historically significant maps and charts, as well as dealers with the resources to locate maps for a fee.

Government Sources

Two government agencies in Washington, D.C., represent the lion's share of existing antique maps. The Geography and Map Division of the Library of Congress holds one of the world's largest collections of antique maps and atlases—more than three-and-a-half million maps and charts in all. The National Archives has two million maps and charts produced by the federal government between 1750 and 1950. Both the Library of Congress and the Archives have reproduction services for their collections. (See "Uncle Sam's Treasure ·Chests.")

The Directory of Historical Societies in the United States and Canada (published by the American Association for State and Local Historical Societies in Nashville, Tenn.) and *Map Collections in the United States and Canada: A Directory* (published by the Geography and Map Division of the Special Library Association in New York) are the best sources for finding local map collections and are included in many libraries' reference sections. Another publication, *Facsimiles of Maps and Atlases: A List of Reproductions for Sale by Various Publishers and Distributors* ($4.50), is a useful guide for locating published reproductions of old maps. It is available through the Library of Congress or at Government Printing Office bookstores.

Federal government agencies that have older maps on file for study and reproduction include the USGS (dating back to 1879) and the National Ocean Survey (various marine and navigation charts from the eighteenth century on; Civil War maps detailing certain marches and campaigns).

Portion of a 1775 map of Virginia and Maryland. Courtesy Historic Urban Plans, Ithaca, N.Y.

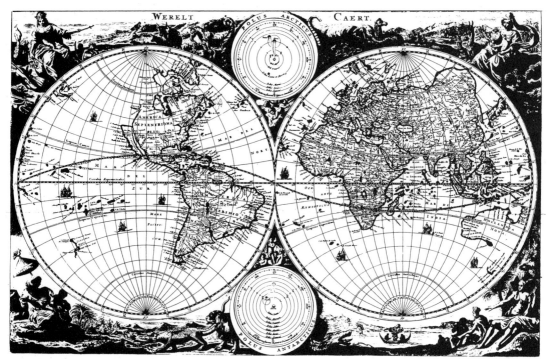

A Dutch "Bible-map" from 1690, probably created by Daniel Stoopendaal, a pre-eminent Dutch map maker.

Commercial Sources

One source for antique maps is a beautiful 10″ × 14″ calendar, *Old Maps*, published each year by Beaufort Books (distributed by Kampmann & Company, 9 East 40th Street, New York, NY 10016; 212-685-2928). The $8.95 calendar, available in bookstores, includes twelve full-color reproductions of antique maps.

Three commercial map publishers carry one or more series of antique map reproductions:

■ **American Map Corporation** (46-35 54th Road, Maspeth, NY 11378; 718-784-0055) sells wall murals of Mercator's World Map, 1636, and the British Empire in America, 1733; various seventeenth- and eighteenth-century facsimiles of military campaigns and explorations.

■ **Bartholomew** (available through Hammond, address below) distributes various seventeenth-century map reproductions of the Americas, the world and the British Empire.

■ **Hammond** (515 Valley Street, Maplewood, NJ 07040; 201-763-6000) sells sets of antique maps grouped as the world and Africa; Europe and the Western Hemisphere; European Naval and Great

Britain; France and Italy; Colonial America; and New France.

These organizations specialize in map reproductions:

■ **American Heritage Publishing** (10 Rockefeller Plaza, New York, NY 10020; 212-399-8900) sells antique maps of America.

■ **British Museum Publications** (6 Bedford Square, London WC1B 3RA, England) distributes reproductions of maps held in the British museum system.

■ **Historic Reprints** (3918 Leland Road, Louisville, KY 40207; 502-458-5286) sells old city and county maps of America.

■ **Historic Urban Plans** (P.O. Box 276, Ithaca, NY 14850; 607-273-4695) sells reproductions of old city plans, both U.S. and foreign.

■ **International Society for the History of Cartography** (The Honorary Treasurer, Imago Mundi, c/o Lympne Castle, Kent, England) has reproductions of landmark cartographic works.

▶ See also "City Maps," "County Maps," "Emergency Information Maps," "Indian Land Maps," "Land Ownership Maps," "Military Maps," "Railroad Maps," and "World Maps."

Uncle Sam's Treasure Chests

The world of maps is so vast that you practically need a map to find one. Two of the best resources for historic map research are the map collections of the Library of Congress and the National Archives, both in or around Washington, D.C. Funded and operated by the federal government, both collections contain millions of maps, charts, atlases, and globes, as well as a myriad of valuable research tools for the study of cartographic information.

Library of Congress, Geography and Map Division (Washington, DC 20541; 202-287-6277). When the Library of Congress was established in 1800, some of its earliest acquisitions were maps and atlases. In 1897, the Geography and Map Division was given its own room; it has since moved to specially designed quarters on Capitol Hill. The collection, the largest in the world, consists of more than three-and-a-half million maps, 44,000 atlases, 2,000 plastic relief models, 300 globes, and 8,000 reference works. Among its most prized possessions are three sailing atlases and nineteen sailing charts dating back to the fourteenth through seventeenth centuries. There also are numerous early American maps and charts, some predating the Revolutionary War, and the Sanborn Map Company's nineteenth century fire insurance maps, which detail the growth of 12,000 American cities and towns. The rest of the world is well represented, too, including rare Asian maps in the Hummel and Warner collections.

Although there is no single catalog of all of the division's holdings, there are specialized card and book catalogs, as well as a computerized magnetic tape listing newer maps. The library publishes selected lists on specialized topics, including annotated lists of Civil War maps, railroad maps, land ownership maps, and Indian land maps. The Geography and Map Division's List of Publications is free upon request. The Geography and Map Division's collections are meant for research purposes only, and lending privileges are restricted to members of Congress, federal agencies, and authorized libraries. A reference service is available to the public, and staff can handle phone and mail requests. The library's Photoduplication Service can make reproductions of maps and atlases for a fee, except where copyright or other restrictions apply.

The Library's Photoduplication Services handle all reproduction orders. Prices range from $5 for a 2″ × 2″ color slide (minimum order of three) and $8.50 for a black-and-white photodirect paper print, to literally hundreds of dollars for exhibition-quality prints, depending on size and reproduction quality desired. The minimum reproduction time is six weeks.

National Archives, Cartographic and Architectural Branch (841 South Pickett Street, Alexandria, VA 22304; 703-756-6700). The Archives' Cartographic and Architectural Branch holds one of the largest collections of American maps in the world. Established as the repository for maps commissioned or created by the government, its holdings date from 1750 to 1950. The Archives Cartographic Branch has more than two million maps and charts, 800,000 in manuscript form, as well as 300,000 architectural drawings and engineering plans and eight million aerial photos.

The maps of the Lewis and Clark and other explorations of North America are among the treasures in the collection. Virtually every aspect of American society and expansion can be found in the files of the branch, located in a suburb of Washington, D.C. A number of special catalogs and reference information papers are available through the Archives, their subjects running the gamut from eighteenth century Indian lands to twentieth century transportation growth. The free pamphlet *Cartographic and Architectural Branch, National Archives and Record Service*, available from the General Services Administration, lists many of the categories and reference materials in the collection. Reproduction services of varying degrees of quality and price are available; orders usually require four to six weeks for completion.

The Archives staff can make black-and-white photocopies of maps while you wait for $1.65 per square foot of original. If you need a better-quality reproduction, the Archives Reproduction Services can make a variety of types of copies. Prices range from $2.65 for a 2″ × 2″ color slide, or $9.35 for a 4″ × 5″ color negative, to as much as $166.50 for a 30″ × 40″ color slide. Reproduction time is six to eight weeks.

Bicycle Route Maps

Over the years, bicycling has grown from a Sunday pastime to a full-blown sport, complete with high-tech equipment, designer racing gear—and detailed route maps. Whether you're looking for a morning glide through a neighborhood park or a cross-country endurance test, there are maps to keep you on track.

The quality of bike route maps varies among publishers. Some maps are simply road maps with a line drawn to indicate a bike route. Other maps provide detailed information about weather conditions, repair or supply services available, and points of interest.

State highway departments or bureaus of tourism often produce bike route maps that are free or inexpensive. Write to the appropriate office (see Appendix B) or get in touch with a local bicycle group. Many groups publish their own maps and most know the best sources for maps of their area. If no bicycling group is listed in a local phone book, try one of the following national organizations, whose publications often cover biking activities and map products around the country:

National Bicycle Organizations

Bicycle Federation of America (1818 R Street NW, Washington, DC 20009; 202-332-6986), a non-profit membership group that publishes a monthly newsletter, *ProBike News*, including reports on mapping and bicycle organizations.

Bicycle USA (also known as The League of American Wheelmen, Suite 209, 6707 Whitestone Road, Baltimore, MD, 21207; 301-944-3399), a membership organization (membership: $22/individual; $27/family) that produces a monthly magazine, *Bicycle USA*, and an annual *Almanac* ($5; available only to members) containing a state-by-state listing of biking information, including organizations, mapping and travel services, and tourism departments.

BikeCentennial, the Bicycle Travel Association (P.O. Box 8308, Missoula, MT 59807; 406-721-1776), which publishes a touring magazine, *BikeReport*, nine times a year, and provides member discounts on the maps and biking accessories.

Commercial and Other Sources

There are thousands of maps created by hundreds of bike groups and publishers. Following are producers of maps or books containing maps for a variety of routes throughout the U.S.:

American Youth Hostels (AYH) (1332 I Street NW, Washington, DC 20005; 202-783-6161) AYH offers *The American Bicycle Atlas* ($7.95 postpaid) by Dave Gilbert. This 272-page book has 96 touring routes, ranging from ten-mile jaunts to a 457-mile-long odyssey. Maps vary in scale and include topographic information and cue sheets. There are routes in all states except Alaska, Hawaii, Iowa, Maine, North Dakota, Oklahoma, South Carolina, Utah, Wisconsin, and Wyoming. Campgrounds, rest areas, and other important travel features are included in the atlas. Local AYH branches sometimes produce bike route maps for their areas. To obtain a list of branches, write to AYH at the above address.

BikeCentennial produces a route network series of state-of-the-art bike maps covering the U.S. The maps, most of which are printed on a special waterproof paper (called Chemtex) with waterproof ink (called Tufftex), are sized to fit in handlebar map cases. Illustrated in shades of blue and green, the maps are drawn at a scale of about 1:250,000. They provide such information as local bike laws, weather, stopovers, and special attractions. The maps feature detailed riding information ("Turn left on Elm, right on Main," etc.), and matchlines enable bikers to move effortlessly from one route map to the next. Bikecentennial maps are available in some map and sporting goods stores and directly from the company (include $2 for shipping and handling). Bike routes published by Bikecentennial include:

■ "The TransAmerica Trail" ($5.95 each; $59.95 for the set of 12 maps), covering the 4,250-mile, coast-to-coast bike route.
■ "The Washington to Minnesota Bicycle Route" ($5.95 each; $20.95 for the set of 4 maps), an 1,815-mile route through Washington, Idaho, Montana, and North Dakota.

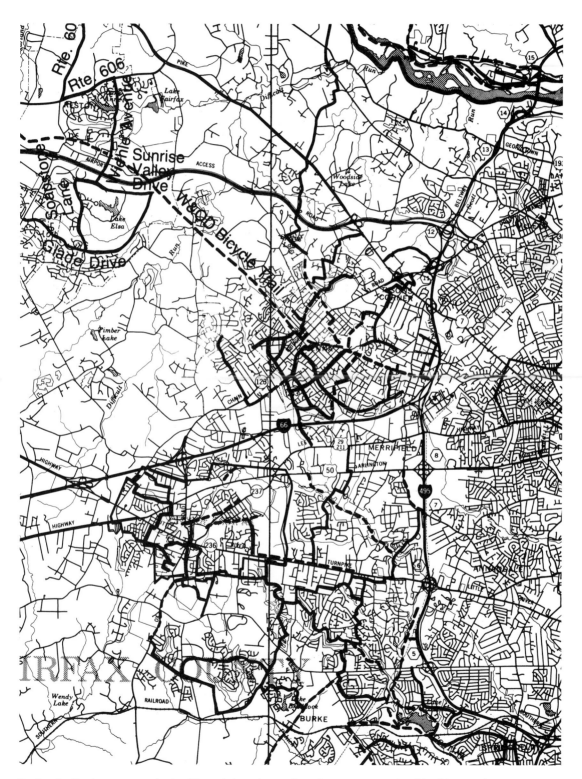

Portion of a bicycle route map, showing bike paths in and around Washington, D.C., produced by the Metropolitan Washington Council of Governments.

■ "Iowa to Maine Bicycle Route" ($5.95 each; $20.95 for the set of 4 maps), a 1,725-mile route that winds from the corn fields to the Atlantic.
■ "The Virginia to Florida Bicycle Route" ($6.95 each; $25.75 for the set of 5 maps), a 1,330-mile route from Richmond, Va. to Ft. Myers Beach, Fla.
■ "The Canada to California Bicycle Route" ($6.95 each; $13.75 for the set of 2 maps), a 780-mile route that skips through Canada and down the Pacific coast to California.
■ "The Great Parks North Bicycle Route" ($5.95 each; $10.95 for the set of 2 maps), 740 miles through the parks of the northern Rocky Mountains
■ "The Great Parks South Bicycle Route": ($6.95), a 680-mile route through the Colorado Rockies.
■ "The Great River North Bicycle Route" ($5.95 each; $10.95 for the set of 2 maps) an 860-mile river route from Fargo, N.D. to Davenport, Ia.
■ "The Great River Central Bicycle Route" ($5.95), a 720-mile route along historic river sites from Iowa to Tennessee; includes a three-color, non-waterproof map and separate service directory.

Pantheon Books (201 East 50th Street, New York, NY 10022; 212-751-2600) publishes *Bicycle Touring in the Western United States* ($9.95). Authors Karen and Gary Hawkins provide maps for tours covering 7,500 miles of terrain through Arizona, California, Colorado, Idaho, Montana, Nevada, New Mexico, Oregon, Utah, and Wyoming. Also included is information about weather conditions, places to stay, repair and supply sources, and topographic details.

Southwest Trails Association (P.O. Box 191126, San Diego, CA 92119; 619-464-1323) publishes two booklets with mapped bike routes. *Southwest*

American Bicycle Route ($3.95) has an overall map at a scale of about 1:3,000,000 that traces a 1,748-mile route from Oceanside, Calif. to Larned, Kan., including travel and topographic information. *Southern Overland Bicycle Route* ($7.95) is a 168-page booklet with 17 maps of varying scale covering a route of 1,607 miles from Austin, Tex. to Los Angeles, following the trails of western pioneers, along with historical, geographical, and travel information.

Foreign Bike Routes

Information about bike routes through foreign countries are often available from tourist boards of those countries (see Appendix C). In addition, two organizations publish foreign maps:

BikeCentennial offers two books for cycling in foreign lands: *Bicycling Vancouver Island & The Gulf Islands* ($10.95, plus $1.50 postage), offers maps for 108 tours of this eight island region, as well as overview maps of the entire area; *Grape Expeditions in France* ($9.95 plus $1.50 postage), provides 32 detailed maps through the French wine provinces of Bordeaux, Burgundy, Champagne, Loire, Provence, and Cotes du Rhone. The accompanying text serves as a wine appreciation guide and gives historical and cultural perspective on each region.

The Cycle Touring Company (P.O. Box 6547, Silver Spring, MD 20906) offers a self-guided tour through Switzerland and surrounding countries ($7.50, postpaid). The 35 large-scale map cards and accompanying text trace a 750-mile route for all levels of cyclists through some of the most challenging bike trails in Europe.

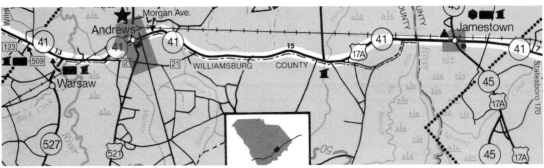

Section of BikeCentennial's Virginia-to-Florida Bicycle Route, showing the Santee River area in South Carolina.

Boundary Maps

When it comes to drawing the line, nobody does it better than Uncle Sam. The federal government has worked diligently to draw and maintain the intricate boundaries that separate it from Canada and Mexico, as well as those dividing the contiguous 48 states from each other. The United States isn't alone in this endeavor: the surveyors of most other countries have long strived to divide conquered kingdoms and define lands given as gifts in royal marriages or annexed after a war. Throughout the world, boundary maps are helpful to police, border guards, and customs agents as well as to geographers, landowners, developers, historians, and statesmen.

Though they are perhaps the simplest and most direct maps in the world—they merely show where one country, state, county, city, town, or land plat ends and another begins—there is a certain romance to a boundary map. To appreciate the mythical proportions some boundaries take, one need only recall Jean Renoir's classic film about World War I, *The Grand Illusion*. In the final scene, German soldiers cease their fire at escaping Frenchmen who have just made it over the

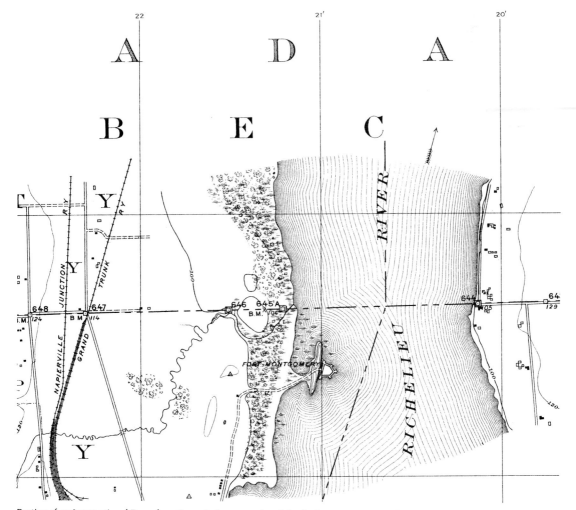

Portion of an International Boundary Commission map, sheet 3 in the St. Lawrence River-St. Croix River series, which illustrates the U.S.-Canadian boundary between New York and Quebec.

Swiss border. There are less dramatic scenes daily at borders, as it is necessary to determine where to build, whom to sue, how to tax, and many other issues that are trivial to all but a few interested parties.

The men and women who survey boundaries follow a long tradition that includes such renowned American surveyors as Daniel Boone and George Washington. From drawing out the lines of a cattle ranch or sheep farm to setting the borders of growing metropolises, the history of boundary mapping is one of expansion and intrigue. Surveyors like Charles Mason and Jeremiah Dixon, who tackled the eighteenth-century American wilderness to pinpoint the North-South dividing line that bears their names, did so with a battery of axemen in the lead to battle the vegetation, and often the Indians.

Boundary maps, however, are not the last word on borders. They are merely references drawn to illustrate the border lines set forth in treaties, annexations, or other agreements. Surveyors creating boundary maps must take the word-for-word descriptions in the border agreements and draw lines accordingly. If this sounds easy, consider the border specifications—simplistic by today's standards—of the first charter of Virginia as declared by England's King James in 1606:

> ...situate, lying, or being all along the Sea Coasts, between four and thirty degrees of *Northerly* Latitude from the Equinoctial Line and five and forty degrees of the same Latitude, and in the main Land between the same four and thirty and five and forty Degrees and the Islands therunto adjacent, or within a hundred miles of the coast thereof.

Sometimes, the process of correcting boundary lines that were carelessly mapped can require more words than the original boundary specifications. In a 1875 document, the North Carolina Geological Survey described the incorrect mapping of the state's borders:

> ...it appears from the South Carolina geographical State survey of 1821-1825 that the course from the starting point is N. 47 degrees 30' W., and instead of pursuing the parallel of 35 degrees, it turns west about

ten miles south of that line, and then, on approaching the Catawba River, turns northward, pursuing a zigzag line to the forks of the Catawba River....

The report estimated that such mapping errors caused the state to lose between 500 and 1,000 square miles of territory. The course of boundary maps may not run smoothly, but their importance can be boundless.

Boundary maps are available through a number of federal agencies, as well as through local and state land management offices and the cartographic offices of foreign countries.

Government Sources

The lines drawn on boundary maps produced by the federal government contain lines that either are solid (if their accuracy is absolutely established) or broken (if they are believed, but not certain, to be accurate). Monuments such as engraved stones or monoliths built as border markers also are shown along boundary lines, usually with a small square symbol. Lines within states are usually mapped by local or state agencies, and these boundaries are then incorporated into federal maps.

International Boundary Commission, United States and Canada (425 I Street NW, Room 150, Washington, DC 20001; 202-632-8058) has boundary maps that show the detailed border locations separating the United States and Canada. The maps, drawn in 1922, are printed on heavy paper and show the vegetation, major waterways, and some topography in shades of blue, green, and brown. The 226 IBC maps that represent the entire U.S.-Canadian border are divided into the following subsections:

■ Source of the St. Croix River to the Atlantic Coast (18 maps)
■ Source of the St. Croix River to the St. Lawrence River (61 maps)
■ Northwesternmost Point of Lake of the Woods to Lake Superior (36 maps)
■ Gulf of Georgia to Northwesternmost Point of Lake of the Woods (59 maps)
■ 49th Parallel to the Pacific Ocean (1 map)
■ Tongass Passage to Mount St. Elias (13 maps)
■ 141st Meridian from the Arctic Ocean to Mount St. Elias (38 maps)

The cost of each map is $3 and prepayment must accompany all orders. Write to the IBC for complete listings of maps within each subsection to help determine which maps you need.

International Boundary and Water Commission, United States and Mexico (The Commons, Building C, Suite 310, 4171 North Mesa, El Paso, TX 79902; 915-541-7300) United States boundary sectional maps created for flood control use in the region. There are maps of the Lower Rio Grande Project, the El Paso project, the Elephant Butte Dam region to the Gulf, and Falcon Dam to the Gulf. The maps cost $4 each and are produced in full color. Also available are photomosaic treaty boundary maps of the region. These colorful maps, created from aerial photographs, can be obtained in the form of color mylar prints for fifteen cents per square inch. (The maps measure 24" × 36"; thus, a full print is $10.)

Bureau of the Census. The Census Bureau produces state subdivision boundary maps for all states (although a few are combined), Guam, Puerto Rico, and related U.S. holdings, and several other U.S. maps showing state and county boundaries. The maps are accurate as of 1983, when most were published. They are available from the Government Printing Office (Appendix A). Census boundary maps available include:

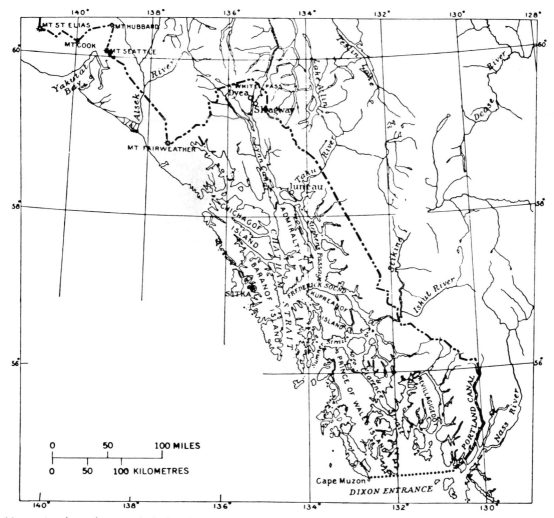

Map tracing the southeastern Alaska boundary between Canada and the United States. Courtesy USGS.

■ Alabama: County and Place Boundaries ($3.75): 36″ × 48″

■ Alaska: Borough, Census Area, Census Subarea, and Place Boundaries ($3) 42″ × 60″

■ Connecticut, Massachusetts, and Rhode Island: County, County Subdivision, and Place Boundaries ($2.50) 22″ × 34″

■ Delaware, District of Columbia, and Maryland: County, County Subdivision, and Place Boundaries ($3.50)

■ Hawaii: County and Place Boundaries ($4) 42″ × 60″

■ Guam and Trust Territory of the Pacific Islands, Including Northern Mariana Islands and American Samoa ($4) 42″ × 60″

■ North Carolina: County, County Subdivision, and Place Boundaries ($4) 42″ × 60″

■ Puerto Rico and the Virgin Islands: Municipio, Municipio and Island Subdivision, and Place Boundaries ($4) 60″ × 44″

■ Tennessee: County and Place Boundaries ($3.75) 36″ × 48″

■ West Virginia: County, County Subdivision, and Place Boundaries ($3.50) 34″ × 44″

There also are two editions of United States county outline maps:

■ Black Edition ($3.50): Shows state, county, and county equivalent boundaries as of January 1, 1980, in black, with state boundaries drawn with heavier lines. 30″ × 42″

■ Black and Green Edition ($3.50): Same as Black Edition, but shows state boundaries in black and county boundaries in green. 30″ × 42″

Most maps produced by the **U.S. Geological Survey** include boundary lines for the area mapped. Topographical quadrangle maps include boundary lines drawn by local or state authorities. Only the maps of West Virginia contain boundaries established by the USGS at the request and compliance of the state. (See "Topographic Maps" for more information on topographic quadrangles and ordering.)

USGS also publishes copies of the Bureau of Land Management's "Principal Meridians and Base Line Map" governing the U.S. Public Lands Surveys ($3.10), which shows the United States, Alaska, and Hawaii, with dates and boundaries for surveyed public lands.

The **Government Printing Office** publishes an in-depth study of the history and regulations of boundary establishment, *Boundaries of the United States and Several States* ($7.50), a 1976 Geological Survey Professional Paper by Franklin Van Zandt that includes dozens of black-and-white and color boundary maps. The 191-page book is available from GPO or USGS.

The **Central Intelligence Agency** publishes hundreds of maps of foreign countries that include internationally accepted boundary lines. The maps are available from the National Technical Information Service; a few are available in GPO bookstores. (See "CIA Maps" for details.)

Both the **Library of Congress** and the **National Archives** have boundary maps in their vast collections. The Library's collection consists of both American and international boundary maps, some dating back to the 1300s. The Archives' collection, which spans the two centuries between 1750 and 1950, contains American boundary maps commissioned by the federal government. While many of the best boundary maps are created privately by hired surveyors and rarely are made public, the Library and the Archives have collected and made available many such maps of both domestic and foreign origin. Reproduction services are available from both collections. (See "Uncle Sam's Treasure Chests" for details.)

State and Local Boundary Maps. These often may be obtained through local land management or survey departments. Most cities have a records office where early land ownership agreements and boundary maps may be available for study; local historical societies are another good source for boundary maps of significance to an area. Some state cartographic offices provide maps or can point you in the direction of good resources (see Appendix B).

Foreign Boundary Maps. These often are available through each country's cartographic agencies (see Appendix C). Another source may be national tourism bureaus (Appendix C).

▶ **See also: "Foreign Maps," "Land Ownership Maps," "Nautical Charts and Maps," "State Maps," and "U.S. Maps."**

Business Maps

For the traveling salesman, the road map is as vital a tool as the telephone and the motel, but it isn't the only kind of map available to people in sales and other aspects of business. Maps are being used increasingly in businesses large and small, as computer and other data are combined with territorial maps to create visual representations for a variety of business applications, primarily in the areas of sales and marketing.

Business maps come in many shapes and forms. Among them:

■ demographic maps ranking areas by population, income, age, race, and other factors;
■ thematic maps showing manufacturing and trade areas;
■ simple, uncluttered black-and-white or color

maps of countries, states, counties, cities, and major transportation routes;
■ zip code maps with population data;
■ maps showing the major television and radio markets;
■ travelers' maps and atlases showing efficient routes, convention centers, hotels, and other amenities;
■ various marketing and sales atlases combining many of the above elements.

Most of these are manufactured by a few large companies that either specialize in, or have departments devoted to, business maps. The federal government's contribution to the business map field comes in the form of census maps (see "Census Maps"), many of which are also available, of-

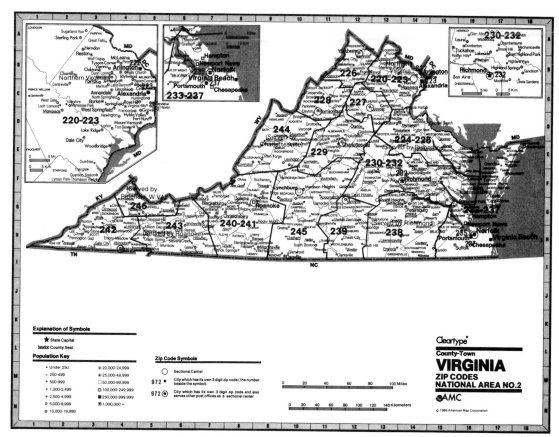

An American Map Corporation zip code map of Virginia.

ten with enhancements, from commercial publishers. The cartographic offices of foreign countries (Appendix C) can often locate the necessary business maps for their regions.

Government Sources

Several Census Bureau maps are available through the Government Printing Office, including:

- "Metropolitan Statistical Areas (CMSAs, PMSAs and MSAs)" ($4.25): This 1984 map shows the locations of three standardized census regions—consolidated metropolitan areas (CMSAs), primary metropolitan Areas (PMAs), and metropolitan statistical areas (MSAs)—for the United States and Puerto Rico. The map (35" × 47") is printed on both sides; the continental U.S., Alaska, Hawaii, and Puerto Rico is on the front and a large map of New England is on the back.
- "Per Capita Retail Sales by County, 1977" ($2.75): This 1983 30" × 44" map, based on 1977 data, illustrates per capita sales around the nation in shades of yellow, orange, and brown.
- "Population Distribution in the United States: 1980" ($3.25): This 29" × 40" map, known also as the "Nighttime View," illustrates the densely populated areas of the United States with spots of white on a black background.

Commercial Sources

Many of these were made with utility in mind: some atlases can slide into glove compartments; larger maps are designed to be mounted and displayed for presentation. Graphics tend to be minimal, as are details about tourist attractions or other extraneous features found on most general use maps.

American Map Corporation (46-35 54th Road, Maspeth, NY 11378; 718-784-0055) produces a variety of products. Its "Cleartype" series is a collection of black-and-white outline maps in varying sizes showing place-names and borders for U.S. cities, counties, and states, as well as maps of Canada and the world. Cleartype maps are suited for drawing or writing on and are available with a variety of mounting styles. When ordering by mail,

there is a minimum order of two maps for sizes 22" × 17" or smaller. The selection includes:

- "Canada Province Outline" in three sizes: 38" × 25" ($5), 22" × 17" ($2.50), and 11" × 8½" ($.55).
- "U.S. State Outline" shows the continental United States, Alaska, and Hawaii with each state outlined and identified. There are ten sizes available, from to 8½" × 6" ($.25) to 74" × 50" ($24).
- "U.S. County Outline" shows outlines of all U.S. counties, with nine sizes available, from 8½" × 11" ($.40) to 74" × 50" ($27).
- "Individual States/County Outline" shows all counties within a single state. Maps are available for all 50 states, in either 8½" × 11" ($.40) or 17" × 22" ($1.25).
- "Individual States/County and Town Outline" are the same as above, but show both towns and counties.
- "World Outline" shows outlines and names of continents and countries on a map drawn on a Mercator Projection. The seven sizes and prices available range from 8½" × 11" ($.55) to 64" × 44" ($22).
- "Continents and Oceania Outline Maps" show outlines of countries, individual continents, and Oceania. The two available sizes are 8½" × 11" ($.55) and 17" × 22" ($2.50).

Other Cleartype maps include sets of principal United States, Canadian, and world cities; major U.S. metropolitan areas; and individual countries in Europe, South America, the Middle East, and Asia.

Cleartype thematic maps available include:

- "U.S. MSA Markets" ($15), a Metropolitan Statistical Area map measuring 44" × 30".
- "U.S. ADI Markets" ($15), Areas of Dominant Influence, industry jargon for major media markets, measuring 44" × 30".
- "U.S. Zip Code County/Town Map" ($30), with zip code areas for places of 2,500 or more population, measuring 44" × 64".
- "U.S.Road Map" ($25), sized 64" × 44".
- "U.S. Railroad Map" ($25), sized 64" × 44".

"Colorprint" maps are similar to Cleartype maps in detail, but are produced in full color. Available maps include:

■ "U.S. County/Town Sales Maps" (38″ × 25″; $17 or 64″ × 44″; $36), showing towns of various population sizes from 2,500 to 10,000.

■ "World Mural," four-color maps available in three sections (110″ × 68″; $140); two sections (86″ × 54″; $60); or a single sheet (64″ × 42″; $23).

■ "World/USA Miniature Murals," four-color murals of world and the United States. Two world map sizes (38″ × 25″; $5 and 8½″ × 11″; $.55) and four sizes of the United States, from 8½″ × 11″ ($.55) to 38″ × 25″ ($5).

Other Colorprint maps available include political reference and political-geophysical wall maps.

The American Map Corporation also produces a number of business atlases, among them:

■ *Business Control Atlas* ($16): This 146-page, spiral-bound book has state-by-state maps of cities and towns with population over 1,000 in the United States, Canada, and Puerto Rico, as well as area code, zip code, and time zone maps and census information.

■ *Executive Sales Control Atlas* ($99): Similar to above, with more comprehensive maps of all areas of the United States, in a binder with write on/wipe off, laminated pages.

■ *Master Sales Control Atlas* ($495): Same as above, in deluxe edition, completely indexed and including pressure-sensitive coding symbols and tapes.

■ *Commercial Sales Atlas* ($65): Same as the *Master Sales Atlas*, but without laminated maps.

■ *Zip Code Atlas* ($14.95): State-by-state maps of three-digit zip code areas, showing county seats, state capitals, postal sectional centers, and multi-coded cities.

Hammond Inc. (515 Valley Street, Maplewood, NJ 07040; 201-763-6000) produces a small series of maps for business use, as well as a comprehensive *Sales Planning Atlas*. Available business maps include:

■ "City/State Sales Planning Maps": Black-and-

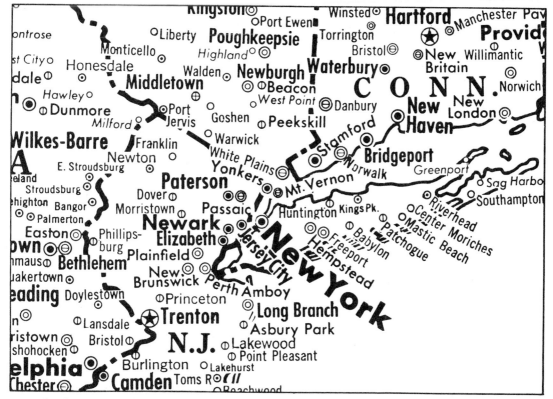

New York and surrounding areas are illustrated in this portion of a "Principal City Map," from American Map Corporation.

white maps showing state boundaries, and major cities/trade centers. Three sizes: 11″ × 17″ ($.95); 19″ × 25″ ($3.50); and 25″ × 38″ ($4.90).

■ "State/County Outline Maps": single state maps showing county outlines, major cities and towns, state capitals, and county seats. An index, zip code directory, and census information are printed on the back of each map. The 8½″ × 11″ maps are sold in packages of ten for $4.

■ "County Outline Map": A 25″ × 38″ wall map of the United States with counties outlined within each state ($3.90).

■ *Sales Planning Atlas* ($14.95): This 128-page atlas includes state-by-state U.S. maps with county outlines and place designations for places with more than 1,000 people, census statistics, U.S. and world time zones, highway mileage and air distances, city weather information, and other pertinent sales and travel planning features. A "U.S. County Outline Wall Map" is included in an inside pocket.

Rand McNally (P.O. Box 7600, Chicago, IL 60680; 800-323-1887, 312-673-9100 in Ill.) has a line of office and business maps that include outline, thematic, and marketing maps, and several business-oriented atlases.

Rand McNally outine maps include:

■ "MarketMaps—Regional Titles": A series of 8½″ × 11″ black-and-white outline state map sets with city and county details of various regions of the United States. Each map is indexed with places having populations of 1,000 or more. Sets in the series are: "Eastern Mid-Atlantic States" (eleven maps; $8.25); "Midwestern States" (twelve maps; $9); "New England/Northeastern States" (eight maps; $6); Southern States (twelve maps; $9); and Western States (fourteen maps; $10.50).

■ "MarketMaps—U.S. Titles": A series of black-and-white outline maps in various sizes and concentrations. U.S. State Outline with state outlines only (five sizes, from 8½″ × 11″; $.50 to 46″ × 66″; $12); U.S. County/State Outline with state and county outline only (five sizes from 8½″ × 11″; $.50 to 46″ × 66″; $15); U.S. City/State Outline—cities designated within state outlines (three sizes, from 8½″ × 11″; $.75 to 21″ × 28″; $5.50); and U.S. City/County/State Outline—cities shown within counties (two sizes, 19″ × 22″; $2.75

and 24″ × 28″; $5.95). There also are single state MarketMaps in both county and city/county outline formats in three sizes: 8½″ × 11″ ($.50); 17″ × 22″ ($1.50); and 21″ × 28″ ($2.75).

■ "Color MarketMaps II": This is a color version of the black-and-white MarketMaps series. Color MarketMaps include U.S. City/County/State outlines in three sizes: 24″ × 28″ ($14.95); 33″ × 42″ ($24.95); and 46″ × 66″ ($44.95). There is also a 21″ × 28″ U.S. City/State outline ($14.95).

■ "Sectional Sales Control Maps": These show sections of the U.S. in black-and-white detail, featuring state and county names, county seats, and cities with populations of 1,000 or more, as well as insets of major metropolitan areas. Four of the five maps (the North Central, Northeast, Southeast and Southwest), are available in two sizes and prices: 25½″ × 36″ ($7) and 41″ × 45½″ ($10); the Western Sales Control Map is available only in 41″ × 45½″ ($16).

■ "Zip Code Map of the U.S.": A four-color map with state and county names, showing names of zip code sectional areas and other zoned cities, with large-scale insets of thirteen major metropolitan areas. Two sizes: 21½″ × 27½″ ($14.95) and 25″ × 32″ ($19.95).

Rand McNally thematic business maps include:

■ "Map of Population": Based on updated census information, this 19½″ × 27½″ map shows population density in the United States ($14.95).

■ "Map of Trading Areas": Outlines and names the fifty top U.S. trade centers and the 494 Basic Trading Areas, 21½″ × 27½″ ($14.95).

■ "Map of Metropolitan Statistical Areas": Shows the census-defined MSAs, PMSAs, and CMSAs, with population tables, 21½″ × 27½″ ($14.95).

■ "Map of Retail Sales": Shows retail sales in each county, 19½″ × 27¾″ ($14.95).

■ "Map of Manufacturing": Uses the Census of Manufacture to show economic growth across the country, 19½″ × 27¾″ ($14.95).

■ "Map of Major Military Installations": Shows all major U.S. installations indicating branch of force, 20½″ × 27½″ ($14.95).

■ "Map of College Population": Shows student population in schools with 100 or more students, 20½″ × 27½″ ($14.95).

Rand McNally business atlases include:

■ *Business Travelers Road Atlas* ($9.95): This 160-page wire-bound atlas contains the standard *Rand McNally Road Atlas* maps, plus maps of major airports and reference data on area codes, state gas taxes, and driving time. Also included is a state-by-state list of convention facilities, toll-free hotel and car rental telephone numbers, and expense account information.

■ *Business Travelers City Guide* ($9.95): This briefcase-sized, 440-page guide has 72 full-color maps of metropolitan areas, plus information on frequent flyer programs, lodging, dining, and entertainment in these cities.

■ *Commercial Reference Maps and Guides* ($11.95): There is a guide for every state, and each is designed for in-depth study of the area's commercial importance, growth, and potential. Population, marketing, and other demographic data are included, plus an index of air and major transportation services and five-digit zip codes. A full-sized road map and a desk-sized commercial map are included.

■ *Handy Railroad Atlas of the United States* ($9.95): This 64-page paperback includes one- and two-color maps of the American and Canadian rail systems. U.S. railroad distance tables also are included.

■ *Sales and Marketing Atlas* ($15.95): This 168-page, spiral-bound atlas has full-page black-and-white maps suitable for coloring or shading to illustrate business plans. Fully indexed, with demographic information.

■ *Zip Code Atlas* ($17.95): This 142-page paperback has color maps of every state to illustrate three-digit zip codes areas, plus county boundaries and seats, major cities, and population centers. Demographic information about population size and distribution is included, as are zip code maps for major cities.

▶ **See also: "Atlases," "Census Maps," "Energy Maps," "Land Ownership Maps," "Map Software," "Natural Resource Maps," and "Utilities Maps."**

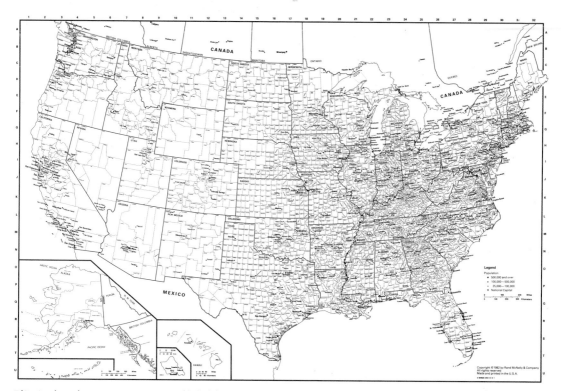

This simple and concise U.S. map is published by Rand McNally for use in sales planning, marketing, and other business applications.

Census Maps

Every ten years, the Bureau of the Census compiles millions of statistics about Americans. The bureau calculates such tidbits as the number of pets per family, the number of children per street, and the number of people per mile, which are added to other data to create a national statistical portrait. The bureau turns some of these facts and figures into demographic maps that illustrate where and what people are in this country. Using a kind of paint-by-numbers method, the bureau produces a new series of maps after every census, updating them regularly as new data are gathered. The bureau also produces several maps, map series, and atlases. Summary reports of these series usually include the series' maps on a smaller scale, along with text that provides an analysis of the information. Census maps are useful to businesses looking for prospective markets; to developers in search of home, office, or factory buyers; to sociologists concerned with population trends; and to anyone else with an interest in the numbers, distribution, incomes, life styles, and so on of Americans.

The maps in the Census Bureau's 1980 "Number of Inhabitants Series" are either state or county outline base maps. In addition to an overall U.S. population map, Census map titles include "Major Acquisitions of Territory of the United States and Dates of Admission to States," "Urbanized Areas of the United States: 1980," "Center of Population for the United States: 1790 to 1980," "Regions and Census Divisions of the United States," and "Population and Geographic Centers of the United States: 1980." The series also includes maps that trace changes in total, rural, urban, and metropolitan populations from 1960 to 1970 and from 1970 to 1980. There are also maps of urban population density and percentage by county.

All of these maps, as well as charts illustrating population trends, are available separately or together in the "U.S. Summary Report of the Number of Inhabitants" series, available from the Census Bureau. Among the titles in the "Maps in the 1980 General Population Characteristics" series are: "Number of Black Persons by State,"

"Number of American Indian, Eskimo, and Aleut Persons by State," and "Number of Asian and Pacific Islander Persons by State." This series also includes maps of regions and county divisions and subdivisions. The U.S. *Summary Report* of this series includes all of these maps and related charts.

Standard Metropolitan Statistical Areas (SMSAs) are the most commonly mapped sections of the country by the Census Bureau. Copies of SMSA maps are available for all fifty states and Puerto Rico in the "Number of Inhabitants" report series. SMSA maps also can be found in the "Urban Atlas Series," which contains 65 atlases of SMSAs, displaying on individual maps twelve characteristics for each, including population density per square mile, percentage of the population under eighteen or over 65, percentage of high school graduates over the age of 25, interrelationship of family income and educational attainment, and median housing value and contract rent. The atlases, which are available from the Government Printing Office, are somewhat out of date; the most recent maps are based on the 1970 census.

Among the other Census Bureau maps:

■ A "U.S. County Outline Map" and "State and County Subdivision" maps for the fifty states, Puerto Rico, the Virgin Islands, Guam, American Samoa, and the Pacific and Northern Mariana Islands. All are basic outline representations, without other census information, and are available from GPO.
■ The GE-70 Special Maps Series, which includes a notable "1980 Population Distribution Map (Nighttime View)" illustrating population by depicting the United States at night, with brightly lit patches representing larger metroplitan areas and unlit or pinpoints of light representing less populated areas. It is available through GPO.
■ Other maps in the Special Maps Series include 1970 urban and rural population distribution, distribution of older Americans in 1970, and primary home heating fuel by county, all available directly from the Census Bureau.

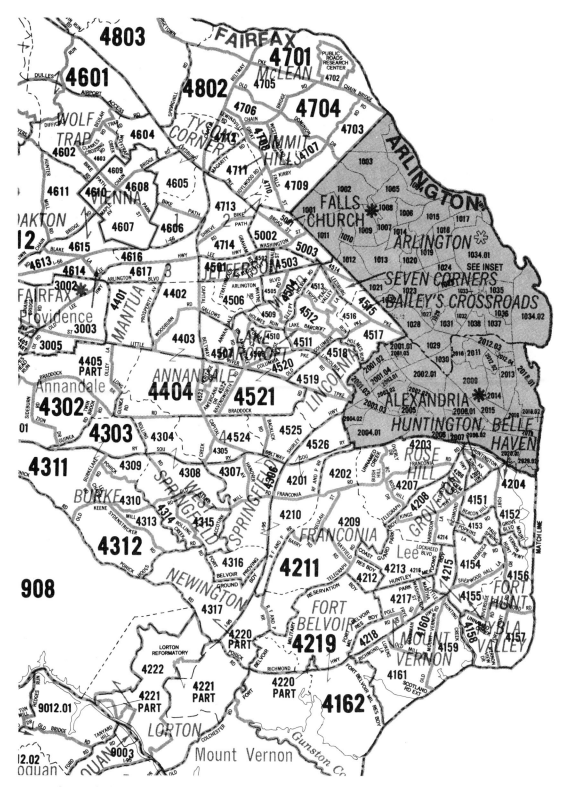

Portion of a Standard Metropolitan Statistical Area census tract, illustrating the census districts of northern Virginia.

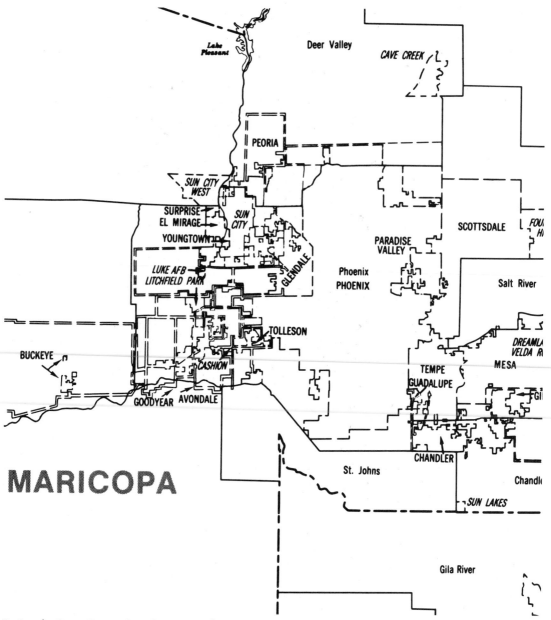

Portion of a Census Bureau State/County map of Arizona.

■ The *Congressional District Atlas* has maps of the 435 congressional districts of the 98th Congress, which convened in 1983. Place and county names are incorporated and indexed alphabetically. The atlas is available from GPO.

■ A large series of statistical maps, some of which have been updated recently. These include maps of ethnic, income, educational, sex, and age distri-

bution, as well as per capita sales, changes in employment, and housing information. All are available directly from the Census Bureau.

▶ **See also: "Business Maps," "City Maps," "Energy Maps," "Indian Land Maps," and "U.S. Maps."**

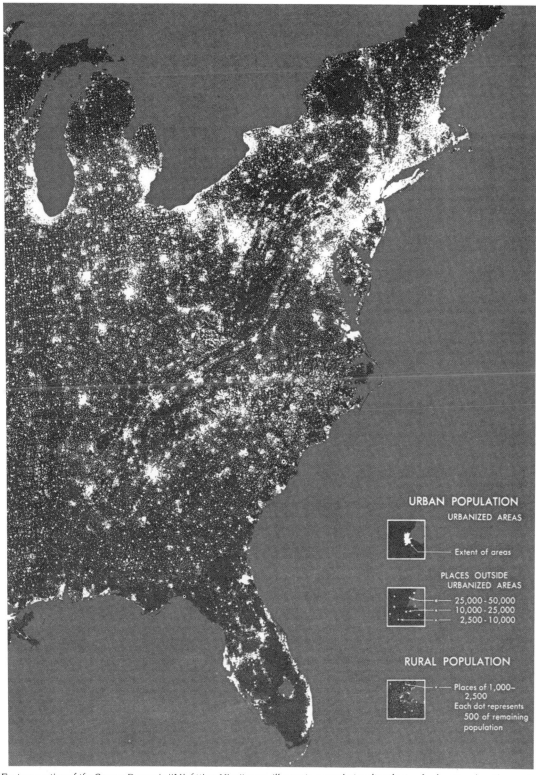

URBAN POPULATION

URBANIZED AREAS

Extent of areas

PLACES OUTSIDE
URBANIZED AREAS

25,000 - 50,000
10,000 - 25,000
2,500 - 10,000

RURAL POPULATION

Places of 1,000–
2,500
Each dot represents
500 of remaining
population

Eastern portion of the Census Bureau's "Nighttime View" map, illustrating population distribution by depicting how the country might appear from above at night.

CIA Maps

If James Bond had needed a map while in the United States, he probably would have turned to the CIA for help. The Central Intelligence Agency, known to insiders as "the Company," may be known worldwide for its clandestine operations, but when it comes to creating and updating maps of foreign countries, this cloak-and-dagger outift comes in from the cold, readily sharing its wealth of information.

The CIA creates maps of practically every place on earth, from Aden to Zimbabwe. These maps were created to aid the CIA in its overseas intelligence operations, and they are very straightforward: no sightseeing gimmicks or hotel rates are listed in the margins. Depending on the map, roads, railroads, airports, and communications centers are noted, as are topography, resources, and other pertinent information about the land. Some maps detail the political structure of a country's ruling party, the areas of its border disputes, or the demographics of its natives. Maps vary in size, scale, and design, depending on the subject matter, but all are useful as basic overviews of the layouts of foreign countries.

The CIA uses the state of the art in computer cartographic tools to create these maps. Its "World Data Bank II" data base uses digitalized representations of the natural and manmade features around the world to aid in mapping. This data base is combined with the agency's Cartographic Automatic Mapping Program, an IBM/360 Fortran program that performs a number of cartographic functions, including updating road maps; changing the shape of the topography as buildings, landfills, or other manmade structures appear on the land; and providing various scales and levels of maps for most areas of the world.

The CIA also produces several atlases with attached or pull-out maps. These atlases, most of which are five to ten years old, are comprehensive guides to sensitive or strategic areas (the Soviet Union, Peoples Republic of China, or Earth's polar regions, for example) or as specific studies of political structure or land use. The atlases include text, graphs, and charts of statistics as well as maps.

Maps published before 1980 are available through the Library of Congress Photoduplication Service (Library of Congress, Washington, DC 20540; 202-287-5650). Most maps published after January 1, 1980 are available from the National Technical Information Service (5285 Port Royal Road, Springfield, VA 22161; 703-487-4650); the atlases and a few maps are available from the Government Printing Office. When ordering CIA maps, include the full name and publication number of each map. By government standards, the maps and atlases are rather expensive—prices range from $4.50 to $10—but are worth it for the expertise and technology with which they were created.

A catalog, CIA *Maps and Publications Released to the Public,* is available from the CIA's Public Affairs Office (Washington DC 20505; 703-351-2053), as are bulletins about publication of new maps.

CIA Maps Available from NTIS

1985 Maps

Africa ($7.50; PB 85-928002)
Africa Ethnolinguistic Groups ($7.50; PB 85-928008)
Afghanistan, Major Insurgent Groups ($10; PB 85-928040)
Belgium & Europe ($10; PB 85-928037)
Comoros ($7.50; PB 85-928005)
Egypt, Azimuthal Equidistant Projection Centered on Cairo ($7.50; PB 85-928036)
Europe, Eastern ($7.50; PB 85-928402)
Guyana ($7.50; PB 85-928003)
Indochina ($7.50; PB 85-928208)
Israeli Settlements in the Gaza Strip and Western Indian Ocean ($10; PB 85-928038)
Lebanon, Population and Religious Affiliation ($7.50; PB 85- 928039)
Mexico ($7.50; PB 85-928009)
Nigeria ($7.50; PB 85-928033)
North America and South America ($10; PB 85-928028)
Permafrost Regions in the Soviet Union ($7.50; PB 85-928101)
Soviet Union ($7.50; PB 85-928108)
USSR, Soviet Union Administrative Divisions,

ECONOMIC ACTIVITY

AGRICULTURE	MANUFACTURING	MINERALS
Coffee	Oil refinery	D Diamond mine
Cotton	Rail shops and yards	Au Gold mine
Sisal	Cement plant	Sn Tin mine
Cashew	Tires	C Coalfield
Pyrethrum	Textiles	Fe Iron deposit
Tobacco	Fertilizer plant	Ph Phosphate deposit
Cattle	Sugar refinery	Na Salt
Tea	Meatpacking	
Cloves	Powerplant	
Major cattle scheme outside of main cattle areas	Oil pipeline	

CIA map of Tanzania showing agricultural, manufacturing, and mining regions.

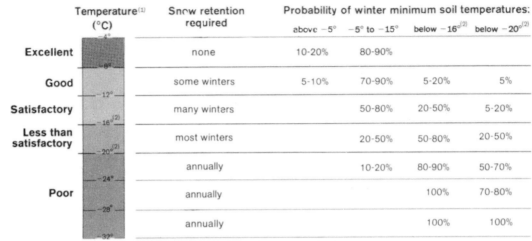

Temperature[1] (°C)	Snow retention required	Probability of winter minimum soil temperatures:			
		above −5°	−5° to −15°	below −16°[2]	below −20°[2]
Excellent	none	10-20%	80-90%		
Good	some winters	5-10%	70-90%	5-20%	5%
Satisfactory	many winters		50-80%	20-50%	5-20%
Less than satisfactory	most winters		20-50%	50-80%	20-50%
	annually		10-20%	80-90%	50-70%
Poor	annually			100%	70-80%
	annually			100%	100%

(1) average of absolute minimum soil temperatures at depth of tillering node (3 cm)

(2) critical soil temperature at depth of tillering node for winter wheat is −16°C and for winter rye, −20°C.

Wintering conditions
winter grains and perennial grasses

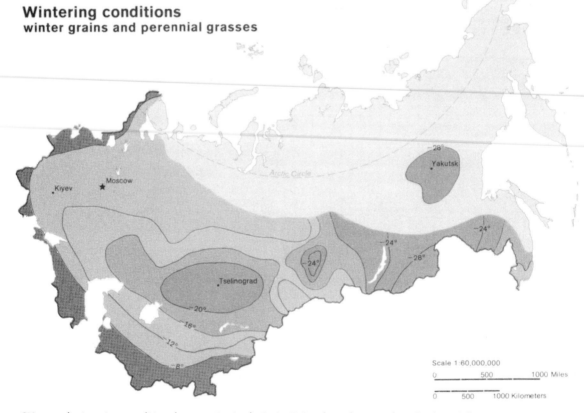

CIA *map showing winter conditions for vegetation in the* Soviet Union, *from the* Agricultural Atlas of the USSR.

1984 East and South Asia ($10; PB 85-928109)
Turkey ($7.50; PB 85-928001)
World Political Map ($7.50; PB 85-928034)

1984 Maps
Africa—Penetration of Islam ($7.50; PB 84-928050)
Albania ($7.50; PB 84-928017)
Antarctic: Research Stations and Territorial Claims ($7.50; PB 84-928002)
Arabian Peninsula ($7.50; PB 84-928016)
Beijing ($9.50; PB 84-928208)
Beirut ($7.50; PB 84-928051)
China: Clothing Recommendations for Travel ($7.50; PB 84-928026)
China Military Regions ($7.50; PB 84-928207)
East Asia and Oceania ($7.50; PB 84-928042)
Hong Kong and Macau ($7.50; PB 84-928209)
Johannesburg and Vicinity ($7.50; PB 84-928010)
Libya ($7.50; PB 84-928006)
Muslim Distribution ($7.50; PB 84-92805)
Peru-Ecuador: Area of Boundary Dispute ($7.50; PB 84-928010)
Qatar ($7.50; PB 84-928041)
Upper Volta ($7.50; PB 84-928004)
U.S. Foreign Service Posts & Department of State Jurisdictions ($7.50; PB 84-928009)
Zhonggo Pinyin Ditu ($7.50; PB 84-928210)

1983 Maps
Antigua and Barbuda ($7.50; PB 83-928003)
China: Fuels, Power, Mineral & Metals ($7.50; PB 83-928207)
Narcotics Smuggling: Major Routes and Cultivation Areas ($9.50; PB 83-928037)
Peoples of Yugoslavia ($7.50; PB 83-927916)
Strait of Hormuz and Vicinity ($7.50; PB 83-928034)

CIA Maps Available from GPO

Southwest Asia ($3.40; S/N 041-015-00139-6)
Persian Gulf ($3.40; S/N 041-015-00140-0)
Afghanistan ($3.40; S/N 041-015-00141-8)
China Map, Pinyin Edition ($3.40; S/N 041-015-00106-0)
The Middle East ($3.40; S/N 041-015-00031-1)
Middle East Area: Oilfields and Facilities ($3.50; S/N 041-015-0030-2)

CIA Atlases Available from GPO

Indian Ocean Atlas (1979; $8.50; S/N 041-015-00080-2) covers the usual geographic information, as well as the economic, historical, and cultural background of the region. Includes one insert reference map and a number of illustrative maps.

People's Republic of China, Administrative Atlas (1976; $8; S/N 041-000076-4) includes detailed maps of each Chinese province, along with lists of administrative divisions, illustrating the political changes the country has seen since its conversion to communism in 1949. Includes pronunciation guides.

USSR *Agricultural Atlas* (1974; $4.75; S/N 041-015-0073-0) explores the Soviet agricultural system and its impact on the country's economy and politics. Land use, technology, irrigation, and farming are studied in depth.

Polar Regions Atlas (1978; $8.50; S/N 041-015-0094-2) discusses the development of the Arctic and Antarctic, focusing on exploration, climate, natural resources, geography, topography, and transportation.

Leningrad Street Guide (1977; $8; S/N 041-015-0087-1) is a pocket-sized book illustrating the transportation system, plat numbers, and points of interest in Leningrad and environs. Includes index and glossary.

▶ **See also: "Foreign Maps."**

City Maps

"All cities are mad: but the madness is gallant. All cities are beautiful: but the beauty is grim," writes Christopher Morley in *Where the Blue Begins*. All cities are confusing, he might have added, which can be both maddening *and* grim. Getting lost at least once in a new city is almost a given, but it needn't become habit. A good map can be a valuable guide to the gallant madness and grim beauty of any modern metropolis. City maps are as useful to the native urbanite as they are for the urban neophyte; some cities can take a lifetime to learn.

Basic city maps come in a variety of sizes, shapes, forms, and detail. There are simple pocket and glove compartment maps showing major roads and official buildings, there are wall maps showing most streets, there are indexed atlases with detailed maps of every neighborhood and district. There's more: land plats showing the location and use of buildings and parks, tourist maps pinpointing locations of award-winning eateries. There are even aerial and satellite photomaps of most American cities.

Large cities like New York or Los Angeles appear on countless maps by both national and local map makers, while many smaller cities and towns have been mapped only by a local chamber of commerce, city hall, or bank. There are probably hundreds of city maps made for internal use by local, state, and federal governments, from sewer maps to taxation maps, but these usually aren't available or helpful to the typical visitor. The number, type, and quality of maps available for any city is usually directly related to the size of its tourist trade.

There are hundreds of commercial map makers specializing in creating city maps for a particular region or state. Many such companies do not sell directly to the public, but sell promotional maps that banks, Realtors, and other businesses distribute to customers. There also are companies specialize in certain kinds of city maps. Historic Urban Plans of Ithaca, N.Y., for example, produces full-color reproductions of antique maps of American and European cities.

The best sources for free city maps are a local tourist bureau, chamber of commerce, or city planning office. State and county goverments produce general tourism and highway maps of their regions; morever, they often can advise you on where to find local maps. Although the federal government includes city outlines on some of its general use maps, it does not produce detailed, street-by-street maps of American cities. (The CIA does, however, have a pocket street guide to the Soviet city of Leningrad—see "CIA Maps.")

More detailed street maps and atlases, or specialized theme maps, probably will be more expensive. They may be purchased at a local bookstore, travel store, or through the producing companies themselves. Many aerial and Landsat photomaps of cities are available from the federal government through its EROS Data Center and other distributing agencies. There also are several commercial producers of Landsat images and numerous commercial aerial photo companies who can provide photomaps of cities (see "Aerial Photographs" and "Space Imagery").

For older or antique city maps, the best national resources are the map collections of the Library of Congress and the National Archives.

The Archives collection includes city plans and plats mapped by the government up to 1950. The Library of Congress maps include thousands of commercially made city maps, as well as those made by federal, state, county, and local governments.

One of the Library's most prized possessions is its set of Sanborn city fire insurance maps, which trace the history of hundreds of American towns from the mid-nineteenth century (see "Emergency Information Maps"). Also in the Library of Congress is a large collection of panoramic city views, a history and checklist of which, *Panoramic Maps of Cities in the United States and Canada* ($6), is available from the Library of Congress or the Government Printing Office.

Local map collections, university libraries, and historical societies are also good resources for finding older city maps and plans.

Section from Dr. Karl Koenig's "Jazz Map of New Orleans." The circles indicate places of historical interest.

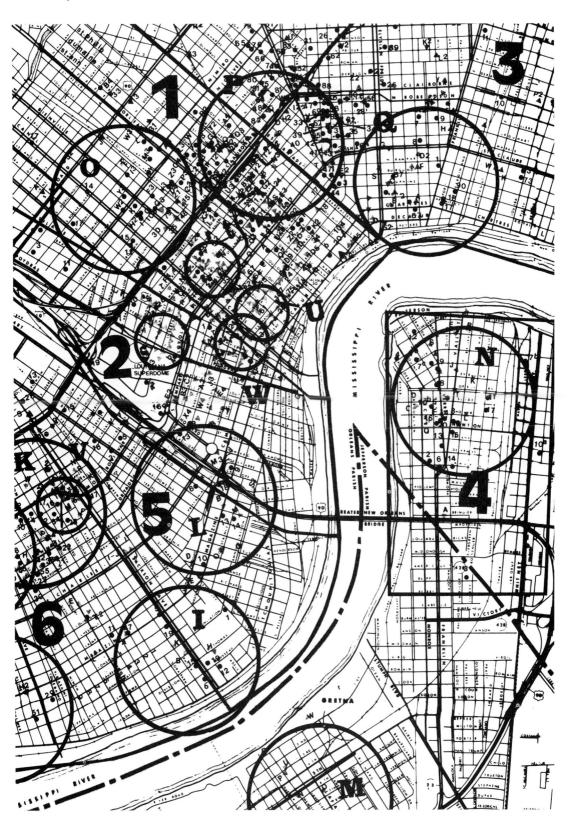

A sampling of the city maps created by publishers around the country.

- ■ "Pictorial Map of Nashville in the 1880s" ($1.25) measures 24″ × 41″.
- ■ "Pictorial Map of Memphis" ($1.25) measures 16″ × 23″.

Local, county and state boards of tourism and chambers of commerce are other good resources for finding city maps.

Commercial Sources

Hippocrene Books (171 Madison Avenue, New York, NY 10016; 212-685-4371) is the U.S. distributor of Cartographia city maps ($2.95 each), artistic maps of mostly Eastern European cities, including Belgrade, Bucharest, Krakow, Leningrad, Moscow, Naples, Rekjavik, Sofia, Thessaloniki, and Warsaw. Also available from Hippocrene are several Bollman picture and street city maps ($6.95 each), which are drawn from an aerial perspective using fifteenth-century techniques to create a unique and accurate bird's-eye view of Amsterdam, Bremen, Cologne, Dusseldorf, Luxembourg, Rothenburg, and Stuttgart.

Prentice Hall Press (200 Old Tappan Rd., Old Tappan, NJ 07675; 800-223-2348) distributes Baedeker's City Guides ($10.95 each), the famed travel guides for the intrepid urban adventurer. These guides feature full-color indexed city maps and fascinating texts to make the city come alive. Available guides include Amsterdam, Copenhagen, Jerusalem, London, Moscow, New York, Paris, Rome, San Francisco, Singapore, and Venice.

American Map Corporation (46-35 54th Road, Maspeth, NY 11378; 718-784-0055) distributes Hallwag city maps ($4.25 each), with three-dimensional sketches of important landmarks. Available maps include Amsterdam, Athens, Barcelona, Berlin, Berne, Budapest, Copenhagen, Costa Brava, Florence, Istanbul, Rome, Tokyo, Vienna, and Zurich. There are also maps of the London, Munich, and Paris subway systems.

Creative Sales Corporation (762 West Algonquin Rd., Arlington Heights, IL 60005; 312-956-0870) publishes the *City Map Atlas*, ($12.95), which contains detailed maps for most major cities in the United States, including street maps and public

Government Sources

Tennessee Valley Authority. TVA has a series of inexpensive lithographic reproductions of pictorial historical maps for four cities in its region. The lithographs, made from artists' sketches of the cities from an oblique aerial view, are suitable for framing. Available lithographs (include 50 cents postage for each map when ordering) are:
- ■ "Pictorial Map of Knoxville" (File No. 455 K 94; $1.25) measures 22″ × 29″.
- ■ "Pictorial Map of Chattanooga" (File No. G MD 455 K 558; $1.25) measures 23″ × 30″.

transportation maps. It is one of the most comprehensive sources of city maps available.

Commercial Sources—Regional

Commercial producers of city maps include:

■ **ADC** (6440 General Green Way, Alexandria, VA; 703-750-0510) produces street atlases and sheet maps for various cities in Delaware, District of Columbia, Georgia, Maryland, North Carolina, Pennsylvania, and Virginia.

■ **Flashmaps Publications, Inc.,** (P.O. Box 101, Chappaqua, NY 10514) produces instant guides for the following major cities: Chicago, District of Columbia, Los Angeles, and New York.

■ **Gousha Maps and Atlases** (Dept. C P.O. Box 6227, San Jose, CA 95150; 408-296-1060) produces detailed street maps of most major American cities.

■ **Marshall Penn-York Co. Inc.,** (538 Erie Blvd. West, Syracuse, NY 13204; 315-422-2162) publishes city maps and atlases of New York, Pennsylvania, and Southern New England under the Visual Encyclopedia trademark.

■ **Metro Graphic Arts Incorporated** (P.O. Box 7035, Grand Rapids, MI 49510) produces maps and street guides of various cities in Alabama, Georgia, Indiana, Michigan, Tennessee, West Virginia, and Wisconsin.

■ **National Survey** (Chester, VT 05143; 802-875-2121) produces maps of New England cities.

■ **North American Maps** (P.O. Box 5850, San Francisco, CA 94101; 415-333-3490) produces maps of California and other western and southwestern states.

■ **Pittmon** (930 S.E. Sandy Blvd., Portland, OR 97214; 503-232-1161) produces city maps of Oregon and Washington state.

■ **Thomas Bros. Maps** (17731 Cowan St., Irvine, CA 92714; 714-863-1984) produces a wide range of spiral-bound street guides, road atlases, and wall maps covering California and parts of Arizona, Oregon, and Washington.

Commercial Sources—Local

Other sources for cities in their regions include:

Alabama:
Atlantic Aerial Surveys, Inc., 803 Franklin Street, Huntsville, AL 35804.

Alaska:
Alaska Map Service, 723 W. 6th Avenue, Anchorage, AK 99502.

Arkansas:
Triangle Company of Arkansas, 3917 Rogers Avenue, Fort Smith, AR 72901.

California:
Pacific Coast Map Service, 12021 Long Beach Blvd., Lynnwood, CA 90262; **Renie Admap Company,** 12728 W. Washington, Blvd., Los Angeles, CA 90017.

Colorado:
Allco Maps & Services, c/o Scarrow & Walker, Inc., 204 8th Street, Glenwood Springs, CO 81601.

Connecticut:
Majorie C. Hatch (Ltd.), Town Clerk's Office, Town Hall, Durham, CT 06422.

Florida:
Champion Maps, 4863 N.E. 12th Avenue, Fort Lauderdale, FL 33304; **Lyons Map Company,** 312 Dade Commonwealth Building, 139 N.E. First Street, Miami, FL 33132.

Louisiana:
Houma Reproduction & Map Co., 550 South Van Avenue, Houma, LA 70360; **The New Orleans Map Company,** 110 Exchange Place, New Orleans, LA 70130.

Maine:
Main Graphics, 55½ Main Street, Lincoln, ME 04457.

Maryland:
Ad Art Associates, Inc., 13447 New Hampshire Avenue, Silver Spring, MD 20907.

Massachusetts:
J.L. Hammett Company, 48 Canal Street, Boston, MA 02111.

Michigan:
Great Lakes Map Company, 24634 Ford Road, Dearborn, MI 48226.

Minnesota:
The Hudson Map Company, 1504 Hennepin Avenue, Minneapolis, MN 55403.

Montana:
State Publishing Company, Airport Road, Helena, MT 59601.

Nevada:
Arrow Blueprint Company, 415 Carson Avenue, Las Vegas, NV 89109.

New Jersey:
Geographia Map Company, 317 St. Paul's Avenue, Jersey City, NJ 07306.

New York:
Geographia Map Company, P.O. Box 688, Times Square Station, New York, NY 10036; **Historic Urban Plans,** Box 276, Ithaca, NY 14850.

North Carolina:
Superior Map Company, 126 North Main, Highpoint, NC 27260.

Ohio:
Surveying & Mapping, 275 South Hickory Street, Chillicothe, OH 45601.

Oklahoma:
Triangle Company, 314 South Cincinnati Street, Tulsa, OK 74119.

Pennsylvania:
Pen-Oh-Wes Map Company, 511 Magee Building, 336 Fourth Pittsburgh, PA 19132.

Texas:
Allstate Map Makers, 1205 Henderson at West Freeway, Fort Worth, TX 76101; **Midland Map Company,** 106 N. Marienfeld Street, Midland, TX 79701.

Washington:
Kroll Map Company, Inc., 2700 Third Avenue, Seattle, WA 98101.

Wisconsin:
Milwaukee Map Service, Inc., 4519 W. North Avenue, Milwaukee, WI 53201; **Smith-Sjolander, Inc.,** 701 Front Street, West, Ashland, WI 54806.

Wyoming:
J.A. Waatti Map Company, 246 South Center Street, Casper, WY 82601.

▶ **See also:** "Aerial Photographs," "Antique Maps," "Atlases," "Business Maps," "Census Maps," "CIA Maps," "Emergency Information Maps," "Highway Maps," "Land Ownership Maps," and "Tourism Maps."

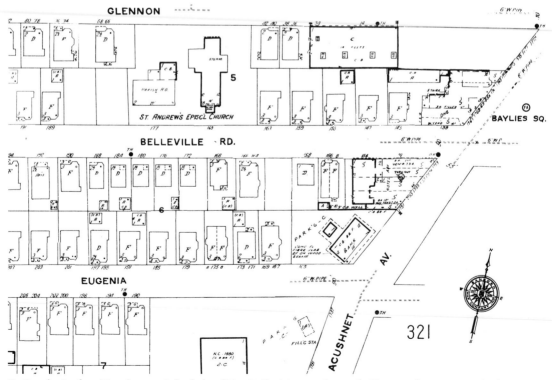

Portion of a Sanborn Map Company's land plat of New Bedford, Mass., showing building numbers, streets, and other specific features of the city.

Congressional District Maps

Congressional district maps tell many tales. The history of congressional representation can be found in the shadings and the boundaries that outline the voting realms—as well as the history of political deal-making and redistricting, known also as "gerrymandering."

The game of gerrymandering is one of the oldest in politics: redrawing the boundaries of a legislative district to create an imbalance of power, giving one political party an unfair advantage at the voting booth. At times, congressional district boundaries wound around and through an area so sinuously as to include only the voters on the left side of one street, and only the voters on the right side of the street a block away. To look at maps of these districts, one might think the boundaries were astrological symbols—sea horses or snakes slithering across the United States with no apparent method to their madness. Without the maps to accurately define the district lines, few would believe the crazy-quilt patterns to be legal divisions of voting boundaries.

The term "gerrymander" was coined when Elbridge Gerry was elected Governor of Massachusetts in 1812 with the aid of a bit of creative state-wide redistricting. A clever cartoonist, noting the serpentine shape of the new boundaries, drew a caricature of the "gerrymander," a salamander-like namesake of the governor.

Gerrymandering has helped more than a few politicians win elections in areas where they normally would have had little support. The Supreme Court sought to abolish the practice in a 1963 ruling, which established the "one man, one vote" precedent. Now, legislative districts must have relatively equal populations, effectively putting an end to the days when 500 bankers could elect three members of Congress, while 5,000 farmers elected just one. But even within these constraints, state legislatures still have the right to carve up voting districts as they see fit.

In most states, the party in power in the legislature has the right to carve up district boundaries. In the end, the district maps have the final say: once drawn, voters and politicians must follow their guidelines until a shift in power sparks the next bout of redistricting.

Some older, gerrymandered congressional district maps are works of art, colored and intricately drawn to include just the right citizenry. More recent maps are a bit less ornate—and less obvious about the purposes of redistricting—and though they may not be as pretty to look at, they paint an accurate portrait of the U.S. population's physical and political distribution.

Congressional district maps are useful to more than just members of Congress: businesspeople use them to study population concentration; fund-raisers use them to pinpoint areas where certain political loyalties may create a donation base; teachers use them to educate students about American history and government. Anyone with an interest in the political make-up and U.S. population distribution will find congressional district maps enlightening, even entertaining.

The federal government creates (and updates with each new Congress) a number of congressional district maps and atlases, as do several commercial map producers. Older congressional district maps are available from map dealers specializing in American history maps, or in reproduction form from a number of map libraries, including the Library of Congress and the National Archives.

Government Sources

Government Printing Office. The following congressional district maps and atlases created by the Bureau of Census are available from GPO:

■ *Congressional District Atlas: Districts of the 99th Congress* (S/N 003-024-06132-5; $15). This 583-page atlas contains maps of all congressional districts during the 99th Congress (1985-87).
■ *Congressional District Atlas: Districts of the 98th Congress* (S/N 003-024-05005-6; $12). 474 pages.
■ "Congressional Districts of the 99th Congress of the United States" (S/N 003-024-06075-2; $3.50). This 35" × 47" map is drawn at a scale of 1:5,000,000.

The Defense Department also produces a congressional district atlas available from GPO: *Conus Army Installations/Activities by Congressional District*

(GPO 1984-421-652-814/2585; $3.75), which has state-by-state maps of congressional districts, naming congressional representatives by army installations. The atlas was created in 1984, which makes it out of date but still useful for matching up installations with placement in districts.

The standard reference volume for congressional information, available from GPO, *The Congressional Directory* (paperback: S/N 052-070-05994-0, $13; cloth binding: S/N 052-070-05995-8, $17;

hardcover: S/N 052-070-05996-6, $21) contains a section in the back of the book devoted to black-and-white maps of congressional districts. The book is updated annually.

U.S. Geological Survey. USGS's National Atlas program produced a colorful map in 1975 that is still available, "Congressional Districts for the 94th Congress" (#00446 38077-AT-NA-07M-00; $3.10).

Section of the Census Bureau's "Congressional Districts of the 99th Congress of the United States," showing the southeastern U.S.

County Maps

William Faulkner's Yoknapatawpha County may have been fictional, but it embodied the regional distinctiveness and closely knit culture many American counties possess. County maps are both useful and fascinating reflections of these national dividing lines that are smaller than states but bigger than cities.

The boundaries of U.S. counties usually are subdivided into townships, cities, or villages. There are some states, especially those in the West, that do things a bit differently, however: New Mexico's counties are divided into election precincts and two Indian reservations, for example, and Wyoming's counties are divided into election districts, although a large portion of the state is given over to Yellowstone Park, which has no county affiliation. Louisiana has no counties at all; it is divided into parishes.

Some counties have personalities of their own. New York's Westchester County, for example, is known as one of the richest in the nation. California's ultra-hip Marin County has been parodied in the movie "The Serial." Harlan County, Kentucky, was the title and subject of a well-known documentary film about coal miners. As a microcosm of American life, the county often represents a portrait of its region or the resources around which it has grown.

County maps both illustrate and mirror the variety of county life and land in America. There are basic county maps showing the subdivisions, highways, parks, and industrial areas. County census maps show a myriad of demographics. County congressional district maps provide a political reference for an area. County recreational maps show lakes, parks, and forests open for public use.

The federal government creates a number of topographic, agricultural, geologic, and recreational maps of counties. State and county governments also create county maps, many of which are distributed free to the public. County and regional historical societies and map collections are good places to find older county maps for research purposes. And there are a number of commercial map companies specializing in the production of county and regional maps.

Government Sources

Census Bureau. The Census Bureau creates maps of counties from statistics it gathers during its surveys. For more information on these maps, see "Census Maps."

Tennessee Valley Authority. TVA has inexpensive blueline and lithographic prints of historical maps of the region, several of which detail counties and county outlines. Include 50 cents for postage when ordering these maps, which include:

■ "Railroad and County Map of Tennessee" (453 D 754-7; $.50), a blueline print of a map published by E. Meoendenhall in 1864.
■ "County Map of Virginia and North Carolina" (no order number; $1.25), a reproduction from a mid-1800s atlas showing counties in parts of West Virginia.
■ "County map of Kentucky and Tennessee" (no order number; $1.50), a reproduction from the same atlas as the above map.
■ "Map of Tennessee" (453 K 315; $1), a blueline print of an 1824 map showing county outlines and county seats.

U.S. Geological Survey. USGS has several county geologic, topographic, and other thematic maps. See appropriate chapters and Appendix A.

Commercial Sources

The "City Maps" section lists companies specializing in local and regional maps. Most of the companies listed also produce county maps. Others include:

■ **Marshall Penn York Company Inc.** (1538 Erie Blvd., West Syracuse, NY 13204; 315-422-2162) produces high-quality, inexpensive county maps of New England, New York, Pennsylvania, and New Jersey, most under $5.
■ **Milwaukee Map Service Inc.** (4519 West North Avenue, Milwaukee, WI 53208; 414-445-7361) produces full-color city maps that list city streets, house numbers, zip codes, freeways, parks, schools, and hospitals. Titles include "Milwaukee

County/Waukesha County Map & Guide,"
"Ozaukee County/Washington County Map," and
"Dane County Street Atlas with City of Madison &
Vicinity Maps." Prices range from $4 to $12.95.
■ **Pittmon Map Company** (930 S.E. Sandy Blvd.,
Portland, OR 97214; 503-232-1161) publishes
county maps for Oregon and Washington state.
Prices range from $1 for some county outline
maps to $75 for some county wall maps.

■ **ADC** (6440 General Green Way; Alexandria, VA
22312; 703-750-0510) has street maps for counties
in Virginia, Maryland, Delaware, North Carolina,
Georgia, and Pennsylvania. Prices range from
$2.95 to $6.95.

▶ **See also: "Business Maps," "Census Maps,"
"City Maps," "Congressional District Maps,"
and "Topographic Maps."**

Portion of a USGS base map of the United States showing county names and boundaries.

Emergency Information Maps

The adage "forewarned is forearmed" is especially true when it applies to rising flood waters or tremors signaling a major quake. Maps of potential or past disaster can often avert serious injury and property loss. But mapping for emergencies can be a tricky thing. Not knowing what emergency will occur, or when and where it might strike, makes it virtually impossible to plan for every event. Still, areas that are flood- or earthquake-prone, seaside towns frequently hit by hurricanes or tidal waves, and any place with a history of disaster, will probably have maps for evacuation and insurance purposes.

Emergency maps have been around for as long as there have been emergencies. Over the centuries, there have been "plague maps" showing the spread of disease, flood and fire maps showing damage to life and property, and countless other diagrams, charts, and maps attempting to illustrate and evaluate the havoc nature, man, or both

can have on the environment. There have been preventive maps as well: countless lives and valuable property have been saved by use of maps of flood plains, faults, unstable areas prone to mudslides and avalanches, and tornado "alleys" that seem to attract nearby twisters.

Among the most common emergency information maps are flood maps. While flooding damage takes it toll in billions of dollars and hundreds of lives annually, flood maps have been highly successful in helping potential victims prepare for the onslaught of mud and water. In some regions, simply having a map of flood plain locations—and avoiding building on them—can make the difference between financial ruin and survival.

Seismicity maps of earthquake regions is another frequently compiled emergency map. Their usefulness for pinpointing regions where earthquakes have occurred or may strike make them

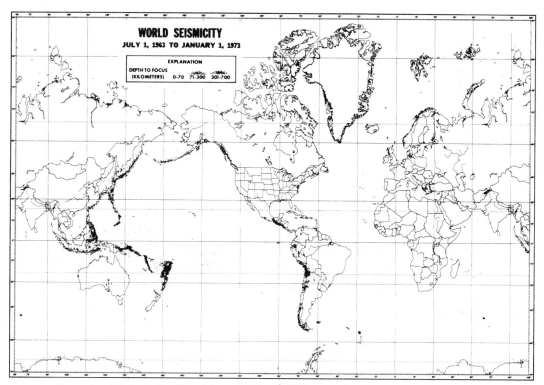

USGS *map illustrating global seismic activity between 1963 and 1973.*

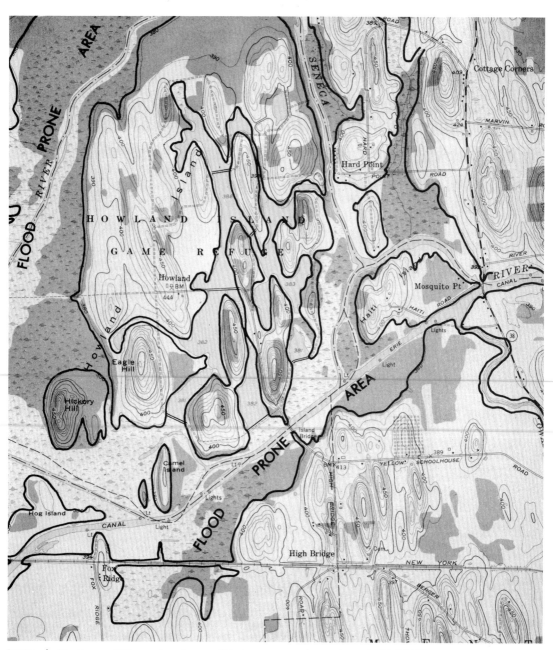

Portion of a Montezuma, N.Y., quadrangle map of flood-prone areas, drawn at a scale of 1:24,000.

valuable tools for planning and constructing new roads, industries, or communities. Seismicity maps are also helpful in the study of faults, shifts, and movement in the Earth's crust.

Other emergency maps available include civil evacuation maps, maps of dangerous tides or currents, maps of active volcano regions, and maps predicting or tracing the paths of such natural di-

sasters as avalanches and hurricanes. But emergency information maps are useful in another way: they have historical value as well.

The fire insurance maps the Sanborn Company began creating in 1867 were certainly utilitarian at the time. Now, however, they are among the Library of Congress' most prized collections. Because of the regularity with which Sanborn updated its maps, historians use the company's works to study the growth of hundreds of American towns and cities. The maps are so detailed that over a single decade one can trace the advances made in building materials or the changing demographics of a neighborhood. Even the earliest Sanborn map in the Library's collection, an 1867 fire atlas of Boston, categorizes building materials, construction, and contents by level of fire hazard.

Certain emergency maps, especially those for civil evacuation, are created by local, county, or state officials rather than by the federal government. Uncle Sam does, however, produce numerous seismicity, flood plain, storm tracking, and tidal warning maps through agencies, including the U.S. Geologic Survey and the Federal Emergency Management Administration.

Government Sources

U.S. Geological Survey. USGS has several seismicity maps pinpointing the earthquake potential of various U.S. regions. The maps are brightly col-

ored and are equally suitable for decoration and reference. Prices range from $1.50 to $6. USGS also has a "World Seismicity Map" for $2.80. Maps may be ordered from the USGS or purchased at retail stores carrying USGS products.

Other USGS maps relating to emergency conditions show potential drought areas and flood plains. Prices and scales vary, but listings for available maps can be obtained from USGS.

Federal Emergency Management Agency. FEMA runs the National Flood Insurance Program, which creates and distributes free "Flood Hazard Boundary Maps" and "Flood Insurance Rate Maps." The maps in both series are created in two forms: the "flat map format" contains a map index, a legend on the cover sheet, and 11" × 17" map panels covering the community; the "multiple fold map format" (also known as the "Z-Fold" format) resembles a standard folding road map and includes a map index only if more than one map panel is required for the community.

Another FEMA series are "Flood Hazard Bound-

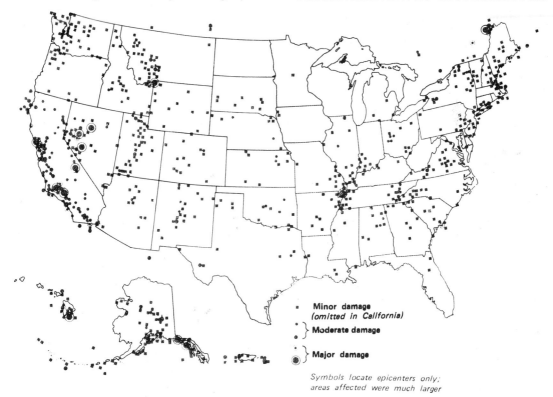

Minor damage
(omitted in California)

Moderate damage

Major damage

Symbols locate epicenters only;
areas affected were much larger

National Oceanic and Atmospheric Administration map pinpointing the epicenters of damaging earthquakes in the United States.

ary Maps," which show hazard areas where flooding may occur within communities. "Special Flood Hazard Areas" are depicted with shading against a base grid of the community. A free pamphlet, "How to Read Flood Hazard Boundary Maps" (GPO-1982 0-384-218), is available upon request from FEMA. "Flood Insurance Rate Maps" (or "FIRMs") takes the Flood Hazard Boundary Map one step further, illustrating base flood elevations and varying degrees of flood hazard zones. FIRMs aid in establishing flood insurance rates for specific properties within a community. A free pamphlet, "How to Read A Flood Insurance Rate Map" (GPO 1985 0-527-832), is available from FEMA.

The best way to obtain these maps for your area is to call the National Flood Insurance Program toll-free (800-638-6620) and tell them where you live. You may also write (FEMA, Flood Map Distribution Center, 6930 A-F, San Tomas Road, Baltimore, MD 21227) and request the Flood Insurance Order Form (FEMA form 81-52, Dec. 83), as well as the free explanatory pamphlets. The order form is especially useful for obtaining several maps of different areas.

Government Printing Office. GPO publishes a "Storm Surge and Hurricane Safety with North Atlantic Tracking Chart" (S/N 003-018-00092-0; $2). This 1979 pamphlet unfolds into a grid for tracking storms along the North Atlantic Coast and includes information on safety precautions during hurricanes.

Commercial Sources

The geologic departments of colleges and universities sometimes produce maps of earthquake regions. One such map, created by Tim Hall, a former professor in the geology department at Foothill College in Los Altos Hills, Calif., is a colorful work titled "Geology and Active Faults in the San Francisco Bay Area," which depicts areas of stable and unstable bedrock, unconsolidated soil, mud and fill in the Bay Area region. The map ($3) is produced by the Coastal Park Association (Point Reyes National Seashore, Point Reyes, CA 94956; 415-663-1115), and is available through many map stores.

Although emergency information maps are difficult to find in the realms of commercial map publishers, **Hagstrom** (American Map Corporation, 46-35 54th Road, Maspeth, NY 11378; 718-784-0055) has an "Emergency Map of New York City" (No.615-2; $2.95), which diagrams emergency routes and stations, including hospitals and fire companies.

▶ **See also: "Geologic Maps" and "Weather Maps."**

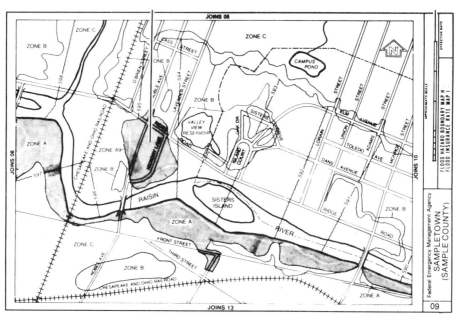

Sample Flood Insurance Rate Map illustrating property areas and risk zones, from the Federal Emergency Management Agency's Flood Insurance Program.

Energy Maps

From lightbulbs to limousines, we are as dependent on electricity, gas, and oil as our primitive ancestors were on clubs, stones, and knives. The search for new energy sources has become a serious endeavor for scientists and engineers—and mappers. Without the means to pinpoint these resources, the wealth of the earth's natural energy would remain hidden.

There are energy maps for every type of energy source. Sunshine maps show the spots on Earth where solar energy is most plentiful; coal and oil investigations maps point out where shale and crude oil can be found. There are maps of hydroelectric and nuclear power plant sites, gas pipelines, and oil refineries, as well as maps of the sediment on the ocean floor where retrievable hydrocarbons can be found.

The federal government produces many energy maps, reports, and charts that are used by those in both the public and private sectors. Other sources of energy maps are some utilities, mining, or oil companies, as well as geologic map companies or groups.

Government Sources

The U.S. government is a primary source for energy maps because of its subsidized utilities projects (such as the Tennessee Valley Authority) and its awareness of the strategic importance for energy independence. Here are some of the energy maps in Uncle Sam's vast collection:

Federal Energy Regulatory Commission (FERC).
FERC produces maps illustrating electric facilities and gas/oil pipelines in the United States. Most are available from the Government Printing Office. Its products include:

■ "Major Natural Gas Pipelines" (13" × 18"; $1.75) shows major existing pipelines, as well as those

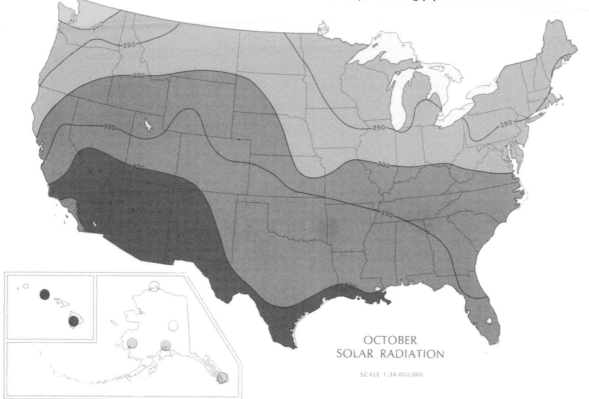

OCTOBER
SOLAR RADIATION

SCALE 1:34,000,000

Inset map depicting nationwide levels of mean solar radiation in the mid-twentieth century during October, from a National Atlas *sheet of solar radiation maps.*

proposed or under construction; locations of natural gas fields; and imports and exports of gas from Canada and Mexico.

■ "Crude Oil Pipelines of the United States and Canada" (40" × 57"; $75) traces the paths of American and Canadian pipelines. The map was created by FERC but is only available from Penn Well Books (P.O. Box 21288, Tulsa, OK 74121). When ordering, specify map P-5156.

■ "Principal Electric Facilities in the United States" (43" × 59"; $3.50) includes generating stations, transmission lines, and ownership (based on reports filed with the FERC to June 1978).

■ *Hydropower Sites of the United States* ($140): This 1981 atlas contains a compilation of 85 river basin maps showing site locations of conventional, pumped storage, and retired hydropower sites.

Government Printing Office. GPO distributes several Regional Assessment volumes from the 1982 National Hydroelectric Power Resources Study, each of which contains two related maps in an attached pocket:

■ Volume 14, *Northeast Power Coordinating Council* ($8.50; S/N 008-022-00171-9).

■ Volume 15, *Mid-Atlantic Area Electric Reliability Council* ($6; S/N 008-022-00172-7).

■ Volume 17, *East Central Area Reliability Coordinating Agreement* ($6.50; S/N 008-022-00177-8).

■ Volume 18, *Mid-America Interpool Network* ($6; S/N 008-022-00179-4).

■ Volume 19, *Mid-Continent Area Reliability Coordination Agreement* ($7; S/N 008-022-00174-3).

■ Volume 20, *Southwest Power Pool* ($8; S/N 008-022-00175-1).

■ Volume 21, *Electric Reliability Council of Texas* ($5.50; S/N 008-022-00176-0).

■ Volume 23, *Alaska and Hawaii* ($7.50; S/N 008-022-00178-6).

Also available from GPO is a Central Intelligence Agency map, "Middle East Area, Oilfields and Facilities" (35" × 39"; $3.50), a multi-colored map created in 1980, showing oilfields, pipelines, tanker terminals, and refineries against a terrain background (S/N 041-015-00130-2).

Central Intelligence Agency. The CIA has several international energy maps available through the

National Technical Information Service (NTIS), including:

■ "China: Fuels, Power, Minerals and Metals" ($7.50; PB 83-92807).

■ "Eastern Europe: Major Power Facilities" ($10; PB 82-927905).

■ "Soviet Union, East & South" Includes electric and other power facilities, minerals, and petroleum refining sites ($10; PB 82-928113).

National Climatic Data Center. A good source for historical maps of solar energy is the National Climatic Data Center (Federal Building, Asheville, NC 22810; 704-259-0682), which produces *A History of Sunshine Data in the United States, 1891-1980* ($.65; available in fiche only) as part of its "Historical Climatology Series." The study gives digitized, summarized monthly, and annual totals, when available, of "duration of sunshine" from 239 observation sites between 1891 and 1980. An accompanying map shows the sunshine station network as it existed in 1891, 1900, 1920, 1940, 1960, and 1980.

U.S. Geologic Survey. For maps concentrating on more recent solar energy information, USGS's National Atlas Program has two sunshine map sets available:

■ "Monthly Sunshine" This set, created in 1968, has a map of theoretical maximum and mean actual hours of yearly sunshine for selected locations, as well as twelve monthly maps of mean actual sunshine ($3.10; 00478 38077-AI-NA-17M-00).

■ "Annual Sunshine, Evaporation, and Solar Radiation." This eight-map set from 1969 contains three maps of mean actual sunshine, annual pan evaporation, and May-October evaporation, and five maps of annual solar radiation and mean solar radiation for January, April, July, and October. ($3.10; 00565 38077-AJ-NA-17M-00).

Also available from USGS are a number of gas, oil, and coal investigations maps, many of which are produced by the Bureau of Mines. For listings of these maps, write or call the nearest USGS National Cartographic Information Center (see Appendix A).

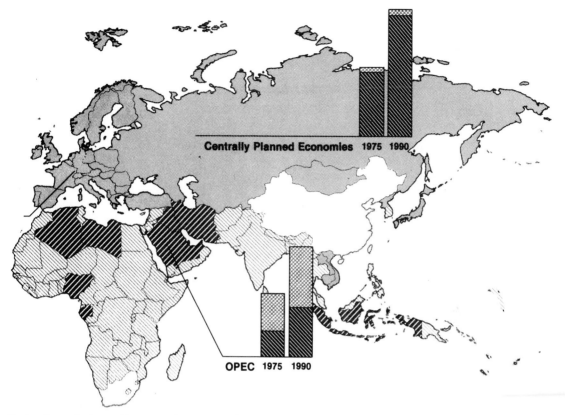

Portion of map showing world energy trade in 1975, with projections for 1990, from the State Department's Atlas of United States Foreign Relations.

Tennessee Valley Authority. TVA produces several series of maps illustrating the transmission lines and private utilities of TVA's roughly 40,910-square-mile territory, covering parts of Tennessee, Alabama, Georgia, Kentucky, Mississippi, North Carolina, and Virginia. Some maps also show the service areas for cooperative and municipal distributors of TVA electric power. The "L" series maps ($2.50 each plus $2.50 for mailing tube and postage) are available in east-half and west-half segments; each half measures 32" × 48" at a scale of 1" = ten miles. The "S" series maps ($1 plus $.50 for postage) are drawn at a scale of 1" = 25 miles and measure 17" × 22".
■ "Transmission Lines" (order from map series L-1 or S-1).
■ "Transmission Lines and Municipal and Cooperative Distributors" (order from map series L-2 or S-2).
■ "Municipal and Cooperative Distributors" (order from map series L-3 or S-3).

Other government sources for energy maps include state geologic departments (see Appendix B) for investigations maps and local utilities boards or commissions.

Commercial Sources

Some of the best sources for energy maps are geologic map companies or associations. Here are several that produce high-quality maps:

The American Association of Petroleum Geologists (AAPG bookstore, P.O. Box 979, Tulsa, OK 74101; 918-584-2555) is a membership organization for petroleum geologists. Although members receive a discount on AAPG products, the publications are also available to non-members. Products include:

■ Geothermal Gradient Maps ($10 each; $250 per set; $3 and up for shipping): This portfolio of 39

computer-contoured and labelled maps covers all of North America.
■ "Sedimentary Provinces of the World" ($18 plus $3 shipping): This 40"x 54" map uses the latest data to classify, inventory, and rate those sedimentary deposits that may contain recoverable hydrocarbons. A 36-page booklet included with the map lists each province and shows potential hydrocarbon productivity.
■ "Geological Provinces: Contiguous 48" ($6 plus $1.50 shipping): This code map by the AAPG Commitee of Statistics of Drilling was prepared for reporting well information from a standardized index map. The map lists codes for the 48 contiguousstates.
■ "Geologic Provinces: Alaska" ($6 plus $1.50 shipping): Same as above, for Alaska.

Williams & Heintz Map Corporation (8119 Central Ave, Capitol Heights, MD 20743; 301-337-1144) produces, but does not sell, many kinds of geologic maps. The maps are made to order for a number of companies, state geologic offices, and

other groups needing specialized work. There are a number of Williams & Heintz energy maps available from these sources, including:

■ "Alaska Oil and Gas Leasing Program" ($10): This 1984 map is drawn at a scale of 1:2,500,000. Available from Alaska Map Service (P.O. Box 10279, Anchorage, AK 99511).
■ "Alaska Oil & Gas Map" ($24.95): Explanatory handbook accompanies the map, drawn at a scale of 1:2,500,000. Available from Continental Maps (P.O. Box 210246, Anchorage, AK 99521).
■ "Arctic Slope Petroleum Facility" ($30): Scale of 1:8000. Available from: Alaska Map Service.
■ "Coal Industry in Illinois" ($3): Scale of 1:500,00. Available from the Illinois Geological Survey (615 E. Peabody Dr., Champaign, IL 61820).
■ "Geothermal Resources and Temperature Gradients of Oklahoma" ($2): This 1984 map is drawn at a scale of 1:500,000. Available from the Oklahoma Geological Survey (830 Van Vlette Oval, Norman, OK 73019).
■ "Intrastate Gas Map of Louisiana" ($6): This

(continued on page 71)

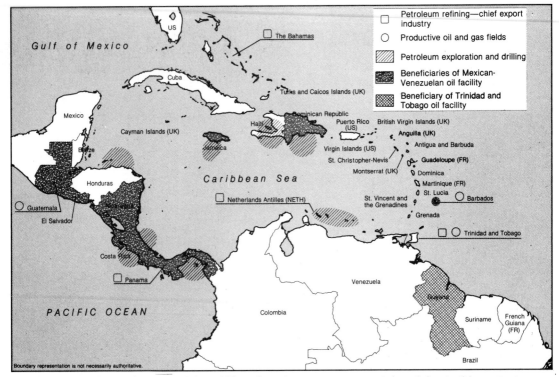

Map depicting petroleum and resources of the Caribbean, from the State Department's Atlas of the Caribbean Basin.

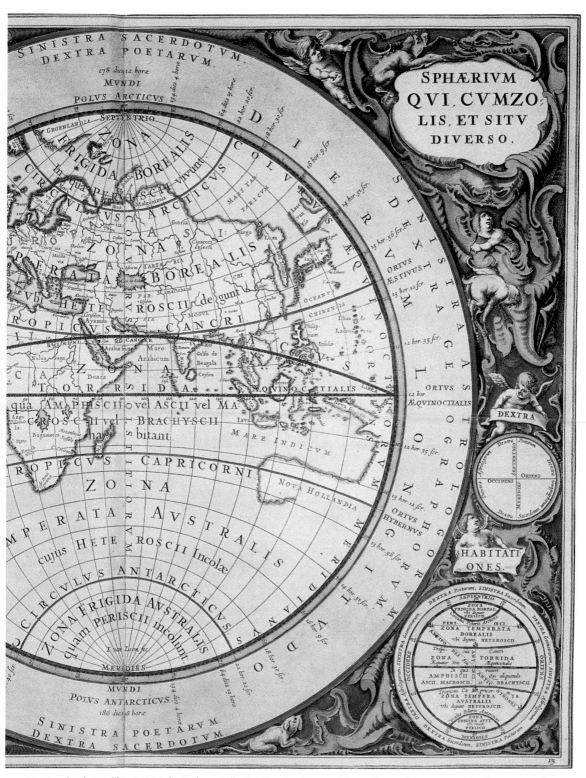

Portion of ''The World in 1660,'' by Andreas Cellarius. Courtesy Hansen Planetarium and University of Utah, Marriott Library, Special Collections, Salt Lake City, Utah.

Aerial photograph of Wilmington, Del. Courtesy U.S. Geological Survey.

Space imagery of the Grand Canary Island by the French satellite Spot. Courtesy Spot Image Corporation.

"Indiana Adventure Map," the combined effort of the Association of Indiana Convention & Visitors Bureaus, the Tourism Development Division of the Indiana Department of Commerce, and Rowe & Field Inc. of Evansville, Ind.

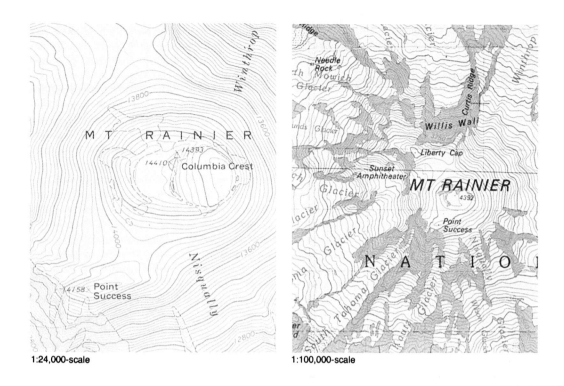

1:24,000-scale

1:100,000-scale

1:125,000-scale

Topographic maps of Mt. Rainier, Wash., illustrating three perspectives of the same region at different scales. Courtesy U.S. Geological Survey.

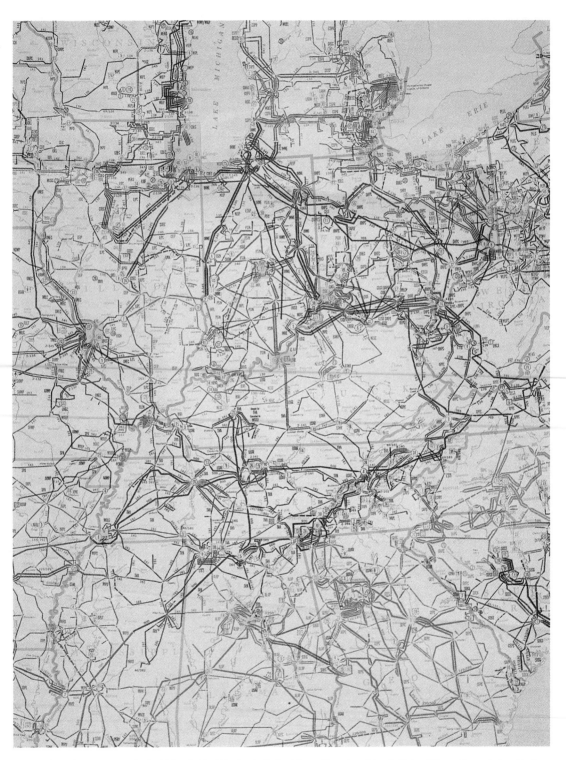

Portion of a utilities map, "Principal Electric Facilities in the United States," produced by the Federal Power Commission. Various colors indicate different types of transmission lines.

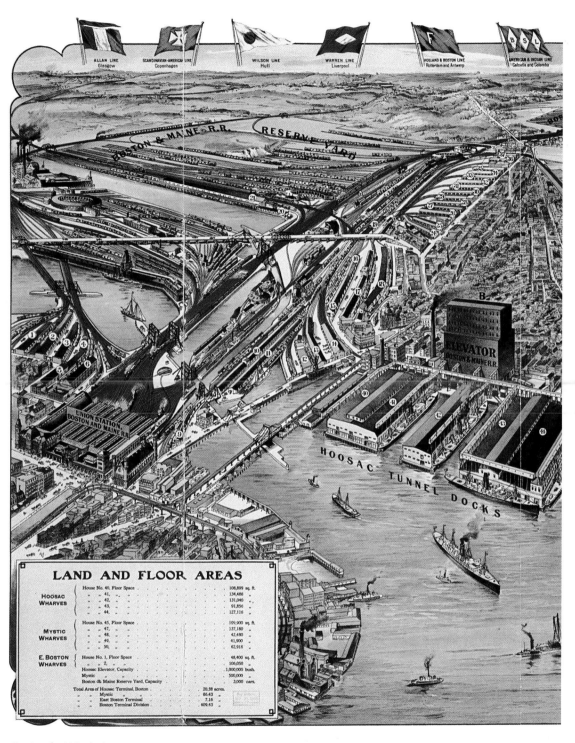

Portion of a 1905 bird's-eye-view map of Boston's railroad and shipyards, identifying individual buildings and facilities. Courtesy Library of Congress.

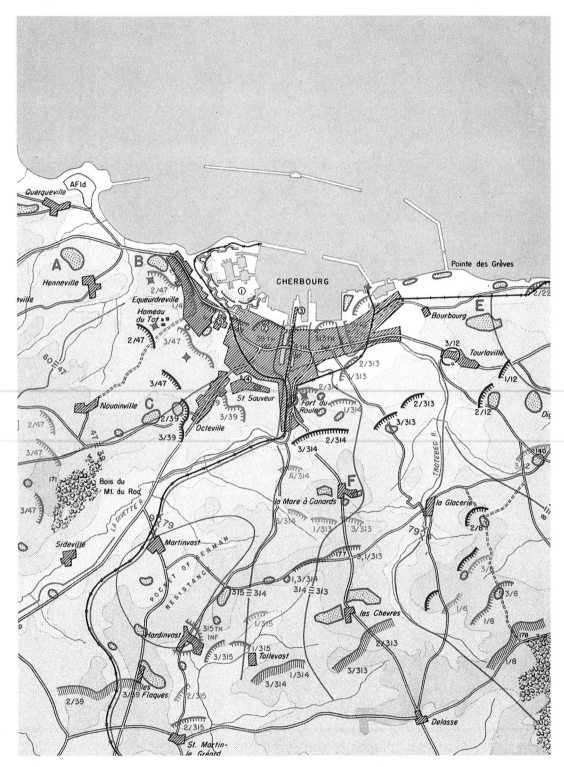

Portion of "The Final Drive On Cherbourg," a World War II military map showing the "night positions reached by forward elements" on June 21-25, 1944. Courtesy Government Printing Office.

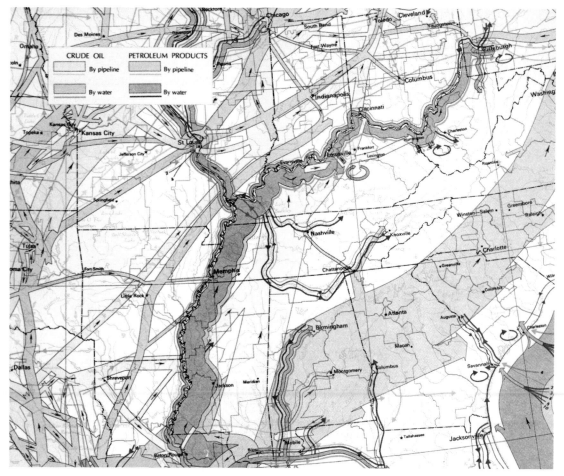

Portion of a map illustrating the flow of petroleum movement within the U.S. in 1974, from the 1970 edition of the National Atlas.

(continued from page 62)
1983 map is drawn at a scale of 1:500,000. Available from the Louisiana Geological Survey (P.O. Box G, University Station, Baton Rouge, LA 70893).

■ "Oil and Gas Basins Map" ($10): This 1983 map by Arlen Ehm is drawn at a scale of 1:2,500,000. Available from the Alaska Division of Geological and Geophysical Survey (794 University Ave., Fairbanks, AK 99701).

■ "Technical Map of the Geothermal Resources of California" ($8.50): This 1983 map by Hasmukhral H. Majmundar is drawn at a scale of 1:750,000. Available from the California Division of Mines and Resources (1416 9th St., Sacramento, CA 95814).

Other geologic companies and societies that produce energy maps include:

■ **Australian Mineral Foundation:** Conyngham St., Private Bag 97, Glenside 5065, South Australia.

■ **Canadian Society of Petroleum Geologists:** #505, 206 7th Ave., S.W., Calgary, Alberta T2P 0W7.

■ **Circum-Pacific Council for Energy and Mineral Resources:** Halbouty Center, 5100 Westheimer Rd., Houston, TX 77056.

■ **Geologic Society of America:** 3330 Penrose Pl., P.O. Box 9410, Boulder, CO 80301.

■ **International Union for Conservation of Nature and Natural Resources:** CH-1196 Gland, Switzerland.

■ **Petroconsultants (CES) Ltd.:** 36 Upper Brook St., London W1Y 1PE, England.

▶ **See also: "Geology Maps," "Land Use Maps," "Natural Resource Maps," and "Utilities Maps."**

Foreign Country Maps

The cartographic agencies of most foreign countries are the best sources for maps relating to specific subjects or regions within those lands (see Appendix C). But several agencies of the federal government, including the U.S.Geological Survey, the Central Intelligence Agency, and the Defense Mapping Agency, also produce foreign maps. There are general outline maps of most foreign countries, as well as thematic maps and atlases that depict such things as agricultural resources in the Soviet Union or oilfields in the Middle East.

The larger map companies like Hammond and Rand McNally produce a number of maps and atlases of foreign countries for general and travel reference. Travel-related map producers, including the American Automobile Association, Michelin, and Bartholomew, also publish maps for other countries. Other sources of foreign maps include the embassies and tourist bureaus that most maintain in Washington, D.C. or New York City.

Government Sources

Central Intelligence Agency. The CIA, one of the federal goverment's most prolific map makers, has more than a hundred maps of foreign countries available to the public. The CIA also creates a few atlases that include pull-out or fold-out maps. The National Technical Information Service sells most CIA maps, although the Government Printing Office is the distributor for several full-color CIA maps and all of its atlases. See "CIA Maps" for details.

Defense Mapping Agency. DMA produces topographic, hydrographic, and related maps and charts of foreign countries. DMA map series of foreign countries include the following: (Stock numbers for individual sheets in multisheet series are listed in DMA's "Public Sale Catalog;" see Appendix A.)

■ "Area Outline Maps" (Series 1105; $5 per sheet), a series of black-and-white planimetric maps drawn at a scale of 1:20,000,000, which delineate international and major subdivision boundaries,

national capital cities of major importance, and water drainage patterns. There entire world is covered in this series of 27 sheets, each of which is about 14″ × 11″.

■ "Europe" (Series 1209; $3.50 per sheet), based on a British topographic map of Europe created by the British Mapping and Charting Establishment Royal Engineers. This series of six sheets shows international boundaries, major civil subdivisions and administrative boundaries, city and town populations, road classifications (by importance and weatherability), operable railways and airports, and other key topographic features. The sheets are drawn at a scale of 1:2,000,000 and are designed to fit together to form a single large wall map. The average size of each sheet is 43″ × 62″.

■ "Middle East Briefing Map" (Series 1308; Stock Number 1308XMEBRMAP; $3.50), measuring 34″ × 38″ and drawn at a scale of 1:1,500,000. This multicolored physical map shows armistice demarcation lines and international boundaries, populations of significant towns, roads, railways, airfields, and oil pipelines.

■ "Africa" (Series 2201; $6.75 per sheet), a multicolored topographic map series comprised of 36 sheets drawn at a scale of 1:2,000,000. Shown are international and major administrative boundaries and major topographic features, including cities, towns, transportation routes, and vegetation. The average size of each sheet is 29″ × 26″.

■ "Administrative Areas of the USSR" (Series 5103; Stock No. 5103XADMAUSSR: $3.50) is a multicolored planimetric, political administrative map showing boundaries, towns, transportation features, hydrographic features, and pipelines. A glossary and administrative list with abbreviations are also included.

A description of DMA's hydrographic products can be found under "Nautical Charts and Maps."

Portion of a 1:25,000-scale sheet from the Swiss Federal Office of Topography's National Map series, illustrating the basic features of the Swiss countryside, including roads, railroads, cities, towns, and bodies of water.

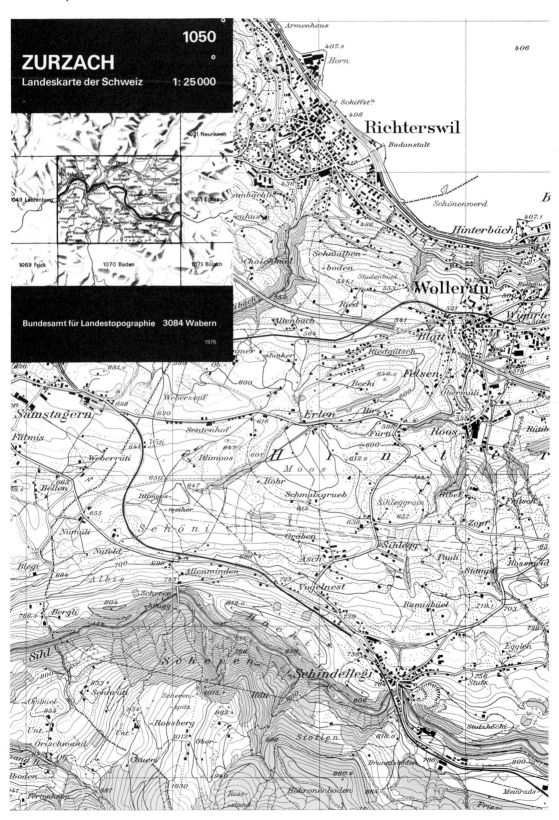

1050

ZURZACH

Landeskarte der Schweiz   1: 25 000

Bundesamt für Landestopographie   3084 Wabern

1976

Government Printing Office. The State Department's Bureau of Public Affairs produces several atlases of foreign countries, available from GPO, including:

■ *Atlas of the North Atlantic Treaty Organization* (S/N 044-000-02039-4; $1.75) contains basic information about NATO as well as nineteen maps displaying NATO's membership and structure, military strength, members' role in world affairs, and relations with the USSR and Warsaw Pact countries.
■ *Atlas of the Caribbean Basin* (S/N 044-000-02022-0; $1.50) includes maps and charts illustrating the Caribbean Basin's economic and political features.
■ *Atlas of U.S. Foreign Relations* (S/N 044-000-01973;$5) a 1983 atlas containing basic information about U.S. foreign relations, divided into six sections dealing with various aspects of foreign relations. There are ninety maps and charts. Each section is also available separately in slightly expanded form as *Atlas of United States Foreign Relations*: "Development Assistance" (S/N 044-000-01894-2; $2.50); "Elements of the World Economy" (S/N 044-000-01899-3; $2.50); "Foreign Relations Machinery" (S/N 044-000-01928-1; $2.50); "International Organizations" (S/N 044-000-01905-1; $3); Trade and Investment" (S/N 044-000-01888-8; $2.75); and "United States National Security" (S/N 044-000-01898-5; $3.25).

Also available from GPO are four editions, from 1948-1951, of the *Foreign Relations of the United States: The Near East, South Asia* (Volume 5 in the series each year). These large volumes, several of which are nearly 2,000 pages long, have numerous maps and charts of the region as it appeared during the time of publication. The books were reprinted in the past decade and may be ordered as follows: 1948 edition (S/N 044-000-01607-9; $19); 1949 edition (S/N 044-000-01646-0: $24); 1950 edition (S/N 044-000-01679-6;$28); and 1951 edition (S/N 044-000-01914-1; $21).

Commercial Sources

Hammond Incorporated (515 Valley Street, Maplewood, NJ 07040; 201-763-6000) distributes Bartholomew's World Travel Map series ($6.95 each), featuring full-color reference maps for most countries of the world. The maps, in a variety of sizes and scales, are of frameable quality. Available maps include:

■ "Africa, Central and Southern" (6549-6) illustrates the African continent from the Cape to the Republic of Zaire, with an inset of Madagascar. The map measures 40" × 30" and is drawn at a scale of 1:5,000,000.
■ "Arabian Gulf" (6557-7) covers the Gulf States in unusual detail. The map measures 36" × 26" and is drawn at a scale of 1:5,000,000
■ "British Isles" (6617-4) shows Britain, with insets of Orkney and Shetland, and a trilingual key and distance table for certain towns. The map measures 40" × 35" and is drawn at a scale of 1:1,000,000.
■ "Indian Sub-Continent" (6570-4) depicts India, Pakistan, Bangladesh, and Sri Lanka, with insets of five major cities. The map measures 40" × 30" and is drawn at a scale of 1:4,000,000.
■ "Malaysia/Singapore" (6612-3) includes individual map insets of Southeast Asia, peninsular Malaysia, Singapore, Sabah, and Sarawak at differing scales, with a trilingual legend. The map measures 26" × 39".
■ "Nigeria" (6585-0), illustrates international and state boundaries, expressways, trunk roads, railways, ferries, mangrove swamps, and spot heights. The map measures 40" × 30" and is drawn at a scale of 1:1,500,000.

The Bartholomew series also includes maps of Africa, East Africa, northeast Africa, West Africa, North America, South America, the Arabian Peninsula, South East Asia, Australia, Canada, China and Mongolia, Egypt, Eurasia, Central Europe, Eastern Europe, Political boundaries of Europe, Western Europe, France, Greece, Iran, Israel with Jordan, Italy, Japan, Lebanon, New Zealand, Spain and Portugal, and Scandinavia.

Bartholomew also has a series of "Pictorial Maps" ($5.95 each), with full-color illustrations that border and dot the maps themselves. Among the maps available are:

■ "Canada" (6671-9)
■ "Cultural Map of Africa" (6660-3)

- "Ireland" (6690-5)
- "Nigeria" (6655-7)
- "A Scenic Map of Scotland" (6706-5)

Hippocrene Books (171 Madison Avenue, New York, NY 10016; 212-685-4371) is the U.S. distributor for several European publishers with foreign map series. Among these are Hildebrand maps ($5.95), which are attractive, comprehensive maps of popular and unusual travel destinations, including Algarve, Australia, Balearic, China, Cuba, Cyprus, Egypt, Grand Canary, Gulf of Naples, Majorca, Mauritius, Peloponnese, Seychelles, Sri Lanka, Teneriffe, and the United States.

Also available from Hippocrene are Cartographia's high-quality maps, as good for daydreaming as for travelling. Cartographia's regular maps ($2.95) can lead the way through Austria, Czechoslovakia, France, Germany, Great Britain, Netherlands, Rumania, Scandinavia, and Yugoslavia, among other places. Cartographia's

A sample of the many maps of foreign lands created by private publishers.

"Handy Maps" ($5.95) provide more in-depth coverage of Algeria, Angola, China, Iceland, Libya, the Middle East, Mozambique, and Europe. Cartographia's city maps ($2.95) can get you around Belgrade, Sofia, Thessaloniki, Moscow, and Krakow, among other metropolises.

National Geographic Society (17th and M Streets NW, Washington, DC 20036; 202-921-1200) offers several maps of foreign countries, including:

■ "Asia" (02812; $4), measuring 37½" × 31½", in full-color.
■ "People's Republic of China" (02835; $3), measuring 37½" × 30½", with illustrations and text on both sides.
■ "Soviet Union" (02396:$4), measuring 37" × 23", in full-color.
■ "Greece and the Aegean" (02834; $3), measuring 30" × 23", in full-color.
■ "Spain and Portugal" (02284; $3), measuring 30" × 23", in full-color.

Rand McNally (P.O. Box 7600, Chicago, IL 60680; 800-323-1887; 312-673-9100 in Ill.) is the American distributor of Kummerly & Frey products. These include highway maps, long-distance road maps, and European atlases covering Austria, the British Isles, Costa del Sol, Finland, Germany, Israel, Poland-Czechoslovakia-East Germany, Romania-Bulgaria, Tunisia, and Yugoslavia-Hungary. Prices range from $6.95 to $13.95. Kummerly & Frey's regional maps ($6.95 to $7.95) cover the British Isles, France, Germany, Italy, Eastern Austria, Greece, Hungary, some Mediterranean countries, Morocco, Northwestern Africa, Portugal, West Germany, and Yugoslavia.

Rand McNally itself publishes cosmopolitan maps ($1.95 to $2.95) for Canada, Mexico, Europe, United States (Alaska only), South America, Africa, and the West Indies/Carribean.

▶ **See also: "Antique Maps," "Atlases," "Bicycle Route Maps," "CIA Maps," "Military Maps," "Political Maps," "Space Imagery," "Tourism Maps," and "World Maps."**

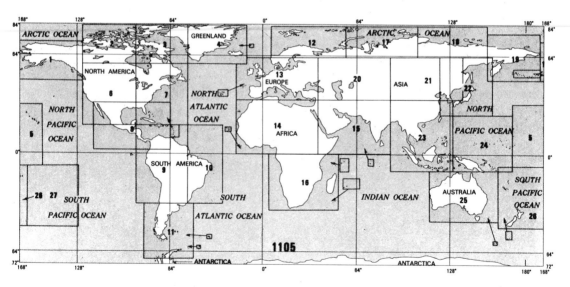

Index of available DMA Area Outline maps in the 1105 series.

Geologic Maps

More than any other type of map, geologic maps are portraits of the Earth. Like any good portrait, a geologic map shows not only the face of its subject but also something of its inner nature.

Geologic maps show the Earth's face by delineating the characteristics and distribution of exposed rocks and loose surface materials. And they make it possible to infer the Earth's "inner nature"—the size, shape, and position of rock masses and any mineral desposits, fluids, or openings they may contain—by means of symbols. This "inner nature" is often interpreted with the help of slices, or cross-sections, made by combining surface observations with whatever subsurface information may be at hand from drill holes, mine workings, caves, or geophysical measurements.

Geologic maps are models of both space and time. The history of an area can usually be reconstructed using a geologic map because the relative ages of rocks can often be determined, and even their ages in years estimated, if they contain certain naturally radioactive elements that decay at known rates. Geologic maps have been used to plot the pathways of meltwaters from glaciers that disappeared tens of thousands of years ago, leading, for example, to the discovery of both immense reservoirs of underground water and great oil pools in the midwestern United States.

Because they must carry so much information, geologic maps are considerably more complex than topographic maps, which simply trace the contours of the Earth (see "Topographic Maps"). Using a topo map requires mastering only two ideas beyond those needed to use a standard road map: the contour line and the interval between lines. Geologic maps, in contrast, represent a whole new realm of information, thought, and experience. Some idea of the complexity of geologic maps may come from realizing that rocks, once formed—on the ocean floor, on river flood plains, beneath glaciers, or around and below volcanoes—can erode away; be lifted or lowered thousands of feet; be folded into troughs, basins, arches, domes, and far more intricate shapes; or be broken by great fractures and dragged or

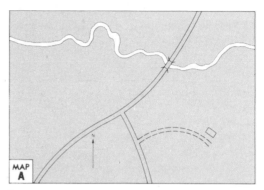

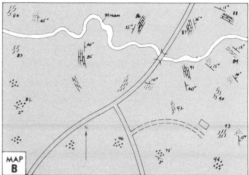

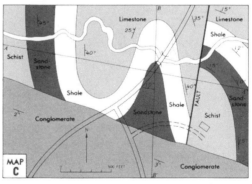

The development of a geologic map, from base map (top), to field map (center), to finished product (bottom).

pushed hundreds of miles from their place of origin. Moreover, the Earth has been actively engaged in making, deforming, eroding, and remaking rocks for more than four-and-a-half billion years. All of these data can be condensed into symbols, colors, and patterns on geologic maps.

A geologic map plays three distinct roles:

■ It is a convenient means of recording observations about rocks in a way that preserves their spatial relationships to each other.
■ Along with the cross-sections that can be drawn from it, it is a device for study and analysis of many kinds of geologic features, such as sequence and thickness of rock formations, their geologic structure, and their history.
■ It is the most compact way for a geologist to record the significant geologic relationships of an area so that they can be readily grasped and used by others.

Scientists and engineers in many fields use geologic maps as basic tools. Because we know, for example, that certain kinds of rock or geologic structures are associated with certain kinds of mineral deposits, geologic maps can help an exploration geologist find oil, copper, uranium, and many other minerals. Hydrologists use geologic maps to locate sources or movement paths of underground water. And because soil is commonly a product of the disintegration of the bedrock beneath, geologic maps are helpful to soil scientists in classifying soil for agricultural purposes.

Geologic maps can be used for these and other purposes whether or not the geologist who made them had such purposes in mind. A map prepared initially to solve a specific geologic problem may later help an engineering geologist choose between potential construction sites; a map made as part of a program of petroleum exploration may turn out, ultimately, to have far greater value in a search for uranium or potash.

The U.S. Geologic Survey makes many kinds of geologic maps as part of a continuing program to ". . .examine the geologic structure. . .of the national domain," as its mission is described. These maps may be published singly or in one of several series:

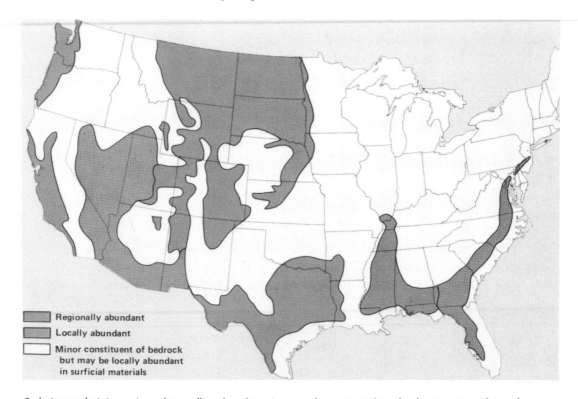

Regionally abundant

Locally abundant

Minor constituent of bedrock but may be locally abundant in surficial materials

Geologic map depicting regions where swelling clay, the main cause of expansive soil, is abundant in near-surface rocks.

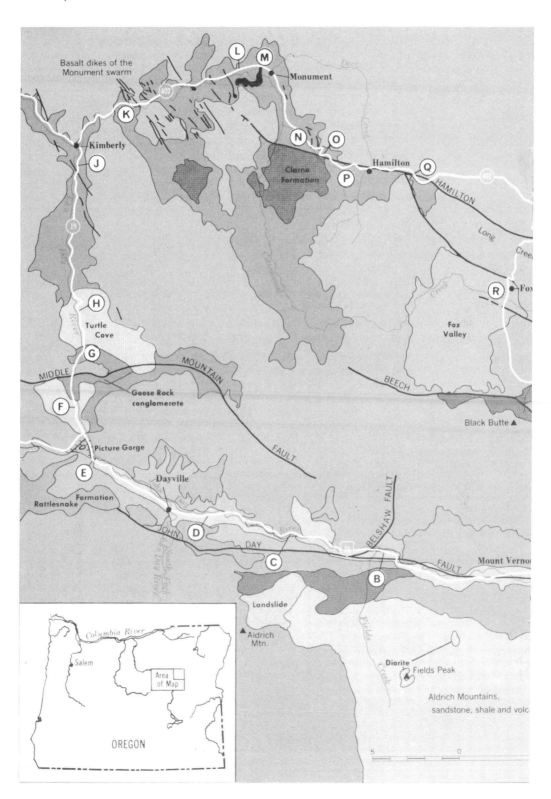

Map of the John Day region of Oregon, depicting its unusual geology.

■ **Quadrangle maps** comprise a four-sided area, bounded by parallels of latitude and meridians of longitude used as an area unit.
■ **Mineral resource maps** show the location and distribution of minerals.
■ **Oil and gas maps** show the location and distribution of those resources.
■ **Hydrologic investigations maps** are used to study a variety of water-related topics, including water availability, flood-prone areas, and water quality.
■ **Geologic reconnaissance maps**, prepared by the Institute of Polar Studies at Ohio State University, show views of Antarctica at 1:250,000 scale.

Geologic maps also may be published as folded sheets in envelopes bound with book-type reports, such as bulletins, water-supply papers, and professional papers, the texts of which contain descriptive and interpretive material that the maps alone cannot provide.

USGS-published geologic maps range in scale from 1:20,000 to 1:2,500,000, depending on the type of information to be portrayed. (See "Topographic Maps" for more on map scales.) The smaller-scale maps, for example, are used for general planning and resource evaluation over large regions. Larger-scale maps may be used for detailed planning, zoning, site selection, and resource evaluation. Geologic maps at 1:250,000 or larger scales are available for nearly fifty percent of the United States. The entire country has been mapped by USGS at the 1:2,500,000 scale; only fifteen percent of the United States has been mapped at the largest scale.

Government Sources

Geologic maps are available directly from USGS and its National Cartographic Information Center (see Appendix A). While USGS maintains no overall catalog of its maps, it does have several free publications related to region (all areas east of the Mississippi River, for example) or type of map (all hydrologic investigations maps, for example). Indexes are available for areas east of the Mississippi River (including Minnesota, Puerto Rico, and the Virgin Islands) and for areas west of the Mississippi River (including Alaska, Hawaii, Louisiana, Guam, and Samoa).

There are also several full-color 19″ × 28″ the-

matic maps from USGS's authoritative National Atlas Program: "Land-Surface Form" (1968), "Classes of Land-Surface Form" (1964), and "Tectonic Features" (1968), all covering Alaska; "Geology" (1966), which shows the distribution of sedimentary, volcanic, and intrusive rock types; and "Surficial Geology" (1979), showing the distribution of transported, untransported, and other deposits for the United States. Each is $3.10, available from USGS.

State and local maps. Regional USGS Public Inquiries Offices also sell maps of local areas and books of local and general interest. In addition, most states' geological survey, bureau of mines, or department of natural resources publish and sell geologic maps. The Louisiana Geological Survey (P.O. Box G, University Station, Baton Rouge, LA 70893; 504-342-6754), for example, publishes a "Geologic Map of Louisiana," which it sells for $9 rolled, $7 folded; Pennsylvania's Department of General Services (State Book Store, P.O. Box 1365, Harrisburg, PA 17105; 717-787-5109) sells a map titled "Rock Types of Pennsylvania" for $4.40. See Appendix B for other state agency addresses.

Commercial Sources

AAPG Bookstore (P.O. Box 979, Tulsa, OK 74101; 918-584-2555) is affiliated with the American Association of Petroleum Geologists and distributes a series of "highway maps" that include compilations of state and regional geologic data with an overlay depicting major highways and landmarks. The entire country is covered in twelve maps at a scale of one inch per thirty miles; price is $4.50 each. AAPG's "Map of the World Project" consists of maps produced by the International Union of Geological Sciences. The six titles include "Tectonic Map of South America" ($20), "Tectonic Map of Europe" ($14), "Tectonic Map of South and East Asia" ($75), "Metamorphic Map of Africa" ($14), "Metaphoric Map of Europe" ($48) and a *Geologic World Atlas* ($245), a large-format atlas designed to cover world geology with 22 sheets.

Geological Map Service (P.O. Box 920, Sag Harbor, NY 11963; 516-725-0780) offers a wide range of international geologic maps, including many hard-to-find foreign-produced maps, some translated into English. Among its products is the *Atlas* of *Lithological-Paleogeographical Maps of the World* ($84), the result of "years of research by top-notch men of Moscow's Academy of Geological Science," with both Russian and English text, according to the company's catalog; and the "International Tectonic Map of the World" ($94), which shows "for the first time" tectonic and oceanic platforms, "which allows for a visualisation [*sic*] of structure and history of main tectonic elements of Earth."

National Geographic Society (17th and M Streets, NW, Washington, DC 20036; 202-921-1200) sells "Earth's Dynamic Crust" ($4; 33" × 42") and "Earth's Dynamic Crust/Shaping of a Continent" ($4; 36" × 28½"), both plastic-coated maps illustrating world geology and tectonics.

Williams & Heintz Map Corporation (8119 Central Avenue, Capitol Heights, MD 20743; 301-336-1144) sells two "geologic portfolios" designed for teaching geology: Portfolio No. 1, "Physical Geology," consists of eight full-color geologic maps and sections, with accompanying text; Portfolio No. 2, "Historical Geology," consists of thirteen full-color maps that cover the major geologic provinces of the United States. Each portfolio is $8.50. Another teaching package is Quadrangle Portfolio No. 1 ($5), consisting of four full-color geologic maps of four quadrangles with interesting geology and accompanying text.

▶ **See also "Emergency Information Maps," "Energy Maps," and "Natural Resource Maps."**

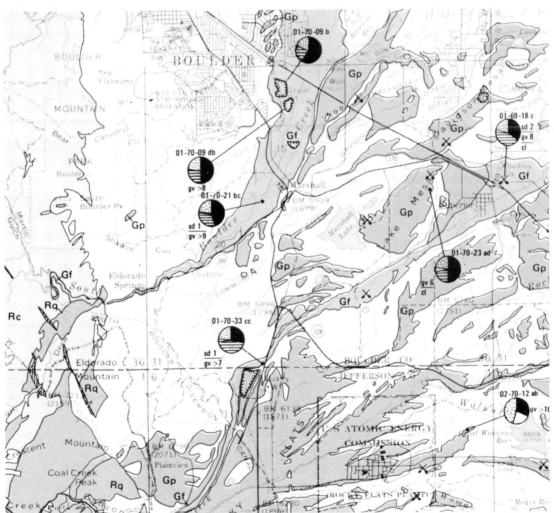

Map illustrating gravel and aggregate resources around Boulder, Colo.

Highway Maps

Even the King of the Road needs a map. So does anyone who plans to travel the interstate, state, county, and other highways that snake across the North American landscape. Highway maps, with their colors, folds, and spaghetti-tangle of expressways and turnpikes, are among the most widely used maps made. But there is also a functional mysticism surrounding highway maps, born out of the gas stations and rest stops that comprise our earliest memories of road trips.

Highway maps are perhaps the easiest—and least expensive—maps to obtain. Although the day of free gas station maps is all but gone, the transportation and tourism bureaus of all fifty states provide free highway maps. The state-produced maps are of a uniformly high quality, and are updated frequently.

State-produced maps are the best bet when it comes to intrastate travel. But when you need a wider view, nothing beats commercial road atlases. These range from glove compartment editions for under $5 to "deluxe" volumes with simulated leather binding that can set you back the price of a tank's worth of gas. There are highway atlases for U.S. and European vacationers, businesspeople, and everyday travel. Many atlas publishers also produce single sheet highway maps for various states and regions.

Automobile and travel clubs like the American Automobile Association provide highway maps, trip planning, and other services to members. AAA members also can obtain road maps for seventeen other countries through eighteen affiliated foreign auto clubs (see "Tourism Maps").

Government Sources

Government Printing Office. GPO distributes "United States Road Symbol Signs" (S/N 050-000-00152-1; $2.25), a useful guide to supplement highway maps and atlases. This folder illustrates different kinds of symbol signs, colors, shapes, and highway route markers for each state.

U.S. Geological Survey. Many USGS map products, especially topographic and general reference maps, include major highways and roads. These aren't necessarily the best to take on a driving trip, but they can help in planning one. See "Topographic Maps" for more information.

Commercial Sources

American Map Corporation (46-35 54th Road, Maspeth, NY 11378; 718-784-0055) has Hallwag's international road atlases and street maps, including:

- *Europa Road Atlas* ($19.95), a comprehensive atlas for Europe's highways, showing car ferries, campgrounds, scenic routes, and street maps for 97 cities and towns.
- "Regional Road Maps" ($6.25), indexed in four languages, for regions including the Alpine countries, Austria and Upper Italy, Eastern Europe, Northern Europe, Northern Germany, Southern Germany, Hungary-Czechoslovakia-Poland, Northern Italy, Southern Italy, Kenya/Tanzania, and the Mediterranean.
- "Country Road Maps" ($6.25), indexed in four languages, covering Austria, Denmark, Finland, Greece, Italy, Morocco/Canary Islands, Southern Scandinavia, Sweden, and Yugoslavia.

General Drafting Company (P.O. Box 161, Convent Station, NJ 07961; 800-367-6277) produces the "Travel Vision" line of road maps and atlases, with maps and sets for the entire United States and Canada as well as for individual states, regions, and cities. Products include:

- "Road Maps USA" ($19.95), a set of 25 road maps covering the entire United States.
- "State Maps" ($1.25 each), available for all states.
- "City Maps" ($1.25 each), available for many major cities in the United States.
- "Regional Maps" ($1.50), the United States, divided into eastern and western regions, plus one map for the entire country.
- "Maps of Canada" ($1.50 each), road maps for Canadian provinces.
- *Road Atlas* ($2.95), covering the United States, Canada, and Mexico.

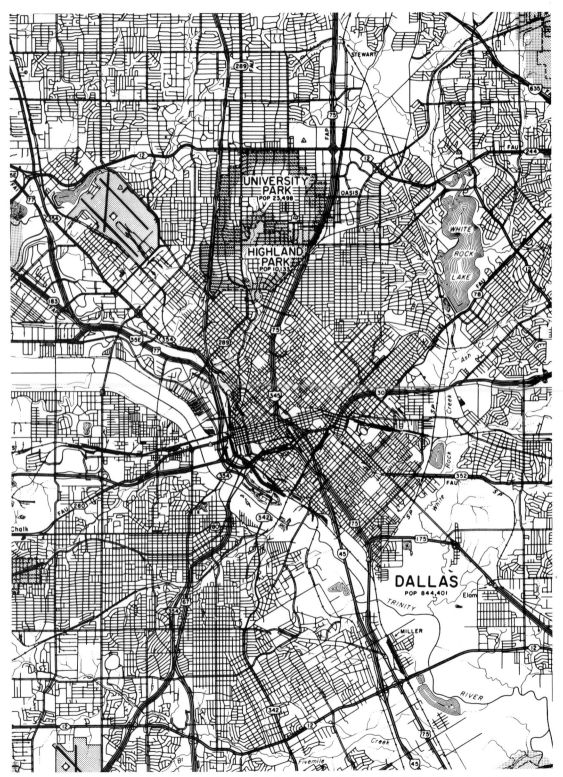

Portion of a Dallas County, Tex., highway map drawn at a scale of 1:125,000, prepared by the Texas Department of Transportation in cooperation with the U.S. Department of Transportation.

Prentice Hall Press (200 Old Tappan Rd., Old Tappan, NJ 07675; 800-223-2348) sells Baedeker/ Shell Road Maps ($4.95 to $7.95), the cream of the crop of international driving maps. Roadside attractions, motels, scenic routes, and speed limits are all detailed. Maps include Africa, the Alps, Europe, France, Germany, Great Britain, Greece, Italy, Mexico, the Middle East, Scandinavia, Spain/Portugal, and Yugoslavia.

Rand McNally (P.O. Box 7600, Chicago, IL 60680; 800-323-1887; 312-673-9100 in Ill.) creates many high-quality travel and road atlases that are updated regularly and filled with maps and information to enhance any trip. Products include:

■ *Road Atlas* ($5.95), the classic road and highway guide for planning and taking vacations or business trips.
■ *Interstate Road Atlas* ($2.95), which has interstate highway and road maps for the United States, Canada, and Mexico.
■ *Pocket Road Atlas* ($1.50), a handy road and highway reference for the United States, Canada, and Mexico that fits easily in a glove compartment.
■ *Motor Carriers' Road Atlas* ($12.95), a road and highway atlas for truckers.
■ *City and Highway Road Atlas* ($3.95), another atlas to slip into your glove compartment.
■ "The Map Collection" ($22.50), a set of 39 Rand McNally road maps covering the fifty states, Canada, and Mexico.

Rand McNally is also the American distributor of Kümmerly & Frey international road maps and atlases. Products available include:

■ "Road Maps to Countries and Selected Areas" ($6.95 each), with maps for most European countries.
■ "Regional Titles" ($7.95 each), with maps for regions in the British Isles, France, Germany, and Italy.
■ *Europe Road Atlas* ($13.95 with index, $9.95 without).
■ "Europe, Long Distance Roads" ($7.95).

Readers Digest Books (distributed by Random House, 201 East 50th Street, New York, NY 10022; 800-638-6460, 800-492-0782 in Maryland) offers

America from the Road ($25.95), a book containing 125 tours designed to help road travelers see the most of America. One hundred and fifty color-coded maps guide the way.

▶ **See also: "Atlases," "Business Maps," "City Maps," "County Maps," "Foreign Country Maps," and "U.S. Maps."**

A sample of the free highway maps available from state transportation and tourism offices.

Historical Sites

Civil War battlefields, presidents' homes, and monuments to long-gone explorers dot the American landscape, as do countless other historical sites of major and minor importance to our national heritage. Some sites are operated under the auspices of the federal government or a local historical society. Others are privately run. For virtually all, there is a map available to guide one to and through the places where history was made.

Government Sources

National Park Service. The National Park Service is the guardian of national historic sites. The "House Where Lincoln Died," Bunker Hill, and Mesa Verde are three of the hundreds of historical sites operated and preserved under the Park Service's care. Maps are usually available at these sites or through the agency's Office of Public Inquiries.

U.S. Geological Survey. USGS pinpoints certain historic landmarks on its maps of America. There must be a substantial object (a house, a battlefield, or a grave, for example) for the site to be included on a USGS map; small monuments or signs do not merit note. Maps depicting historical sites and areas are available through district or regional USGS branches.

Government Printing Office. GPO has maps and guidebooks to several popular historical sites. Prices range from $2.25 for a simple guidebook to $10 or more for comprehensive texts, complete with maps, of various sites. Examples of maps and guides available from GPO include "Carl Sandburg Home" ($6.50; S/N 024-005-00253-7), "Dinosaur Quarry: Dinosaur National Monument, Colorado and Utah" ($4.50; S/N 024-005-00093-3), "Fort Vancouver National Historic Site, Washington" ($7; S/N 024-005-00816-1), and "Guide to United States Army Museums and Historic Sites" ($5.50; S/N 008-020-00561-4).

Other Sources

State historical societies (see Appendix B) and building preservation societies sometimes publish maps or guides to historical sites preserved by states or local jurisdictions. State tourist agencies (Appendix B) and local chambers of commerce often publish walking tour maps or guidebooks to area attractions.

▶ **See also: "History Maps," "Park and Forest Maps," "Recreation Maps," and "Water Recreation Maps."**

A PERSPECTIVE VIEW
of the
Mansion, Outbuildings, Gardens, etc.,
with a key thereto

A map of George Washington's home in Mount Vernon, Va. Courtesy Mount Vernon Ladies' Association of the Union.

History Maps

Maps of history are modern diagrams that illustrate a region's trends or events over decades or centuries. Instructors use history maps to teach everything from archaeology and anthropology to military history and literature. Scholars use them to track trends in a society or culture. As study tools, they provide valuable overviews of the evolution of a society's traditions, explorations, and advances.

There is a wide range of history maps available. There are maps that trace the routes of famous explorers, maps of the history of medicine, religion, theater, poetry, art, and technology. There are maps of most significant developments in the history of civilization. Many history maps are poster-size and intended for both decoration and study. Others are accompanied by texts that provide both background and analysis of the events illustrated on the maps.

The best overall sources for history maps are the larger commercial map publishers, especially those with an educational market. Historical maps, as well as atlases of American and world history, military history, and social history, are produced in great numbers by these publishers. Many smaller companies often publish history maps related to the other products in which they specialize. The federal government produces little in the way of history maps, but some state and local governments produce maps related to local development.

Commercial Sources

American Map Corp. (46-35 54th Road, Maspeth, NY 11378; 718-784-0055) publishes bible atlases in English and Spanish and produces a set of seventeen illustrated bible wall maps. The atlases cost $2.95 each; the set of maps is $25.50.

George F. Cram Company Inc. (P.O. Box 426, Indianapolis, IN 46206; 313-635-5564) publishes two series of 52″ × 40″ maps, one of American history, the other of world history, for use in schools. The American History Series contains 35 titles, ranging from "Spanish Exploration and Settlement to 1580 A.D." to "Mineral Production of

the United States." The World History Series, with 46 titles, includes "Mohammedan Conquests at Their Height, 750 A.D." and "Europe, September 1, 1938." Both series include maps of major wars, explorations, and expansions. Each series costs $335, with mountings extra.

Hammond Inc. (515 Valley Street, Maplewood, NJ

to United States
1,000

3,00

2,500 to United States

Immigration figures are expressed in thousands.

Regions with net migration surplus

Regions with net migration deficit

07040; 201-763-6000) publishes several atlases of world history in cooperation with Times Books of London, as well as a small series of its own, including bible atlases and atlases of American and world history. Hammond also is the American distributor for Bartholomew Maps, which has a series of historical maps of British possessions, including England and Wales, Ireland, London, Scotland, and Wales. Maps in this series illustrate castles, battles, historical characters, and the coats of arms of cities and towns. Bartholomew also produces several pictorial maps on historical subjects, including "Castles and Palaces," "Cathedrals and Abbeys," and "Historic Houses." Atlases range in price from $7.95 for some softcover editions to $75 for hardcover editions. Bartholomew historical maps are $4.95; pictorial maps, $5.95.

Hearne Brothers (24632 Gibson, Warren, MI 48098; 800-521-0300, 313-755-3700 in Ala. and Mich.) publishes a six-foot-square, two-sided map of United States history for use in schools. One

A *map showing world immigration patterns from 1950-74, from the State Department's* Atlas of United States Foreign Relations.

side illustrates the history of the area east of the Mississippi, the other side the area west of the Mississippi. Inset maps of explorations and acquisitions, as well as miniature portraits and biographies of historical figures, are on both sides.

National Geographic Society (17th and M Streets NW, Washington, DC 20036; 202-921-1200) produces one of the largest selections of history maps. Titles include "Historical Japan," "Shakespeare's Britain," "North America Before Columbus," and "Classical Lands of the Mediterranean." NGS also publishes several historical charts, including "Alaskan Ice Age Mammals," "History Salvaged from the Sea," and "Mythical Realms of Gods and Heroes." National Geographic maps are full-color with illustrations and are often suitable for framing. Write to National Geographic for price list.

Nystrom (3333 Elston Avenue, Chicago, IL 60618; 800-621-8086) specializes in learning materials for schools. Its series of American and world history maps are 50″ × 38″. Among the 33 maps in the American history series are "Indian Tribes and Settlements in the New World, 1500-1750" and "Transportation Unites the Nation." Titles in the 32 world history map series include "Christian Europe and the Crusades" and "U.S.S.R. Territorial Expansion." Prices of single maps range from $37 to $73, depending on type of mounting. Prices of sets range from $308 to $666.

Rand McNally (P.O. Box 7600, Chicago, IL 60680; 800-323-1887, 312-673-9100 in Ill.) produces three sets of American history and one set of world history maps intended for school use. It also distributes the Breasted-Huth-Harding series of world history maps. The three U.S. series are "American History Maps" (for intermediate grades), "American Studies Series" (all levels), and the "Our America Series," which includes time lines and text on each map. The world history series covers the development of civilization in most areas of the globe. The 62 maps in the Breasted-Huth-Harding Series include "Barbarian Migration" and "Air Age." Write to Rand McNally for a price list.

Government Sources

While the U.S. government is primarily involved in

publishing maps about present-day America, some local or state agencies produce or distribute maps describing local history. Write to the local historical society for further information, or contact state mapping agencies where applicable. (See Appendix A.)

Other Sources

Following is a sampling of the history maps produced by smaller map companies or organizations involved with studying or promoting specific subjects.

■ **Basin St. Press** (1627 South Van Buren, Covington, LA 70433) produces a "Jazz Map of New Orleans" ($8.06, including postage) by Dr. Karl Koenig, which pinpoints the city's existing jazz clubs; the accompanying 30-page booklet outlines a walking tour of Storyville, the French Quarter, and St. Charles Street, tracing the rich history of jazz in New Orleans.

■ **Celestial Arts** (P.O. Box 7327, Berkeley, CA 94707; 800-841-2665, 415-524-8755 in Calif.) publishes a "wall visual" poster ($9.95) called "The Aztec Cosmos," a stylized ancient historical map demonstrating the Aztec culture's artistic, mathematical, and stone-carving accomplishments. The map includes a 32-page booklet describing the Aztec's symbols and religion.

■ **Facts On File Publications** (460 Park Avenue South, New York, NY 10016; 800-322-8755, 212-683-2244 in N.Y.) produces *Historical Maps on File* ($145). The 300 uncopyrighted maps contained in this loose-leaf collection are simple black-and-white diagrams of major historical trends or events. Titles include "The Ten Years (or Maori) War," "Prohibition before the Eighteenth Amendment 1919," and "The Silk Road." These maps are useful for students or researchers who need to copy a map for reports and presentations.

■ **Geological Society of America** (3300 Penrose Place, P.O. Box 9140, Boulder, CO 80301; 303-447-2020) publishes a wall-sized geologic "time scale" in black and white ($8.50), which traces the geologic development of the North American continent.

■ **Modern School** (524 East Jackson Street, Goshen, IL 46526; 800-431-5929) produces thirteen U.S. history maps for classroom use, including "Colonization," "Territorial Expansion to

1848—The Mexican War," and "The United States at Present." The series is available in three different mountings, ranging from $158 to $208.

■ **Williams & Heintz Map Corp.** (8119 Central Avenue, Capitol Heights, MD 20743; 301-336-1144), primarily a producer of maps for private industry, it also publishes a series of geologic maps. Its

"Historical Geology" portfolio ($8.50) has thirteen maps that trace the geologic history of major geologic provinces of the United States.

▶ **See also: "Antique Maps," "Atlases," "Historical Site Maps," "Military Maps," and "Railroad Maps."**

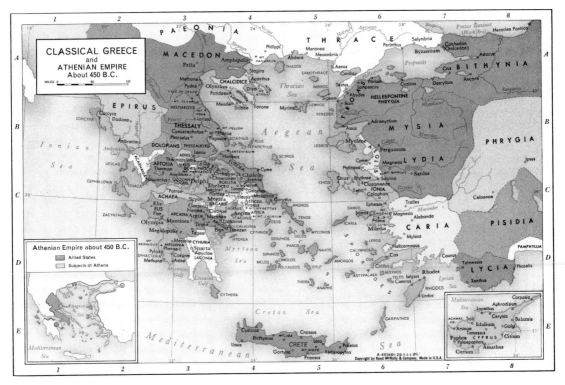

Map of Classical Greece and the Athenian Empire, from Rand McNally's Historical Atlas of the World, *one of the many historical atlases produced by private publishers. (See also "Atlases.")*

Indian Land Maps

A legacy of government mapping was born in 1804, when Thomas Jefferson sent Meriwether Lewis and William Clark in search of the mysteries of what later became the western part of the United States. And so began the federally recorded history of the absorption of Indian territory into the body of the fledgling country.Within a short time, the mapping of Indian lands became routine.

The Lewis and Clark maps showed general locations of Indian tribes, bands and villages, as well as the number of tents, lodges, and "souls." Later maps reflected the growing conflict between Indians and whites: they stated the number of warriors in a tribe, for example, or the favorite haunts of raiding parties. Although the War Department was charged with duties that included those "relative to Indian affairs," Uncle Sam learned quickly that burying the hatchet was a better tactic in winning land from Indians. So, in 1824, the Bureau of Indian Affairs was established within the War Department to handle the nonmilitary aspects of Indian affairs. The Bureau (transferred to the Department of the Interior in 1849), with its various divisions covering everything from Indian forestry to population statistics, created the need for maps of Indian land and life.

Still more maps were produced to redefine boundaries each time a treaty was drawn up between the government and an Indian tribe or nation. Westward expansion and development led to the creation of specialized maps of Indian lands, showing railroad rights-of-way across Indian territories and hydroelectric facilities near reservations, among other things.

Sometimes the process of mapping itself spurred the erosion of Indian land ownership. The General Allotment Act of 1887 charged the government with surveying Indian reservations to establish land values for agricultural purposes. If agricultural worth was significant, the land was allotted to qualifying Indians, the catch being that any surplus allotted lands were usually bought up by the government. Legislation in the 1930s prohibited future sales of Indian land, but by that time the Indians had lost some 100 million acres

of treatied land to the government's allotment program.

Aside from depicting the steady loss of territory over the years, Indian land maps can be helpful in studying irrigation, crop rotation, and other land use, as well as social structure and community planning of various tribes. Although the major

wave of Indian land mapping abated at the beginning of the twentieth century, the federal government includes reservations in many of its overall mapping projects (census, topography, and utilities, for example), and several thousand earlier maps have been carefully preserved in map libraries. Indian maps are also produced by a number of map companies as American history teaching tools, and by organizations involved in the study and understanding of Native American cultures.

Government Sources

Bureau of the Census. The decennial census of 1860 was the first to treat the Indian population as a separate race, but it wasn't until 1890 that the census counted the number of Indians living in their own territories or on reservations. (The Bureau of Indian Affairs Statistics Division, abolished in 1947, surveyed the Indian population long before the Census Bureau got around to the task.) Some BIA population maps are included in the holdings of the National Archives, as are early

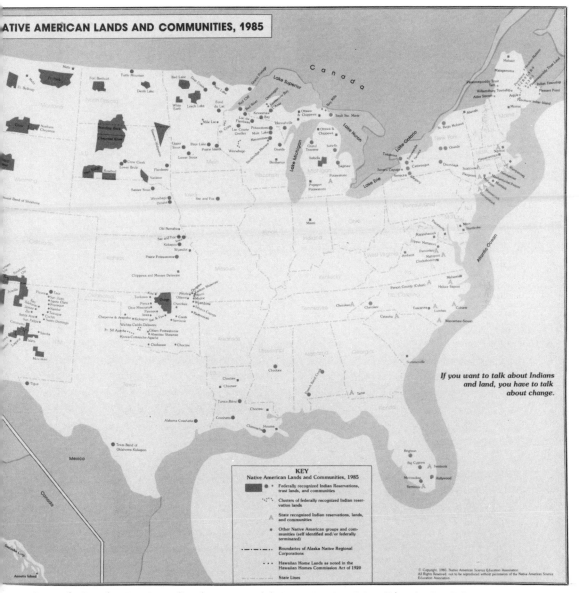

If you want to talk about Indians and land, you have to talk about change.

A map showing where American Indians live, courtesy of the Native American Science Education Association.

census maps. The Census Bureau currently produces and distributes several maps depicting recent Indian population studies (see "Census Maps" for information):

■ "Number of American Indians, by Counties of the United States" (34″ × 42″; $1.75). This map from the GE-50 Series was developed from 1970 census statistics.
■ American Indian Reservation maps (scales and prices vary). There are maps for twenty reservations in this series developed from 1980 census information. Details of roads, dwellings, and other structures are included.

Tennessee Valley Authority. Not only does the TVA produce power from its battery of transmission stations, it is also one of Uncle Sam's more prolific map makers. The TVA has several Indian-related maps available, including:

■ Reservation Property Maps. These blueline print maps show TVA boundary line data and adjoining property corners. There are several sheets covering each reservoir, and indexes for each reservoir area are available free of charge. Scales, prices, and postage costs vary.
■ Reservation Property Maps, Reduced ($.50 each plus $.50 postage). These maps are black-and-white prints of the above blueline prints, reduced to 11″ × 17″, at various scales.
■ "A Draft of the Cherokee Country" (11″ × 17″; $.50 plus $.50 postage). This print of Henry Timberlake's 1762 map shows the Little Tennessee River, Indian governors, Indian villages, and forts.
■ "Cherokee 'Nation' of Indians 1884" (12″ × 15″; $1.50 plus $.50 postage).

U.S. Geological Survey. USGS, part of the Interior Department, produces maps that include BIA information. USGS topographic and other maps depicting boundaries illustrate Indian lands according to BIA categorization: tribal lands (reservations owned by an entire tribe that are subject to tribal laws, and are intact), Indian lands allotted in part (reservations, including both tribal lands and tracts of land allotted to individual indians) and allotted and open (reservations with individually owned land tracts, other tracts open to

the public, and any remaining tribal lands); former Indian reservations generally are not noted.

As part of the National Atlas Program, the USGS also produces a general map of Indian lands, titled "Early Indian Tribes, Culture Areas, and Linguistic Stocks" ($3.10). This multi-colored map, created in 1967, includes explanatory text on the back.

Library of Congress and **National Archives.** The map collections of both the Library of Congress and the National Archives are full of old Indian land maps. The maps in the library's Geography and Mapping division date back to the colonial explorers who set out to diagram the wilds of the New World for their sovereign nations. Most of these maps are general exploration studies that note Indian villages and territories along with other interesting features of the land.

More comprehensive and specific is the enormous collection of Indian maps in the Cartographic and Architectural Branch of the National Archives, composed of several collections from various federal mapping agencies. Maps of Indian lands and life made by the BIA, the Census Bureau, the Corps of Topographical Engineers, and the War Department's Office of Explorations and Surveys, to name a few, are included in the Archives holdings. Some maps are as recent as 1950, although most date from 1781 to 1883. Included in the collections are such maps as:

■ "Sectional Map from the Coast of Maryland, Virginia, and North Carolina from Cape Henlopen." This 1781 map was drawn by John Purcell under the instructions of Lt. Col. Thomas Brown, Superintendent of Indian Affairs in the Southern District. The map is in six sections and measures 73½″ × 75″.
■ "A Map of Lewis and Clark's Tract Across the Western Portion of North America, from the Mississippi to the Pacific Ocean, by Order of the Executive of the United States in 1804, 5 & 6." This map, in manuscript on tracing paper, was copied by Samuel Lewis from the original drawing of William Clark. The map includes the positions of numerous Indian tribes, villages, and bands, as well as some population information.
■ "Map Illustrative of the Route of H.R. Schoolcraft, U.S. Ind[ian] A[gent] between L. Supe-

rior & Mississippi R. in the summer of 1831. By D. Houghton, Surgeon 7 Nat[uralist] to the Exp[edition]." This map illustrates parts of the Chippewa, Sioux, Menominee, and Winnebago Territories, including names of Indian chiefs and population numbers for Indian villages along the route and on area lakes and rivers.

■ "Map of the Indian Reservations within the limits of the United States." This 1883 map, drawn by Paul Brodie, shows Indian reservations by color and includes population figures.

Reproductions of maps from both the National Archives and Library of Congress may be obtained through the reproductions services of each collection. For further information, see "Uncle Sam's Treasure Chest."

Commercial and Other Sources

There are several educational map producers that create Indian land and history maps for classroom use, among them:

The George F. Cram Company Inc. (P.O. Box 426, Indianapolis, IN 42606; 317-635-5564) publishes an American History Series, which includes "Indians During Early Explorations and Settlement" (52″ × 40″; $63 markable, $59 nonmarkable), depicting in full-color the location and physical features of American Indian tribes at the time of the white man's arrival and settlement.

Modern School (524 East Jackson Street, Goshen, IN 46526; 800-431-5929) produces a set of six 28½″ × 22½″ reproducible geography charts, including one titled "Indian Tribes" ($24), showing the location of American Indian tribes and cultures before the arrival of Columbus.

Nystrom (3333 Elston Avenue, Chicago, IL 60618; 800-621-8086) produces a set of colorful American history maps as part of its social studies series. Two relate to Indians: "Indian Tribes and Settlements in the New World 1500-1750" (50″ × 38″; $37 folded and eyeletted for hanging; $57 in spring roller), illustrating the locations of natural resources and Indian cultures, as well as Cortez's conquest of Mexico and Pizarro's conquest of Peru; and "The Roots of American Culture: Westward to the Mississippi" (same prices and size as

above), depicting the old Southwest and Northwest and showing sites of major Indian battles.

Rand McNally (P.O. Box 7600, Chicago, IL 60680; 800-323-1887; in Ill., 312-673-9100) produces two series of American history maps for schools that include Indian maps: American History Maps for Intermediate Grades, "Homelands of the American Indians—North America" (50″ × 50″; $57), a brightly colored markable and tear-resistant map depicting the homelands of the major Indian nations before the arrival of Columbus; and Our America Series, "Early Indians and their Culture" (44″ × 38″; $54), a full-color map showing seven major and eighteen other linguistic areas, as well as pictorials of food sources, products, habitats, and culture.

Other producers of Indian maps and charts include:

■ **Celestial Arts** (P.O. Box 6326, Berkeley, CA 94707; 800-841-2665; in Calif., 415-524-1801) sells a wall chart, "The Aztec Cosmos" ($9.95 plus $2 shipping and $.65 tax for Calif. residents), illustrating the cultural and artistic accomplishments of the Aztec civilization and religion. A 32-page explanatory booklet is included.

■ **National Geographic Society** (17th and M Streets NW, Washington, DC 20036; 202-921-1200) produces several Indian maps including: "Indians of North America" (32½″ × 37½″; $3 plus $1.25 postage), a full-color ethnological map created in 1982; "Indians/Archaeology of South America" (23″ × 37″; $3 plus $1.25 postage), a two-sided map including illustrations, chronology, notes, and text; "North America Before Columbus" (32½″ × 37½″; $3 plus $1.25 postage), an archaeological map that includes an inset chart highlighting the "prehistory" of North America; and "Visitors Guide to the Aztec World" (25″ × 20″; $4 plus $1.25 postage), illustrating the Valley of Mexico on one side and Mexico City on the reverse.

■ **Native American Science Education Association** (1228 M St. NW, Washington, DC 20005; 202-638-7066) produces "Indian Lands and Communities, 1985" (20″ × 30″; $10 plus $2 folded or $3.50 in a mailer tube), a colorful comprehensive map of current Indian country in the United

States, featuring federal- and state-recognized, and other tribal communities and trust lands.

Indian Map Distributors

■ Apache Trading Post, Highway 90 West of Alpine, Alpine, TX 79830.
■ The Chinook Bookshop, 210 North Tejon Street, Colorado Springs, CO 80902.
■ The Indian Store, Greenville, ME 04441.

■ Navajo Center, Inc., 5720 E. Highway 80, Yuma, AZ 85364.
■ Shoshone Valley Trading Company, 1340 Sheridan, Cody, WY 82414.
■ Totem Pole, Inc., 733 Turnpike Street, Route 114, North Andover, MA 01845.

▶ **See also: "Boundary Maps," "Land Ownership Maps," and "Topographic Maps."**

Land Ownership Maps

From land grant maps to county plat maps, the portrayal of lands bought, granted, or inherited paints a picture of our perpetual need to own land. The detail with which some of these maps are drawn—every house, street corner, park, and fire hydrant in town diagrammed and labeled—preserves on paper one moment in the history of America's urbanization. By studying older ownership maps, one may locate the first house where immigrant grandparents lived. By studying current

WINNEBAGO T. 26 N–R.11 E.

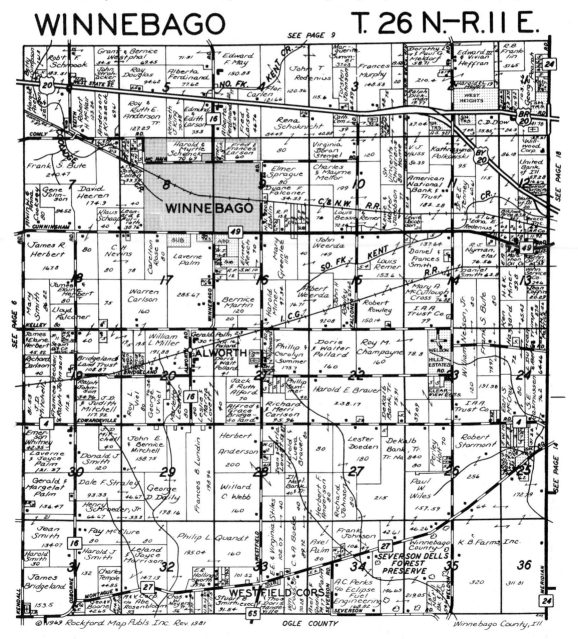

Land plat of Winnebago County, Ill. Courtesy Rockford Map.

ones, one might ascertain information about the land-holdings of neighbors and other residents.

The mapping of land ownership dates back to the Babylonian cadastral maps that delineated individual land-holdings. Somewhat later, according to legend, Ramses II established a cadastral survey in the thirteenth century B.C., but little of the papyrus on which the maps were made has survived. By the Renaissance, the mapping of European estates was commonplace, and by the eighteenth century, maps of counties were being published in England, with specific houses and residents named.

In the nineteenth century, the development of American county "land plats"—simple but detailed grid maps showing buildings, public lands, roads, and other features—became a necessity for the rapidly expanding nation. The importance of diagrams showing exactly who owned what and who lived where was immeasurable in a country where land grant acts and squatters rights were hotly debated. Today, county land plats, updated regularly by both commercial and goverment mappers, still serve as valuable land planning tools; older plats serve as portraits of an area's past.

Everyone from genealogists to geographers uses land ownership maps. Planners, builders, and investors can outline prospective developments by examining land ownership blueprints. These maps sometimes reveal lands granted to, then taken from, native Indians, or the plantations of slave owners. And the exploding growth of cities, towns, and industrial centers is all recorded on land ownership maps.

Boundary maps (see "Boundary Maps") are one form of land ownership maps, but most land ownership maps do more than merely illustrate property lines. While boundary maps designate where one land plot ends and another begins, many land ownership maps disclose to whom those lands belong.

Current land ownership maps are available from several federal agencies, among them the USGS, the Army Corps of Engineers, and the National Park Service. Older boundary, land grant, and plat maps may be found in the collections of the Library of Congress and the National Archives. State, county, and local mapping departments create their own land ownership maps for taxation

purposes, and some are available to the public. Land plat books and other ownership maps also are published by commercial map and blueprint companies around the country.

Government Sources

Uncle Sam owns a lot of land, and the surveying of this wealth of real estate is a job undertaken zealously by the federal government. Land ownership maps are produced by several agencies or departments to diagram the continuing use of the land.

The Bureau of Land Management (BLM) is the

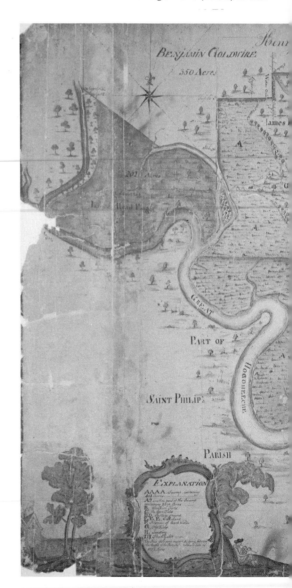

A 1769 map illustrating the land holdings in and around t

largest federal source for plats of townships surrounding public land. In many cases, BLM's surveys were the first to establish boundary lines, and subsequent maps have detailed the growth of many American towns. The plats are simple black-and-white representations of an area, noting streets, houses, lakes, and parks. Other features, such as cultural centers and noteworthy topography, are included when possible. BLM no longer distributes its own land plats, but they can be obtained through two sources: BLM township plats of Illinois, Indiana, Iowa, Kansas, Missouri, and

Ohio are available through the National Archives and Records Service; township plats of other public-land states can be obtained from USGS.

The National Park Service keeps track of the purchase and development of federally protected parks. Maps showing the extent of each park's land-holdings are available at the parks themselves or from the Park Service. (See "Park and Forest Maps.")

The Army Corps of Engineers produces maps showing public water recreation areas. Land ownership maps depict the boundaries of these lands

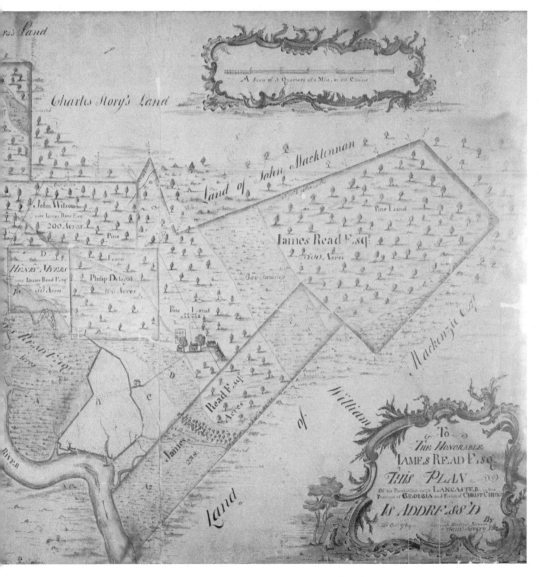

...antation of James Reed along the Ogeechee River in Georgia. *Courtesy National Archives.*

and their potential for safe recreational use. The maps are inexpensive and are available from the Army Corps of Engineers District Offices. (See Appendix A.)

The Tennessee Valley Authority has land maps and reservation property maps available for its 40,910 square-mile region, encompassing parts of Tennessee, Alabama, Georgia, Kentucky, Mississippi, North Carolina, and Virginia. TVA maps show property corner markers, boundaries, bearings, and distances for areas or reservations affected by TVA reservoirs. There are several sheets covering each reservoir area, and free indexes for these sheets are available.

Holdings by the Library of Congress of pre-twentieth century land ownership maps include 1,449 county maps representing approximately one-third of all U.S. counties. The Library publishes *Land Ownership Maps: A Checklist* ($5.50), available from the Library or the Government Printing Office, which lists these maps and gives a brief history of the collection. Copies of maps listed may be ordered from the Library's Photoduplication Service. The Library also has 1,269 county land ownership maps contained on 105-millimeter microfiche. Individual diazo microfiche copies may be purchased for $2 per fiche ($10 minimum), with the complete set available on positive silver halide microfiche for $5,000. A free brochure listing the number of fiche required for each state is available from the Library's Photoduplication Service. Another microfiche collection is entitled "Ward Maps of United States Cities" and includes 232 pre-twentieth century ward maps for 25 major cities. They are available from the Photoduplication Service on individual diazo microfiche ($2 each, with a $10 minimum) or as a complete set on either diazo microfiche ($645) or positive silver halide microfiche ($975).

The National Archives map collection includes the surveys of the Land Grant Office and later maps from the Bureau of Land Management. Indexes of these maps are available for study at the Archives' map research facilties in Alexandria, Va. Copies may be ordered through the Archives' reproductions service.

State, county, and local governments often produce land ownership maps for such uses as settling zoning disputes or raising property taxes, and may be available through local records or land offices. Other local sources include historical societies and long-established land sales companies, which may have ownership maps available for study and reproduction.

Commercial Sources

Publishing land ownership maps is one of the oldest sources of income for commercial map companies. No sooner did any town spring up than did the mappers arrived to plot boundaries and ownership agreements. Producers of land ownership maps, especially land plats, may be found in most counties or population centers. Examples of maps being produced by such companies include:

■ **Pittmon Map Company** (930 S.E. Sandy Blvd., Portland, OR 97214; 503-232-1161) produces city and county maps of Oregon and Washington. Products include the "Portland Metro Area Large Wall Map," a twelve-foot-square black-and-white land ownership and city street map published in fifteen sections that may be purchased separately. Street names, house numbers, parks, schools and other city features are clearly labeled. Cost is $30 per section; $300 for the whole map.

■ **Rockford Map Publishers** (P.O. Box 6126, 4525 Forest View Avenue, Rockford, IL 61125; 815-399-4614) has been producing county plat books since 1944, with more than 600 County Land Atlases and Plat Books currently in publication. The Land Atlas and Plat Books measure $8\frac{1}{2}'' \times 11''$ and are wire bound, with black-and-white plat maps of cities and population centers, as well as a black, red, and white county land ownership map in the center of the volumes. Rockford has County Land and Plat Books available for counties in Alabama, Florida, Idaho, Illinois, Indiana, Iowa, Minnesota, Mississippi, Missouri, New York, Oklahoma, Pennsylvania, South Dakota, West Virginia, and Wisconsin. Prices range from $17 to $25.

■ **Sanborn Map Company Inc.** (629 Fifth Avenue, Pelham, NY 10803; 914-738-1649) began producing detailed city maps in 1866 and by the mid-1950s had diagrammed most U.S. communities with more than 2,500 people. Renowned for its nineteenth-century Fire Insurance maps (now a prized collection in the Library of Congress), the Sanborn Map Company has maps or atlases available for most cities. The maps and atlases, produced in both black-and-white and color, show roads, buildings, parks, fire hydrants, and other features, as well as places labeled by usage and type of structure. Sizes range from 11″ × 13″ to 22″ × 28″, and prices vary. The archival collection of Sanborn Fire Insurance Maps, 1867-1950, held by the Library of Congress, is available on microfilm.

Following are selected companies that produce and sell blueprints, plats, and other commercial forms of land ownership and development maps for their regions:

Alabama: Birmingham Blue Print Co. Inc., 2121 Third Avenue, Birmingham, AL 35203; 205-323-1563.

Arizona: Chandler Blueprint & Map Co., 337 North Arizona Avenue, Chandler, AZ 85224; 602-963-8779; Mesa Blueprint, 50 South MacDonald, Mesa, AZ 85201; 602-969-6901.

Arkansas: Fort Smith Blueprint, 1642 ''A'' Street, Fort Smith, AR 72901; 501-782-4686,

California: Ace Blueprint Co., 2491 Long Beach Blvd., Long Beach, CA 90801; 213-424-0468.

Colorado: 4 Corners Land Surveyors, 344 East Main Street, Cortez, CO 81321; 303-565-6558; Pueblo Blueprint Company, 218 South Victoria Avenue, Pueblo, CO 81003; 303-544-2414.

Delaware: Wilmington Blue Print Service, 817½ Tatnall Street, Wilmington, DE 19899; 302-652-3366.

Florida: Bonifay Abstract Company, 124 East Virginia Avenue, Bonifay, FL 32425; 904-547-2025; A.R. Cogswell Blue Print and Supply Company, 800 North Myrtle Ave, Jacksonville, FL 32207; 904-356-4271.

Georgia: J.B. McRary Engineering Corp., 6075 Roswell Road, Suite 125, Atlanta, GA 30301; 404-255-9544.

Indiana: Evansville Blue Print Co., 600 Court Street, Evansville, IN 47701; 812-424-2484.

Kentucky: Pride Engineering Company, 122 Milton Avenue, Glasgow, KY 42141; 502-651-8311.

Louisiana: Allen's Blue Print & Supply, 501 10th Street, Alexandria, LA 71301; 318-443-1877; Baton Rouge Blue Print & Supply Company, 297 Ferdinand Street, Baton Rouge, LA 70801; 318-383-2208.

Michigan: Rowe Engineering, Annex Building, 429 North State, Caro, MI 48723.

Minnesota: Trygg Land Office, Junction Highway 21 & Moss Ridge, Ely, MN 55731; 218-365-4668.

Mississippi: Neely Reprographics, 519 East Pearl Street, Jackson, MS 39201; 601-354-3523.

Missouri: Springfield Blue Print & Photocopy Company, 417 South Robberson Avenue, Springfield, MO 65806; 417-869-7316.

New York: Historic Urban Plans, Box 276, Ithaca, NY 14850; 607-273-6633.

North Carolina: Raleigh Blue Printers, 126 West Martin Street, Raleigh, NC 27602; 919-832-2841.

Texas: Brazoria County Abstract Company, 111 East Magnolia, Angleton, TX 77515; 409-849-6453; Miller Blue Print Company, 501 West 6th Street, Austin, TX 78701; 512-478-8793.

Vermont: The National Survey, Chester, VT 05143; 802-875-2121.

West Virginia: C&B Blueprint Company, 701 8th Avenue, Huntington, WV 25701; 304-525-2175.

▶**See also: "Boundary Maps."**

Land Use Maps

In a world where every conceivable resource, from sunshine to soil to salt water, has a utilitarian purpose for people and nature, maps depicting land use are essential for keeping track of where and how our land is being used. Land maps can provide answers to such questions as what percent of a region is used for industry, or how much of an agricultural region is cropland rather than pasture, and which land is prime for residential development.

Environmentalists, industrialists, foresters, farmers—anyone who needs to understand what land is being used and where it is being over- or underexploited—find land use maps necessary tools of their trade. The development of virtually any transportation route, utility, energy, or urban renewal project depends on the information found on such maps. The "big picture" about past,

present, and future land use aids in making the best possible use of a region's soil, rock, sediment, vegetation, wildlife, and water.

Modern technology has led to the digitization of much of the Earth's surface, resulting in a new generation of extremely accurate land use maps. The early stages of these digitized maps look a bit like a paint-by-numbers art kit. The field of the map is usually a basic light blue topographic map, with major roads, rivers, forests, and parks outlined and named. The sections of the land given to specific uses are outlined with thin black lines (many of the outlined areas being so small that they resemble tiny ameoba on the map) and numbered according to use. These early versions, although not particularly pretty or simple to read, are quite adequate for most land use purposes.

The next step in the process produces more at-

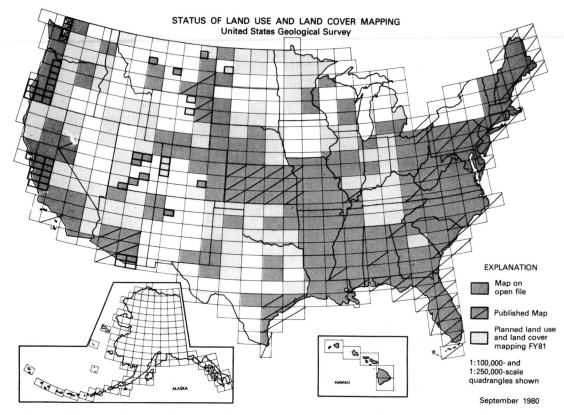

STATUS OF LAND USE AND LAND COVER MAPPING
United States Geological Survey

EXPLANATION

Map on open file

Published Map

Planned land use and land cover mapping FY81

1:100,000- and 1:250,000-scale quadrangles shown

September 1980

ALASKA

HAWAII

USGS map illustrating the status of land-use and land-cover mapping programs in the United States.

tractive and readable land use maps. With computer assistance, or even diligent hand coloring, these basic maps can be turned into vivid illustrations of land use. Splashes of red, orange, and green are applied according to the digitized information within each outline, and the once dull-looking map suddenly rivals the most lovely satellite image for beauty and vibrance.

The U.S. Geological Survey is presently involved in using such digital methods to map the land use and land cover for the entire United States. Land cover maps illustrate, in less detail than topographic maps, the type of natural or man-made "cover" (buildings, vegetation, and water, for example) over the Earth's surface. Because land cover is often an indicator of past, present, or potential land use, these maps are helpful supplements to land use maps.

The USGS project, begun in 1975, uses a two-level classification system to depict the various types of land use and land cover in America. The first classification level is divided into nine segments relating to different land characteristics: urban or built-up land, agricultural land, rangeland, forest land, water, wetland, barren land, tundra, and perennial snow and ice. These classifications are divided into subclassifications, comprising the second level of classification. The result is that USGS's system for describing the land use and cover of, say, barren lands, is broken into such subcategories as dry salt flats; beaches; strip mines, quarries, and gravel pits; and transitional areas.

All this is less complicated than it sounds, and the highly specific system of delineating land types and uses actually simplifies the process further by taking the guesswork out of map reading. At a glance, one can now see exactly what kind of farming or ranching is taking place on a given plot of land; earlier land use maps were considerably more vague about depicting such specifics.

Aside from USGS maps, other sources of land use maps are the state, county, or local departments involved with land use and development. Regional boards or bureaus of agriculture, natural resources, and land zoning are good starting points for finding specific kinds of land use maps. (See Appendix B for addresses of many of these state agencies.)

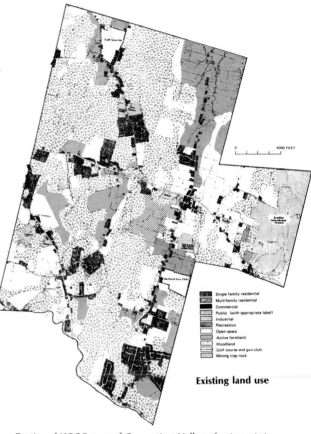

Existing land use

Portion of USGS *map of Connecticut Valley, showing existing land use in East Granby, Conn.*

Government Sources

U.S. Geological Survey. USGS is the best source for maps created specifically for land use and land cover studies. USGS's maps are available as stable-base film positives, semi-stable diazo foils, and paper diazos. Prices vary; a price list may be obtained free from the National Cartographic Information Center (see Appendix A). Also free from USGS is the pamphlet "Index of Land-Use and Land-Cover and Associated Maps."

Other sections in this book describe maps that often have land use applications.

▶ **See also: "Agricultural Maps," "Business Maps," "Geologic Maps," "Energy Maps," "Natural Resource Maps," "Park and Forest Maps," "Recreation Maps," "River, Lake, and Waterway Maps," "Utilities Maps," and "Water Recreation Maps."**

Military Maps

Among the precious few consolations of war are the resulting technological advances that often have application in nonmilitary life. Over the years, the need for accurate military maps has led, time after time, to the creation of newer and more sophisticated mapping techniques.

In 1777, the Military Cartographic Headquarters was established at Ringwood, N.J., to create maps for General George Washington's campaign against the British. The attacks and marches planned with these maps led the Americans to an unprecedented victory against Mother England, and the legacy of American military mapping began.

In the decades that followed, the young nation found itself embroiled in a series of conflicts with other nations, and finally, within itself. Cartographic agencies were created to keep pace with the changing needs of the military, and these agencies in turn gave birth to numerous advances in surveying and mapping techniques.

The War of 1812 pointed out the need for nautical military maps to accommodate an expanding Navy, resulting, in 1830, with the establishment of the Navy Depot of Charts and Instruments. The Civil War led to the development of aerial reconnaisance mapping, with surveyors rising above the fray in hot air balloons to diagram enemy territory. In 1907, aerial reconnaisance reached new heights with the establishment of the Aeronautical Division of the Army Signal Corps.

The Spanish-American War gave U.S. military cartographers their first real chance at mapping foreign soil, an exercise that paid off during the trench and field battles of the first World War. The use of aerial photography for military purposes was also perfected during World War I. The fine art of cartographic cooperation was honed during World War II, as the federal government's civilian map agencies joined with the Army Map Service and the Navy Hydrographic Office to help battle the Nazi menace.

Government Sources

The mapping agencies of the Defense Department were combined in 1972 into the Defense Mapping

Agency. Today, DMA's Topographic, Hydrographic, and Aerospace Centers produce many of the maps used by the American military. Aside from updating and producing a steady stream of military maps for everyday use, the DMA is currently creating a digitized map of the world to help guide missiles and other military systems. (See "Mapping the Future" for more on these efforts.) Many of DMA's regular maps are available to the public, although they are among the most expensive in the federal government's map collection.

Besides DMA, there are several other government sources of military maps:

■ The National Oceanic and Atmospheric Administration distributes military aeronautical and nautical charts and maps.
■ The Central Intelligence Agency creates maps of foreign countries (see "CIA Maps"), which are distributed by the National Technical Information Service and the Government Printing Office.
■ The Defense Department, State Department, and other agencies produce maps sometimes used for military purposes; they are distributed by GPO.
■ The collections of the Library of Congress and the National Archives are filled with military maps available for study. The Archives contains maps created by government mapping agencies, while the Library of Congress' collection includes both domestic and foreign military maps. For a fee, the reproductions services at both collections make copies of their maps.
■ Maps of historic battlegrounds that are preserved by the federal government can be obtained from the National Park Service, while state and local bureaus of tourism or historical preservation usually hand out free maps of the memorials or battlegrounds under their auspices.

If you're searching for a military map, here are some strategic places to look:

Government Sources

Government Printing Office. GPO has several publications containing military maps. One inter-

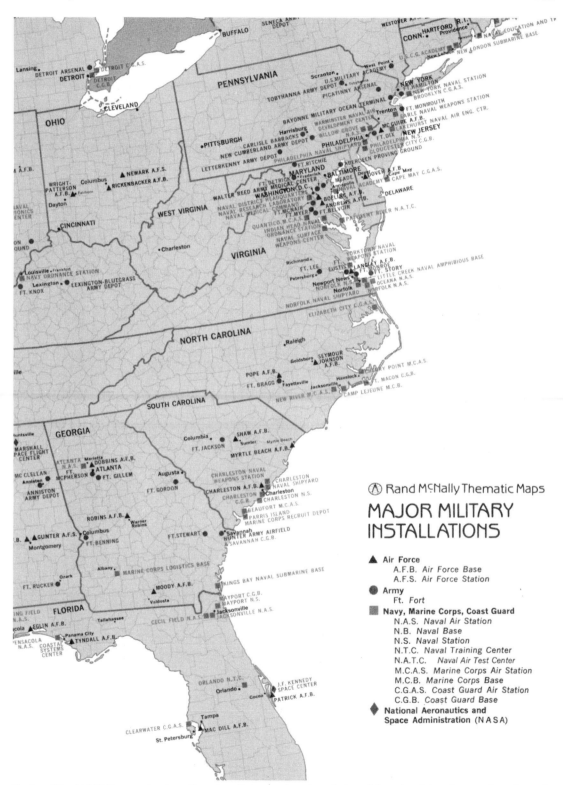

Portion of Rand McNally map of major military installations in the U.S., including all branches of the military, military hospitals, and landing strips.

esting example is *American Revolution, 1775-1783: Atlas of the 18th Century Maps and Charts, Theatres of Operations* (S/N 008-046-0043-3, $13.50), presenting a selection of maps that were available to military and civil leaders of both sides during the Revolutionary War. Also included is geographical coverage of various battlefields involving naval forces.

Also available from GPO is a good guide to the National Ocean Survey's collection of Civil War maps. *National Ocean Survey Cartobibliography: Civil War Collection* (S/N 003-017-00483-0; $4.50) contains listings of many of the collection's maps created during the war by twelve of the Confederate states plus Pennsylvania and West Virginia.

Other military books with maps available from GPO, most priced between $10 and $30, include:

- *United States Army in the Occupation of Germany, 1944-1946* (S/N 008-029-00090-3).
- *China-Burma-India Theater: Stillwell's Command Problems* (S/N 008-029-00074-1).
- *Stillwell's Mission to China* (S/N 008-029-00013-0).
- *Time Runs Out in CBI* (S/N 008-209-00014-8).
- *European Theater of Operations: Ardennes, Battle of the Bulge* (S/N 008-029-00069-5).
- *Breakout and Pursuit* (S/N 008-029-00021-1).
- *Cross Channel Attack* (S/N 088-029-00020-0).
- *Logistical Support of the Armies, Vol. 1* (S/N 008-029-00023-7).
- *Logistical Support of the Armies, Vol. 2* (S/N 008-029-00024-5).
- *Lorraine Campaign* (S/N 008-029-00019-9).
- *Supreme Command* (S/N 008-029-00076-8).
- *The Siegfried Line Campaign* (S/N 008-029-00068-7).

Tennessee Valley Authority. TVA produces several inexpensive blueline lithoprint reproductions of original Civil War maps from campaigns in the Tennessee Valley region. When ordering, include fifty cents postage for each map. Available maps include:

- "Map of the approaches and defense of Knoxville during the Civil War" (File No.455 K 90; $1.50), a blueline print measuring 25″ × 31″, surveyed in 1863.
- "Map of the Army movements around Chattanooga made to accompany the report of Major General Grant in January, 1864" (File No. G MD

453 G 754; $1), a lithoprint measuring 18″ × 24″.
- "Battlefield of Chickamauga, Georgia, April, 1864" (File No. G MD 453 G 754-1; $1), a blueline print measuring 18″ × 22″.
- "Map showing the operations of the National Forces under the command of General W.T. Sherman during the campaign of Atlanta, September 1864" (File No. G MD 453 G 754-2; $1), a blueline print measuring 16″ × 21″.
- "Chattanooga and its approaches" (File No. G MD 453 K 754-3; $1.50), a blueline print measuring 22″ × 28″ that shows the Union and Rebel

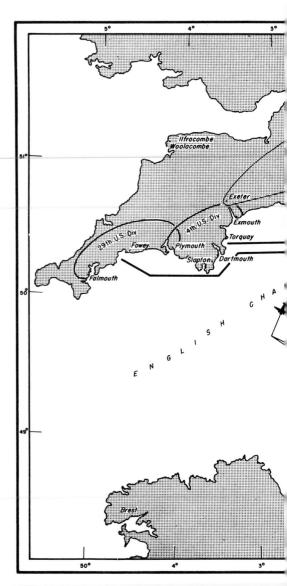

Map showing the routes of the Allied assault on D-Day, from a

works during the battles of November 1863.

■ "Maneuver Ground, Chickamauga Park and Vicinity" (File No.G CF 8141 G; $1), a blueline print measuring 18″ × 24″ of a topographic map made in April 1910.

■ "Map of Battlefields of Chattanooga" (File No.5-438; $1), a blueline print measuring 18″ × 24″ dated 1901 showing movement against Orchard Knob.

■ "The First Epoch of the Atlanta Campaign, from Chattanooga to Oostanaula River" (File No. 453 K 754-6: $1.50), a blueline print measuring 22″ ×

35″. This map shows the positions held by Generals Sherman and Johnston.

■ "Military Map Showing the Marches of U.S. Forces Under General Sherman, 1863-1865" (File No. 453 M 754-8; $1.50), measuring 23″ × 38″.

U.S. Geological Survey. USGS's topographic mapping program, which covers the National Park System, has mapped many historic forts, battlegrounds, and military memorials and parks. A free map pinpointing topographic maps, "Index to USGS Map Coverage of the National Park System," is available from USGS. The maps in the Na-

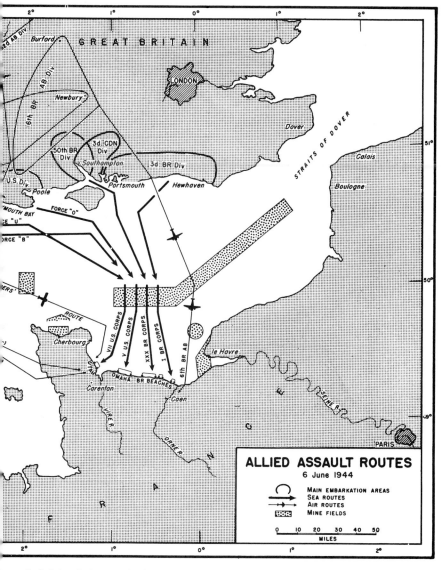

maps included with the GPO *book* Utah Beach to Cherbourg.

tional Park Series cost $3.60 each and are drawn at various scales, some parks requiring more than one sheet. (See "Topographic Maps" and "Park and Forest Maps" for more information.)

National Archives and **Library of Congress.** The collections of maps in the Archives and the Library of Congress include thousands related to military history. The Archives collection has maps created by the federal government, while the Library of Congress' collection extends beyond our shores, to maps from Asian and European wars.

National Oceanic and Atmospheric Administration. For reasons no one can explain, NOAA maintains an extraordinary collection of Civil War charts and diagrams drawn by the cartographers of the Confederate Army. A catalog of NOAA's Civil War collection is available from GPO.

The collections of the Library of Congress, National Archives, and NOAA are available to the public for study only. Reproduction facilities are available at each collection, although reproductions can take up to eight weeks. See "Uncle Sam's Treasure Chests" for more information on the collections of the Library of Congress and National Archives.

Commercial Sources

Older maps of military campaigns or battles can be found through antique map and military paraphernalia dealers; many print and art dealers carry antique military map reproductions. Fine-quality reproductions can also be obtained from the bookstores of many museums and libraries.

Other sources for military maps include those commercial map companies that produce classroom maps tracing military campaigns or battles. Some companies also publish reproductions of military maps for decorative purposes, as well as up-to-date, utilitarian maps pinpointing current military bases.

Another good source for historical military maps are local or regional military clubs for devotees of a certain era or war. Pennsylvania and West Virginia have several Civil War organizations, for example, while the New England area is rife with Revolutionary War buffs. The museums and gift shops of military battlefields and parks are also good hunting grounds for military maps.

Several educational map publishers produce maps depicting military history. Here's a sampling:

George F. Cram Company Inc. (P.O. Box 426, Indianapolis, IN 46206; 317-635-5564) produces several large, full-color maps of military history for classroom use. The maps, which range in cost from $59 each for non-markable versions to $63 for markable versions, measure 52″ × 40″. Maps in Cram's American History Series include "The Revolution in the Middle and Northern Colonies," "The Revolution in the South and West," "The Mexican War and Compromise of 1850," and "The Civil War, 1861-1865." Maps in the World History Series include "World War I—1914-1918," "World War II, European Theater," and "World War II, Pacific Theater."

National Geographic Society (17th and M Streets, Washington, DC, 20036; 202-921-1200) has "Battlefields of the Civil War" (02824; $3), a full-color illustrated map that measures 30″ × 23″.

Nystrom (3333 Elston Avenue, Chicago, IL 60618; 800-621-8086, 312-463-1144 in Ill.) has two colorful series of history teaching maps similar to Cram's. The Nystrom maps ($36 to $57, depending on mounting) measure 50″ × 38″. Titles relating to military history in the American series include "The Revolutionary War," "The War of 1812," "The War Between the States 1861-1865," and "Korean War; Vietnam War." Maps in the World History series include "Mongol-Turkish Conquests," "Napoleonic Empire, 1812," "World War II in Europe and Northern Africa," and "Russian and Japanese Expansion in the Far East."

Rand McNally (P.O. Box 7600, Chicago, IL 60680; 800-323-1887, 312-673-9100 in Ill.) has a "Map of Major Military Installations" (21585-X; $15), which measures 27½″ × 20½″ and uses different symbols to depict all major military installations for each branch of the Armed Services.

▶ **See also: "Aerial Photographs," "Aeronautical Charts and Maps," "Antique Maps," "Atlases," "CIA Maps," "Historical Maps," "Historic Site Maps," and "Indian Land Maps."**

Natural Resource Maps

The modern world is paradoxically dependent on the natural world: the more technology we invent, the greater our need for the resources to build or fuel this technology. From minerals to forests, natural gas to sunshine, all that the Earth, sea, and air have to offer has been mapped, charted, and diagrammed.

The "ecology" movement of the 1960s and 1970s, with its philosophy of conservation rather than depletion, led the way to a new consciousness about the Earth. "Use it or lose it" became "save it or else." Today, forests that are harvested are simultaneously replanted, "exotic" technologies such as solar and wind power are becoming second-nature, and the search for new sources of traditional energy sources has intensified. Maps often lead the way to finding and exploiting these resources wherever they lie—below the ground, beneath the ocean floor, or shining from above.

In 1871, when John Wesley Powell and his brother-in-law, Almon Harris Thompson, set out on a mapping survey of the American West, they were expected merely to fill in the details of an earlier, less-comprehensive map. But Powell had a new vision of the untamed land: He wanted to go beyond the preconceived notions of geologic and topographic mapping. Earlier maps had concentrated on geology for merely historical or industrial purposes. Topography, likewise, was treated with a narrow-minded eye toward the shape of the land and its suitability for agriculture and ranching. Powell believed that understanding the land and the way it was formed led to a deeper understanding of its usefulness for man. By surveying and mapping the land in relation to its ongoing development and specific uses, Powell predicted that future discovery and development of natural resources would be enhanced.

The Powell-Thompson maps are geologic landmarks, concentrating for the first time on mineral and soil development as well as study of the catalysts for the chosen path of a river or formation of a mountain. These studies shed new light on the search for and extraction of natural resources. One cartographic idea that Powell espoused but was never able to see carried out was the concept of "scientific classification" of the land. He believed that topographic maps were not specific enough in the nature of available resources; he wanted mappers to categorize the land in more

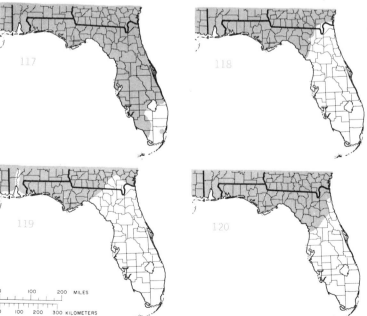

Series of maps showing the Florida growing regions of certain species of oak trees: bluejack oak (top left), laurel oak (top right), blackjack oak (bottom left), and swamp chestnut oak (bottom right). From the GPO's Atlas of United States Trees.

specific terms of usefulness. Instead of "farm-land," for example, Powell believed maps should read "irrigation land" or "pasturage land," while mining lands should be labeled with the type of mineral or coal beneath the surface rather than just the generic term "mining." Although Powell's idea did not catch on at the time, his concept of mapping land classification now plays an important role in the exploration and use of natural resources.

The mapping of natural resources in America is an ongoing process for both government and commercial cartographers. As older resources are depleted, new ones found, and different methods of retrieval created, there are maps made to reflect the changes. And because even greater care is taken to protect the environment and nurture its riches, there will always be work for mappers of natural resources.

Energy and mining companies, farmers, builders, foresters, conservationists, and anyone else interested in land use find natural resource maps invaluable. The diagramming of natural resources include solar energy atlases, forests, oil fields, and mineral, coal, and gas investigations maps. There are maps of past, present, and potential energy sources, as well as maps detailing lands where the energy exploration is prohibited. These and other maps are available from the goverment and from selected commercial mappers or organizations.

Government Sources

U.S. Geological Survey. USGS's National Atlas Program includes the following maps on natural resources:

■ "Major Forest Types" (38077-AM-NA-07M-00; $3.10), a 1967 map showing the distribution of eastern, Hawaiian, and Alaskan forest and nonforest lands.
■ "Networks of Ecological Research Areas" (38077-AO-NA-07M-00; $3.10) shows the location of research areas designated by public and private agencies as secure sites for basic and applied studies of natural processes.
■ "Principle Lands Where Exploration and Development of Mineral Resources are Restricted" (38077-AP-NA-07M-00; $3.10). This 1983 map shows areas of 5,000 acres or more where mineral

development is prohibited or severely, moderately, or slightly restricted. Alaska and Hawaii are included on the reverse.

USGS also produces coal, oil, and gas investigations maps (see "Energy Maps") as well as a series of "Mineral Investigations" maps and studies. Write to the nearest USGS office for listings of available maps and surveys. (See Appendix A.)

Government Printing Office. GPO has the following atlases on natural resources:

■ "Atlas of United States Trees: Volume 5, Florida" (S/N 001-000-03728-5; $6.50). This 23-page volume, published in 1978, has maps of forest resources in Florida.
■ "Forester's Atlas of the Northeast" (S/N 001-001-00601-7; $9.50). This 1985 atlas provides a cartographic display of forest resource information and other data related to the forests of the Northeast.
■ "Solar Radiation Energy Resource Atlas of the United States" (S/N 061-000-00570-6; $18). This 182-page atlas from 1981 describes and illustrates solar radiation energy resources available throughout the United States.

Tennessee Valley Authority. TVA has a mapping services branch that creates maps and charts for the local region, including:

■ "Geologic Map and Mineral Resources Summaries" ($2.50 each plus $1.50 postage). These geologic maps cover separate portions of Tennessee and come with a mineral resources summary in a seven-and-a-half-minute quadrangle format. A free listing of these maps is available upon request from TVA.
■ "Mineral Resources of the Tennessee Valley Region" ($4 plus $2 for mailing tube and $1.50 postage). This 1970 map measures 35″ × 49″ and is printed in full color.
■ "Mineral Resources and Mineral Industries of Tennessee" ($2.50 plus $2 for mailing tube and $1.50 postage). This 40″ × 66″ map describes Tennessee's mineral riches.

Other government sources of natural resource maps include state, county, and local departments of natural resources, ecology, forestry, and mining. (See Appendix B for addresses.)

Commercial Sources

Several commercial map publishers and geologic organizations produce maps of natural resources:

National Geographic Society (17th and M Streets NW, Washington, DC 20036; 202-921-1200) offers "America's Federal Lands" (02005; $4). This 1982 map includes descriptive notes and a listing of natural resources by region. The map measures 42½" × 29½".

Williams & Heintz Map Corporation (8119 Central Avenue, Capitol Heights, MD 20743; 301-336-

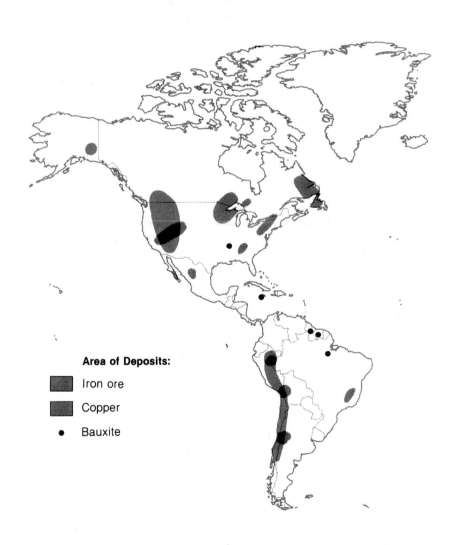

Area of Deposits:

Iron ore

Copper

• Bauxite

Portion of map showing mineral deposits of iron ore, copper, and bauxite, from the State Department's Atlas of United States Foreign Relations.

1144) produces but does not sell geologic maps, although some organizations offer some of its products relating to natural resources, including:

■ "Geothermal Resources and Temperature Gradients of Oklahoma" ($2; order number GM-27) and "Geologic Map in Geology & Mineral Resources of Payne County" ($19 cloth, $15 paper; Bulletin 137, Plate 1 and 3), both from Oklahoma Geological Survey, 830 Van Vlette Oval, Norman, OK 73019.
■ "Mineral Resources Map, Offshore Oregon" ($6; order number GMS-37) from Oregon Department of Geology and Mineral Industries, 910 State Office Building, Portland, OR 97201.
■ "Ground-Water Hydrology of the Minor Tributary Basins of the Ohio River, West Virginia" ($10) from Chief, Division of Water Resources, West Virginia Department of Natural Resources, 1201 Greenbrier Street, Charleston, WV 25311; Attn: Public Information Office.

American Association of Petroleum Geologists (AAPG Bookstore, P.O. Box 979, Tulsa, OK 74101; 918-584-2555) publishes "Circum-Pacific Mineral Resources Map Series" ($12), a series of six working mineral resources maps of the Circum-Pacific region depicting mineral deposits by colored symbols showing location, geologic or geometric class, size of deposit, and age of mineralization.

George F. Cram Company Inc. (P.O. Box 426, Indianapolis, IN 46206; 317-635-5564) has the following natural resource maps for classroom use from its American history series:

■ "Coal, Iron, Petroleum, Gas Regions of the United States" ($63 markable, $59 non-markable; order number 526), showing percentages of total production in figures as well as in different colors. The map is 52″ × 40″.
■ "Mineral Production of the United States" ($63 markable, $59 non-markable; order number 527), showing where important minerals are found, with percentages of the total production indicated in figures and colors. The map is 52″ × 40″.

Rand McNally (P.O. Box 7600, Chicago, IL 60680; 800-323-1887, 312-673-9100 in Ill.), which distributes the Denoyer-Geppert "Our America" series of classroom maps, has "Manufacturing and Minerals" ($54; order number 214-10534-2), showing the locations of manufacturing centers and mineral resources.

▶ **See also: "Agricultural Maps," "Energy Maps," "Geologic Maps," "Park and Forest Maps," and "Recreation Maps."**

Park and Forest Maps

Every year, millions of visitors pour into America's parks and forests for camping, recreation, or sightseeing. Whether it's a weekend in the wilderness or a cross-country family trek, maps are a necessity for enjoying thousands of public parks and forests.

Maps of public wilderness lands are produced by a number of government agencies. Most relate to specific parks, forests, or wildlife refuges, while a few provide overviews of the entire national park and forest system. These overview maps are good for planning a vacation or locating a nearby park, while the more detailed maps can lead an adventurous hiker to a spectacular view, or a thirsty camper to water.

The Department of the Interior administers most of the agencies that produce maps of federal recreation lands. Among these agencies are the Bureau of Land Management, the Fish and Wildlife Service, the National Park Service, and the U.S. Geological Survey. Maps are also available through the Department of Agriculture's National Forest Service, and selected maps can be purchased in Government Printing Office bookstores, as well as through commercial dealers. Forests and parks that are protected by state or local governments are administered by state, county, and city land management or environmental protection agencies (see Appendix B). Maps for state and local parks and forests can usually be obtained through the administering agency or local tourist board. Organizations devoted to the preservation and enjoyment of the wilderness, such as the Sierra Club, also produce their own maps for use by members and for sale to the public.

Government Sources

Bureau of Land Management. BLM, which grew out of the now defunct General Land Office, administers more than 446 million acres of public land known as the "National Land Reserve." Most of BLM's holdings are in the West, although there are small sections in the South and North that fall under its jurisdiction. There are more than 3,600 miles of marked trails in BLM territory, as well as over 3,000 federal recreation areas open to the

public. BLM maps for these trails and recreation areas can be obtained from district, state, or regional BLM offices (see Appendix A).

Fish and Wildlife Service. The more than thirty million acres of wildlife refuges in this country providing sanctuary to wild birds, mammals, and many other creatures fall under the protective wing of the Fish and Wildlife Service. While fishing and hunting are usually prohibited at the refuges, camping, hiking, and nature study are allowed and encouraged. Free or inexpensive maps are usually available at the refuge, and the U.S. Geological Survey has maps of all the National Wildife Refuges. "National Wildlife Refuges" is a fold-out map showing the locations of almost 300 refuges, available from GPO for $1.

Portion of the "National Park System Guide and Map" created by the National Park Service, pinpointing National Parks and Historical Sites around the country.

Government Printing Office. GPO also has the following forest maps and atlases available:

■ *Atlas of United States Trees: Volume 5, Florida* (S/N 001-000-03728; $6.50) covers Florida forest land, which contains more species of trees than any other state except Hawaii. There are 262 maps in this 1978 volume.

■ *Foresters Atlas of the Northeast* (S/N 001-001-00601-7; $9.50), a 98-page volume that provides a cartographic display of this region's forest resources.

National Forest Service. There are 122 National Forests, and the NFS has maps for all of them. The Forest Service produces various types of maps for its lands, including a large, 1:7,500,000-scale sheet from the *National Atlas of the United States* titled "National Forests and other Lands Administered by the Forest Service." There are also forest visitors' guides and maps, wilderness area maps, and Special Designated Area maps. Visitors' maps include location keys for points of interest as well as camping and recreation grounds. Wilderness and Special Designated Area maps provide detailed information on wilderness and other specially designated areas within the bounds of national forests. Maps can be ordered through the NFS regional and national offices, and selected maps are available through GPO. Requests for maps should, if possible, include a note about which parts of a particular forest interest you, because many of the larger forests are contained on several maps, divided by ranger stations. NFS can be of even more help in selecting appropriate maps if you indicate what activities are planned for a given area; NFS produces different maps for hikers, campers, and geologists to meet their specific needs.

National Park Service. The National Park Service administers millions of acres of park land, as well as nine national seashores and the Pictured Rock National Lakeshore. There are schematic and topographic maps available for most of these parks, as well as recreational and historic site maps. Nearly all national parks have folders containing maps and information, available free to the public. They can be obtained either at the parks themselves or through the Public Inquiries Office of the National Park Service. GPO publishes and sells several Park Service maps and guides, including "Guide and Map: National Parks of the United States" ($1.25), "The National Parks: Lesser Known Areas" ($1.50), and "Access National Parks: A Guide for Handicapped Visitors" ($6.50).

U.S. Geological Survey. USGS is the government's largest mapping agency, as well as its most complex. Maps depicting the topography, geology, and recreational use of national forests, parks, and refuges are available from USGS for a small fee, usually under $4. Depending on the size and importance of the public recreation area, details of these lands may be included in larger-scale maps that cover the area around the park. Detailed boundaries of these areas are usually shown if they are of substantial size. Smaller patches of public land may not be shown, but wildlife refuges and game preserves always appear on USGS maps. USGS maps can be obtained through local or district USGS branches.

State agencies involved with environmental protection and preservation or fish and game management are good places to obtain maps of state protected recreation land. (See Appendix B.) Maps of locally protected public parks or forests are often obtained through city or county sources, such as the board of tourism.

Other Sources

Sierra Club Books (distributed by Random House, 201 East 50th Street, New York, NY 10022; 800-638-6460, 800-492-0782 in Md.) publishes a series of paperback guides to parks and natural recreation areas, which include between ten and eighteen full-color maps per title. There are two series: *The Sierra Club Guides to the Natural Areas of the United States* (with separate titles for California; Colorado and Utah; New Mexico, Arizona, and Nevada; and Oregon and Washington) and *The Sierra Club Guides to the National Parks* (with separate titles for parks of the desert Southwest; the East and Middle West; the Pacific Northwest and Alaska; the Pacific Southwest and Hawaii; and the Rocky Mountains). Another series, *The Sierra Club Totebooks*, feature hiker's guides that feature maps for a variety of wilderness areas, including the Smokies, the Grand Canyon, the North Cascades, Virginia, the Swiss Alps, the John Muir Trail, and Yellowstone backcountry, among others.

Following is a listing of outdoor groups that offer maps for hikers, bikers, campers, and nature lovers. There may be some restrictions on the availability of maps, especially to non-members of some membership organizations.

■ **Adirondack Mountain Club** (172 Ridge Street, Glen Falls, NY 12801; 518-793-7737) has maps of New York's Adirondack Mountains.

■ **Appalachian Trail Conference** (P.O. Box 236, Harpers Ferry, WV 25425; 304-535-6331) has maps of the Appalachian Trail's fourteen-state route.

■ **Buckeye Trail Association** (P.O. Box 254, Worthington, OH 43085) distributes maps of Ohio's 900-mile Buckeye Trail.

■ **Colorado Mountain Club** (2530 West Almeda Street, Denver, CO 80219) has maps of the mountains in Colorado.

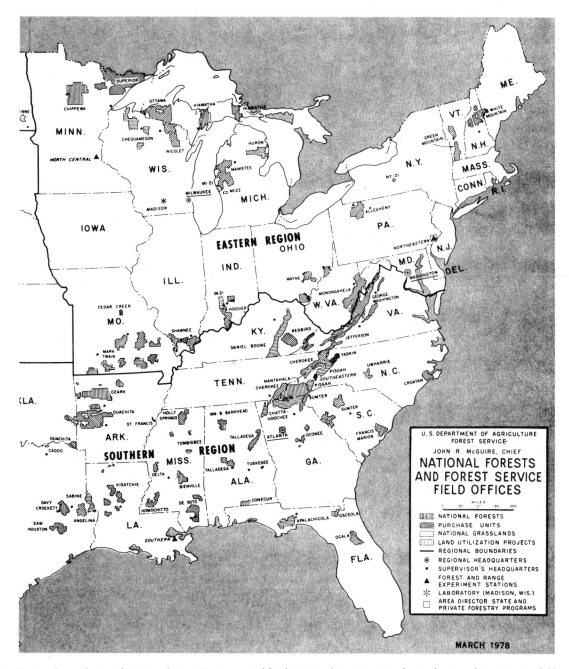

Portion of map showing the National Forest System, created by the National Forest Service, showing forests and Forest Service field offices.

■ **Connecticut Forest & Parks Association** (P.O. Box 389, East Hartford, CT 06108; 203-289-3637) has maps and a "Walk Book" of Connecticut wilderness areas.

■ **Dartmouth Outing Club** (Box 9, Robinson Hall, Dartmouth College, Hanover, NH 03755; 603-646-2428) has maps of New Hampshire trails and countryside.

■ **Florida Trail Association** (P.O. Box 13708, Gainesville, FL 32604) has maps of the Florida Trail.

■ **Green Mountain Club** (Box 889, Montpelier, VT 05602; 802-223-3463) has maps of Vermont's 260-mile-long trail.

■ **International Backpackers Association** (P.O. Box 85, Lincoln Center, ME 04458; 207-794-6062) has schematic and topographic maps of national and international backpacking routes.

■ **Potomac Appalachian Mountain Club** (1718 N Street NW, Washington, DC 20036; 202-638-5306) has maps of trails in Washington, D.C., Maryland, Pennsylvania, and Viginia.

▶ **See also: "Agricultural Maps," "Bicycle Route Maps," "Historical Site Maps," "Land Use Maps," "Natural Resource Maps," "Recreation Maps," "Tourism Maps," and "Wildlife Maps."**

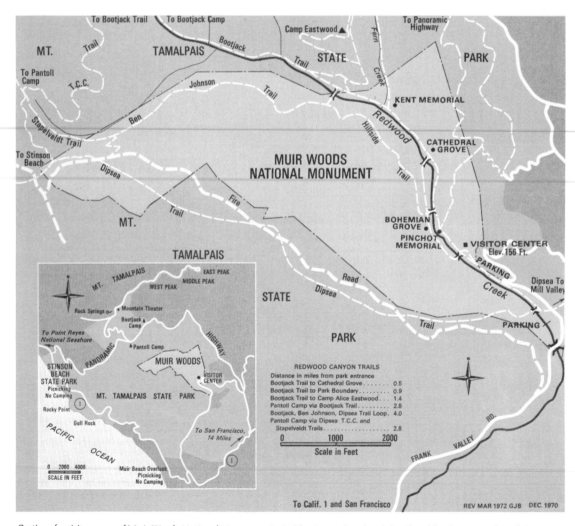

Section of a visitors map of Muir Woods National Monument in California, produced and distributed by the National Park Service.

Political Maps

There are two types of political maps. In strict cartographic terms, a political map refers to maps that outline the political boundaries of the world. With their color-coded outlines of states and nations, these are the basic maps found in virtually every classroom, library, and home atlas—the ones that taught us early on that Italy looks like a boot "kicking" the island of Sicily, or that Mississippi was on the left and Alabama was on the right. This type of political map is created by practically every map-making company, as well as by most countries' governments. They can be found elsewhere in this book; see especially "Atlases," "Foreign Country Maps," "Globes," "State Maps," "U.S. Maps," and "World Maps."

The other type of political map does more than simply divide nation from nation or state from state—they provide political characteristics, illustrating, for example, a ruling party's influence and role, or tracing a region's political development over time. These are "political" in the truest sense of the word, showing areas of human rights abuse, for example, or countries under dictatorial rule.

One of the best collections of political maps may be found in a book, *The New State of the World Atlas*, by Michael Kidron and Ronald Segal (New York: Simon & Schuster, 1984; $10.95), a paperback chock full of four-color maps. Each compares the world's nations in some qualitative way, the choices and titles of which clearly reflect the authors' political leanings. Examples: "Shares in the Apocalypse" (which nations have how many of what kinds of weapons), "The First Slice of the Cake" (the percentage of gross national product spent by each nation's government), "Webs and Flows" (each country's share of transnational parent corporations), and "Exploitation" (a ratio of the price of manufactured products compared to the wages of the workers who make them). In the back of the book, the concept and rationale be-

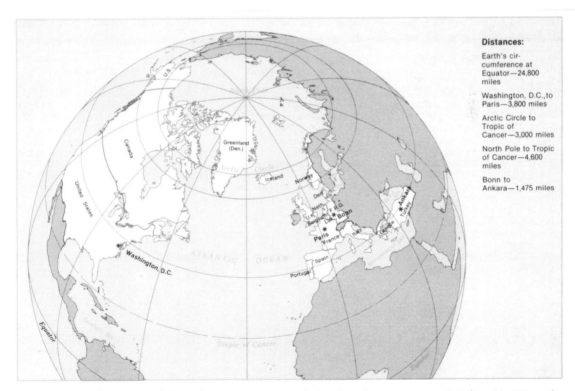

Distances:

Earth's circumference at Equator—24,800 miles

Washington, D.C., to Paris—3,800 miles

Arctic Circle to Tropic of Cancer—3,000 miles

North Pole to Tropic of Cancer—4,600 miles

Bonn to Ankara—1,475 miles

Map showing member countries of the North Atlantic Treaty Organization, from the State Department's Atlas of NATO, *available from GPO.*

hind each map is explained in understandable prose. For those at either end of the political spectrum, this atlas provides a wealth of thought-provoking maps.

While some commercial map publishers and government agencies produce a few political maps, most come from other sources, particularly public interest groups, political interest groups, or private foundations. There is no directory of such organizations or the maps they produce. The gems must be uncovered. One example is "Devolving Europe" (CoEvolution Quarterly, Box 428, Sausalito, CA 94966; 415-332-1716), a full-color map that pinpoints 28 "fiercely different movements for independence or self-rule." The map (11″ × 15″; $2) comes with an explanatory article that helps put things into perspective.

Government Sources

Central Intelligence Agency. The CIA creates several political maps, many of which are available from the National Technical Information Service. A few, including atlases, can be obtained from the Government Printing Office. CIA's political maps and atlases include:

■ "Major Insurgent Groups of Afghanistan" (NTIS PB 85-928040; $10).
■ "Administrative Divisions, 1984, East and South

Asia, and USSR" (NTIS PB 85-928109; $10).
■ "Lao People's Revolutionary Party: Organization and Structure" (NTIS PB PB 82-9927919; $9.50).
■ *Administrative Atlas of Peoples Republic of China* (GPO S/N 041-015-00076-4; $8), illustrating the politics of China.

For more information, see "CIA Maps" and Appendix A.

Commercial Sources

National Geographic Society (17th and M Streets NW, Washington, DC 20036; 202-921-1200) offers several maps of foreign countries, including:

■ "Africa: Political Development" (02311; $4), a 23″ × 29″ map with illustrations and text on both sides.
■ "Mideast in Turmoil" (02840; $4), measuring 21″ × 14″, depicting recent unrest in the Middle East.
■ "Ireland: Political/Historical" (02843; $4), measuring 14″ × 21″.
■ "Phillipines: Political/Historical" (20010; $4), measuring 20½″ × 27″, printed on both sides.

▶ **See also "Atlases," "Census Maps," "CIA Maps," "Foreign Country Maps," "Military Maps," and "World Maps."**

Map of the military balance in the Caribbean, from the State Department's Atlas of Foreign Relations.

Railroad Maps

The railroads of America crisscross the country, connecting coast with coast and small town with metropolis. For 150 years, they have carried settlers to the West and presidents to the White House. Maps of railroad lines are mirrors of America's past and, in some cases, projections for its future. Railroad maps are also useful tools for travelers, engineers, planners, military strategists, transportation buffs, and historians.

The Baltimore & Ohio Railroad (B&O) was under construction—and surveyance—by 1830, opening fourteen miles of track before the end of that year. Dozens of other railroads soon followed as rail travel for passengers and freight became popular in the expanding nation. The first American railroad map was probably a 1809 survey of the Leiper Railroad in Pennsylvania. The original didn't survive, but a long-named reproduction, "Draft Exhibiting...the Railway Contemplated by John Leiper Esq. from His Stone Sawmill and Quarries...to His Landing on Ridley Creek," can be found in an 1886 book, *A Short Account of the First Permanent Tramway in America*, by Robert P. Robins. The book itself is part of the Library of Congress collection.

Railroad maps are available from a wide range of sources, including the federal government, commercial map publishers, the railroad lines themselves, and as reproductions from libraries and map collections. Some are made specifically for or about a railroad, while others are general use maps that include railroad lines.

Commercial Sources

The following companies publish railroad maps in various forms. Some are contained in trade publications; others are history teaching tools; still others are designed as business or travel maps. All are available directly through the publishers, although a few may also be found in book, travel, or map stores.

American Map Corporation (46-35 54th Road, Maspeth, NY 11378; 718-784-0055) publishes a Cleartype "U.S. Railroad Map" (64" × 44"; $25 plus postage) that covers the United States and parts of Canada and Mexico. Railroad names are printed on the map and included in an index. There also are large-scale insets of dense metropolitan areas on this simple line map designed for travel or business planning.

George F. Cram Company Inc. (P.O. Box 426, Indianapolis, IN 46206; 317-635-5564) publishes a series of American history maps for classroom use, and two in the series are colorful depictions of the growth of the American railway network. "Transportation, Early Railroad Period, 1840-1880" and "Transportation, Principal Railroads Since 1880" (52" × 40"; $59-$63) are available singly or in sets.

National Railway Publication Company (424 West 33rd St., New York, NY 10117; 800-221-5488, 212-714-3148 in N.Y.) publishes, as part of the International Thompson Transport Press, a series of trade books for the travel and freight industries. The books may be purchased through subscription or on a single-copy basis. The maps in the books are utilitarian, black-and-white line drawings of specific routes. Three books include railroad maps: *The Official Railway Guide* (Freight Service Edition: six issues, $80; single copy, $28)—each of the six issues concentrates on a single freight line, with locator and route maps for all areas of the country serviced by freight railroads; *The Official Railway Guide* (Travel Edition six issues, $44; single copy, $28)—updated six times a year to provide the latest pricing and departure information from major passenger carriers including Amtrak, National Railways of Mexico, and VIA Rail Canada, as well as partial listings for a number of international carriers; *Railway Line Clearances* (1986-87 issue, $28) covering rail clearance and weight limitations across America. The maps identify routes and correspond to information in the accompanying charts and tables. Orders may be made by phone or by mail; New York State residents should add appropriate sales tax. Major credit cards are accepted, but payment must accompany single copy orders.

Rand McNally (P.O. Box 7600, Chicago, IL 60680; 800-323-1887, 312-673-9100 in Ill.) publishes two railroad business references: *Handy Railroad Atlas of the United States* ($9.95), a 64-page atlas including distance tables and individual maps, in one and two colors, of major metropolitan areas in the U.S. and Canada; and *Map of the Principal Railroads* ($15 for 48" × 33"; $20 for 66" × 46"), identifying all major railroads in the U.S., southern Canada, and northern Mexico. Also available from Rand McNally is Denoyer-Geppert's classroom teaching map, "Development of Transportation, 1829-1860" ($54). This full-color, 44" × 38" map, part of an educational American history series called "Our America," is markable and washable; special markers are included.

Maps from Railroads

Most railways have maps available upon request by letter or phone. Following is a list of major U.S. and foreign carriers:

Australia. Railways of Australia, c/o Australian Tourist Commission, Suite 467, 630 Fifth Ave., New York, NY 10111; 212-489-7550.

Austria. Austrian Federal Railways, c/o Austrian National Tourist Office, 545 Fifth Ave., New York, NY 10017; 212-944-6880.

Belgium. Belgium National Railroads, 745 Fifth Ave., New York, NY 10051; 212-758-8130.

Britain: Britrail Travel International, 630 Third Ave., New York, NY 10017; 212-599-5400.

Canada: VIA Rail Canada, Suite 400, 2 Place Ville-Marie, Montreal, PQ Canada; 514-286-2311.

France: French National Railroads, 610 Fifth Ave., New York, NY 10020; 212-582-2816.

Germany: German Federal Railroad, 33rd Floor, 747 Third Ave., New York, NY 10017; 212-308-3100.

Italy: Italian State Railways, 666 Fifth Ave., New York, NY 10036; 212-397-2667.

Japan: Japanese National Railways, 45 Rockefeller Plaza, New York, NY 10020; 212-757-9070.

Mexico: Chihuahua Pacific Railway Co., (Ferrocarril de Chihuahua al Pacifico), P.O. Box 46, Chihuahua, Chih., Mexico; 2-22-84. National Railways of Mexico, (Ferrocarriles Nacionales de Mexico), Centro Administrativo, Av. Central No. 140,

Mexico 3,D.F., 905-547-8971, 905-547-5240. Pacific Railroad, (Ferrocarril del Pacifico), Calle Tolsa No. 336, Guadalajara, Ja., Mexico, Tel. 26-31-02. Sonora-Baja California Railway, (Ferrocarril Sonora-Baja California), Terminal Station, Final Ave., Ulises Irigoyen, P.O. Box 182, Mexicali, B.C. Mexico, Tel. 723-86, 721-01 (from U.S. & Canada, 706-567-2386).

Netherlands: Netherlands Railways, 576 Fifth Ave., New York, NY 10036; 212-245-5320.

South Africa: South African Railways, c/o South African Tourist Corp., 610 Fifth Ave., New York, NY 10020; 212-757-4679.

Switzerland: Swiss Federal Railways, c/o Swiss National Tourist Office, 608 Fifth Ave., New York, NY 10020; 212-757-5944.

United States: Amtrak, 400 North Capitol Street, NW, Washington, D.C. 20001; 202-383-3000.

Government Sources

The U.S. Geological Survey publishes a number of maps that depict the U.S. rail system. Topographic maps of the states include illustrations of past, present, and planned railroads (see "Topographic Maps"). The rails are depicted according to the condition and use of the tracks rather than by type of train travel: mainline tracks are drawn as solid line-and-crossties, those under construction are shown as dashed lines, abandoned but still intact tracks appear as double crossties, and dismantled tracks are indicated by a dashed trail symbol and the legend "Old Railroad Grade." The maps also distinguish between standard- versus narrow-gage tracks and single- versus multi-rail routes. One advantage of topographic maps is that you can see at a glance the history and future of railroads along a specific section of land.

Railroads are also depicted on two other USGS maps: "U.S. Base Map" (24" × 36"; $1.50) includes markings for railroads along with other standard features such as roads, parks, and cities (No. 10-A); "U.S. General Reference" (19" × 28"; $3.10) is a colorful, single-sheet map from the *National Atlas* depicting major features, including railroad tracks.

The Tennessee Valley Authority (TVA) has a topographic map of that region that includes railroad routes. The map (48" × 62"; $10, plus $2 for the required mailing tube plus $1 handling), a

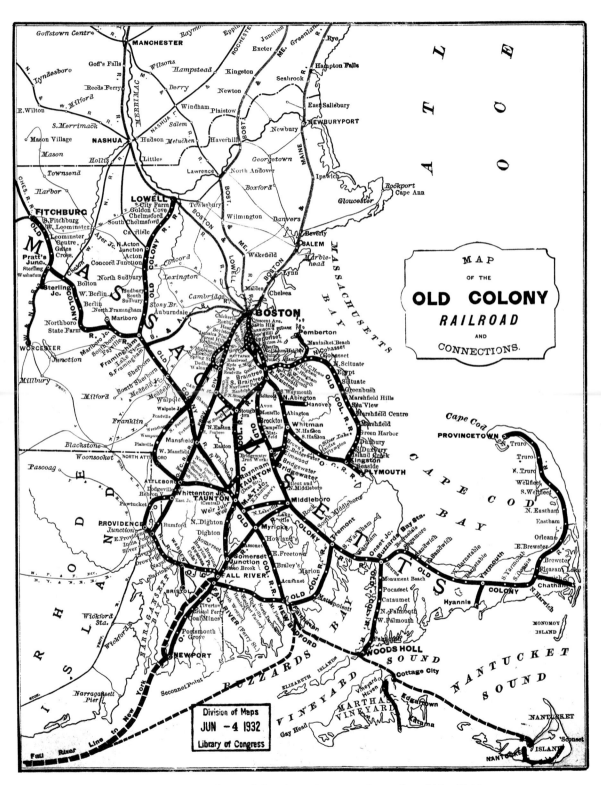

Portion of 1891 railroad map, from the collection of the Library of Congress' Geography and Map Division.

1979-80 full-color edition of TVA's principal base map, also is available with an overprint of an index to the maps available in the region. Also available through TVA is a blueline print of a map published in 1864, "Railroad and County Map of Tennessee" ($1).

The Federal Railroad Administration (FRA) has several map sets that can be purchased through the Government Printing Office. "United States Transportation Zone Maps" ($10.90) is a set of maps with pages punched for three-ring binders, which is more than two inches thick when bound. The continental United States is divided into 486 transportation zones, with two maps (one of rail systems and major highways, the other with rail systems, signal systems, number of tracks, freight density, and trackage rights) for each zone, comprising 972 maps in all.

GPO also sells sets of FRA state maps ($9.75), containing 82 maps showing track ownership, rail junctions, distances between rail intersections, and other pertinent track information, as well as information on major highways and waterways. These FRA map sets are available at some GPO bookstores and may be ordered from GPO by mail.

Also available from GPO are two books on railroad maps produced by the Library of Congress. *Railroad Maps of North America: The First 100 Years* ($28; 1984) is a 208-page history of American railroad maps, beautifully illustrated and containing full-color as well as black-and-white map reproductions, as engrossing to scan as it is to study. *Railroad Maps of the United States: A Selected Annotated Bibliography of Original Maps in the Geography and Map Division of the Library of Congress* ($5.50; 1975) is a 117-page paperbound volume presenting a concise history of the railroad maps held in the Library of Congress, with commentaries of many. The illustrations are in black and white.

The Library of Congress, as suggested by its publication of these volumes, has an extensive collection of old railroad maps, many dating to the early- and mid-nineteenth century. Among the 3,000 railroad maps stored in the vaults of the Library's Geography and Map Division: Frank H. Galbraith's hand-colored railway service maps dating from 1897, using humorous illustrations to show mail stops to help railroad postal workers remember place-names along the way; a map of the North Pennsylvania Railroad and its connections, printed in 1853, including a lengthy proclamation of the railroad's virtues; J.H. Colton and Company's "Map of the New York and Erie Rail Road and Its Connections," published in 1853, with the railroad network printed in red over an outline map of the area and a printed border on the map drawn to simulate a wooden frame. Reproductions may be ordered from the Geography and Map Division's Photoduplication Department.

Like the Library of Congress, the National Archives holds thousands of railroad maps in its collection of maps and charts tracing the history of transportation in America, as surveyed by the government. The first railroad to request and receive federal assistance for mapping its line was the B&O, in the early 1830s, which was quickly followed by numerous eastern railroads vying for government surveyors. The federal government also became involved in mapping railroads to show right-of-way privileges and land grants in the booming West. These and other railroad-related maps (including maps of postal routes that used the railroads to carry mail, and railroad routes through Indian reservations) are stored in the Archives collection.

The Archives maps are filed under collection headings, and most railway surveys may be found in the following collections:

- "Railroad Rights-of-Way" (6,350 items)
- "State Railroad Rights-of-Way" (289 items)
- "Railroad Profiles" (233 items)
- "Railroad Land Grants" (446 items)

The Archives has a reproduction service that can provide copies of these and other maps for a fee.

Recreation Maps

Getting there, as they say, is half the fun. Without a good map, it can be half the headache. Whether it's a Sunday in the park or a month in the mountains, recreation maps can help find the best route to a nearby or far away hiking trail, swimming hole, camp site, or amusement park—or, it may reveal some new and exciting "discovery" you weren't expecting. And once you've gotten there, knowing the lay of the land is as important as finding the land in the first place.

Which section of a lake has lifeguards? Where is

market for guides to vacation lands.

Finding a recreation map can be as easy as walking into a local sporting goods store. Many retailers, especially large chains such as Herman's World of Sports or Eddie Bauer, sell maps along with their canoes, skis, and parkas. Other sources include the many outdoors, conservation, and sports organizations that provide maps to members and the public, sometimes to promote their activities. Name an outdoor sport, hobby, or pastime and chances are there's a map to match.

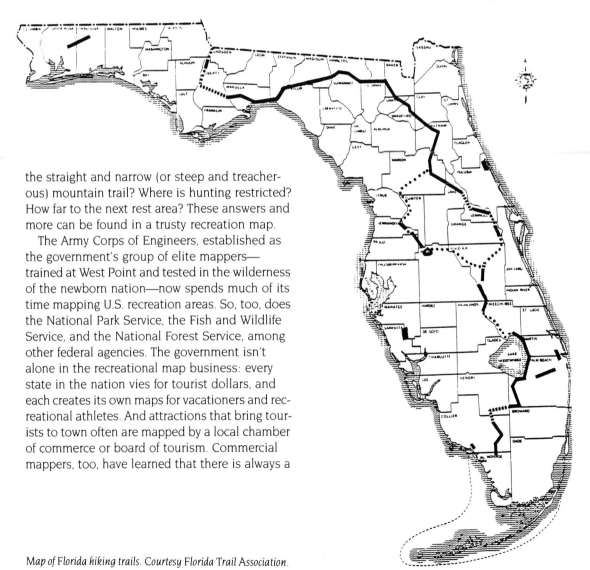

the straight and narrow (or steep and treacherous) mountain trail? Where is hunting restricted? How far to the next rest area? These answers and more can be found in a trusty recreation map.

The Army Corps of Engineers, established as the government's group of elite mappers—trained at West Point and tested in the wilderness of the newborn nation—now spends much of its time mapping U.S. recreation areas. So, too, does the National Park Service, the Fish and Wildlife Service, and the National Forest Service, among other federal agencies. The government isn't alone in the recreational map business: every state in the nation vies for tourist dollars, and each creates its own maps for vacationers and recreational athletes. And attractions that bring tourists to town often are mapped by a local chamber of commerce or board of tourism. Commercial mappers, too, have learned that there is always a

Map of Florida hiking trails. Courtesy Florida Trail Association.

Government Sources

Tennessee Valley Authority. TVA produces multi-colored pocket-size recreation maps of TVA lakes, showing highways, roads, mileages, cities and rural communities, public access areas, commercial recreation areas, boat docks, private clubs, group camps, public parks, wildlife management areas, boat launching sites, and lands open to public use. Available maps include: Cherokee, Douglas, and Nolichuky Lakes; Chickamauga Lake; Fort Loudoun Lake; Guntersville Lake; Kentucky Lake; Norris Lake; and Wheeler and Wilson Lakes.

National Park Service. The Park Service has a variety of trail and other recreational maps for the lands under its jurisdiction. See "Park and Forest Maps" for further information.

National Forest Service. Information about maps for the lands of the Forest Service may be found under "Park and Forest Maps."

Army Corps of Engineers. The Corps of Engineers creates maps and guides for the federal government's water recreation lands, including lakes and reservoirs. See "Water Recreation Maps" for details.

Commercial Sources

There are a vast number of companies producing maps for recreational use, most of which appear in other chapters. For maps of hiking and other recreational trails, see "Park and Forest Maps"; for maps of bicycle routes, see "Bicycle Route Maps"; for maps of fishing and boating areas, see "Water Recreation Maps."

Other sources include publishers of maps for business use. These are often free or inexpensive and are created to illustrate the recreational or tourist facilities of a certain region. One such map producing company is **The National Survey** (Chester, VT 05143; 802-875-2121), which produces a variety of recreation maps for state and local governments and retailers. One example is National Survey's free, ad-filled "Eastern Ski Map," showing ski and winter recreation resorts around the eastern United States.

Rand McNally (P.O. Box 7600, Chicago, IL 60680; 800-323-1887; 312-673-9100 in Ill.) has a series of "Recreation Maps and Guides" ($1.95 each) that include entertainment and dining information for Boston, Chicago, Dallas/Ft. Worth, Houston, Los Angeles, New Orleans, Orlando, Phoenix, San Diego, San Francisco, and Washington, D.C.

▶ **See also: "Bicycle Maps," "Natural Resource Maps," "Nautical Charts and Maps," "Topographic Maps," " Water Recreation Maps," and "Wildlife Maps."**

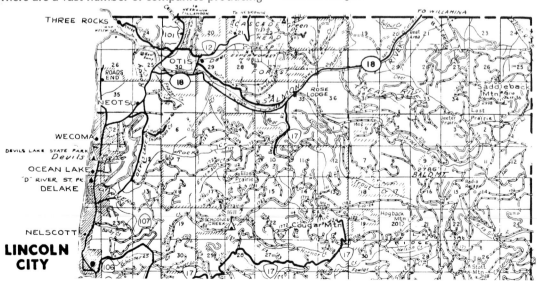

Portion of a Pittmon Map Company recreation map of Lincoln County, Ore., illustrating hiking trails, hunting areas, and beaches.

Space Imagery

Modern science has created new tools that are not only revolutionizing techniques for making maps, but are also giving rise to new types of map products. Among the most important of these tools is "remote-sensing," the process of detecting and monitoring chemical or physical properties of an area by measuring its reflected and emitted radiation.

The earliest remote-sensing experiments took place using photographs aboard the first manned Earth-orbiting missions: Mercury, Gemini, and Apollo. Astronauts used hand-held cameras to produce historic pictures that were examined by scientists worldwide, although no actual maps were made from the pictures.

In 1969, the first scientific space photographic experiment was performed on Apollo 9. Four 70-mm cameras were mounted on a metal frame that fit the spacecraft's command module hatch window. Taking a variety of pictures of the Phoenix, Ariz., region, scientists later interconnected them—a process called "mosaicking"—and printed them as a single image to produce a standard line map. Although crude by today's standards, the experiment led the way for what would become highly sophisticated photo-mapping techniques using manned and unmanned spacecraft.

Landsat I (originally called the Earth Resources Technology Satellite, or ERTS), launched in 1972, was the first American spacecraft designed specifically to record images of the Earth. Since then, subsequent Landsat satellites have recorded hundreds of images of the planet. At an altitude of 567 miles, each satellite circles the globe fourteen times daily, scanning a particular scene every eighteen days, or more than 40 times a year. Each image covers an area approximately 115 miles square, and Landsat can detect an image as small as 100 feet square. Since 1972, images from the four Landsat satellites have become valuable tools for farmers, oil companies, geologists, foresters, foreign governments, and others interested in land resource management. In 1985, ownership of Landsat was transferred by the federal government to the Earth Observation Satellite Co. (Eosat), a partnership of Hughes Aircraft Co. and RCA Corporation.

Although Landsat produces pictures of Earth, its principal viewing instruments are not cameras but two digital sensor systems known as multispectral scanner systems. Digital cameras have several advantages over other cameras in terms of signal-to-noise ratio, weight, reliability, and simplicity of operation, and so have been flown on almost all planetary probes. Another advantage is that their digital information can be manipulated in a computer, allowing enhancement or suppression of images.

In multispectral scanner systems, satellites record information in two visible (red and green) wavelengths and two infrared wavelengths not visible to the human eye. The procedure results in four separate black-and-white images, combined into a "false-color" portrait, in which different colors describe the land below:

■ Healthy vegetation appears in shades of red and contrasts with unhealthy vegetation, which appears as blue-green.
■ Water appears as dark blue or black unless it is sediment laden, in which case it takes on a light blue tone.
■ Most buildings, streets, and other "cultural features" appear as a steely blue-gray.

Another, newer space-imagery vehicle is "Spot," a French-owned satellite launched in 1986, the first commercially owned satellite sensing system. Spot's sensing abilities enable it to record images as small as 10 meters (about 33 feet) square—about half the size of a tennis court—and at a higher resolution than Landsat. Airplanes, bridges, ships, roads, even some houses can be detected by Spot with impressive clarity. One reason is that Spot uses a system of mirrors that can "look" to the side as well as straight down, enabling the satellite to "view" an object from two or more directions. Among other things, this allows for production of stereoscopic images that create a three-dimensional perspective of land images. Still, Landsat can produce bigger pictures than Spot, in more wavelengths of light.

The uses of space imagery are widespread and growing. There is the sheer beauty of space maps,

A *Landsat image of La Paz, Mexico.*

of course—some have been likened to French impressionist paintings—but there are a myriad of practical uses. Space imagery, for example, has been used to:

■ Analyze geological structures, from earthquake faults to mountain ranges, and to detect oil and mineral deposits.
■ Manage water resources and improve stream flow characteristics and water quality in lakes, rivers, and bays.
■ Map, measure, and analyze glaciers and ice caps to predict reservoir inflow and potential flooding.
■ Create thematic maps of forested and cultivated land and coastal waterways.
■ Produce computer-aided mapping and land use analysis.
■ Monitor forest fires, air pollution, oil well fires, and changes in vegetation.
■ Analyze archaeological sites, detect road alignment, and monitor wildlife migration.

Ordering Space Imagery. The EROS Data Center (EDC), near Sioux Falls, S.D., operated by the Earth Resources Observation Systems program of the Department of the Interior, reproduces and sells copies of Landsat imagery, as well as that of Skylab, aerial photography (see "Aerial Photos"), NASA aircraft data, and other remote-sensing products. EDC reproduces and sells copies of imagery, photographs, geophysical data, and computer products collected by sixteen different organizations.

Landsat Images. Landsat images are available for the 50 states and for most of the Earth's land surface outside the U.S. Landsat, for example, has several products available for any given location, including:

■ Single black-and-white images, available as film negatives, film positives, or paper prints.
■ Complete sets of four black-and-white images and a false-color composite. All false-color composites are available as film positives or paper prints.
■ Computer tapes containing digital data.

Each Landsat image covers about eight million acres. Images do not reveal outlines of small areas, like houses or small towns and villages, but provide views of broad areas and large features, such as mountain ranges and the outlines of major cities.

Landsat images are available through the U.S. Geological Survey's National Cartographic Information Center (see Appendix A) and its Earth Resources Observation Center (EROS) Data Center in Sioux Falls, S.D. When ordering, it is important to describe the exact area in which you are interested, including, if possible, the geographic coordinates or a map marked with the specific area. You also should indicate:

■ the type of product (black-and-white or false-color);
■ the minimum image quality acceptable;
■ the maximum percent of acceptable cloud cover (10 percent to 90 percent); and
■ the preferred time of year.

To order images of the 48 contiguous United States, you can use the form *Selected Landsat Coverage* (NOAA Form 34-1205, available free from EROS and USGS), which includes a map of the U.S. showing the locations of individual Landsat images selected for their clarity and lack of cloud cover. USGS also has prepared a number of photomaps, mosaic, and other images produced by Landsat, including an impressive view of the entire United States. Prices for most of these range from $2.50 to $6, not including postage and handling charges for mail orders.

Spot Images. Spot's images may be obtained directly from Spot Image Corporation (1897 Preston White Drive, Reston, VA 22091; 703-620-2200), the wholly owned subsidiary of the French company created to market Spot's services. Spot data are available as digital information in computer-compatible tapes and as black-and-white or color prints and transparencies. Prices depend on several factors, including which of the three types of radiation that Spot records (two bands of visible light and one of near-infrared radiation) is desired, resolution quality (either 20-meter resolution or the sharper 10-meter resolution), and the size of the print or transparency. For example: a 9½"-square black-and-white transparency showing all three bands at a scale of 1:400,000 and 20-

meter resolution is $705—a color transparency at a scale of 1:250,000 (corrected for distortion to the point that it can be used to overlay on a printed map with high accuracy) and 10-meter resolution is $1790. Prints are a bit less pricey: they range from $370 for some black-and-white to $790 for the top-of-the-line color shot. At such prices, Spot images, however spectacular, are not intended for mere decoration.

Other Space Imagery. Also available are older space-based images that predate Landsat and Spot, including those made from traditional photographic processes using both fixed on-board and hand-held cameras. A limited number of photographs from space are available from the Gemi-

ni and Apollo programs, for example, made between 1965 and 1970, and from the Skylab program in 1973 and 1974. The Gemini and Apollo images are limited by those spacecrafts' flight paths and cover primarily the Southwest, the Gulf Coast, and Florida. Skylab, however, includes extensive photographic coverage of most of the U.S., much of South America, and parts of Africa, Europe, and the Middle East. These photos are available from NCIC and EROS. Two forms may be helpful in ordering: *Manned Spacecraft Photograph Order Form* and *Geographic Search Inquiry Form*, both of which include ordering instructions.

▶ **See also: "Aerial Photographs" and "Weather Maps."**

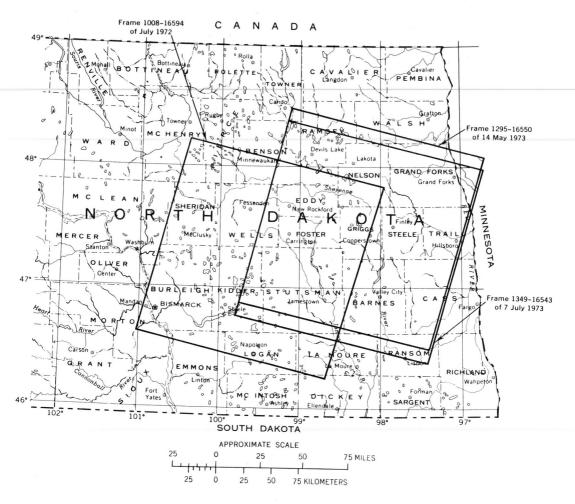

Index map compiled from USGS data showing coverage provided by three Landsat images in a primary waterfowl-breeding area of North Dakota.

State Maps

Like national and county maps, state maps encompass much of the cartographic spectrum. In addition to state road maps and tourist maps, there are land plat maps, geologic maps, topographic maps, recreation maps, boundary maps, and many other charts, surveys, and maps which depict certain resources or features. All are described in their respective chapters elsewhere in this book.

The wide variety of available state maps is reflected in the number of producing companies and agencies. Among the many kinds of state maps that Uncle Sam creates are the U.S. Geological Survey's topographic, geologic, and natural resource investigations maps; the National Oceanic and Atmospheric Administration's hydrologic maps; Landsat and aerial photomaps available from the EROS Data Center; and the Census Bureau's demographic maps.

For purposes of getting from here to there, the best source of free, up-to-date road maps are the state tourism offices (see Appendix B). Most are straightforward road maps, although a few are spiced up with interesting graphics or themes. (Indiana, for example, distributes an illustrated "Adventure Map," with state activities and attractions geared toward entertaining and educating children.) But that's just the beginning of maps published by states. Most states produce and distribute one or more of the following: geologic maps, soil maps, natural resource maps, recreation maps, and maps related to travel, land use, and industry within their borders. Local commercial publishers produce state atlases, road maps, travel guides, recreational, and business maps, and basic wall maps for use in schools and businesses.

Older state maps can be found in the collections of the National Archives and the Library of Congress, as well as in the holdings of state, county, and local historical societies or agencies.

Following are selected sources of state maps:

Government Sources

The federal government produces many types of state maps, all covered in other chapters of this book:

■ The USGS produces a series of state topographic maps, covering an entire state or specific areas; scales vary by coverage. Other USGS products that encompass state maps include the National Atlas Program, geologic and energy investigations maps, seismicity maps, and Bureau of Land Management land plat maps for public lands. (See "Atlases," "Emergency Information Maps," "Energy Maps," "Geologic Maps," "Land Ownership Maps," "Natural Resource Maps," and "Topographic Maps.")

■ The Census Bureau produces a number of state maps showing various demographic trends, including population size, ethnicity, income, and age, as well as maps detailing utility use and per capita retail sales. Another Census Bureau publication with state maps is the *Congressional District Atlas*, a regularly updated book with state-by-state maps of congressional districts. (See "Business Maps," "Census Maps," and "Congressional District Maps.")

■ The National Oceanic and Atmospheric Administration creates numerous state maps related to lakes, rivers, and waterways, as well as aeronautical charts that cover certain states. (See "Aeronautical Maps and Charts," "River, Lake, and Waterway Maps," and "Water Recreation Maps.")

■ The Tennessee Valley Authority has topographic, geologic, and utilities maps for states in its region. (See "Energy Maps," "Geologic Maps," "Natural Resource Maps," "Topographic Maps," and "Utilities Maps.")

■ The Federal Emergency Management Agency's Flood Insurance Administration publishes state maps of flood plains. (See "Emergency Information Maps.")

■ The Defense Department produces an annual *Atlas/State Data Abstract for the United States* ($6), available from the Government Printing Office, containing state-by-state maps and information on military bases, personnel, and defense contracts. (See "Military Maps.")

Commercial Sources

Virtually every major map company in America produces some kind of state map. Any map store and most book stores carry state maps, at least local ones. Other sources include most of the publishers listed under "City Maps," as well as those listed in Appendix E. Here are four examples:

American Automobile Association (8111 Gatehouse Road, Falls Church, VA 22047; 703-222-6000) has free state travel maps available to AAA members only. The maps may not be ordered through the mail, but must be obtained at local AAA offices.

General Drafting Co. (Canfield Road, Convent Station, NJ, 17961; 800-367-6277) produces the Travel Vision series of road maps, which includes 25 state maps covering the entire United States.

Gousha Maps and Atlases (P.O. Box 6227, San Jose, CA 95150; 408-296-1060) has forty full-color state maps covering the entire United States, available singly ($1 each) or complete as the "State Map Library" ($38.50).

Rand McNally (P.O. Box 7600, Chicago, IL 60680; 800-323-1887, 312-673-9100 in Ill.) produces a series of state travel maps ($1.50 each), as well as a set of mural wall maps of 33 states ($9.95 each).

Portion of state tourism map of Idaho, distributed by Idaho Transportation Department.

Topographic Maps

A topographic map is a line-and-symbol representation of natural and selected man-made features plotted to a definite scale. "Topos," as they are often called, show the shape and elevation of the terrain in precise detail by using contour lines. Topos show the location and shape of objects as big as mountains and as small as creeks and dirt roads.

The many uses of topographic maps make them the workhorses of cartography. They are of prime importance in planning airports, highways, dams, pipelines, and almost any type of building. They play an essential role in ecological studies and environmental control, geologic research, water-quality research, conservation, and reforestation. And, of course, they are widely used by hikers, hunters, bikers, and other outdoors types. Topographic maps are also used as the basis for a wide range of other cartographic products, from aeronautical charts to road maps.

Topo maps come in a variety of scales, usually stated as a ratio or fraction showing the measurement of the map in relation to the land it covers. In a 1:24,000 (or 1/24,000) topo map, for example, one unit (an inch, centimeter, or whatever) on the map equals 24,000 of the same unit on the ground.

Map scale is the basic classification of topographic maps, and each scale series fills a range of map needs:

■ Large-scale maps, such as 1:24,000, are useful for highly developed or rural areas where detailed information is needed for engineering planning or similar purposes. Large-scale topo maps are the ones used most often by hikers and campers and for use in other recreational activities.
■ Intermediate-scale maps, ranging from 1:50,000 to 1:100,000, cover larger areas and are best suited for land management and planning.
■ Small-scale maps—1:250,000, 1:500,000, and 1:1,000,000—cover very large areas on a single sheet that are useful for comprehensive views of extensive projects or for regional planning.

For more than a century, the U.S. Geological Survey has been creating and revising topographic maps for the entire country at a variety of scales. There are about 60,000 USGS-produced topo maps, covering every square inch of U.S. territory. Each map covers a specific quadrangle (or "quad"), defined as a four-sided area bounded by parallels of latitude and meridians of longitude. Generally, adjacent maps of the same quadrangle can be combined to form a single large map.

USGS produces five series of topographic maps, each covering a different-sized quad:

■ In the seven-and-a-half-minute series, each quad covers an area seven-and-a-half minutes square (a minute is one-sixtieth of a degree in latitude and longitude). In this series, the scale is 1:24,000 (1:25,000 for Alaska and 1:20,000 for Puerto Rico); one inch represents about 2,000 square feet, and each quad covers about 49 to 71 square miles.
■ In the fifteen-minute series, each quad covers an area fifteen minutes square. In this series, the scale is 1:62,500 (1:63,360 for Alaska); one inch represents about one mile, and each quad covers about 197 to 282 square miles.
■ In the intermediate-scale quadrangle series, each quad covers an area thirty minutes by one degree. In this series, the scale is 1:100,000; one inch represents about one-and-a-half miles, and each quad covers about 1,145 to 2,167 square miles.
■ In the U.S. 1:250,000 series, each quad covers an area one degree by two degrees. In this series, as the name indicates, the scale is 1:250,000; one inch represents about four miles, and each quad covers about 4,580 to 8,669 square miles. Maps of Alaska and Hawaii vary from these standards.
■ In the International Map of the World series, each quad covers an area four by six degrees. In this series, the scale is 1:1,000,000; one inch represents about sixteen miles, and each quad covers about 73,734 to 102,759 square miles.

For comparison purposes, the area covered by one 1 × 2 degree map requires four 30 × 60 minute maps, thirty-two 15-minute maps, sixty-four 7.5 × 15-minute maps, and one hundred and twenty-eight 7.5-minute maps.

When it comes to topos, the basic topographic map is just the tip of the cartographic iceberg. USGS also produces other special-purpose maps and related map data. These include:

■ Orthophotomaps, produced for selected topographic quadrangles, show land features primarily by color-enhanced photographic images that have been processed to show detail in true position. Orthophotomaps may or may not include contours. Because imagery naturally depicts an area in a more true-to-life manner than on a conventional topographic map, the orthophotomap provides an excellent portrayal of extensive areas of sand, marsh, or flat agricultural areas.

■ Orthophotoquads are a basic type of photoimage map prepared in a quadrangle map format. They can be produced quickly because they are printed in shades of gray without image enhancement or cartographic symbols. Orthophotoquads are valuable as map substitutes in unmapped areas and as complements to existing line maps.

■ A number of county maps at scales of 1:50,000 or 1:100,000 have been prepared cooperatively with some states. The maps are multicolored, show political boundaries, a complete road network, and a variety of topographical and cultural features. A series of 1:100,000-scale quad maps provide much of the detail shown on larger-scale maps yet cover enough geographic area to be useful as base maps for county-wide and regional study.

■ State maps at scales of 1:500,000 and 1:1,000,000 are available for all states except Alaska and Hawaii, which are covered by state maps at other scales. There also are shaded-relief editions for many states.

■ The National Park Series, at various scales, covers many parks, monuments, and historic sites. Many of these maps are available with shaded-relief overprinting in which the topography is made to appear three-dimensional by the use of shadow effects.

■ U.S. maps are available in sizes and scales ranging from letter size (1:16,500,000) to a two-sheet wall map (1:2,500,000). The complete series includes two maps, one at 1:6,000,000 and one at 1:10,000,000, that show all fifty states in their correct position and scale.

■ USGS also is engaged in a mapping program for Antarctica. The Antarctic maps are published at several scales, primarily 1:250,000, with shaded relief.

Although most topographic maps are produced by the USGS's National Mapping Program, other federal agencies—including the Defense Mapping

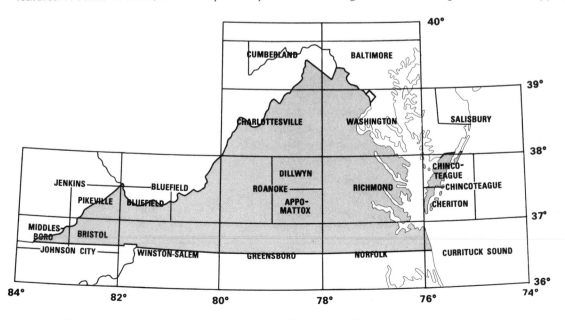

Index of 1:250,000- and 1:100,000-scale topographic maps of Virginia, from USGS state index.

Agency, National Ocean Survey, Tennessee Valley Authority, and the National Park Service—also prepare topographic maps as part of their regular activities, although such maps have been incorporated into the topographic map series published by USGS. They also may be obtained from the producing agencies (see Appendix A).

Colors, lines, and symbols. More than on most other map types, symbols are the graphic language of topographic maps. Color plays a key role, too:

■ symbols for water features are shown in *blue*;

■ man-made objects like roads, railroads, buildings, transmission lines, and political boundaries, are shown in *black*;

■ *green* distinguishes wooded areas from clearings;

■ *red* represents or emphasizes the more important roads, route numbers, fence lines, land grants, and the lines of townships, ranges, and sections of states subdivided by public-land surveys;

■ heavily built-up areas larger than three-quarters of a square mile are given a *pink* tint;

■ features added from aerial photographs during map revision are *purple*;

■ the contour lines that show the shape and elevation of the land surface are *brown*.

Color is just the beginning. The type of lines on a topographic map also provides valuable informa-

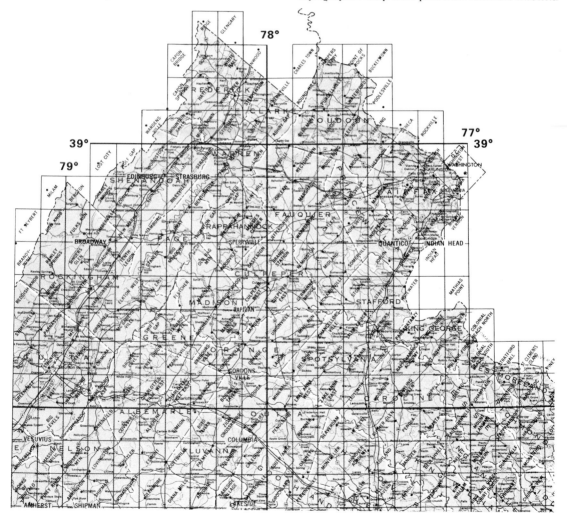

Portion of USGS Virginia state index for 7½-minute (1:24,000 scale) and 15-minute (1:62,500 scale) series topographic maps.

tion. For example, one type of black line designates national boundaries, another shows state boundaries, and still others indicate counties, parishes, civil townships, precincts, towns, barrios, incorporated cities, villages, hamlets, reservations, small parks, cemeteries, airports, and land grants. Still other black lines denote certain types of roads, trails, railroads, telephone lines, bridges, and tunnels. Similarly, there are a dozen or so different blue lines that designate various types of rivers, streams, aqueducts, and canals.

Symbols are another key feature. Some topo map symbols are "pictographs," resembling the objects they represent—a pick and axe designates a mine or quarry, for example; an exposed boat wreck appears as a partially submerged vessel.

All told, there are about 140 different topographic map lines and symbols. A complete directory of colors, lines, and symbols are contained in a free brochure, *Topographic Map Symbols*, available by mail from USGS distribution centers. In person, pick up the brochure from the distribution centers, the fourteen sales counters, or the many commercial dealers that sell USGS topographic maps.

How to order topographic maps. USGS publishes a series of free indexes to topographic maps that are helpful in picking the exact map you seek. There is a separate index for every state, an index for the National Park system, and one index each for the small-, medium-, and large-scale maps covering the entire United States. Each index includes outlines of the region overlaid with various grids showing the different map scales available for that region. There is also a series of free catalogs showing topographic and other published maps for each state; each catalog includes an order blank and related information. USGS catalogs and maps are available from distribution centers (see Appendix A) and sales counters as well as from commercial dealers.

Prices for topographic maps vary by scale and type. Both the seven-and-a-half-minute and fifteen-minute series maps are $2.25 each; 1:100,000-, 1:250,000-, and 1:1,000,000-scale maps are $3.60 each; most other maps are under $5. Prices of USGS maps sold through commercial dealers may vary.

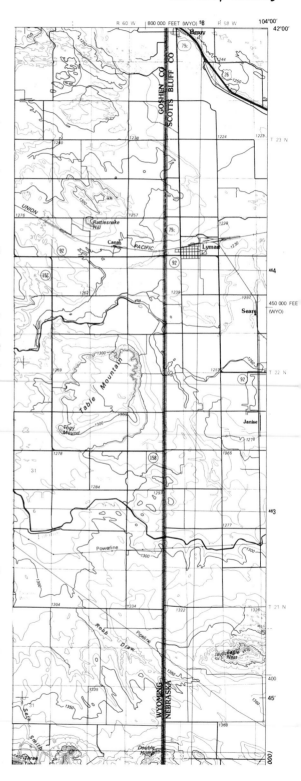

Portion of USGS *topographic map of Chugwater, Wyo.*

Tourism Maps

Without a good map, a dream vacation can quickly turn into a nightmare. Knowing where you're going and how to get there, as well as what facilities, attractions, and recreation areas are nearby, can save a lot of headaches. Tourism maps can help plot out this information and more to help make the most of your hard-earned time-off.

Tourism maps tend to be the freebies of the map world, because they often carry advertising or promote some attraction or region. Most states offer free maps to tourists that pinpoint popular vacation spots and provide helpful travel information. At the very least, a state will provide, free of charge, a highway map and a pamphlet describing the area's "R 'n' R" virtues.

The fact is, if you plan to vacation in an established tourist area, there are likely to be more free maps available than you could possibly use. Many major attractions, including amusement parks, museums, festivals, and shopping complexes, produce maps for use in their areas. So do chambers of commerce and city halls of smaller cities and towns. A few phone calls (probably toll-free ones) can bring an abundance of free tourist maps in the return mail.

Many tourism bureaus and embassies of foreign countries provide free maps, too. Many travel agencies also provide tourist maps for areas in which you have made reservations, as do many hotel, motel, and resort chains. Free or inexpensive maps also are available to members of a number of travel associations, including American Express and the American Automobile Association. Moreover, AAA members also may obtain maps from eighteen affiliated international travel associations in seventeen countries, including auto clubs in Austria, Australia, Chile, Denmark, England, Greece, Israel, Italy, Japan, Luxembourg, the Netherlands, New Zealand, Norway, South Africa, Switzerland, Venezuela, and West Germany,

The only hitch in a tourist map is that you may have to wade through insets and margin notes advertising every imaginable attraction and its virtues. This can make map reading fun, or difficult, depending on whether you want to be entertained or informed. If all you really need is a good road map, specify this when you write away or call. All states and many jurisdictions provide clear, readable highway maps free upon request.

Tourism maps and atlases also are produced by several general or travel-oriented map companies, including Rand McNally, Michelin, and Bartholomew. Prices vary, but most are free of advertising and of a better quality than those from, say, some far off local wax museum.

Government Sources

Government Printing Office. GPO has a small sampling of maps and guides for tourism in the United States and abroad, including:

■ "Welcome to Washington" (S/N 024-005-00823-3; $2.25), which includes maps of downtown Washington, D.C., and the metropolitan Washington area, with information on possible day trips.
■ "Devils Tower" (S/N 024-005-00810-1; $3.50), a history and travel guide that includes maps and tourist information for the famous volcanic rock tower in the Black Hills of Wyoming.

Tennessee Valley Authority. TVA publishes several lake recreation maps, available for 75 cents each; see "Water Recreation Maps" for details. Also available from TVA is an 1838 lithograph of an "Aboriginal Tourist Map of Tennessee" (File No. 453 G 77;$1), which shows steamboat routes, towns, county outlines, and drainage. The print measures 15" × 21".

Commercial Sources

American Map Corporation (46-35 54th Rd., Maspeth, NY 11378; 718-784-0055) has Hallwag's European travel guides and maps, including: *Euro-Guide* ($29.95), a large, complete guide for travelling in Europe, with road, regional, city, and resort area maps, as well as other important travel information; and Special Holiday Maps ($6.25), detailing points of historical interest, cities, restaurants, and other necessary travel stops. There are holiday maps available for Corfu, Crete, Cyprus, France, Greece/Peloponnesus, Mallorca, Malta, and Rhodes.

Hammond Inc. (515 Valley Street, Maplewood, NJ 07040, 201-763-6000) distributes Bartholomew Pictorial and Tourist Route maps. The pictorial maps ($5.95 each), which depict popular themes and attractions in Britain and Europe, are illustrated and include the following titles:

- "Castles and Palaces" (6673-5).
- "Cathedrals and Abbeys" (6674-3).
- "Cumbria Lake District" (6739-1).
- "Whiskey Map" (6718-9).
- "Wine map of the World" (6720-0).

The maps in the Tourist Route Series ($6.95 each) have keys in English, German, and French, showing scenic areas, town plans, toll bridges, golf courses, beaches, and other tourist attractions. The maps measure 40" × 30" and are available for Northern England, Southern England, Ireland, Scotland, Europe, and Wales. Also available from Bartholomew is the "Durable Great Britain" tourist map (6899-1; $9.95), a sturdy weather and tearproof map for the most intrepid British traveler; and "50 Miles Around London" (6499-6; $5.95), showing day trips into the British countryside.

    "Handy Maps" ($6.95 each), another Bartholomew line, are sturdy, weatherproof, acccordianfold maps packaged in clear plastic wallets. These are the perfect "back pocket" maps. There are Handy Maps for Europe, Britain and Ireland, London, North England, South England, and Scotland.

    Hammond is also U.S distributor of Clyde Leisure Maps ($6.95 each), created by Clyde Surveys Ltd. of Great Britain. These are beautifully rendered full-color tourist maps for some of the less-traveled regions of the world. Titles include:

- "Athens and Peloponnese" (6961-0).
- "Corfu" (6950-5).
- "Crete" (6951-3).
- "Cyprus" (6959-9).
- "Egypt" (6952-1).
- "Jersey" (6960-2).
- "Madeira" (6954-8).
- "Majorca" (6955-6).

Michelin Guides and Maps (P.O. Box 3305, Spartanburg, SC 29304; 803-599-0850) has European country maps ($2.50 to $3.95), including Austria,

Benelux, Germany, Great Britain/Ireland, Portugal, Spain, and Switzerland. Also available are detailed maps ($2.50 to $7.95) of Switzerland/Northern Italy and France (detailed and regional); *Hotel and Restaurant*, known as the "Red Guides" ($3.95), are annual paperback guides for London and Paris. In hardback, the "Red Guides" ($14.95 to $15.95) cover France, Germany, Greater Britain and Ireland, Italy, Spain/Portugal, Benelux, "Europe, the Main Cities (English)." Michelin's sightseeing and cultural information handbooks, the English editions of the "Green Guides" ($7.95 to $9.95), cover Canada, United States (New England and New York City only), Austria, Germany, Italy, Portugal, Scotland, Spain, England/The West Country, Switzerland, London, Paris, Rome, Brittany, and France. The French editions of the "Green Guides" ($7.95 to $9.95) cover Belgium/Luxemburg, Canada, Greece, Holland, Morroco, United States (New York City only), Paris, and regional guides for France.

Passport Books (4255 West Touhy Avenue, Lincolnwood, IL 60646; 800-323-4900) publishes *Passport's European Travel Atlas* ($17.95), a comprehensive road and touring atlas for getting the most out of traveling in Europe. The book includes itinerary planning maps and city maps.

Prentice Hall Press (200 Old Tappan Rd., Old Tappan, NJ 07675; 800-223-2348) has two series of tour books with excellent maps: *Access Travel Guides* ($7.95 to $11.95, with most books under $10) take the traveler along on a seven-day, seven-boulevard tour for a taste of the town. City, street, and subway maps are included. There are *Access* guidebooks for Hawaii, Las Vegas, London, Los Angeles, New Orleans, New York, Paris, Rome, San Francisco, Tokyo, and Washington, D.C. Another guidebook series, *Insight Guides* ($15.96 to $16.95), are filled with pictures and maps, with text written by journalists.

Rand McNally (P.O. Box 7600, Chicago, IL 60680; 800-323-1887, 312-673-9100 in Ill.) has several road atlases for travelers. See "Highway Maps" and "Foreign Maps" for details.

Readers Digest Books (Dist. by Random House, Inc., 201 East 50th Street, New York, NY 10022; *(continued on page* 143)

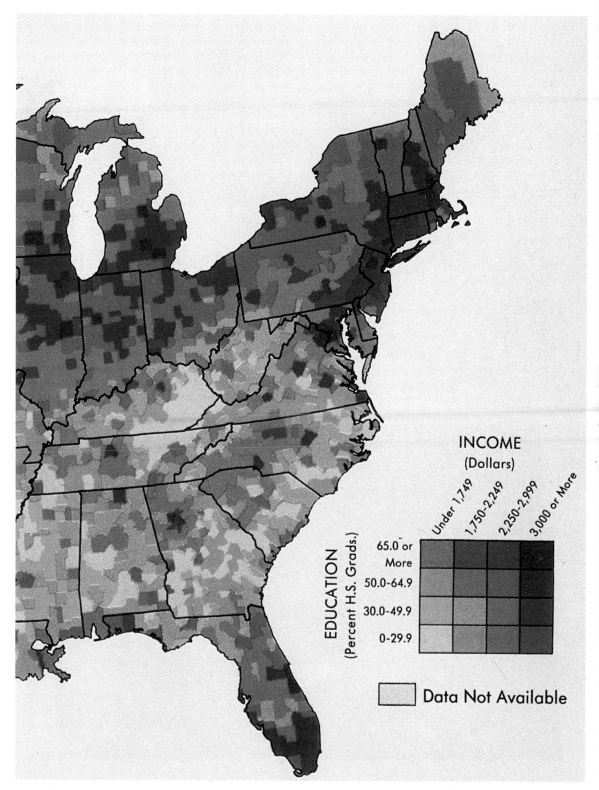

Portion of a Census Bureau statistical map, "Relationship of Educational Attainment to Per Capita Income, 1969."

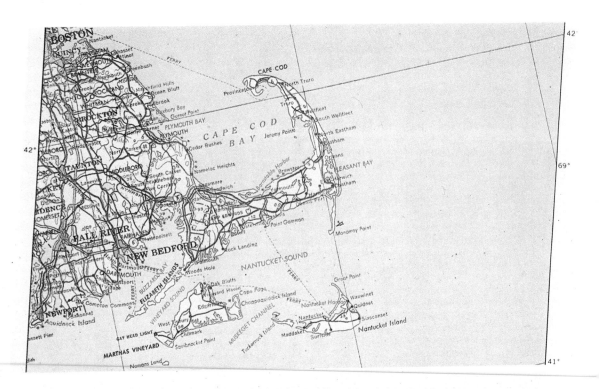

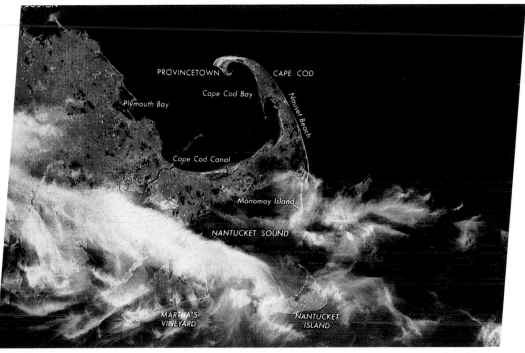

Two views of Cape Cod, Mass. Top, part of the Boston sheet of the Defense Mapping Agency's "International Map of the World." Below, a Landsat image covering the same region. Courtesy U.S. Geological Survey.

A *polar projection map of the North Pole from the Nimbus-5 weather satellite. Colors indicate variations in microwave radiometric temperature.*

''Map of the Universe,'' compiled and designed by Tomas J. Filsinger, showing astronomical and astrological phenomena. The Milky Way and other highlights glow in the dark on this poster-sized map. Courtesy Celestial Arts.

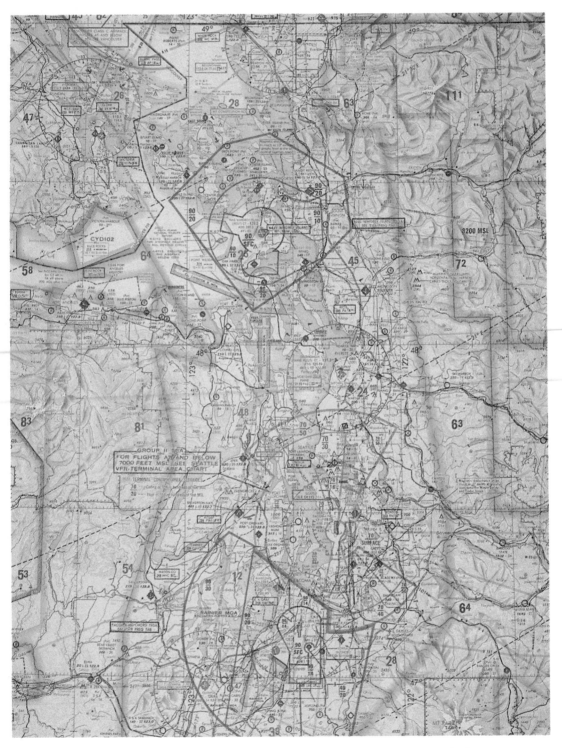

Aviation map of western Washington, including Seattle, the San Juan Islands, and part of Vancouver Island, B.C.

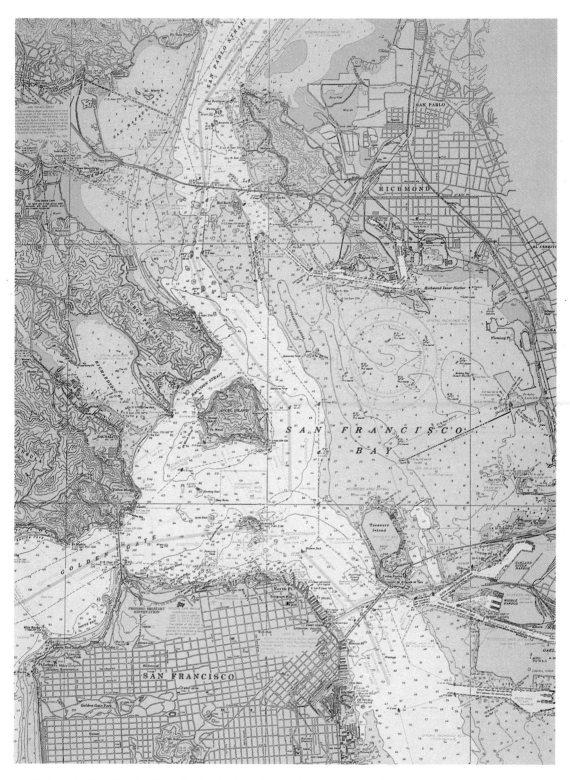

Nautical chart of San Francisco Bay, showing depth markings and other information for sailors.

Computer-processed wetland map of the Chincoteague Bay salt-marsh complex in the Virginia Eastern Shore.

(continued from page 134)
800-638-6460, 800-492-0782 in Md.) publishes *Scenic Wonders of America* (ISBN 0-89577-009-1; $21.95), which leads the way to more than a thousand of America's scenic natural wonders, with fifty full-color maps.

▶ **See also: "Atlases," "Foreign Country Maps," "Highway Maps," "Natural Resource Maps," "Park and Forest Maps," "Recreation Maps," "U.S. Maps," "Water Recreation Maps," and "World Maps."**

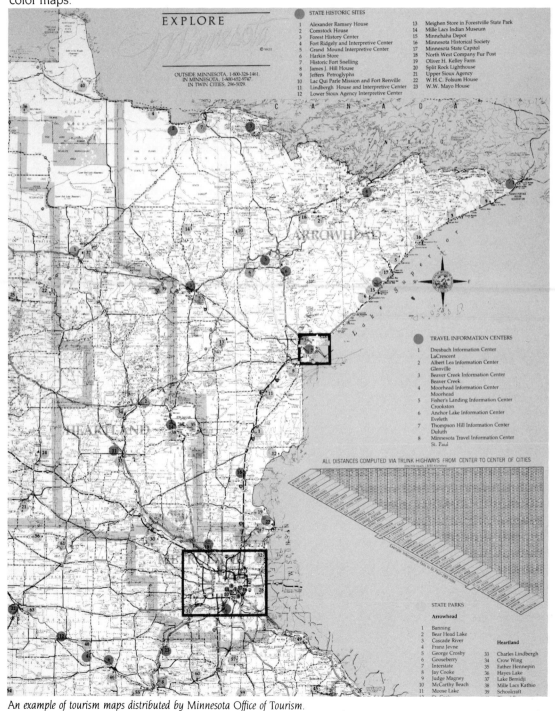

An example of tourism maps distributed by Minnesota Office of Tourism.

Treasure Maps

Is there a more romantic, exotic, or heart-pounding map legend than "X marks the spot"? Tales of pirate gold, Spanish doubloons, and buried jewels have always made the pulse quicken and the mind wander to dreams of wealth and power. Treasure maps are the keys to both the fantasy and reality of lost riches.

Finding treasure maps is not an easy task. Unlike maps of hidden natural resources, there's no scientific way to determine where there may be a cache of cash. The only guidelines are the legends handed down and the original maps created by those who hid the treasures. Many such maps are held in the collection of the Library of Congress and are available for study or reproduction. But don't get your hopes up: the Library's maps have already been examined exhaustively by treasure seekers.

Map from 1898 advertisement for the Denver & Rio Grande Railroad capitalized on the Klondike gold rush by offering relatively quick transportation to the gold fields.

It's likely that there are still hundreds of buried treasures out there, hidden in the tomb of some forgotten king or lying beneath the shifting sands of an ocean floor, the legacy of many a capsized galleon or royal treasure ship. But zealous treasure seekers have since discovered much of this lost booty. In short, the chances of stumbling across a real, undiscovered treasure map are slim. And looking in the usual places—map stores, libraries, archives—doesn't broaden the outlook. If a treasure has remained hidden this long, it's probably because there isn't a known map showing its location.

How to find treasure, then? Look for maps and historical information that point to shipwrecks, gold mines, or pirate coves. Topographical maps often show the location of old gold mines and the ex-haunts of pirates. The records of shipping companies and royal navies often note which ships carried treasure and which of those were lost at sea. The wrecks' locations may be tracked from local newspapers, which often ran horrific stories of shrieking sailors' demise, along with maps and diagrams depicting where it all happened. Studying old weather charts, maps, and records also may proffer clues to areas where hurricanes might have caused shipwrecks.

In essence, finding treasure maps today consists of the art of tracking down hidden sources that are not, on the surface, treasure maps, but which may point to possible treasure sites. There are also several stores specializing in treasure-hunting equipment that sell facsimiles of old treasure maps. Short of these resources, finding a treasure map takes imagination, patience, and perseverance. And more than a little luck.

Government Sources

U.S. Geological Survey. USGS produces several mineral investigations maps and surveys available (see "Natural Resources Maps" and "Energy Maps").

Bureau of Mines. The Bureau of Mines produces several maps and publications helpful to those seeking the natural treasures of the Earth. The Bureau's library (202-634-1116) contains many out-of-date maps and surveys related to American mining. Another source is the Bureau's Mineral Industry Location System (202-634-1138), which has a file of maps and overlays depicting the locations of mineral deposits in the United States.

If you're thinking of doing a little prospecting on your own, you'll want a free copy of the Bureau's *Mine Map Repository* collection, available from the Bureau's Office of Technology Information (Room 1035, Columbia Plaza, Washington, DC 20241; 202-634-1001), which describes old or abandoned mine passageways open to the public.

Library of Congress. The Library of Congress has a checklist, *Treasure Maps in the Library of Congress*, now out of print but which may be studied in the map room of the Library's collection, as can the maps listed in the book. The Library's Geography and Map Division has an extensive collection of treasure maps that can be studied or, for a fee, reproduced. See "Uncle Sam's Treasure Chests" for more information.

Commercial Sources

The following stores sell reproductions of treasure maps:

■ Huth's Rock & Treasure Hunters, 128 N. Frontier, Wickenburg, AZ 85358.
■ Raydon Treasure Land, 3030 A6 E, Main Street, Farmington, NM 87401.
■ The Treasure Shop, Newport, VT 05855.
■ Underground Detections Unlimited Division, Puffs Hobby Shop, U.S. Highway No. 9, Waretown, NJ 08758.

▶ **See also: "Antique Maps," "Geologic Maps," "Nautical Charts and Maps," and "Weather Maps."**

U.S. Maps

"It was wonderful to find America, but it would have been more wonderful to miss it," wrote Mark Twain in *Pudd'nhead Wilson's Calendar*. For many, finding America—in all its many cartographic forms—is nearly a national pastime. From tourists to teachers, biologists to bus drivers, nearly everyone uses maps of the U.S. in their quest to find America. And there's a U.S. map for nearly everyone, too.

When Thomas Jefferson authorized purchase of the Louisianna Territory from Napoleon in 1803, the size of America more than doubled overnight. Little was known about the new land, and even less known about the trails and passages that were purported to exist through this vast wilderness. There was believed to be a single, small mountain range running across the center of the territory, through which passage to the Pacific Coast could be easily maneuvered. But when the Lewis and Clark expedition, ordered by Jefferson to find this "Pacific Passage," discovered instead the nearly impenetrable Rocky Mountains, the mysteries of the new territory became evident.

The Lewis and Clark team brought back maps that illustrated everything from the number of "souls" in Indian villages to the placement of tributaries along the West's major rivers. It would take many subsequent explorations before the extent, treachery, and wealth of the land was fully understood and mapped.

Today, the spectrum of U.S. maps is vast and comprehensive. The agencies of the federal government produce hundreds of maps, ranging from general reference works to specific thematic maps of U.S. history, resources, transportation, agricultural, industrial, military, and recreational areas—and anything else that can be mapped. Commercial map makers also produce thousands of general and thematic U.S. maps, in forms ranging from atlases to classroom wall maps to small, pocket-sized road maps.

The vaults of map libraries, historical societies, and local land offices hold a wealth of U.S. maps within their protective care. Although the originals of some of these maps may be examined only on the premises, the national collections—the Library of Congress and the National Archives—as well as many of the smaller ones provide reproduction services for a fee.

Whether seeking maps of America's soil or soul, its parks or pipelines, they likely exist in abundance. Most chapters of this book contain some kind of U.S. map, although there are others that defy simple classification. Here is a sampling of U.S. maps not included elsewhere in this book:

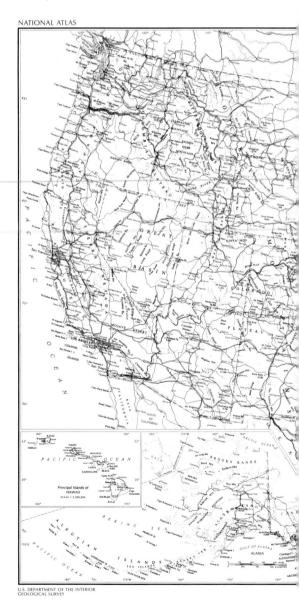

NATIONAL ATLAS

U.S. DEPARTMENT OF THE INTERIOR
GEOLOGICAL SURVEY

General reference sheet of the United States from the colorful Nation

Government Sources

Every map-producing agency of the federal government creates maps of the United States in one form or another. The National Archives and the Library of Congress have extensive collections of U.S. maps that are available to the public for study or reproduction through the collections' facilities. (See "Uncle Sam's Treasure Chests.") Most sources of U.S. maps fall under other headings in this book. Others federal sources include:

Tennessee Valley Authority. TVA has several inexpensive blueline and lithographic reproductions of aboriginal and historical maps of the United States, including:

■ "Aboriginal Map of Eastern U.S." (File No. G MD 453 G 552; $1), a lithoprint of a 17″ × 22″ map made by a Frenchman in 1718 that shows towns and drainage.

■ "Map of Eastern U.S. Made to Accompany 'History of American Revolution'" (File No. G MD 453

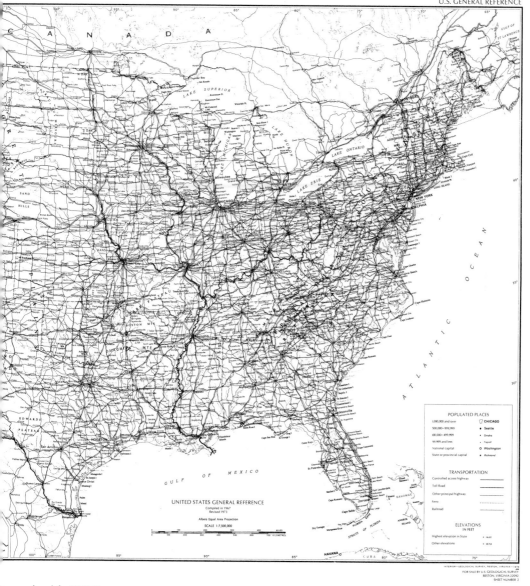

...s, produced by USGS.

K 701; $1.50), a blueline print from a map reprinted in 1811.
■ "North West Section of Map of the United States" (File No. 453 K 274; $1.50), a blueline print of a 1784 map.
■ "United States and Mexico" (File No. G MD 453 P 754-4; $2), a blueline print of an 1860 map.

When ordering these maps, include fifty cents for postage and handling.

U.S. Geological Survey. USGS produces and distributes many U.S. maps, far too many to list in detail here. A sampling of USGS U.S. maps includes:

■ National Atlas Progam's "U.S. General Reference Map" (File No. 00438, Ref. Code: 38077-AA-NA-07M-00; $3.10), an all-purpose map suitable for use as a basic reference tool. The map measures 19″ × 28″ and is drawn at a scale of 1:17,000,000. Several thematic U.S. maps are also available from the National Atlas Program, many of which are mentioned elsewhere in this book.
■ "Routes of the Explorers" (Sheet No. 8-A), a colorful historical map tracing the paths of principal explorers of North America from 1501 to 1844, measuring 18″ × 25″.
■ Base, contour, outline, and physical division maps of the United States, available in various scales, colors and sheet sizes. Prices range from sixty cents to $5.50. Many of these maps are mentioned in other chapters; see "Geologic Maps," "Natural Resource Maps," and "Topographic Maps."

Commercial Sources

There are thousands of U.S. map and atlas publishers. All major companies produce maps of the U.S. for a wide range of purposes, from business maps to travel maps, general reference maps, and historical maps, among many others. Most of these are mentioned in elsewhere in the book. Here are a few more, intended for general reference uses:

American Automobile Association (8111 Gatehouse Road, Falls Church, VA 22047; 703-222-6000) produces road maps of the United

States that are available free to AAA members, but which are not for sale to the general public. The maps may be obtained in person at local AAA offices.

Historic Urban Plans (P.O. Box 276, Ithaca, NY 14850; 607-273-4695) has several quality reproductions of older U.S. maps, including "United States: 1820" ($5), measuring 14″ × 22″, a beautiful reproduction printed in subdued colors and suitable for framing. Another attractive map from Historic Urban Plans is "Colonial America: 1718" ($5), measuring 15½″ × 20½″, which, among other things, is a reproduction of the first map to use Texas as a place name.

National Geographic (17th and M Streets, Washington, DC 20036; 202-921-1200) has several general maps and atlases of the United States, including:

■ "United States" (02003; $4), measuring 42½″ × 29½″, in full color. An index is available (02004; $1.50).
■ "United States" (02008; $6), part of the enlarged map series, printed on heavy chart paper in full color. The map measures 69½″ × 48½″.
■ *Atlas of North America; Space Age Portrait of a Continent* (00605; $29.95), containing maps of North America that show physical features in astounding detail. The atlas is also available in a hardcover deluxe edition with a magnifier (00607; $39.95).

Rand McNally (P.O. Box 7600, Chicago, IL 60680; 800-323-1887, 312-673-9100 in Ill.) produces a "United States Map" ($2.95), ideal for decorating an office or boardroom. The map is finely detailed and subtly colored and measures 52″ × 34″.

▶ **See also: "Agricultural Maps," "Antique Maps," "Boundary Maps," "Business Maps," "Census Maps," "Congressional District Maps," "Energy Maps," "Geologic Maps," "Highway Maps," "History Maps," "Indian Land Maps," "Military Maps," "Natural Resource Maps," Park And Forest Maps," "Railroad Maps," "Recreation Maps," "Space Imagery," "Topographic Maps," "Tourism Maps," and "Wildlife Maps."**

Utilities Maps

You come home at night, switch on cable TV to catch the latest news via satellite, turn on the kitchen light, pop your frozen lasagne in the microwave, and when your mother calls long distance using her credit card, you answer on your combination speakerphone-answering machine. At this moment, you, the quintessential modern man or woman, are tied to more strings than a marionette. Utilities have become as essential in our lives as candles and wood-burning stoves were to those who lived before the industrial revolution. Keeping track of all the electric, gas, and phone lines, television cables, water pipes, and other delivery systems of modern technology re-

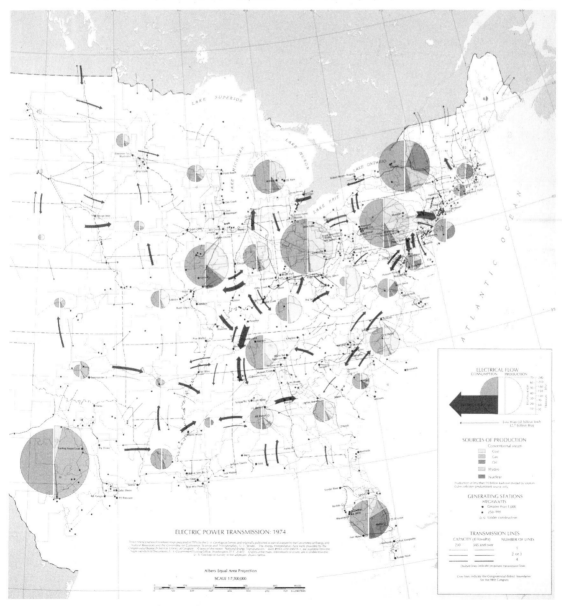

Map from the National Atlas *showing electric power transmission in 1974.*

quires more than a home computer: it takes maps.

Utilities maps generally aren't suitable for framing or gift-giving (unless the recipient is a lineman for the county); they are typically black and white, with perhaps a color or two to delineate utilities lines. Still, they are necessary tools for developers and construction workers as well as for utilities companies themselves. Even the weekend gardener may have need of these maps to avoid that awful moment when hoe meets underground cable. As important as it is to know where utility lines are, it sometimes helps to know where they aren't.

The typical utility map is a straightforward representation of the lines, pipes, cables, and wires carrying one or more commodities, as well as pinpointing the stations or sources generating them. Utilities maps run the gamut from simple diagrams of phone lines, gas pipes, and water mains, to complex depictions of sewer systems, television cables, hydroelectric plants, and any other utility that serves a broad area.

The best sources for local utility maps are the companies themselves. Sewer and water systems maps are created and distributed by local and county departments of public works. Several branches of the federal government produce or distribute national and regional maps of power plants and telephone systems. Federal producers of utilities maps include the Tennessee Valley Authority, which has a number of power maps for its region, the Bureau of the Census, with a statistical map on home heating fuel use, and the Central Intelligence Agency, which produces several maps detailing energy sources in the Soviet Union and the Middle East. The Government Printing Office also distributes a number of utilities maps from various federal agencies. Cartographic departments of foreign countries can assist in finding utilities maps for those lands, while the local tourism, sanitation, or utilities commissions of specific provinces may also be of help in locating maps for their regions.

Government Sources

Government Printing Office. GPO has two publications that include telephone utility maps and charts: *Telephone Areas Serviced by Bell and Independent Companies in the United States* (S/N 003-000-00579-8; $5.50), compiled in 1982. This 125-page book contains a series of maps showing the different operating areas served by Bell and the various independent telephone companies in the United States, plus state-by-state listings for more than 1,400 telephone companies. The headquarters and the land areas of each state's major telephone companies are also listed in an easy-to-read table format; and *World's Submarine Telephone Cable Systems* (S/N 003-000-00636-1; $11), a 422-page volume published in 1984, with 257 "Seacable System Data Profiles," detailed information on all undersea telephone cable systems in the world that were in service at the end of 1983, and a section on fiber optic submarine telephone cable systems.

Census Bureau. The Bureau of the Census publishes "Primary Home Heating Fuel by Counties of the United States: 1950, 1960, and 1970" ($1.90). This demographic map, spanning three decades of census information, is No. 3 in the GE-70 special reference map series.

▶ **See also: "CIA Maps," "Energy Maps," "Hydrologic Maps," and "Natural Resource Maps."**

Wildlife Maps

Ah, wilderness! While we toil and play daily in our concrete and glass jungles, wildlife, by and large, has been relegated to a relative handful of sanctuaries, refuges, and other protective enclaves. Thanks largely to the federal government, though, there is plenty of wildlife left, although the number of endangered species increases almost daily. And campers, bikers, hikers, entomologists, ornithologists, and zoologists are among those who use wildlife maps to keep track of Mother Nature.

Uncle Sam, through its Fish and Wildlife Service (part of the Department of the Interior), is landlord to more than 30 million acres of wilderness—home to more than 1,200 species of mammals, birds, reptiles, amphibians, and fish—much of which consists of protected wildlife refuges and preserves. These are lands where the only shoot-ing permitted is done with a camera, where winged, finned, and furred creatures reign, and where humans are mere guests. The Fish and Wildlife Service administers these lands and provides maps to the public for each of its holdings. The National Park Service and the U.S. Forest Service also provide maps for the lands, rich with flora and fauna, that they administer.

State, county, and city governments are another good resource for free wildlife maps, especially in regions where there is an abundance of locally protected forest and game land. Write to the appropriate conservation board or fish-and-game bureau to learn what maps are available.

As for foreign wildlife, the travel and tourism bureaus for some countries known for their unusual wildife (including Australia and various Afri-

Fish and Wildlife Service map of the National Wildlife Refuge System, showing regional offices and boundaries.

can nations) provide wilderness maps to visitors, as do privately run game parks both in the United States and abroad.

Other sources for wildlife maps include many of the organizations that promote conservation and protection of the environment, and scientific associations that study various species (although these are often technical and available only to members). Zoological parks and museums also can help locate local wildlife maps. If there's nothing in their bookstores and gift shops, check with a curator or resident expert.

See ''Recreation Maps'' for sources of hunting maps, and ''Water Recreation Maps'' for maps of fishing areas.

Government Sources

Defense Mapping Agency. DMA produces a ''Whale Chart'' ($5.50) that shows whale species and their locations along the North American coastline. The chart can be obtained directly from the DMA or through the Government Printing Office.

Government Printing Office. GPO has a small collection of wildlife maps and atlases, including:

■ *Anglers' Guide to the United States Atlantic Coast, Fish, Fishing Grounds and Fishing Facilities*, a seven-part series of guides that includes a colorful fishing map atlas. The guides provide information on type and location of commonly sought fish. Also available is the *Anglers's Guide to the United States Pacific Coast: Marine Fish, Fishing Ground and Facilities*, similar to the Atlantic Coast guide. See ''Water Recreation Maps'' for ordering information.
■ ''National Wildlife Refuge System'' (S/N 024-010-00514-9; $4), a 1979 map that identifies the system's regional and area offices and boundaries, wetlands management district offices, and national wildlife sanctuaries.
■ *Flyways: Pioneering Waterfowl Management in North America* (S/N 024-010-00653-6; $17) is a 540-page map-filled book studying the migratory habits and habitats of North American waterfowl.

Tennessee Valley Authority. TVA has created a series of topographic maps of wildlife and game refuge areas in the Tennessee Valley region. The

maps illustrate management boundaries, interior trails and roads, checking stations, and private lands within the TVA boundary. Available maps are:

■ ''Catoosa Wildlife Management Area'' ($2).
■ ''Chuck Swan Wildlife Management Area'' ($1.50).
■ ''Prentiss Cooper Wildlife Management Area'' ($1.50).
■ ''Tellico Wildlife Management Area'' ($2).
■ ''Ocoee Wildlife Management Area'' ($2).
■ ''AEDC Wildlife Management Area'' ($1.50).
■ ''Fall Creek Wildlife Management Area'' ($1.50).

Include fifty cents postage for each map ordered.

Fish and Wildlife Service. The Fish and Wildlife Service has free maps and brochures of wildlife refuges and fish hatcheries under federal protection. Boundary maps of each of the Fish and Wildlife Service projects are available, free, at the locations themselves, or by writing to the service's Washington, D.C. headquarters. The maps, which measure $8\frac{1}{2}'' \times 11''$, are black-and-white diagrams showing boundaries, wilderness areas, refuge headquarters, and driving directions from surrounding areas. Also available are three United States maps showing the land under the Fish and Wildlife Service's jurisdiction. The free maps, which are available on $8\frac{1}{2}'' \times 11''$ or $17'' \times 22''$ sheets, are titled ''National Wildlife Refuge System,'' ''National Fish and Wildlife Management Areas,'' and ''National Fish Hatcheries and Fishery Assistance Stations.'' The free U.S. maps, which are black-and-white with red lines denoting regional boundaries, are updated annually.

U.S. Geological Survey. USGS produces a series of topographic maps of the National Park System that include maps of wildlife preserves and refuges under the care of the federal government. The ''Index to USGS Topographic Map Coverage of the National Park System,'' a fold-out map pinpointing park and wildlife areas covered in the topographic program, is available free from the USGS. (See ''Topographic Maps'' and ''Park and Forest Maps'' for more information.) The maps in the National Park Series cost $3.60 each and are

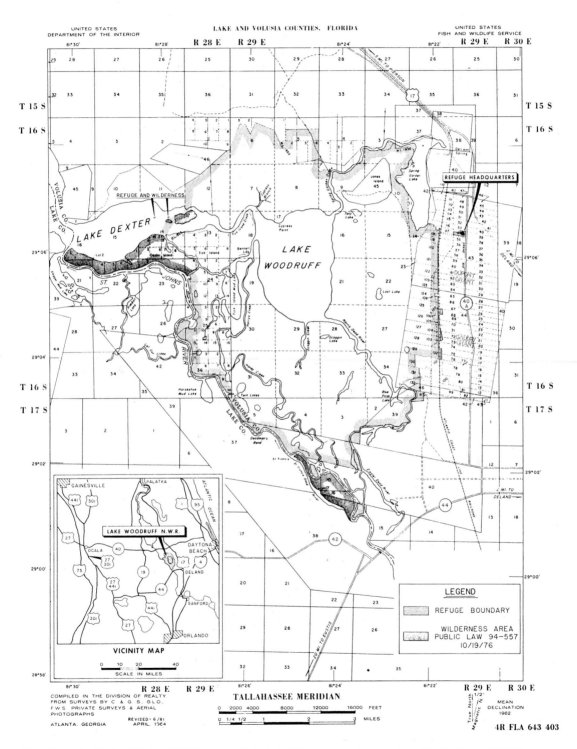

Map of the Lake Woodruff National Wildlife Refuge in Lake and Volusia Counties, Fla., created by the Fish and Wildlife Service.

drawn at various scales; some parks require more than one sheet. Also available from USGS is a series of "Coastal Ecological Inventory Maps" ($3.60 each), which vividly illustrate the ecological setting, including flora and fauna, of the North American coastline. Maps are available for each major ecological coastal area.

Commercial Sources

Hammond Inc. (515 Valley Street, Maplewood, NJ 07040; 201-763-6000) distributes a "Dinosaur Fossil Find Map" (0144-7; $2.95), a 38″ × 25″, full-color map depicting regions where there have been significant findings of dinosaur fossils. Bartholomew maps, distributed in the United States by Hammond, has a Johnston and Bacon pictorial map series that includes a map titled "Loch Ness Monster" (6381-7; $5.95). The map depicts Scotland's Loch Ness and shows where the monster has been sited.

Another pictorial series from Bartholomew includes maps of more accessible wildlife. The maps ($5.95) include illustrations of the subjects as well as migratory patterns, habitat depictions, and other interesting information. Available maps include:

- "Birds of Britain" (6669-7).
- "World of Animals" (6721-9).
- "World of Birds" (6722-7).
- "World of Butterflys" (6723-5).
- "World of Insects" (6728-6).

National Geographic Society (17th and M Streets NW, Washington, DC 20036; 202-921-1200) has several wildlife maps and charts, including:

- "Alaska's Ice Age Mammals" (02252; $3), measuring 31½″ × 23″, with illustrations.
- "Australia—Land of Living Fossils" (02806; $3), measuring 23″ × 30″, depicting flora and fauna in the land Down Under.
- "Bird Migration in the Americas" (02810; $3), measuring 23″ × 36″, with illustrations of birds and migratory routes.
- "The Great Whales" (02820; $3), measuring 30″ × 20½″, with illustrations and notes.
- "Whales of the World" (02819; $3), measuring 30″ × 20½″, with illustrations and notes.

▶ **See also: "Bicycle Route Maps," "Park and Forest Maps," "Recreation Maps," and "Water Recreation Maps."**

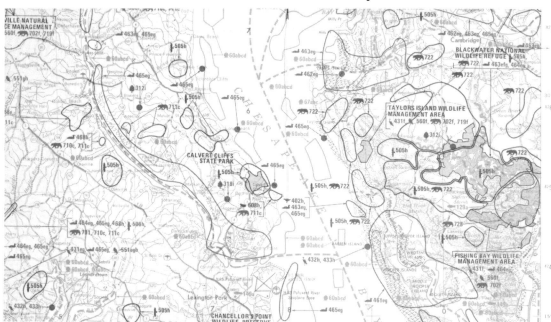

Portion of Fish and Wildlife Service "Atlantic Coast Ecological Inventory" map showing the flora and fauna of the Chesapeake Bay region.

World Maps

It's simply not possible to count the number of world maps that exist—even those currently available. There are thousands of maps, dating from the birth of map making. There are maps of the world when only one continent was known to exist and maps of the world today, with every inch of the globe plotted with astounding accuracy. There are maps of world vegetation, rainfall, mineral reserves, soil types, and industrial strongholds. There are, in short, as many maps as there are ways to interpret and comprehend the modern world.

The uses of world maps are as varied as the maps themselves. Geologic maps of the world are vital to the work of Earth scientists; maps showing annual sunshine that falls on various spots around the world are key to planning energy resources. Maps showing the growth of socialism, the decline in arable land, the shifts of industrial wealth, and the flows of maritime commerce all have their respective professional constituencies.

World maps are created by most cartographic government agencies and private companies. The federal government publishes several general as well as specific world maps, ranging from "mosaics" of Landsat images to a map of illegal drug-growing regions and smuggling routes.

Commercial companies also make a vast range of world maps, as do various geographic, political, and Earth science societies around the world.

Some of the most beautiful world maps are also the oldest, drawn in the days when artists moonlighted as map illustrators. Sources for antique world maps include the collections of the Library of Congress and the National Archives, as well as a number of dealers in antique maps, globes, and atlases specializing in world maps; some may be willing to search for a particular map. (See "Antique Maps.")

But there are some newer gems, too. One example is titled "World Biographical Provinces" ($4; CoEvolution Quarterly, Box 428, Sausalito, CA 94966; 415-415-332-1716), a 22″ × 39″ full-color map based on data from the United Nations Educational, Scientific, and Cultural Organization, illustrating "the way the earth is divided according to plants and animals." It comes with an explanatory article that helps put this unique view of the world into perspective.

Here is a sampling of other world maps:

Government Sources

Central Intelligence Agency. The CIA has several world maps available through the National Technical Information Service, including:

- "Political Map of the World "(NTIS PB 85-928034; $7.50).
- "World Map" (NTIS PB 84-928038; $7.50).
- "Standard Time Zones of the World" (NTIS PB 83-928010; $7.50).
- "U.S. Foreign Service Post and Department of State Jurisdictions" (NTIS PB 83-928009; $7.50), created in 1983, so information may now be slightly out of date.

U.S. Geological Survey. USGS has several world maps available, most popular being the "International Map of the World" ($3.60), a basic multicolored reference map showing borders, capital cities, and other key features to delineate the nations of the world. Another popular USGS world map is the "Relief Edition of the International Map of the World," which has been created in three scales: the 1:20,000,000-scale map ($3.90), a single sheet measuring 42″ × 56″; the 1:22,000,000-scale map ($9.90), consisting of three sheets, each measuring 34″ × 57″; and the 1:14,000,000-scale map ($33.30), consisting of six sheets, each measuring 42″ × 56″.

Also available from USGS is a "World Seismicity Map" ($2.80), which shows different areas of seismic activity on an international level.

Commercial Sources

World maps are the backbone of most map companies, the standard maps that "never go out of style," so finding a map of the world is generally as easy as walking into a local travel, book, or map store. There are thousands of world maps avail-

able; many of a thematic nature are listed elsewhere in this book. Here is a small sampling of
available world maps:

Hammond Inc. (515 Valley Street, Maplewood, NJ
07040; 201-763-6000) distributes the Bartholomew "World Wall Map" (paper: 6623-9; $14.95;
flat laminated: 662-0; $34.95), a dramatic 40" ×
60" full-color map with political boundaries and
topographic features, richly illustrated.

Hammond also produces a series of full-color
wall reference maps, including three 8½" × 11"
world maps ($2.25, folded; $4.50, rolled and
shipped in a tube):

■ "World" (folded: 0-8437-0335-0; rolled: 0-8437-
0135-8), measuring 50" × 33".
■ "World (Spanish)" (folded: 0-8437-0339-3;
rolled: 0-8437-0123-4), measuring 38" × 25".
■ "World-Color Relief" (folded: 0-8437-0310-5;
rolled: 0-8437-0122-6), measuring 38" × 25".

National Geographic Society (17th and M
Streets NW, Washington, DC 20036; 202-921-
1200) has two world maps available: "World Phys-
ical/Ocean Floor" (02359; $4), and "World
Political" (02353; $4), both measuring 42½" ×
29½", with dynamic colors and detail.

Rand McNally (P.O. Box 7600, Chicago, IL 60680;
800-323-1887, 312-673-9100 in Ill.) is the U.S. distributor for Kummerly & Frey, which has several
colorful world maps for general reference
available:

■ "Political World Map" (85789-4; $8.95).
■ "Physical World Map" (21931-6; $30), two-piece
flat map.
■ "Political World Map" (21930-8; $30), two-piece
flat map.

Rand McNally also distributes Wenschow Maps,
large, beautifully detailed, full-color relief maps
developed in Germany. Wenschow has a series of
spring-mounted, 50" × 35" cultural geography
world maps, including:

■ "Population Density" (114-10741-6; $99), show-
ing population density by continent. The map
measures 50" × 35".
■ "Languages" (114-10742-4; $99), showing distri-

bution of thirty of the world's language groups.
The map measures 50" × 35".
■ "Religions" (114-107432-2; $99), showing areas
of dominance for fourteen religions throughout
the world. The map measures 50" × 35".
■ "Cultural Regions and Migrations" (114-10744-
0; $99), which uses arrows to indicate the direc-
tions of population migrations throughout the
world since 1500. The map measures 50" × 35".
■ "World Cultural Geography" (114-10740-8;
$228), which consist of all four maps in the set,
mounted on one cloth-backed sheet on a spring
roller.

There is also a Wenschow "World/Ocean Relief"
(111-10203-0; $195), a 96" × 65" full-color map
with hypsometric tinting depicting the ocean floor
in three dimensions. The map, drawn at a scale of
1:15.000,000, is mounted on a plastic rod but is
available on a spring roller mounting for $228.

▶ **See also: "Antique Maps," "Atlases," "CIA
Maps," "Globes," "Political Maps," and "Space
Imagery."**

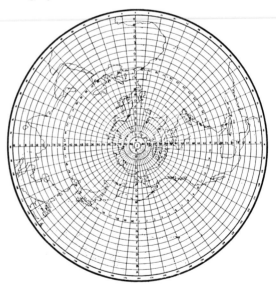

*Sheet reference system for maps of the Northern Hemisphere in
the "International Map of the World" series.*

SKY MAPS

Aeronautical Charts and Maps

Aeronautical charts provide a wealth of fascinating information, regardless of whether you intend to take over the controls of a Piper Cub or a DC-10.

Granted, these are not simple maps to read. At first glance, they seem filled with purple and blue circles, arrows, and other strange markings, and the little text that exists consists primarily of cryptic letters and numbers—"Pickett 3 MOA 4000' to and incl. 10,000'," reads one such code on an aeronautical map of Virginia.

But with a bit of patience, you can spot areas that are prohibited or restricted to fly over— usually military bases and other high-security locations. And you are likely to find dozens of heretofore unknown landing strips in your region— possibly belonging to some tycoon who may have quietly constructed a runway capable of handling a jumbo jet. You'll find out exactly where low-flying aircraft are permitted and where they're banned, perhaps giving you the informational ammunition to inform the Federal Aviation Administration about some commercial airliner that has been repeatedly flying over your home at an altitude a bit too close for comfort. It's all there, if you know how and where to look.

The National Ocean Service, part of the Commerce Department's National Oceanic and Atmospheric Administration, publishes and distributes aeronautical charts of the United States. Charts of foreign areas are published by the Defense Mapping Agency, which makes them available for sale through NOS. In addition to the NOS's five distribution centers, both domestic and foreign aeronautical charts and related publications are readily available through a network of several hundred sales agents, usually located at or near airports. A free publication, *Catalog of Aeronautical Charts and Related Publications*, includes a list of such dealers, as well as detailed descriptions of the various charts and publications distributed by NOS.

The date of an aeronautical chart is important if you are using it for aviation purposes. NOS notes that when charted information becomes obsolete, *use of the chart or publication for navigation may be dangerous.* Changes, many of them critical, occur constantly, and it is important for pilots to obtain up-to-date charts. To ensure that only the latest charts are used, NOS publishes *Dates of Latest Edition*, available free from NOS distribution centers.

NOS publishes and distributes several types of aeronautical charts:

■ **Aeronautical Planning Charts** are used for pre-flight planning of long flights. Selected routes are transferred to more detailed charts for actual flight use. NOS publishes two types of flight planning charts: a "VFR/IFR Wall Planning Chart," at a scale of 1:2,333,232, a large, 82″ × 56″ chart produced in two pieces, which can be assembled to form a composite Visual Flight Rules (VFR) planning chart on one side and an Instrument Flight Rules (IFR) planning chart on the other. The chart is revised every 56 days. A one-year subscription is $45.50; single copies are $6.50. Another planning chart, the "Flight Case Planning Chart," is a smaller, 30″ × 50″ folded chart (scale: 1:4,374,803) designed for pre- and in-flight use. It contains the same information as the VFR/IFR chart, with the addition of selected Flight Service Stations and National Weather Service Offices located at airports, parachute jumping areas, a tabulation of special-use airspace areas, a mileage table listing distances between 174 major airports, and a city/airport location index. This chart is revised every 24 weeks. A two-year subscription is $15; single copies are $3.60.

■ **Visual Aeronautical Charts** are multicolored charts designed for visual navigation of slow- to medium-speed planes. The information featured includes selected visual checkpoints, including populated places, roads, railroads, and other distinctive landmarks. There are three types: "Sectional Aeronautical Charts" (1:500,000; 20″ × 60″) show the airspace for a large region of several hundred square miles; "Terminal Area Charts" (1:250,000; 20″ × 25″) show the airspace designated as "Terminal Control Areas" around airports; and "World Aeronautical Charts" (1:1,000,000; 20″ × 60″), cover much larger areas with much less detail. Single-copy prices are $2.75. One helpful publication is VFR *Chart User's Guide* ($3), a 36-

page, multicolored booklet intended to serve as a learning document for all three types of charts. It includes detailed definitions of the dozens of symbols used on these charts.

■ **Instrument Navigation Charts** provide information for navigation under instrument flight rules.

There are different series for low-altitude flights (below 18,000 feet), high-altitude flights, and instrument approach procedure (IAP) charts.

Defense Department charts distributed by NOS include a variety of "flight information publica-

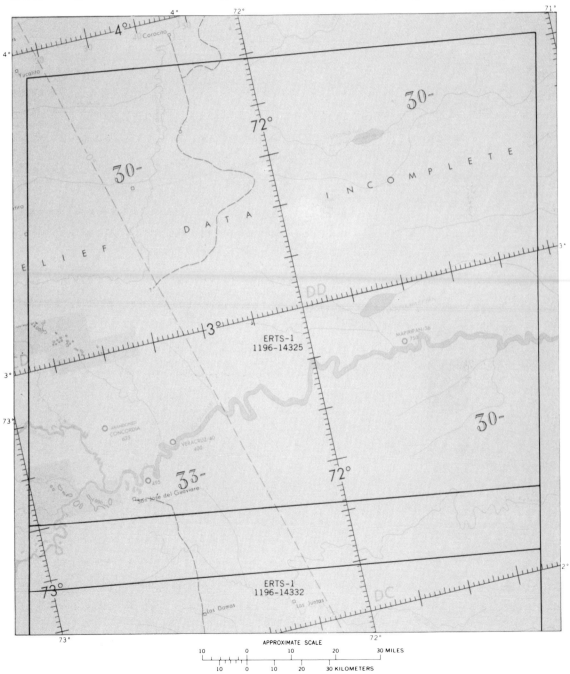

Portion of U.S. Air Force Operational Navigation Chart of southeastern Colombia.

tions," dubbed FLIP, in defense jargon. Many of these will have little practical use, unless you are training to become a Blue Angel.

■ **FLIP Enroute Charts** are available for most parts of the world, from Africa to Asia to Antarctica. Each set of maps provides the information needed for flying in foreign airspace.
■ **Operational Navigation Charts** provide information on high-speed navigation requirements at medium altitudes.
■ **Tactical Pilotage Charts** provide information on high-speed, low-altitude, radar and visual navigation of high-performance tactical and reconnaissance aircraft at very low through medium altitudes.

■ **Jet Navigation Charts** are used for long-range, high-altitude, high-speed navigation.
■ **Global Navigation and Planning Charts** are suitable for flight planning, operations over long distances, and en route navigation in long-range, high-altitude, high-speed aircraft.

Other Defense Department charts provide information for navigation over the polar areas, identify weather observation stations, and show distances between major airports, among other things. All are listed in the NOS *Catalog of Aeronautical Charts.*

Astronomical Maps

The study of the heavens has been an age-old endeavor, enthralling ancient philosophers and modern astrophysicists alike. For centuries, illnesses and disaster were foretold by the stars and royal matches were created or dissolved according to the advice of the court astronomer or astrologer. Man depended on the sky above to tell his future, explain his past, and preserve his current life.

The universe opened up in the early seventeenth century, when Galileo Galilei perfected the first telescope. Like a parting curtain, the heavens were increasingly revealed, leading to the creation of a system of maps and charts to keep track of all the stars, planets, meteor belts, comets, and other nighttime phenomena. More recently, our own man-made "stars"—spacecraft and satellites—joined the stars above us, bringing us a deluge of exquisite images of the canals of Mars and the rings of Saturn. This, in turn, has led to

even better maps and charts of planet surfaces and atmospheres.

We've even sent a map attached as a plaque to the Pioneer 10 spacecraft into the universe. Space scientists hope that, should Pioneer 10 be discovered by some extraterrestrial life-form, the simplistic diagram of human anatomy and our planet's location in the galaxy will explain where and what we are.

There are astronomical maps and charts for every level of Earthlings, too, from schoolchild to scientist. There are spacecraft photomaps and charts of our nearest planetary neighbors, and maps of solar systems, galaxies, and meteor belts light years away, invisible to all but the strongest telescopes. Other maps and charts detail the movements of stars, the craters of moons, and the fiery paths of comets, recording the steps of the ever-changing cosmic dance.

The most commonly used and useful astro-

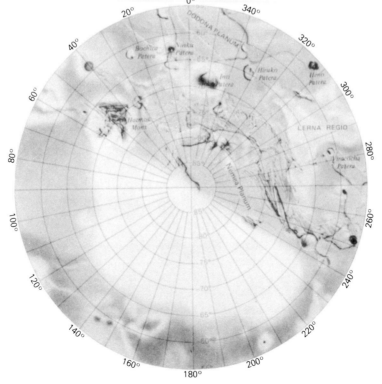

South polar region

Preliminary pictorial 1:2,500,000 topographic map of Io, one of Jupiter's moons, created from images recorded by Voyagers 1 and 2.

nomical maps are star charts and atlases. These illustrate, track, and identify the movements of heavenly bodies in the universe. The charts are re-drawn every fifty years (a period known as an ep-och), with minor updating performed as necessary in the intervening years. Those interested in studying the night sky need a star chart handy to record personal observations and to identify stars, planets, and galaxies. A star chart is, in essence, a tour guide to the heavens.

There are several types of star charts. Some are drawn on a visible grid in black ink on a white field. These are useful for tracking and marking observations as well as for star-identification pur-poses. Other charts, useful only for gazing but not for making observations, are found in guides for amateur stargazers. Drawn in white or yellow on a dark field, many such star charts resemble con-nect-the-dots pictures, illustrating the outlines of constellations. The charts used by astronomers usually plot and number the stars in scientific terms. Galaxies, meteor belts, and other phenom-ena, when depicted on charts, appear as cloudy swirls or bands across their approximate location in the sky.

Stars above a certain magnitude are not illus-trated on every star chart; the selection of stars depends on the use for which the chart is intend-ed. (The magnitude of a star is determined by its brightness. The lower the magnitude, the brighter and more visible the star.) Weekend sky watchers may require only a chart that shows stars visible to the naked eye or with a low-powered telescope, while astronomers in observatories need star charts detailing every known star and phenome-non in the universe.

Although star charts are available separately, the best and most helpful are the chart compila-tions found in star atlases. Most star atlases, cre-ated by several astronomical societies and publishing houses (notably Sky Publishing in Cambridge, Mass.), include supplementary cata-logs that give identification information and plot-ting data. A good star atlas is as essential as a telescope for accurate study of the night sky.

There are a number of qualities to keep in mind when choosing a star atlas. The paper on which it is printed should withstand moisture and other outdoor dangers; charts should be readable at night; the size of the atlas should be convenient for travel and use with a telescope. Don't get an atlas that plots every star unless you need it, be-cause the fewer the stars on the chart, the more readable it is at a glance; an atlas that shows stars to magnitude 8.0 or 9.0 is all most people need. Also, make certain the atlas is current. If you plan to do field studies, make sure there are grids for plotting observations.

Certain atlases are better for the general study of the night sky while others are better for observ-ing and plotting various phenomena. The *Field Guide to the Planets* ($12.95 from Sky Publishing) is one of the best for a romantic evening of stargaz-ing. With informative text and easy-to-read charts, it's the perfect guide for the casual sky watcher. Sky Publishing's *Skalnate Pleso Atlas of the Heavens* ($17) is one of the best for observing and charting the movements of stars, planets, meteors, or any-thing else that catches your eye in the sky. The altas depicts 32,000 stars and 1,850 nonstellar ob-jects, and is excellent for learning about and plot-ting celestial motion.

For those who believe their fate is written in the stars, there are a number of astronomical charts and maps that include astrological signs of the horoscope. One of the most exotic and colorful is the "Map of the Universe" published by Celestial Arts (P.O. Box 7327, Berkeley, CA 94707; 800-841-2665; 415-845-8414 in Calif.). The multi-colored map ($9.95 plus $2 postage) is printed on black with highlights that glow in the dark. Major con-stellations and zodiac signs are vividly illustrated, as are comet paths, meteor showers, among other things. An accompanying sixteen-page booklet explains how to read the map.

But if you need something a bit more specific than a map of the entire sky, there are many avail-able moon, planet, and solar system maps. The National Aeronautic and Space Administration has created several atlases and maps from the in-formation brought back by astronauts and the transmissions of unmanned spacecraft. Atlases of Mars and Mercury, as well as topographic maps of the moon, are among the cartographic gems available from NASA through the Government Printing Office. GPO also has poster maps of the solar system, the planets, and the Pioneer 10 plaque.

Aside from astronomical societies and publishers, other sources for astronomical maps and charts include the National Geographic Society, the Smithsonian's Air and Space Museum, astronomical observatories and museums, and many of the larger commercial map publishers.

When the curtain of the sky rises nightly for the greatest show above Earth, here are some maps that can help you enjoy a front row seat:

Government Sources

Government Printing Office. GPO has the following maps and charts relating to astronomy:

■ *Astronomical Almanac for the Year* (two volumes available: 1983/1982, S/N 008-054-00092-4, $16; 1984/1983, S/N 008-054-0096-7, $14). These almanacs, both over 500 pages long, contain a variety of charts, maps, graphs, tables, and other statis-

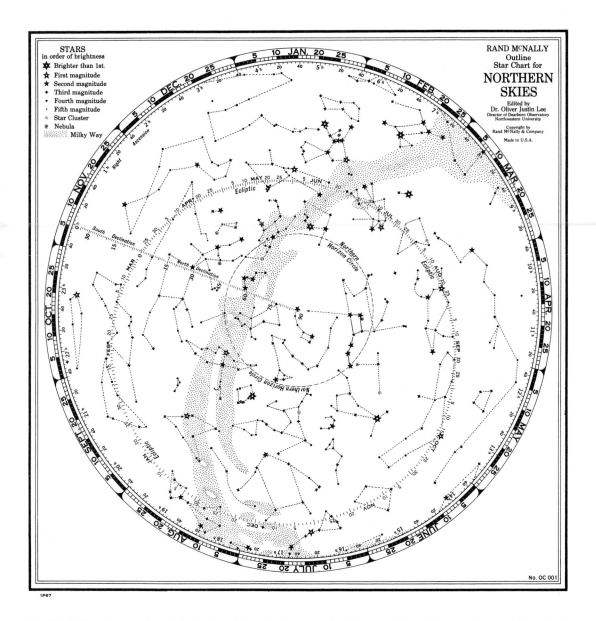

Rand McNally outline star chart of the Northern Skies, showing stars to the fifth magnitude as well as star clusters, nebulae, and the Milky Way.

tics relating to astronomical events during the years covered.

■ *Astronomical Phenomena* (three volumes available: 1983/1980, S/N 008-054-00091-6, $5; 1984/1981, S/N OO8-054-00095-9, $5; 1985/1983, S/N 008-054-00105-0, $4.50). These slim volumes contain astronomical highlights from the *American Ephemeric and Nautical Almanac*, including maps and charts relating to the moon, planetary configurations, stars, and other heavenly phenomena.

■ *Atlas of Mars: The 1:5,000,000 Map Series* (S/N 033-000-00780-9, $11). This 146-page atlas created in 1979 contains small-scale maps and photomosaics covering the entire Martian surface.

■ *Atlas of Mercury* (S/N 033-000-0069501, $21). This 128-page atlas from 1978 consists of photographs taken by the Mariner 10 spacecraft.

■ *Viking Lander Atlas of Mars* (S/N 033-000-00856-2, $22). This atlas contains reduced reproductions of elevation contour and vertical profile maps created from Viking data.

■ "Solar System" (S/N 033-000-000760-4, $2.75). This poster depicts the solar system and Milky Way as seen looking toward the Earth from the moon. Other posters depicting nearby planets include "Comparing the Planets" (S/N 033-000-00744-2, $3.50) and "Ten Years of Planetary Exploration" (S/N 033-000-00861-9, $4.50).

■ "Pioneer 10 Plaque" (S/N 033-000-00878-3, $2.50). This poster is a reproduction of the Pioneer 10 plaque that carries a "map" of our location in our solar system.

■ "Galileo to Jupiter: Probing the Planet and Mapping Its Moons" (S/N 033-000-00763-9, $2.75). This 20-page booklet from 1979 relates the story of the spacecraft Galileo's discovery and mapping of Jupiter's moons.

See "Space Imagery" for sources of satellite and space program products.

Commercial Sources

American Map Corporation (46-35 54th Road, Maspeth, NY 11378; 718-784-0055) distributes Hallwag's astronomy maps ($8.95 each). The following maps, each of which comes with an illustrated booklet, are available:

■ "The Moon," a two-sided photographic map showing both faces of the moon.

■ "The Stars," which depicts zodiac signs, constellations, and a variety of star types.

■ "Mars" illustrates five views of the planet.

■ "The Solar System" depicts orbits as well as the planets' relative positions and sizes.

AstroMedia (a division of Kalmbach Publishing Co., 1027 N. 7th St., Milwaukee, WS 53233; 414-272-2060), in cooperation with Cambridge University Press, publishes *The Star Book* ($7.95) by Robert Burnham, with maps by Richard Berry. The spiral-bound book has easy-to-read maps of the night sky during the early and late phases of each season, with stars and constellations represented in white against a dark blue field. The accompanying text and illustrations provide cogent explanations to aid in identifying stars and constellations.

Hammond Inc. (515 Valley Street, Maplewood, NJ 07040; 201-763-6000) distributes two useful stargazing aids. The "Star Finder" ($2.95) comes with an easy to use "Star Finder Wheel," which shows the principal fixed stars in the Northern Hemisphere. Tables to help track the movements of planets are included. Hammond's "Galaxy 2" illuminating globe ($65) is suitable for those who want to do a little indoor "stargazing." When turned off, this 12" globe depicts the stars and planets as they appear at night. When the internal light is switched on, the globe reveals a portrait of astrological positions in the sky.

Hubbard (P.O. Box 104, Northbrook, IL 60062; 800-323-8368) produces several astronomical teaching charts and tools. Among the products are:

■ "Astrocharts" ($41.50 per set of 6). These 29" × 23" charts are enlarged reproductions of astronomical object photographs taken from the Mt. Wilson and Mt. Palomar observatories. The color, quality, and subjects—which includes depictions of Orion's Great Nebula, Andromeda's Great Galaxy, Sagittarius' Frifid Nebula, make them suitable for classroom reference or decorative use.

■ "Astronomy Study Prints" ($16.50) is a set of twelve 9" × 15" charts for teaching the basics of astronomy. The set includes prints of star charts of the Northern and Southern Hemispheres, as well as prints of the planets, the sun, the moon, and galaxies.

■ "Star Charts" ($29.95) are reversible 44″ × 44″ sky maps of the Northern and Southern Hemispheres. The stars, nebulae, planets, constellations, and phenomena are depicted with light colors against a dark background for easy reference.

■ "Star Finder/Zodiac Dial" ($3.95) is a reversible wheel for finding stars and identifying zodiac constellations.

■ "Universal Celestial Globe" ($105) is a clear model of the celestial sphere that provides a physical demonstration of star and planetary movement. It comes with a meridian ring and horizontal mount, but is also available without these features ($65).

National Geographic Society (17th and M Streets NW, Washington, DC 20013; 202-921-1200) has several astronomical maps and charts, including:

■ "The Earth's Moon" ($3), measuring 42″ × 28″, with descriptive notes and diagrams.

■ "Heavens" ($4), measuring 34½″ × 23″, illustrating the constellations and certain phenomena.

■ "Mars" ($3), measuring 38″ × 23″, with diagrams and a painting of a Martian dust storm on the back.

■ "Solar System/Saturn" ($3), measuring 22½″ × 17″, with illustrations and text on both sides.

■ "The Universe/Sky Survey" ($3), measuring 23″ × 34″, with illustrations and text on both sides.

NightStar Company (1334 Brommer Street, Santa Cruz, CA 95062; 408-462-1049) produces the "NightStar Flexible Star Map" ($49.95). Thirteen years in the making, this inverted "map" is created by deflating a printed plastic ball into a bowl-shaped, flexible chart of the night sky. Unlike flat charts or globes that present a somewhat distorted view of the sky as seen from Earth, NightStar's bowl shape reconstructs what we see when we look into the night sky. NightStar comes with overlay strips of the planets and a fifty-page booklet.

Northstar Imports (P.O.Box 60100, Reno, NV 89506; 702-972-5111) is the United States distributor for Philips' Astronomical Publications, produced in Great Britain by George Philip and Son Ltd. Among the renowned Philips' star maps, atlases, and planispheres available from Northstar are:

■ "Philips' Chart of the Stars" ($ 4.95), a 45″ × 36″ wall chart depicting the middle heavens as well as the North and South polar stars. Stars, constellations, planets, and their relative positions are illustrated.

■ "Philip's Moon Map" ($3.25) measures 29″ × 21″ and illustrates in full-color the near side of the moon with all major surface features identified and indexed. The accompanying text tells the history of the moon and its exploration.

■ "Stars at a Glance" ($2.50) is a fifty-page paperback with maps and charts for quick identification of the night sky at all locations and times of year.

■ "Philips' Planisphere" ($7.50), 10″ in diameter, has two revolving disks that illustrate the night sky when matched up with the date and time noted around the edges. Built of heavy plastic, it is available for four different lattitudes (32 degrees North, 42 degrees North, 51½ degrees North, and 35 degrees South). It comes in a vinyl carrying pouch, with detailed instructions. A "Mini Planisphere" ($4.50) measures 5″ in diameter.

Rand McNally (P.O. Box 7600, Chicago, IL 60680; 800-323-1887, 312-673-9100 in Ill.) publishes a series of astronomical atlases, including:

■ *The Sun* ($9.95), with 300 drawings, diagrams, and photographs, many taken by Skylab and the Solar Maximum space missions.

■ *The Moon* ($9.95), with maps of the moon and 25 full-color photographs.

■ *Jupiter* ($9.95), with photographs and satellite images, many in full-color, taken by NASA space probes.

■ *Saturn* ($9.95 paper, $16.95 hardcover), with images, maps, and photographs from NASA's Voyager missions.

■ *The Solar System* ($19.95), produced in association with the British Royal Astronomical Society. This atlas depicts the solar system with photographs, diagrams, and maps.

■ "Luminous Star Finder and Zodiac Dial" ($4.95), a star wheel printed with glow-in-the-dark ink that illustrates stars to the fifth magnitude, as well as nebulae and the Milky Way.

■ "Map of the Solar System" ($2.95) measures $25\frac{1}{2}" \times 32\frac{1}{2}"$ and is printed in full-color with up-to-date NASA information about the planets.

Sky Publishing Corporation (49 Bay State Rd., Cambridge, MA 02238; 617-864-7360) publishes an extensive line of star atlases. Besides those mentioned earlier, there are:

■ *Popular Star Atlas* ($7.95), helpful for naked-eye or binocular observations, this atlas contains sixteen constellation charts for stars to visual magnitude 5.5, and indicates some bright variable stars, nebulae, and clusters.

■ *Norton's Star Atlas and Reference Handbook* ($24.95), the standard against which other books have been measured since it was first published in 1910. The seventeenth edition contains maps of more than 8,400 stars to visual magnitude 6.35 and more than 600 deep-sky objects. Also included is a two-color map of the moon and an indexed map of Mars.

■ *Sky Atlas* 2000.0 (desk version, with black stars on white background, $15.95; field version, white stars on black field, $15.95; deluxe version, color illustration on white background, $34.95). This atlas has 26 charts depicting 43,000 stars to visual magnitude 8.0, as well as 2,500 deep-sky objects.

■ *Photographic Star Atlas* (Northern Hemisphere editions: A, with black stars on white background, $48; B, with white stars on black field, $60. Southern Hemisphere editions: A, $30; B, $40). Made in Germany by Hans Vehrenberg, these extraordinary atlases are produced from astrophotographs taken in Germany and Africa. The Northern editions have 303 maps, and the Southern editions contain 166 maps.

■ "Lunar Map" (95 cents each), an $11" \times 17"$ sheet with the surface of the moon diagrammed in blue.

■ "Lunar Quadrant Maps" ($8.95), four charts measuring $23" \times 27"$ each, illustrating in detail features of the moon that can be seen through a telescope.

▶ **See also: "Atlases."**

Weather Maps

Weather has always been a provocative and mystical element of the natural world. From the songs and poems it has inspired to the conversations it has started or saved, our romance with blue skies and blustery winds is as old as weather itself. Because weather is often unpredictable and erratic, the maps, charts, and tables that trace its patterns and behavior can be lifesaving tools for pilots, sailors, and others.

Weather maps, by their very nature, are usually out of date within a few days or even hours of their creation. There are exceptions—including historical climatology maps, general tracking guides, do-it-yourself prediction kits, and Weather Service charts—but most specific weather maps are useful only for an extremely limited period of time.

The federal government produces a number of weather maps, charts, atlases, and guides aimed at educating and informing the public. The National Weather Service (part of the Commerce Department's National Oceanic and Atmospheric Agency), which provides the information for the telephone recordings and radio and TV station forecasts upon which many people rely, also issues daily weather charts and maps.

The Weather Service's daily maps (available by subscription from NOAA and the Government Printing Office) show the surface weather of the United States as it is observed at seven o'clock Eastern time each morning. A weekly series, also available by subscription, includes each day's maps for the seven-day period, plus smaller maps showing high and low temperatures, precipitation, and wind patterns. These maps are widely used by airplane pilots and boat captains.

Another set of useful weather maps produced by the Weather Service are the fifteen Marine Weather Services Charts covering the waters of the United States and Puerto Rico, which illustrate the locations of visual storm warning display sites, and of weather radio stations broadcasting Weather Service information.

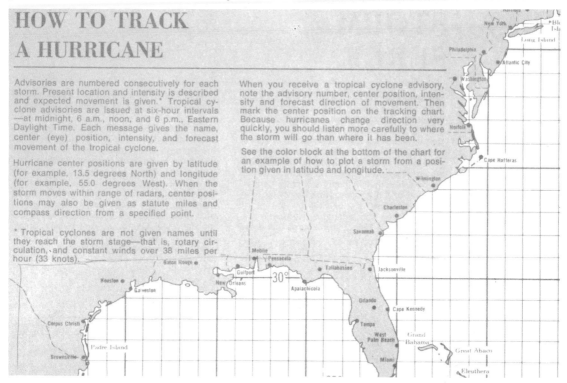

HOW TO TRACK A HURRICANE

Advisories are numbered consecutively for each storm. Present location and intensity is described and expected movement is given.* Tropical cyclone advisories are issued at six-hour intervals—at midnight, 6 a.m., noon, and 6 p.m., Eastern Daylight Time. Each message gives the name, center (eye) position, intensity, and forecast movement of the tropical cyclone.

Hurricane center positions are given by latitude (for example, 13.5 degrees North) and longitude (for example, 55.0 degrees West). When the storm moves within range of radars, center positions may also be given as statute miles and compass direction from a specified point.

* Tropical cyclones are not given names until they reach the storm stage—that is, rotary circulation, and constant winds over 38 miles per hour (33 knots).

When you receive a tropical cyclone advisory, note the advisory number, center position, intensity and forecast direction of movement. Then mark the center position on the tracking chart. Because hurricanes change direction very quickly, you should listen more carefully to where the storm will go than where it has been.

See the color block at the bottom of the chart for an example of how to plot a storm from a position given in latitude and longitude.

Portion of the do-it-yourself storm-tracking chart from GPO's "How to Track a Hurricane."

Other weather maps and charts produced by the federal government include the historical climatology series of maps and atlases published by the National Climatic Data Center, the sunshine and temperature maps that are included in the U.S. Geological Survey's National Atlas Program, and a variety of climatic, storm, and weather pattern data and maps available from the Government Printing Office.

If you like to feel a bit more in control of the weather, there are weather prediction and tracking kits available from both governmental and commercial map sources. The GPO sells a "Cloud Code Chart" ($2.25) that illustrates and identifies various clouds and cloud patterns. If the sky overhead looks more than a little ominous, GPO also has a pamphlet called "Storm Surge and Hurricane Safety" ($2) that includes a North Atlantic hurricane tracking chart. The chart uses a grid to depict the ocean along the land area from Mexico to New England and includes directions for tracking a hurricane's movement along the grid. Hammond, the big commercial map publisher, produces a do-it-yourself weather prediction kit ($2.95), which includes a weather chart and predictor wheel.

Government Sources

Government Printing Office. GPO has several weather- and climate-related maps and atlases available, including:

■ *Climatological Atlas of the World Ocean* (S/N 003-017-00509-7; $11). This 189-page atlas has maps, charts, graphs, and tables that synthesize National Ocean Survey data about temperature and other climatologic information.
■ "Daily Weather Maps, Weekly Series" (S/N 703-021-00000-0; subscription prices: $60 a year/domestic, $75 a year/foreign; single-copy prices: $1.50/domestic; $1.88/foreign). This weekly series includes the daily weather maps created by the National Weather Service. Explanations of the maps and symbols used are included.
■ "Explanation of the Daily Weather Map" (S/N 003-017-00505-4; $2). This 32″ × 21″ chart explains the symbols and other information contained in the Daily Weather Maps.
■ *United States Navy Hindcast Pectral Ocean Wave Model*

Climatic Atlas: North Atlantic Ocean (S/N 008-042-00074-8; $39). This 393-page atlas, created in 1983, is filled with maps, charts, and other historical data about wind and wave climatology of the North Atlantic Ocean.
■ *United States Navy Marine Climatic Atlas of the World.* Two of the volumes in this atlas series contain maps related to ocean climatololgy: *South Atlantic Ocean* (Volume 4; S/N 008-042-00069-1; $18) and *South Pacific Ocean* (Volume 5; S/N 008-042-00070-5; $11).
■ "Clouds" (S/N 003-014-0016-9; $2.50). This chart helps identify common cloud formations through full-color illustrations. Also available is the "Cloud Code Chart" (S/N 003-017-00211-0; $2.25), which uses the International System of Cloud Classification.

■ *Precipitation Frequency Atlases of the Western United States.* These atlases contain maps, charts, and other data relating to precipitation statistics. Most are out of print, although there are two volumes still available for sale: *New Mexico* (Volume 4; S/N 003-017-00518-0; $10) and *Nevada* (Volume 7; S/N 003-017-00161-0; $9.50).
■ *World Weather Records, 1961-1970.* There are three volumes in this series, each of which includes maps, charts, and other data about world weather over a ten-year period: *North America* (Volume 1; S/N 003-018-00096-2; $7); *Europe* (Volume 2; S/N 003-018-00101-2; $8); and *West Indies, South and Central* (Volume 3; S/N 003-018-00108-0; $8).
■ "Storm Surge and Hurricane Safety with North Atlantic Tracking Chart" (S/N 003-018-00092-0; $2). This 1979 pamphlet unfolds into a grid for tracking storms along the North Atlantic coast and includes information on safety precautions during hurricanes.

National Climatic Data Center. The National Climatic Data Center (Federal Building, Asheville, NC 28801; 704 259-0682), part of the National Oceanic and Atmospheric Administration, has an Historical Climatology Series that includes eleven weather-related atlases. The maps in the atlases depict local, regional, or continental climatological parameters, showing climate changes over a relatively long time. A service charge of $4 per order must be included when purchasing the atlases by mail. Available atlases include:

■ *Atlas of Mean Winter Temperature Departures From the Long-Term Mean over the Contiguous U.S., 1895-1983* (Series Title 3-1; $3), with seasonal maps of departures from mean winter temperatures in the U.S. from the late nineteenth to late twentieth centuries.

■ *Atlas of Monthly and Seasonal Temperature Departures,* 1895-1983 (Four volumes, Series Titles: 3-2 (Winter); 3-3 (Spring); 4-3 (Summer), and 3-5 (Fall); $10 each or $36 for all four). This series includes maps of departures from long-term, statewide, average monthly and seasonal temperatures.

■ *Atlas of Monthly Palmer Hydrological Drought Indices* (1895-1930) *for the Contiguous United States* (Series Title 3-6; $12), with maps showing drought conditions in the United States according to the Palmer Hydrological Drought Index, an objective measure of moisture conditions. A companion volume, for years 1931-1983 (Series title 3-7; $17), is also available.

For a complete list of atlases and other products in the Historical Climatology Series, write to the NCDC and ask for the *Environmental Information Summary* (C-24).

National Oceanic and Atmospheric Administration. NOAA will supply free copies of the National Weather Service's weekly series of daily weather maps upon request to NOAA Public Affairs (14th and Constitution Avenue NW, Room 6013, Washington, DC 20230); subscriptions, however, must be purchased through the Government Printing Office. Also available from NOAA, through the National Ocean Service, are the fifteen Marine Weather Services Charts ($1.25 each; $18.75 per set), which can be obtained through the NOS Distribution Branch (N/CG33, Riverdale, MD 20737).

SUNDAY, MAY 25, 1986

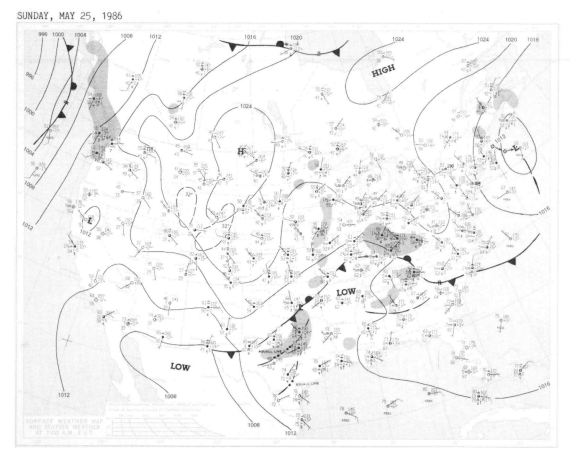

National Weather Service ''Surface Weather Map'' for May 25, 1986, from ''Daily Weather Maps, Weekly Series.''

U.S. Geological Survey. USGS's National Atlas Program includes several weather-related maps. The maps are colorful and suitable for framing, albeit a bit out of date. Prices shown include surface mailing within the United States. The following maps are available:

■ "Monthly Sunshine" (File No. 00478, Ref. Code 38077-AI-NA-17M-00; $3.10), created in 1965.
■ "Annual Sunshine, Evaporation, and Solar Radiation" (File No. 00565. Ref. Code 38077-AJ-NA-17M-00; $3.10), created in 1969.
■ "Monthly Average Temperature" (File No. 00661, Ref. Code AK-NA-17M-00; $3.10), created in 1965.
■ "Monthly Minimum Temperatures" (File No. 00662-38077-AL-NA-17M-00; $3.10), created in 1965.

Commercial Sources

Hammond Inc. (515 Valley Street, Maplewood, NJ 07040; 201-763-6000) produces a "Weather Kit" (0-8437-0180-3; $2.95) for weather prediction. The kit includes a 25″ × 38″ weather chart depicting weather terms, cloud forms, and types of weather fronts. A "weather wheel" is also included to help make accurate predictions.

Northstar Imports (P.O. Box 60100 Reno, NV 89506; 702-972-5111) distributes the "Pocket Weather Forecaster" ($3.75), which uses charts and diagrams of wind direction and cloud type to help predict weather 12 to 36 hours in advance. The forecaster is made of laminated card stock.

▶ **See also: "Aeronautical Charts and Maps," "Emergency Information Maps," "Energy Maps," "Nautical Charts and Maps," and "Tide and Current Maps."**

WATER MAPS

Nautical Charts and Maps

Rivers, lakes, oceans, and other bodies of water are portrayed on both maps and charts, the distinction between which even some veteran old salts don't really understand. *Charts* differ from *maps* primarily in the amount of navigation information shown. Charts are much more detailed, showing a main channel sailing line, for example, as well as safety harbors, the general shape and elevation of river or lake bottom, hazard areas, and other key symbols that enable a boat pilot to wend safely through a potentially treacherous body of water. Maps, in contrast, are much more superficial, primarily showing landmarks. They are limited more to the requirements for small-craft navigation and for general recreation guidance.

The National Ocean Service (NOS), part of the National Oceanic and Atmospheric Administration (itself an agency of the U.S. Department of Commerce), produces several types of maps and charts:

■ **Coast charts** (scales from 1:50,000 to 1:150,000), the most widely used nautical charts, are intended for coast-wise navigation inside the offshore reefs and shoals, entering bays and harbors of considerable size, and navigating certain inland waterways.

■ **General charts** (scales from 1:150,000 to 1:600,000) are designed for use when a vessel's course is well offshore, but when its position can be fixed by landmarks, lights, buoys, and characteristic soundings.

■ **Sailing charts** (scales smaller than 1:600,000) are plotting charts used for offshore sailing between distant coastal ports and for approaching the coast from the open water.

■ **Harbor charts** (scales larger than 1:50,000) are for navigation and anchorage in harbors and smaller waterways.

■ **Small-craft charts** (scales from 1:10,000 to 1:80,000) include specific information pertinent to

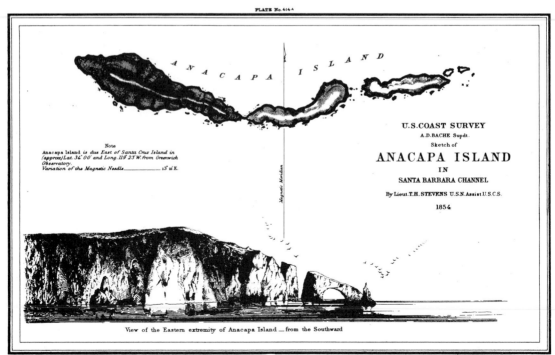

An 1854 U.S. Coast Survey sketch of Anacapa Island, off the southern California coast, engraved by a young James McNeill Whistler during his short career as an illustrator with the Survey.

small-craft operators. They show a great variety of information, such as tide and current data, marina and anchorage facilities, and courses. These charts are published both as folded sheet maps and in book form, for handling convenience on small boats.

■ **Canoe charts**, a series of charts of the Minnesota-Ontario Border Lakes, are designed to suit the needs of small, shallow-draft vessels.

■ **Coast pilots** and **Great Lakes pilots**, published in nine volumes, provide detailed navigation information that cannot be shown conveniently on charts, such as radio service, weather service, port data, sailing directions, and natural features.

■ **Special maps and data**, by-products of the nautical charting program, are generally for nonnavigational use. They include topographic surveys and planimetric shoreline maps, aerial photographs, hydrographic smooth sheets, graphic depth records, descriptive reports of surveys, and sedimentology sample data. (See "Ocean Maps" for details of such map products.)

Government Sources

National Ocean Survey. NOS publishes free chart catalogs—actually large, folded maps—that list nearly a thousand available charts. There are four catalogs: "Nautical Chart Catalog 1" covers the Atlantic and Gulf coasts, including Puerto Rico and the Virgin Islands; "Nautical Chart Catalog 2" covers the Pacific coast, including Hawaii, Guam, and Samoa; "Nautical Chart Catalog 3" covers Alaska, including the Aleutian Islands; and "Great Lakes" covers those lakes and adjacent waterways. The catalogs are useful for another reason: each contains a listing of the hundreds of authorized NOS nautical chart dealers throughout the United States and Canada.

NOS also provides information and indexes on the following lake and river charts: "Lakes" (Cayuga, Champlain, Great Lakes, Mead, Minnesota-Ontario border lakes, Okeechobee, Oneida, Pend Oreille, Franklin D. Roosevelt, Seneca, Tahoe); and "Rivers" (Columbia, Connecticut, Delaware, Hudson, James, Kennebec, Neuse, New, New York State Barge Canal, Pamlico Sound, Penobscot, Potomac, Rappahannock, Savannah, St. Johns, St. Lawrence to Cornwall, York, and others).

A separate free publication, *Dates of Latest Editions of Nautical Charts*, is issued quarterly by NOS to aid mariners in obtaining up-to-date charts. *Notice to Mariners*, also available from NOS, is a pamphlet issued weekly by the Defense Mapping Agency in cooperation with NOS, the U.S. Coast Guard, and the U.S. Army Corps of Engineers to keep mariners advised of new publications and information on marine safety.

Tennessee Valley Authority. Since its inception in 1933, TVA has operated a Mapping Services Branch (formerly the Maps and Surveys Branch), which produces a great variety of nautical maps and charts. Among them are navigation charts and maps, published for the TVA main-river reservoirs, and recreation maps, for each of the TVA lakes. (See also "Water Recreation Maps.") TVA publishes an *Index to Navigation Charts and Maps of TVA Reservoirs* and an *Index to Recreation Maps—Tennessee Valley Lakes*. A price catalog and indexes may be obtained free from the TVA Mapping Services Branch.

U.S. Army Corps of Engineers. The Corps of Engineers publishes nautical charts of selected rivers showing water depths and other navigation data, and indexes showing water areas and the number of charts required to cover them. Covered rivers include the Allegheny, Atchafalaya, Big Sandy, Big Sunflower, Calcasieu, Cumberland, Illinois, Kanawha, Mississippi, Missouri, Monongahela, Ohio, Tennessee, and the Gulf Intracoastal Waterway. Maps and indexes may be obtained from any of the nine Corps of Engineers district offices.

Defense Mapping Agency. DMA, through its Hydrographic Center, publishes a variety of nautical maps covering the United States and foreign regions, most priced around $12. A complete list of nautical charts available from DMA is contained in DMA's *Catalog of Maps, Charts, and Related Products, Part 2—Hydrographic Products*, available from DMA's Office of Distribution Services. The catalog includes DMA's series of "world charts," showing major oceans and shipping regions, and its several hundred "coastal, harbor, and approach charts," covering smaller regions throughout

North America. The DMA catalog is color-coded, indicating which charts are available from DMA, NOS, and the Government Printing Office, and which must be obtained from other nations' hydrographic offices or sales agents. The catalog contains a complete name-and-address listing of DMA nautical chart agents throughout the United States and in forty countries, as well as order forms for ordering charts available directly from DMA.

Commercial Sources

While the federal government is the primary producer of up-to-date nautical maps and charts, at least one source distributes renderings of sailing days long past.

Cartographics (P.O. Box 67, North Stonington, CT 06359; 203-535-3152) sells a variety of original antique nautical maps from the sixteenth through the nineteenth century, showing both U.S. and foreign waters. A catalog providing descriptions of the maps is available for $1. (Example: an 1861 map of California's Tomales Bay, 15" × 24", is $35.) Maps range from $20 to $1,050, the latter for

a 1773 map of New England showing Massachusetts to Maine.

Chartifacts (P.O. Box 8954, Richmond, VA 23225; 804-272-7120) offers originals and reproductions of antique coastal charts and surveys. They specialize in American coast and seaport charts from the earliest USGS surveys, and their knowledgeable cataloging includes detailed histories and descriptions of each map and chart they carry. In general, prices of original maps range from about $25 (for an 1853, 1:40,000-scale reconnaissance map of Sabine Pass between Louisiana and Texas Points) to about $125 (for a rare 1859 Progress Sketch of Florida from Biscayne Bay to Dry Tortugas). Reproductions are generally under $20. Descriptive lists of originals and illustrated catalog pages of reproductions are available from Chartifacts. You are asked to specify your area of interest and include a stamped, self-addressed envelope.

▶ **See also: "Ocean Maps," "River, Lake, and Waterway Maps," "Tide and Current Maps," and "Water Recreation Maps."**

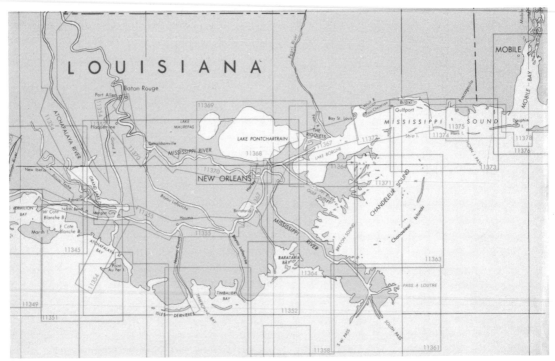

Portion of index for NOAA's National Ocean Service nautical charts and maps from the "Nautical Chart Catalog 1: United States Atlantic and Gulf Coasts, Including Puerto Rico and the Virgin Islands."

Ocean Maps

When it comes to mapping, there are essentially three "oceans." One is the geographical ocean, the ocean as it appears from space. Another is the geological ocean, the nature of the coasts, continental margins, and the deep-sea floor. Still another is the biological ocean: the fishes, plants, and assorted other life forms that populate the deep blue sea. (There is also the nautical ocean, of course, the sailing routes used by pilots of boats and ships. See "Nautical Charts and Maps" for information on those maps.)

The earliest world maps were, in effect, maps of the oceans, which served as boundaries for earlier civilizations' perspectives of their planet. Indeed, some of the earliest surviving maps are European nautical charts that date back to the second half of the thirteenth century. Today's maps of the seas are somewhat more accurate, based on the digital recordings of satellites instead of the visual recordings of seamen.

Scientists have been fascinated with the bottom of the ocean almost as long as they have studied the lands ashore. Geologists in the early nineteenth century speculated that the ocean floors were dull expanses of mud—featureless and flat. For centuries, naturalists thought that the oldest rocks on Earth were on the ocean floors. They believed that the present-day ocean basins formed at the very beginning of the Earth's history and that throughout time they had slowly been filled by a constant rain of sediment from the lands. Data gathered since the 1930s have enabled scientists to view the seafloor as relatively youthful and geologically dynamic, with mountains, canyons, and other topographic forms similar to those found on land. The seafloor, they found, is no more than 200 million years old—a "young" part of the globe's crust compared to the continents that contain rocks nearly twenty times that age.

Research conducted since World War II has produced an ocean of data on the seafloor, much of it based on the studies of the federal National Ocean Survey conducted by the National Oceanic and Atmospheric Administration, an agency of the Commerce Department. Actually, it was the war itself that produced the technology for this research. In testing different sound frequencies to help locate submarines, scientists found that certain frequencies were capable of sending sound waves through the seafloor and getting reflections from deeply buried layers of rock. This revolutionized the study of marine geology, and the quality of maps of the ocean floor.

Among the most spectacular cartographic products of this technology is the glow-in-the-dark "Map of the Ocean Floor" published by Celestial Arts (P.O. Box 7327, Berkeley, CA 94707; 800-841-2665; 415-845-8414 in California). The 36-inch-square map provides accurate and highly illustrated details of the mysterious terrain that underlies our oceans—in effect, what the Earth would look like without water—showing all four hemispheres from several different viewpoints. With the lights out, areas of volcanic activity glow in the dark. The map ($9.95 plus $2 postage) comes with a helpful 28-page "guide and tourbook" to the map.

NOAA produces a variety of ocean maps (see "Nautical Charts and Maps" for other NOAA products). Among them are:

■ **Bathymetric maps**, which are topographic maps of the seafloor. Through the use of detailed depth contours and other data, the size, shape, and distribution of underwater features are vividly portrayed. These serve as the basic tool for performing the scientific, engineering, marine geophysical, and marine environmental studies often required for development of energy and marine resources.

■ **Topographic/bathymetric maps** are multipurpose maps showing both the topography of the ocean floor and of the land nearby. These are cooperatively produced by NOS and the U.S. Geological Survey to support the coastal zone management and environmental impact programs. They also may be used by land-use planners, conservationists, oceanographers, marine geologists, and others interested in the coastal zone and the physical environment of the Continental Shelf.

■ **Bathymetric fishing maps** are topo maps of the seafloor designed primarily for use by commercial and sport fishermen. This series of maps, produced at a 1:100,000 scale, includes information about the type and distribution of bottom sediment and known obstructions on the seafloor, in addition to the basic information found on a standard bathymetric map. It is intended to aid fishermen in identifying where the "big ones" are biting.

■ **Geophysical maps** consist of a base bathymetric map, a magnetic map, a gravity map, and, where possible, a sediment overprint. The bathymetric map, when combined with the others, serves as a base for making geological-geophysical studies of the ocean bottom's crustal structure and composition. There are two series of geophysical maps. The 1:250,000-scale series contains the geophysical data for the Continental Shelf and

Slope. The 1:1,000,000-scale series covers geophysical data gathered in the deep-sea areas, sometimes including the Continental Shelf that lies adjacent.

A free NOAA publication, *Map Catalog* 5 (Distribution Division, National Ocean Service, 6501 Lafayette Avenue, Riverdale, MD 20737; 301-436-6990), provides a U.S. map overlaid with a grid showing the availability of each type of map for all of the United States, including Alaska and Hawaii, along with ordering instructions. Map prices range from $2.50 to $4.30.

▶ **See also: "Antique Maps," "Atlases," "Nautical Charts and Maps," "Space Imagery," "Tide and Current Maps," "Treasure Maps," "Water Recreation Maps," and "World Maps."**

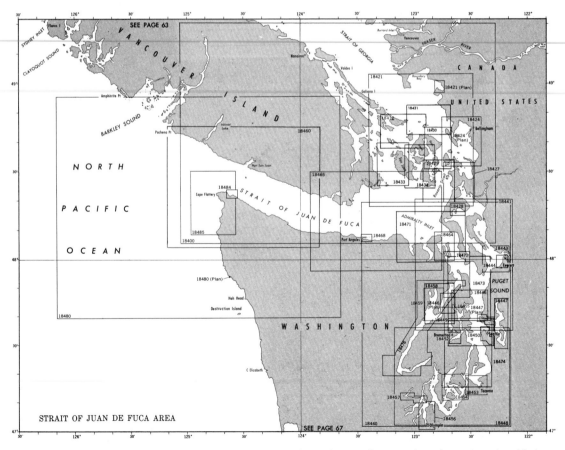

Index of nautical charts available for the Strait of Juan De Fuca in the northern Pacific Ocean, from the DMA catalog of hydrographic products.

River, Lake and Waterway Maps

For mapping purposes, rivers, lakes, and waterways fall primarily into the jurisdictions of three federal agencies: the Army Corps of Engineers, the U.S. Geological Survey, and the Tennessee Valley Authority, all of which are prolific cartographers. Some of their products are covered in two other sections of this book, "Nautical Charts and Maps" and "Water Recreation Maps."

U.S. Geological Survey. General information about individual, major U.S. rivers may be found in a series of free brochures, "River Basins of the United States" produced by USGS. The series, which covers the Colorado, Delaware, Hudson, Potomac, Suwannee, and Wabash Rivers, include general, not highly detailed, maps of the river basins, each of which spans two or more states. Also included is information about each river's early exploration; its headwaters and mouth; its major tributaries; a description of its course, length, width, depth, and rate of flow; the river's dams, reservoirs, and canals; its geologic setting and drainage area; its water quality and use; and the major cities it passes along its route. These brochures are available from USGS publication distribution centers (see Appendix A) and are listed in a free catalog titled *Popular Publications of the U.S. Geological Survey.*

Another USGS series is its State Hydrologic Unit Maps, highly detailed maps showing the hydrographic boundaries of major U.S. river basins that have drainage areas greater than 700 square miles. (Hydrology is the study of the water cycle, from precipitation as rain and snow through evaporation back into the atmosphere.) The four-color maps provide information on drainage, culture, hydrography, and hydrologic boundaries for each of 21 regions and 222 subregions. The maps, which cost from $1.75 to $5 each, are used primarily by water-resources planners for managing water resources and flood potential, and by land-resources planners for managing natural resources and recreational areas. The maps are available from USGS Distribution Centers (see Appendix A). A free brochure, "State Hydrologic Unit Maps," also is available from USGS.

Army Corps of Engineers. The big picture of U.S. waterways is contained in a 15" × 22" black-and-white Corps of Engineers map, "Major Waterways and Ports of the United States." On the map, navigable waterways are shown as heavy black lines, with other rivers shown with less emphasis. For the shipping rivers, and waterways, there are symbols indicating locks, ports, and principal cities.

The Corps also produces maps of major rivers—considerably more colorful than the USGS versions—containing much the same types of information, with one major exception: a detailed chart of recreational facilities along each river, such as boat ramps, sanitary facilities, camping facilities, and picnic tables; the sites on the chart are keyed to the map.

The Corps of Engineers' series of maps of U.S. lakes provides considerably more detail, right down to the lakes' boat ramps, campgrounds, and concession stands. Most helpful is a series of six regional maps: "Lakeside Recreation in the Southeast," "Lakeside Recreation in the Midwest," "Lakeside Recreation in the West," "Lakeside Recreation in the Southwest," "Lakeside Recreation in New England," and "Lakeside Recreation in the Northeast." Each contains a map of the states covered along with a detailed chart, showing the facilities available at each lake—everything from the type of campsites (developed or primitive) to boat launching ramps, showers, hunting, ice fishing, and nearby hotels and restaurants. In addition to the regional maps, there are detailed maps covering dozens of individual lakes. These show recreation areas in considerable detail, including information about all facilities. Both river and lake maps are available directly from the Corps of Engineers.

Unfortunately, each of the Corps' divisions and districts publishes its own maps and publications and there is neither a central distribution center nor a single listing of all Corps of Engineers maps. The Missouri River Division, for example, distributes a "Descriptive List of Maps and Charts for Sale to the Public," which is available from that division's two offices, in Omaha and Kansas City, Mo. Similarly, the Ohio River Division distributes maps and charts of that river, and the Chicago District distributes maps of the middle and upper Mississippi River and the Illinois Waterway to Lake Michigan; lower Mississippi maps come from the Corps' Vicksburg (Mississippi) District. And then there are the Black Warrior, Alabama, Tombigbee, Apalachicola, and Pearl Rivers, all of whose maps come from the Corps' Mobile (Alabama) District. When seeking maps of a particular area, your best bet is to contact the Corps of Engineers office closest to that area (see Appendix A for addresses); you will be redirected if you guessed incorrectly.

Tennessee Valley Authority. TVA's Mapping Services Branch produces a wide range of maps and publications, all listed in a free TVA *Maps Price Catalog*. In addition to its recreation maps of TVA lakes (see "Water Recreation Maps"), there is also a series of thirteen full-color Tributary Watershed Maps, showing drainage basins, topography, highways, railroads, and nearby cities; and a series of full-color Reservoir Area Maps, showing reservoirs and surrounding regions. TVA also publishes navigation maps of its many rivers and tributaries.

▶ **See also: "Nautical Charts and Maps," "Tide and Current Charts," and "Water Recreation Maps."**

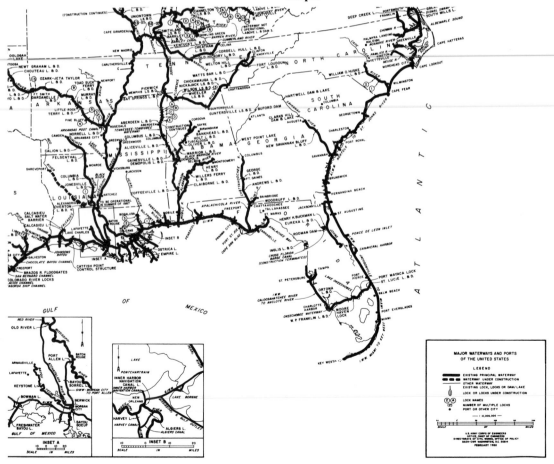

Section from the U.S. Army Corps of Engineers "Major Waterways and Ports of the United States" map, showing existing and planned waterways and ports.

Tide and Current Maps

Among the many remarkable qualities of Mother Earth is her ability to perform certain rituals with uncanny regularity. Tides, for example, can be predicted with astounding accuracy and plotted on Tidal Current Charts. These are available from the National Ocean Service, part of the Commerce Department's National Oceanic and Atmospheric Administration. The NOS tidal current charts each consist of a set of eleven charts that depict, by means of arrows and figures, the direction and velocity of the tidal current for each hour of the tidal cycle. The charts, which may be used for any year, present a comprehensive view of the tidal current movement in the respective waterways as a whole and also supply a means for rapidly determining, for any time, the direction and velocity of the current at various points throughout the water areas covered.

There are twelve available charts (they cost $4 each), covering Boston Harbor, Charleston Harbor, Narragansett Bay (two charts), Long Island and Block Island Sounds, New York Harbor, Delaware Bay and River, Upper Chesapeake Bay, Tampa Bay, San Francisco Bay, and Puget Sound (two charts). All but the Narragansett Bay chart require purchase of one of the NOS Tidal Current Tables ($5.50). There are two: one covering the Atlantic Coast, the other covering the Pacific Coast and Asia. The Narragansett Bay chart requires purchase of the NOS Tide Table ($6.75) covering the East Coast. All of these NOS charts, tables, and relat-

ed publications are available directly from NOS (see Appendix A) or through one of its authorized dealers.

▶ **See also: "Nautical Charts and Maps," "Ocean Maps," and "River, Lake, and Waterway Maps."**

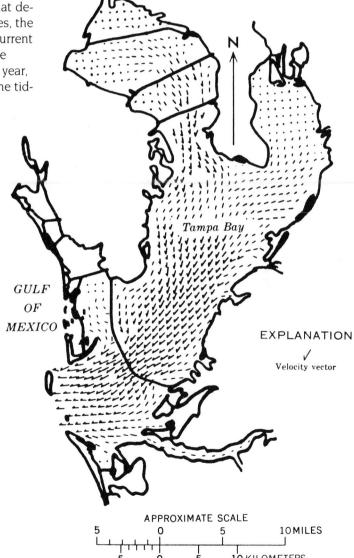

Map showing current flow and velocity in Tampa Bay, Fla., from information compiled from Landsat satellite imagery.

Water Recreation Maps

Whether you're looking to hook a large-mouth bass or a suntanned lifeguard, there's a map that can help. Water recreation maps can point the way to the best fishing, the safest swimming, or the fastest boating.

The Army Corps of Engineers, created in 1838 and responsible for mapping a lot of the Wild West, now spends much of its time preserving and mapping the water recreation lands under its jurisdiction. There are Corps district offices all over the country (see Appendix A), and each has free or inexpensive maps and guides to the lakes, rivers, and beaches it maintains for public recreation and enjoyment.

The National Ocean Service (NOS), part of the Commerce Department's National Oceanic and Atmospheric Agency, has sailing and boating maps covering most of the nation's water recreation areas. The NOS sailing and boating maps and charts are drawn at various scales and show sailing routes, flows of tides and currents, danger zones, and other important sailing and boating information for all craft sizes—from yachts to canoes. Free nautical catalogs diagram the sailing and boating maps and charts available from the NOS. (See "Nautical Charts and Maps" for further information.)

Also available from NOS are bathymetric fishing maps for most known fishing regions along U.S. coastlines. These maps are topographic depictions of the seafloor designed for use by recreational or commercial fishermen. The maps, which cost $4, illustrate and identify the distribution of bottom sediment and obstructions that may give clues to the location of fishing grounds. The NOS series is drawn at a scale of 1:100,000 and is diagrammed in a free catalog available from NOAA.

Several agencies within the Interior Department also produce and distribute water recreation maps. The National Park Service has free maps for the National Wild and Scenic River System, all National Parks (many of which have lakes and rivers within their boundaries), and the nine National Seashores it protects. The department's Bureau of Reclamation provides free maps for the dams

and reservoirs with recreational uses around the nation.

Low-cost recreation maps of reservoirs can also be obtained from the Tennessee Valley Authority, while maps of restricted or protected fishing areas are available from the Fish and Wildlife Service. Nautical charts and maps of foreign water are available from the Defense Mapping Agency.

That's just a beginning. State, regional, county, and local governments in areas where water recreation facilities are available also produce free or inexpensive maps. (See Appendix B for addresses.) And there are also local and national map publishers that produce fishing, boating, and other water recreation maps.

Without a water recreation map, you could end up feeling like a fish out of water. Here are some places to cast your line:

Government Sources

Bureau of Reclamation. The Bureau, part of the Interior Department, has free recreation maps listing facilities and principal recreation uses by region covering the following areas:

- Idaho, Oregon, and Washington.
- Montana, Nebraska, South Dakota, North Dakota, and Wyoming.
- Arizona, California, Utah, and Nevada.
- Colorado, Kansas, Texas, Oklahoma, and New Mexico.

To obtain the maps, contact the Bureau's Office of Public Affairs (Room 7644, Washington, DC 20240; 202-343-4662).

Government Printing Office. GPO sells some of the best overall series of fishing guides available: *Anglers's Guide to the United States Atlantic Coast: Fish, Fishing Grounds, and Fishing Facilities.* These seven guides provide useful information on everything from tides and shoreline configuration to climate variances and fishing water sediment. Included with each guide is a colorful fishing map atlas. The series includes:

■ *Nantucket Shoals to Long Island Sound* (S/N 003-020-00070-3; $9).

■ *Block Island to Cape May, New Jersey* (S/N 003-020-00071-1; $9).

■ *Delaware Bay to False Cape, Virginia* (S/N 003-020-00072-0; $9).

■ *Chesapeake Bay* (S/N 003-020-00096-7; $9).

■ *False Cape, Virginia to Altamaha Sound, Georgia* (S/N 003-020-00097-5; $9).

■ *Altamaha Sound, Georgia to Fort Pierce Inlet, Florida* (S/N 003-020-0098-3; $9).

■ *St. Lucie Inlet, Florida to the Dry Tortugas* (S/N 003-030-00099-1; $9.50).

Also available is the *Anglers' Guide to the United States Pacific Coast: Marine Fish, Fishing Grounds and Facilities* (S/N 003-020-0011301; $8.50), which, like the Atlantic version, contains useful fishing maps and information.

Army Corps of Engineers. The Corps of Engineers creates maps of lake and reservoir areas. There are district offices around the country that can provide maps for specific areas. See ''River, Lake, and Waterway Maps'' for details.

Tennessee Valley Authority. TVA produces multicolored pocket-size recreation maps of its lakes showing highways, roads, mileages, cities and rural communities, public access areas, commercial recreation areas, boat docks, private clubs, group camps, public parks, wildlife management areas, boat launching sites, and lands open to public use. Some of the available maps are: Chickamauga Lake, Kentucky Lake, Wheeler and Wilson Lakes, Guntersville Lake, Fort Loudoun Lake, Norris Lake, and Cherokee, Douglas, and Nolichuky Lakes.

Names and addresses of retailers of water

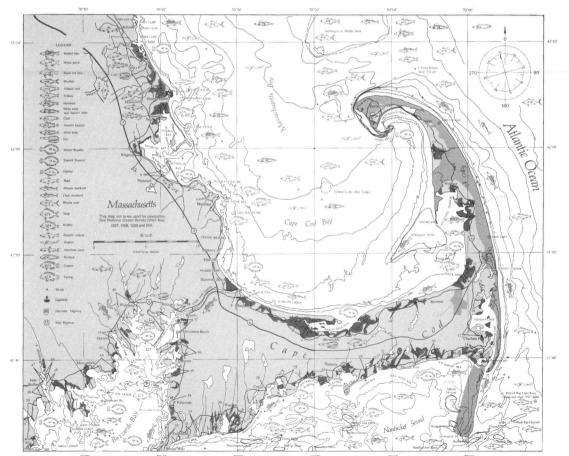

Fishing map of Massachusetts waters showing species and known locations of indigenous fish, from GPO's Angler's Guide to the United States Atlantic Coast: Fish, Fishing Grounds and Facilities: Nantucket Shoals to Long Island Sound.

recreation maps that sell government maps are printed in NOAA catalogs. There are thousands of boating and tackle shops around the country that distribute maps for their regions, and these are the best overall source for finding local maps.

Commercial Sources

Here is a sampling of publishers that produce useful water recreation maps:

ADC (6440 General Green Way, Alexandria, VA 22312; 703-750-05120) has fishing and boating maps of Virginia, Maryland, North Carolina, South Carolina, and Pennsylvania. Prices range fom $1 for simple fishing maps to $8.95 for elaborate off-shore fishing charts.

Adirondack Mountain Club Books (P.O. Box 3256, Glens Falls, NY 12801; 518-793-7737) has two books of maps for canoeing in the waters of the Adirondack's rivers: *Adirondack Canoe Waters—North Flow* (ISBN 0-935272-1305; $10.95), with 34 maps, and *Adirondack Canoe Waters—South Flow* (ISBN 0-935272-23-2; $9.95), with 160 map-filled pages.

Appalachian Mountain Club Books (5 Joy Street, Boston, MA 02108; 617-523-0636) offers several guidebooks with maps for river recreation in the Appalachian region:

■ *New England Whitewater River Guide* (0-910146-33-0; $8.95) has detailed, two-color maps for traversing some of the area's wild waters.
■ AMC *River Guide: Massachusetts, Connecticut, Rhode Island* (0-910146-56-X; $8.95), with eight maps for regional river boating, canoeing, and rafting.
■ AMC *River Guide: New Hampshire, Vermont* (0-910146-49-7; $8.95), with eight maps.
■ AMC *River Guide: Maine* (0-010146-60-8; $8.95), with eight maps.

National Scenic Trail of Florida (P.O. Box 13708 115 NE 7 Avenue, Gainesville, FL 32604; 904-378-8823), a nonprofit membership organization, has a "Florida Canoe Trails" map ($1 plus $1 postage) available for club members only. Memberships are $19 a year for individuals, $24 a year for families.

Rivermap (c/o John Hunter, 2612 Longview Avenue, Louisville, KY 40206; 502-897-5532) is a charmingly rendered map of the recreational features of the Ohio River around the Louisville area. Aside from serving as a basic map of the river, this map ($4) is dotted with helpful insets giving information on such things as obtaining fishing licenses and visiting nearby tourist attractions.

▶ **See also: "Recreation Maps," "River, Lake, and Waterway Maps," "Wildlife Maps," and "Nautical Maps."**

MAP PRODUCTS

Atlases

Mention the word "atlas" and it usually brings to mind the word "world," although "world atlases" represent a mere fraction of atlases published. An atlas is, by definition, any collection of maps in a volume. (The word comes from the giant in Greek mythology of the same name, who was compelled to support the heavens on his shoulders.) There are atlases of nearly every place and thing: agriculture atlases, Bible atlases, country atlases, history atlases, plant and animal atlases, road atlases, celestial atlases, war atlases, and on and on. The Library of Congress, in Washington, D.C., has more than 11,000 books containing the word "atlas" in their titles—representing only books the library has cataloged since 1968!

Just as there seems to be an atlas for every place and thing, there is one of nearly every quality, including size, shape, paper, map size, map scale and detail, and comprehensiveness of index. One frequent criticism of world atlases is that they tend to be biased toward their place of origin. A world atlas published in Europe, for example, may give overwhelming emphasis to countries of that continent, although they constitute a small fraction of the world's nations; the same is true for volumes published in the U.S.

World Atlases

When seeking a world atlas, there are several qualities to consider, among them:

■ **Coverage and scale.** All countries should be well represented, and at favorable scales. Pakistan, for example, should not be portrayed at the same scale of, say, Brazil. Good atlases use a carefully chosen sequence of map scales, which are multiples of one another, and use the same scale for all the sectional maps of a given continent. A serious research atlas should have a minimum scale of 1:10,000,000, except for continental or world maps.
■ **Map quality.** There are several ways, including color and shading, to distinguish different elevations above sea level. Also important is treatment of place-names. Most recent English-language atlases use local spellings of place

names—"Beijing" for Peking, for example, and "Wein" for Vienna—often with the English equivalent in parentheses.
■ **Currency.** About 500 to 1,000 place-names change each year, say cartographers, requiring continual updating of maps and atlases. Unfortunately, the publication date printed on an atlas' copyright page does not always indicate that maps are up to date, as many publishers publish new editions containing old maps. Some atlases, such as the *National Geographic World Atlas* and the *Times Atlas of the World*, issue periodic supplements.
■ **Map types.** There are political maps (containing boundaries and place-names), geographic maps (defining physical features like mountains and rivers), and combinations of the two. Better atlases also contain one or several thematic maps, such as topographic, agricultural, population, natural resource, and historical maps.
■ **Overall quality.** Ultimately, the overall readability of an atlas is the best determining factor. Maps should be easy to read, and the book should include clear, concise symbols and supplementary front matter, such as charts, tables, and special-purpose maps. A comprehensive index listing place-names is vital. Quality of manufacture, such as binding and paper thickness, also is important; a good atlas will get a lot of use over several years.

There are many world atlases from which to choose. (The Library of Congress' computer shows 648 books containing the words "world" and "atlas" in their titles; 160 are specifically titled *Atlas of the World*.) Among the better known and most comprehensive:

■ *Goode's World Atlas* (Chicago: Rand McNally, 1986; 384 pages; $22.95). This is one of the most popular world atlases used in schools (its 1922 through 1949 editions were titled *Goode's School Atlas*) because it provides more than a hundred special-purpose maps typically used by students on subjects like population, economics, and agriculture. Goode's maps are particularly clear and readable, and the book's bindings were designed for rugged school library use.

■ *Great World Atlas* (Maspeth, N.Y.: American Map Corp., 1986; 352 pages; $39.95). One of the newest world atlases, it includes a large section of satellite photos along with 128 pages of well-executed maps, several thematic and statistical maps, and an adequate index.

■ *Hammond Gold Medallion World Atlas* (Maplewood, NJ: Hammond Inc., 1986; 672 pages; $75). Hammond publishes several world atlases, but this is the most comprehensive, with more than 600 maps providing a wide range of data. Hammond also publishes an Ambassador World Atlas (1985; 500 pages; $39.95), a Diplomat World Atlas (1985; 272 pages; $24.95), a Citation World Atlas (1984; 364 pages; $22.95), an International World Atlas (1984; 200 pages; $14.95), and a New Horizon World Atlas (1986; 272 pages; $13.95),

■ *National Geographic World Atlas* (Washington, D.C.: National Geographic Society, 1981; 383 pages; $44.95). Published by this venerable map-making institution, the atlas is a comprehensive and attractive work, featuring clear, easily readable maps. Of particular note is the book's coverage of the oceans and Africa, both presented in detail not generally found in other world atlases. National Geographic also publishes one other atlas, *The Atlas of North America* (1985; 264 pages; $29.95, or $39.95 for the "deluxe" edition with magnifier and slip case).

■ *The New Oxford Atlas* (New York: Oxford University Press, 1978; 108 pages; $29.95). This is a general reference atlas containing 80 maps of the continents and regions of the world, along with 28 special maps of climate, land use, population, environment, geology, vegetation, and climate.

■ *The Rand McNally New International Atlas* (Chicago: Rand McNally, 1986; 568 pages; $150). Compiled by more than a hundred cartographers worldwide, this is known for its generally balanced coverage and attractive maps. It includes detailed maps of major world metropolitan areas of 1:1,000,000 and 1:3,000,000 scales, a helpful glossary giving translations of geographic terms in 52 languages, and an extremely thorough 160,000-name index. Unlike several other atlases, however, this one does not feature thematic or special-purpose maps.

Rand McNally also publishes the *Rand McNally Cosmopolitan World Atlas: New Census Edition* (1984; 392 pages; $55); *Rand McNally Images of the World* (1984; 160 pages; $24.95); *New Rand McNally College World Atlas* (1986; 528 pages; $17.95); *Quick Reference World Atlas* (1977; 48 pages; $2.95); *Family World Atlas* (1986, 256 pages, $14.95); and *Contemporary World Atlas* (1986, 256 pages, $9.95).

■ *Times Atlas of the World* (New York: Times Books, 1985; 520 pages; $139.99). The *Times of London* has published atlases since 1895, and they are consistently lauded for their comprehensive, balanced coverage and top-quality index. In addition to this "comprehensive" edition, the Times also publishes a "concise edition," *The New York Times Atlas of the World* (1983; 256 pages; $49.95), also of high quality.

Other world atlases include:

■ *Aldine University Atlas* (Glenview, Ill.: Scott, Foresman & Co., 1969; $9.75).
■ *Atlas Moderno Universal* (Maplewood, N.J.: Hammond Inc., 1984; $2.95).
■ *Atlas of the Land* (New York: Ballantine Books, 1985; hard $19.95, paper $9.95).
■ *Atlas of World Physical Features* (New York: John Wiley & Sons, Inc., 1972; $9.95).
■ *Bartholomew Mini World Atlas* (Maplewood, N.J.: Hammond Inc., 1984; $6.95).
■ *Franklin Watts Atlas of North America & the World* (New York: Franklin Watts Inc., 1984; $22.95).
■ *Golden Picture Atlas* (New York: Western Publishing Co. Inc., 1984; $16.95).
■ *Great International Atlas* (Milwaukee, Wisc.: George Philip Raintree, 1981; $75).
■ *Hammond Headline World Atlas* (Maplewood, N.J.: 1985; $2.95).
■ *Prentice-Hall Great International Atlas* (Englewood Cliffs, N.J.: Prentice-Hall Inc., 1981; $69.95).
■ *Prentice-Hall Home Reference Atlas* (Englewood Cliffs, N.J.: Prentice-Hall Inc., 1983; $6.95).
■ *Prentice-Hall Illustrated Atlas of the World* (Englewood Cliffs, N.J.: Prentice-Hall Inc., 1982; $29.95).
■ *Prentice-Hall Pocket World Atlas* (Englewood Cliffs, N.J.: Prentice-Hall Inc., 1983; $2.95).
■ *Prentice-Hall University Atlas* (Englewood Cliffs, N.J.: Prentice-Hall Inc., 1984; $27.50).
■ *Reader's Digest/Bartholomew Atlas of the World* (New York: Reader's Digest Association, 1986; $14.95).
■ *Signet-Hammond World Atlas* (New York: New American Library, 1982; $4.50).
■ *VNR Pocket Atlas* (New York: Van Nostrand Reinhold Co. Inc., 1983; $10.95).
■ *World Atlas* (New York: Penguin Books Inc., 1979; $9.95).
■ *World Atlas* (New York: Random House Inc., 1982; $6.95).

United States Atlases

First and foremost in this category is the federal government's authoritative *National Atlas of the United States*, prepared by 84 government agencies and published by the Government Printing Office. Although the most recent edition is 1970, the book remains untouched in its exhaustive thematic maps: climate, geology, history, commerce,

population, public lands, rivers and lakes, and foreign trade regions, among others. Together, these 756 high-quality maps paint a vivid portrait of the nation.

Other U.S. atlases include:

■ *Early Maps of North America* (Newark, N.J.: New Jersey Historical Society, 1961; $6.95).
■ *Gousha Chek Chart U.S. Road Atlas* (New York: New American Library, 1985; $3.50).
■ *Gousha North American Road Atlas* (New York: New American Library, 1985 $5.95).
■ *Grosset Road Atlas* (New York: Ace Books, Division of Charter Communications Inc., 1983; $5.95).
■ *Hammond Glove Compartment Road Atlas* (New York: Ace Books, Division of Charter Communications Inc., 1982; $2.25).
■ *Hammond Road Atlas & Vacation Guide* (Maplewood, N.J.: Hammond Inc., 1986; $2.50).
■ *Hammond United States Atlas, Gemini Edition* (Maplewood, N.J.: Hammond Inc., 1984; $9.95).

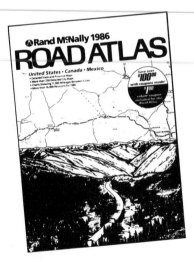

■ *Rand McNally Road Atlas & Vacation Guide* (Chicago: Rand McNally & Co., 1985; $12.95).
■ *Rand McNally Road Atlas: United States, Canada, Mexico* (Chicago: Rand McNally & Co., 1986; $5.95).
■ *Road Atlas America* (Maplewood, N.J.: Hammond Inc., 1986; $4.95).

Specialized Atlases

These vary widely—in form, content, and availability. While there are thousands of specialized atlases, we've listed below some of the more interesting, comprehensive, or useful. Many, but not all, are still in print; a few are difficult to find outside of major metropolitan and university libraries.

State Atlases

■ *Atlas of Alabama* (University, Ala.: University of Alabama Press, 1973; $10.95).
■ *Atlas of California* (Portland, Ore.: Professional Book Center Inc., 1979; $29.95).
■ *Atlas of Colorado* (Boulder, Colo.: Colorado Associated University Press, University of Colorado, 1985; hard $29.50, paper $12.50).
■ *Atlas of Florida* (Tallahassee, Fla.: Florida State University Foundation, 1981; $27.50).
■ *Atlas of Georgia* (Athens, Ga.: Institute of Community & Area, University of Georgia, 1985; $39.99).
■ *Atlas of Hawaii* (Honolulu: The University of Hawaii Press, 1983; $29.95).
■ *Atlas of Illinois* (Madison, Wisc.: American Publishing Co., 1976; $26.95).
■ *Atlas of Iowa* (Madison, Wisc.: American Publishing Co., 1974; $19.95).
■ *Atlas of Kentucky* (Lexington, Ky.: University Press of Kentucky, 1977; $19.50).
■ *Atlas of Maryland* (College Park, Md.: University of Maryland, Department of Geography, 1977; $4.50).
■ *Atlas of Michigan* (Grand Rapids, Mich.: William B. Eerdmans Publishing Co., 1977; $27.50).
■ *Atlas of Mississippi* (Jackson, Miss.: University Press of Mississippi, 1974; $5).
■ *Atlas of New York* (Madison, Wisc.: Diversified Industries, 1978; $29.95).
■ *Atlas of Ohio* (Madison, Wisc.: American Publishing Co., 1975; $26.95).
■ *Atlas of Texas* (Austin, Tex.: Bureau of Business, University of Texas, 1979; $29.95).
■ *Atlas of the State of South Carolina: Prefaced with a Geographical, Statistical & Historical Map* (Easley, S.C.: Southern Historical Press, 1980 reproduction of 1825 edition; $35).
■ *Atlas of Utah* (Provo, Utah: Brigham Young University Press, 1982; $49.95).
■ *Atlas of Wisconsin* (Madison, Wisc.: University of Wisconsin Press, 1974; hard $27.50, paper $15).
■ *California Road Atlas* (Irvine, Calif.: Thomas Brothers Maps, 1985; $12.95).
■ *Illustrated Atlas of Hawaii* (Honolulu: Island Heritage Ltd., 1970; $5.95).

■ *Maine Atlas & Gazetter* (Freeport, Me.: DeLorme Publishing Co., 1984; $9.95).
■ *Nevada Directory of Maps & Aerial Photo Resources* (Santa Cruz, Calif.: Western Association of Map Libraries, 1984; $15).
■ *New Hampshire Atlas & Gazetter* (Freeport, Me.: DeLorme Publishing Co., 1983; $9.95).
■ *New Jersey Road Maps of the Eighteenth Century* (Princeton, N.J.: Princeton University Library, 1981; $5).
■ *New Mexico in Maps* (Albuquerque, N.M.: University of New Mexico Press, 1981; $14.95).
■ *Vermont Atlas & Gazetter* (Freeport, Me.: DeLorme Publishing Co., 1983; $9.95).
■ *Yankee Magazine's Travel Maps of New England* (Dublin, N.H.: Yankee Books, 1984; $4.95).

Foreign Country and Regional Atlases

■ *AA Big Road Atlas of Britain* (Topsfield, Mass.: Merrimack Publications Circle, 1985; $10.95).
■ *Atlas of Africa* (New York: Free Press, 1974; $125).
■ *Atlas of Black Africa* (New York: Irvington Publications, 1984; $14.95).
■ *Atlas of Canada* (Milwaukee, Wisc.: George Philip Raintree, 1982; $8.95).
■ *Atlas of Canada & the World* (Milwaukee, Wisc.: Pernell Reference Books, 1979; $39.95).

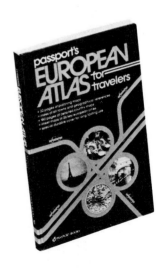

■ *Atlas of Central America* (Austin, Tex.: Bureau of Business Research, University of Texas, 1979; $18).
■ *Atlas of Europe: A Profile of Western Europe* (New York: Charles Scribner's Sons, 1974; $5.95).

■ *Atlas of European Architecture* (New York: Van Nostrand Reinhold Co. Inc., 1984; $34.95).

■ *Atlas of France* (Topsfield, Mass.: Merrimack Publications Circle, 1983; $10.95).

■ *Atlas of the Greek World* (New York: Facts On File, 1981; $35).

■ *Atlas of Ireland* (New York: St. Martin's Press Inc., 1980; $99.50).

■ *Atlas of Israel* (New York: Elsevier Science Publishing Co. Inc., 1970; $276.75).

■ *Atlas of Mexico* (Austin, Tex.: Bureau of Business Research, University of Texas, 1975; $20).

■ *Atlas of Peru* (New York: Ballantine Books Inc., 1984; $9.95).

■ *Atlas of South Asia* (Boulder, Colo.: Westview Press, 1985; $15).

■ *Atlas of the Arab World* (New York: Facts On File, 1983; $16.95).

■ *Atlas of the Third World* (New York: Facts On File, 1983; $85).

■ *Big Road Atlas of Europe* (Topsfield, Mass.: Merrimack Publishers Circle, 1983; $12.95).

■ *Comprehensive Atlas of Canada & the World* (Milwaukee, Wisc.: George Philip Raintree, 1982; $29.95).

■ *Europe Today: An Atlas of Reproducible Pages* (Wellesley, Mass.: 1985; $23.50).

■ *Rand McNally Road Atlas of Britain* (Chicago: Rand McNally & Co., 1985; $12.95).

■ *Rand McNally Road Atlas of Europe* (Chicago: Rand McNally & Co., 1985; $6.95).

■ *Third World Atlas* (Philadelphia: Taylor & Francis Inc., 1984; $15).

Historical Atlases

■ *Atlas of African History* (New York: Holmes & Meier Publishers Inc., 1978; $19.50).

■ *Atlas of African History* (New York: Penguin Books Inc., 1980; $8.95).

■ *Atlas of American History* (New York: Charles Scribner's Sons, 1978; $50).

■ *Atlas of American History* (New York: Hippocrene Books Inc., 1985; $17.95).

■ *Atlas of Ancient Civilizations* (New York: Thomas Y. Crowell Co., 1976; $12.95).

■ *Atlas of Ancient Egypt* (New York: Facts On File, 1980; $30).

■ *Atlas of Ancient History* (New York: Penguin Books Inc., 1967; $6.95).

■ *Atlas of Ancient History* (New York: Hippocrene Books Inc., 1984; $17.95).

■ *Atlas of Anglo-Saxon England* (Buffalo, N.Y.: University of Toronto Press, 1981; $14.95).

■ *Atlas of Archaeology* (New York: State Mutual Book & Periodical Service, Ltd., $60).

■ *Atlas of British History* (Totowa, N.J.: Rowman & Littlefield Inc.; 1979; $8.95).

■ *Atlas of Early American History: The Revolutionary Era* (Princeton, N.J.: Princeton University Press, 1976; $125).

■ *Atlas of Early Maps of the Midwest* (Springfield, Ill.: Illinois State Museum Society, 1983; $10).

■ *Atlas of English Literature* (Darby, Pa.: Arden Library, 1979, reproduction of 1925 edition; $20).

■ *Atlas of Historic Towns: Maps and Plans of Historical Commentaries, from Earliest Times to 1800* (Baltimore,

Md.: Johns Hopkins University Press, 1975; Vol. 1 $50, Vol. 2 $7.50)..

■ *Atlas of Medieval Europe* (New York: Facts On File, 1983; $35).

■ *Atlas of Medieval History* (New York: Penguin Books Inc., 1968; $5.95).

■ *Atlas of Modern History to 1815* (New York: Penguin Books Inc., 1973; $5.95).

■ *Atlas of Russian History: Eleven Centuries of Changing Borders* (New Haven, Conn.: Yale University Press; $10.95).

■ *Atlas of the American Revolution* (Chicago: Rand McNally & Co., 1974; $35).

■ *Atlas of the Greek & Roman World in Antiquity* (Park Ridge, N.J.: Royes Data Corp., 1982; $48).

■ *Atlas of the Greek World* (New York: Facts On File, 1981; $35).

■ *Atlas of the Historical Geography of the* U.S. (Westport, Conn.: Greenwood Press, 1975 reproduction of the 1932 edition; $132.25).

■ *Atlas of the Islamic World: Since 1500* (New York: Facts On File, 1982; $35).

■ *Atlas of the Roman World* (New York: Facts On File, 1982; $35).

■ *Atlas of the Twentieth Century* (New York: Facts On File, 1982; $29.95).

■ *Atlas of the World in the Middle Ages* (New York: Franklin Watts Inc., 1981; $11.90).

■ *Atlas of World History* (New York: Franklin Watts Inc., 1982; $12.90).

■ *Atlas of World History* (Chicago: Rand McNally & Co., 1981; $14.95).

■ *Historical Atlas of the Outlaw West* (Boulder, Colo.: Johnson Books, 1984; $14.95).

■ *Historical Atlas of the World* (Chicago: Rand McNally & Co., 1965; $5.95).

■ *History of Africa in Maps* (Chicago: Denoyer-Geppert Co., 1979; $6.95).

■ *Poland: A Historical Atlas* (New York: Hippocrene Books, 1986; $22.50).

■ *Shepherd's Historical Atlas* (New York: Barnes & Noble Books, 1980; $39.95).

■ *Times Atlas of World History, Revised Edition* (Maplewood, N.J.: Hammond Inc., 1986; $75).

■ *Times Concise Atlas of World History* (Maplewood, N.J.: Hammond Inc., 1986; $19.95).

■ *World Atlas of Archeology* (New York: G.K. Hall, 1985; $65).

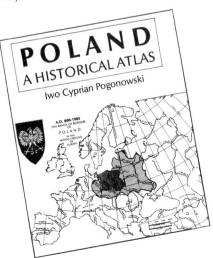

Political, Cultural, and Sociological Atlases

■ *A Comparative Atlas of America's Great Cities* (Minneapolis: Association of American Geographers and University of Minnesota Press, 1976; $95).

■ *Atlas of African Affairs* (New York:- Methuen Inc., 1984; $11.95).

■ *Atlas of British Politics* (Dover, N.H.: Longwood Publishing Group, 1985; $29).

■ *Atlas of Economic Structure & Policies, Vol. 2* (Elmsford, N.Y.: Pergamon Press Inc., $15.50).

■ *Atlas of Human Evolution* (New York: Holt, Rinehart & Winston Inc., 1979; $17.95).

■ *Atlas of Man* (New York: St. Martin's Press Inc., 1978; $25).

■ *Atlas of Man & His World* (New York: Facts On File, 1980; $24.95).

■ *Atlas of Mankind* (Chicago: Rand McNally & Co. Inc., 1982; $35).

■ *Atlas of North American Affairs* (New York: Metheun Inc., 1979; $9.95).

■ *An Atlas of Nuclear Energy* (Atlanta: Georgia State University, Department of Geography, 1984; $7).

■ *Atlas of Soviet Affairs* (Boulder, Colo.: Westview Press, 1986; $6.95).

■ *An Atlas of World Affairs* (New York: Methuen Inc., 1983; hard $17.95, paper $8.95).

■ *Atlas of World Cultures* (Pittsburgh, Pa.: University of Pittsbugh Press, 1981; $14.95).

■ *Atlas of World Population History* (New York: Penguin Books Inc., 1978; $4.95).

■ *Atlas of World Sport* (New York: State Mutual Book & Periodical Service, Ltd., 1982; $69).

■ *Cultural Atlas of Africa* (New York: Facts On File, 1981; $35).

■ *Cultural Atlas of China* (New York: Facts On File, 1983; $35).

■ *New State of the World Atlas* (New York: Simon & Schuster Inc., 1984; $10.95).

■ *Oxford Economic Atlas of the World* (New York: Oxford University Press Inc., 1972; $14.95).

■ *Oxford Regional Economic Atlases: The United States & Canada* (New York: Oxford University Press Inc., 1975; $14.95).

■ *Social & Cultural Atlas of the United States, No. 81012* (Chicago: Denoyer-Geppert Co., 1979; $5.95).

■ *The Stamp Atlas* (New York: Facts On File, 1986; $29.95).

■ *Where In The World? An Atlas for Stamp Collectors* (Albany, Ore.: Van Dahl Publications, 1983; $24.95).

■ The Women's Atlas of the United States (New York: Facts On File, 1986; $29.95).

■ Women in the World: An International Atlas (New York: Simon & Schuster, 1986; hard $19.95, paper $12.95).

■ World Atlas of Revolution (New York: Simon & Schuster, 1983; hard $19.95, paper $10.95).

■ World Atlas of Wine (New York: Simon & Schuster, 1985; $40).

Military and War Atlases

■ Atlas of Ancient & Medieval Warfare (New York: Hippocrene Books Inc., 1982; $25).

■ Atlas of Military Strategy (New York: Free Press, 1980; $29.95).

■ Atlas of Modern Warfare (New York: Putnam Publishing Group, 1978; $22.50).

■ Atlas of the Arab-Israeli Conflict (New York: Macmillan Publishing Co. Inc., 1975; $6.95).

■ Atlas of Weapons & War (New York: Thomas Y. Crowell Co., 1976; $12.95).

■ State of War Atlas: Armed Conflict-Armed Peace (New York: Simon & Schuster Inc., 1983; $9.95).

■ World Atlas of Military History 1860-1945 (New York: Hippocrene Books, 1978; $22.50).

■ World Atlas of Military History 1945-1984 (New York: Hippocrene Books, 1985; $24.95).

Atlases of Religion

■ Atlas of Man & Religion (Elmsford, N.Y.: Pergamon Press, 1970; $6).

■ Atlas of Religious Change in America: 1952-1971 (Atlanta, Ga.: Glenmary Research Center, 1978; $6.50).

■ Atlas of the Bible (Nashville, Tenn.: Thomas Nelson Publications, 1985; $35).

■ Atlas of the Bible (New York: Facts On File, 1985; $35).

■ Atlas of the Bible: An Illustrated Guide to the Holy Land (New York: Random House, 1981; $21.50).

■ Atlas of the Bible Lands (Nashville, Tenn.: Broadman Press, 1979; $3.95).

■ Atlas of the Bible Lands (Maplewood, N.J.: Hammond Inc., 1984; $6.95).

■ Atlas of the Jewish World (New York: Facts On File, 1984; $35).

■ Oxford Bible Atlas (New York: Oxford University Press Inc., 1985; hard $18.95, paper $9.95).

■ Westminister Historical Atlas of the Bible (Philadelphia: Westminister Press, 1956; $18.95).

Celestial Atlases

■ Atlas of Deep Sky Splendors (New York: Cambridge University Press, 1984; $44.50).

■ Atlas of Deep Sky Splendors (Cambridge, Mass.: Sky Publishing Corp., 1983; $39.95).

■ Atlas of the Solar System (North Pomfret, Vt.: David & Charles Inc., 1983; $26.50).

■ National Geographic Picture Atlas of Our Universe (Washington, D.C.: National Geographic Society, 1980; $16.95).

■ Sky Atlas (Cambridge, Mass.: Sky Publishing Corp., 1982; $39.95).

■ U.S. Naval Institute and American Map Corporation Space Atlas (Maspeth, N.Y.: American Map Corp., 1979; $2.95).

Plant and Animal Atlases

■ Atlas of Animal Migration (New York: Thomas Y. Crowell Co., 1974; $14.37).

■ Atlas of Distribution of the Freshwater Fish Families of the World (Lincoln, Neb.: University of Nebraska Press, 1981; $12.50).

■ Atlas of the Living Resources of the Seas (New York: Unipub, 1981; $120).

■ Atlas of the Sea (New York: Thomas Y. Crowell Co., 1974; $10.95).

■ Atlas of Wildlife (New York: Thomas Y. Crowell Co., 1972; $14.37).

- *Atlas of World Wildlife* (Chicago: Rand McNally & Co., 1973; $16.95).
- *Lloyds Maritime Atlas* (Philadelphia: International Publications Service, 1983; $30).
- *Sea Marine Atlas: Southern California* (New York: W.W. Norton & Co. Inc., 1979; $19.95).
- *World Atlas of Agriculture: Europe, U.S.S.R., Asia Minor; South & East Asia, Oceania; the Americas; & Africa*, 5 Volumes (New York: Unipub, Vols. 1 & 3 1972; Vol. 2 1974; Vol. 4 1975; Set 1975; $795).

Railway and Shipping Atlases

- *Atlas of Maritime History* (New York: Arco Publishing Inc., 1975; $35).
- *Rand McNally Atlas of the Oceans* (Chicago: Rand McNally, 1977; $29.95).
- *Atlas of the World's Railways* (New York: Frederick Fell Publications Inc., 1982; $14.95).
- *Railroad Atlas of the United States* (Chicago: Rand McNally, 1973; $3.95).
- *Rand McNally Handy Railroad Atlas of the United States* (Chicago: Rand McNally & Co., 1978; $9.95).
- *World Atlas of Railways* (New York: W.H. Smith Publishers, 1978; $10.95).

Atlases for Young People

- *Illustrated Atlas of the Modern World* (New York: Franklin Watts, 1985; $12.90).
- *Picture Atlas of Our World* (Washington, D.C.: National Geographic Society, 1979; $16.95).
- *Rand McNally Children's Atlas of the World* (Chicago: Rand McNally & Co. Inc., 1985; $11.95).
- *Rand McNally Student's World Atlas* (Chicago: Rand McNally & Co., 1984; $3.95).

Map Software

As with so many other things formerly accessible only to professionals, personal computers have brought the cartographer's craft to the masses. While it isn't yet possible to affordably produce maps of National Geographic quality on your Apple or Atari, several software products are now available that will let you create custom-designed maps for a wide range of uses.

Map software varies widely in capabilities and ease of use. Some products were designed for simple applications; others are capable of sophisticated applications that take full advantage of computers' graphics and ability to deftly turn numbers into pictures. Some such software may be used in tandem with any of several computerized data bases that make demographic or cartographic data available to subscribers.

Below is a sampling of map software available for personal computers, along with brief descriptions. These programs have not been tested for purposes of these listings, but rely on publisher literature and reviews in computer publications. Those who have specific computer-mapping needs are advised to contact the programs' publishers to discuss their suitability of use. Most publishers have brochures or sample print-outs available upon request. Some publishers offer trial arrangements, typically involving sample disks that will run only for a limited time. Others offer 20- or 30-day trial periods, during which you may return the software for a refund.

It is important to pay attention to computer-software compatibility. Most programs run only on certain computers, with specific configurations of memory, disk drives, graphics adapters, and printers. Without the right equipment, a program may not be worth more than the disk on which it is contained.

There are other mapping programs than those listed below, with new programs being published regularly. A full-service computer dealer will be able to locate new products. Meanwhile, here is a sampling of what's available.

■ *Atlas* (Software Concepts Inc., 1116 Summer Street, Stamford, CT 06905; 203-357-0522) is an inexpensive "computerized atlas" that combines the accuracy of a three-dimensional globe, the informational resources of an atlas, and the random-access capability of a personal computer. *Atlas* is billed as a learning tool, usable in several ways: locating a specific city, finding information about a city or country, determining latitude and longitude coordinates, calculating the distance between any two points on the globe in miles, kilometers, or nautical miles. Stored in the program's "Databank" are facts about "nearly every city with a population over 100,000;" as the cursor passes over the globe, you can display such data with a few keystrokes. The program offers no printing capability. Price is $69.95 (a trial version is available for $5; $6.95 for the Macintosh) and requires a 128K IBM PC or PCjr with graphics card, an Apple Macintosh, or a 48K Apple IIe or IIc.

■ *ExpresssMap* (Strategic Locations Planning, 4030 Moorpark Avenue, Suite 123, San Jose, CA 95117; 408-985-7400) is a "complete, automated presentation mapping system." The system consists of an integrated set of programs and geographic data and boundary files that give you the ability to draw maps on a computer monitor, dot-matrix printer, or pen plotter, on paper or transparency material, in up to sixteen colors. *Atlas AMP*, the heart of the four-program system, features such capabilities as "unlimited zooming" within maps, automatic labeling with names or data, varied map styles, color flexibility, and the ability to transfer data from spreadsheet and data base programs, such as *Lotus 1-2-3*, *VisiCalc*, and *dBaseII*. The geographic boundary files include maps of the 50 states, U.S. metropolitan statistical areas (SMSA's), areas of dominant influence (ADI's), and designated marketing areas (DMA's); separate packages include boundary files for U.S. counties and foreign countries. The package is $499-$900, depending on options (an evaluation disk is available for $10), and requires an IBM PC or compatible, with 448K RAM, two disk drives, and a graphics card.

■ *Mapit* (Questionnaire Service Company, Box 778, East Lansing, MI 48823; 517-641-4428) is designed for simple map making. "The intent of

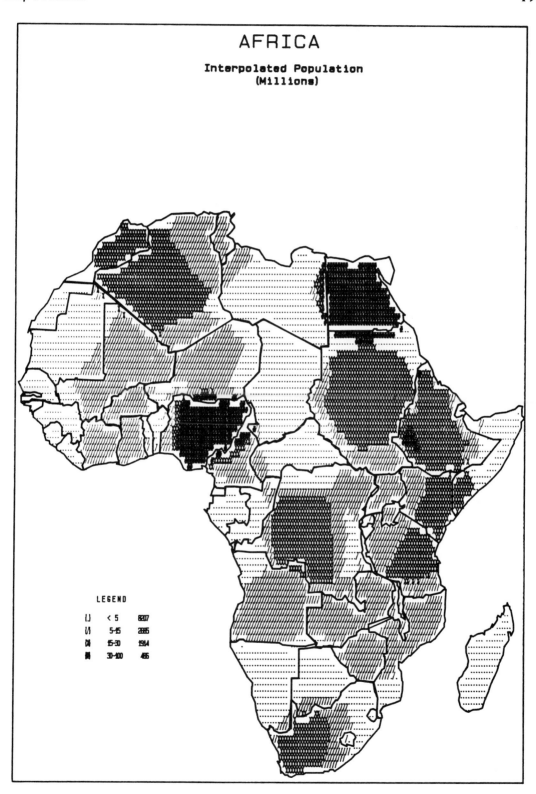

Example of "Mapit" software's computer-generated cartography.

Mapit," says the publisher, "is to make mapping available to anyone with a microcomputer." The package includes state or province map outline files for the U.S., Canada, and Australia, plus country outline files for Europe, Asia, Africa, and South America. The program permits creation of other map outline files that can be stored and re-used. A separate outline file includes county outlines for all states except Alaska and Hawaii. All outline files may be labeled, shaded, and filled in to reflect various types of data. *Mapit* runs on IBM PC and compatibles and other computers that use MS-DOS and CP/M-86 operating systems, with 128K and one disk drive; maps may be printed using most dot-matrix printers or H-P color plotters. Price is $95; the separate county outline data base is $95.

■ *Mapware*-US and *Mapware*-ADI (Computer Mathware Inc., P.O. Box 1327, Princeton, NJ 08540;

609-924-6582) enables you to make maps representing a wide range of marketing, financial, or demographic information. By filling or hatching any state or ADI (Area of Dominant Influence, roughly the same as "media market") with a different color or pattern, you can graphically present sales figures, income levels, ad campaign results, annual rainfall, or just about anything that can be quantified. Different parts of the U.S. may be displayed simultaneously, and you can zoom in on specific areas. The program also enables creation of titles, legends, and annotated text, creating presentation-quality products that may be output on a printer or plotter. The programs are $600 each and require and IBM PC or compatible with 128K memory and one disk drive.

■ *Randmap* (Rand McNally Infomap, Inc., 5535 N. Long, Chicago IL 60630; 312-673-9100) is described by its publisher as a "comprehensive mi-

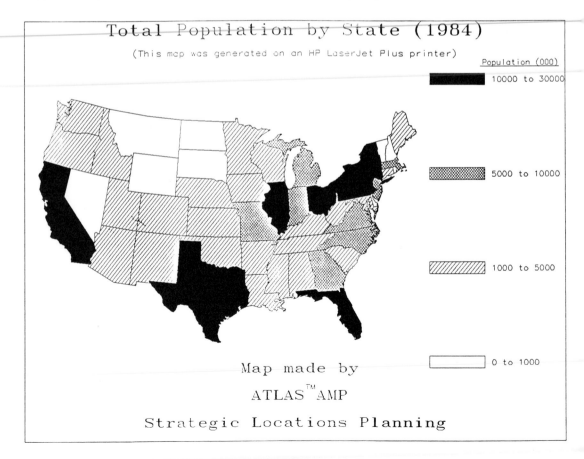

Total-population-by-state map created with "ATLAS AMP" software.

crocomputer mapping software package."
Designed (and priced) primarily for business and
educational use, it enables you to create maps by
state, county, standard metropolitan statistical
area (SMSA), areas of dominant influence (ADI),
dominant market areas (DMA), sales and marketing index (SAMI), zip codes, congressional districts, and any other geographic denomination
you can imagine or create. *Randmap* also lets users
merge their own data created with such programs
as *dBaseII, Lotus* 1-2-3, and *VisiCalc,* and boasts a
wide range of other features. *Randmap* is compatible with several printers and graphics boards and
operates on all IBM PC and compatible computers with 128K memory. The price, $995, includes
state boundary files.

■ U.S.-*Atlas* (Illston PC-Programs, 1930 Hayselton
Drive, Jefferson City, MO 65101; 312-635-3417) is
described as "a convenient tool in computing approximate distances between towns, parks, and
places of interest for the traveler or vacationer." It
is not really a mapping program, although rough
maps do appear on screen (and may be printed)
as part of U.S.-*Atlas'* fact-finding missions. The
program enables you to find the location of a city
or place in a given state, compute distances between cities (or the distances among a giant circle
of cities), determine the latitude and longitude of
any city, locate cities with identical names but in
different places (there are ten cities called "Paris"), find national parks, recreation areas, and other places of interest. U.S.-*Atlas* contains data
about some 30,000 cities and is sufficiently easy
to use that it doesn't require a manual (although
there's one on disk that may be printed). Price is
$49.95 (a free demonstration disk with data for
three states is available); it requires an IBM PC or
compatible with 192K memory.

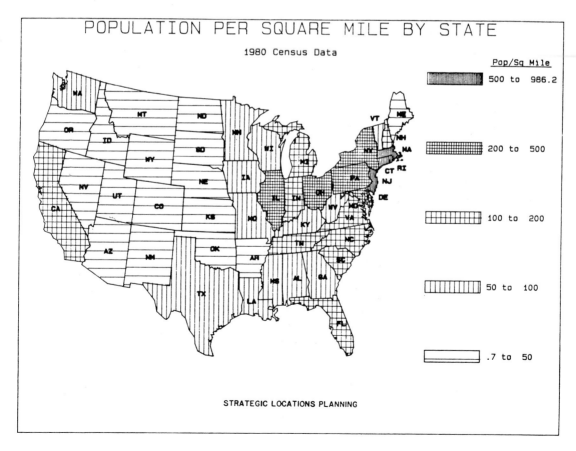

"Strategic Locations Planning" computer population map derived from 1980 Census data.

Globes

The globe—the most accurate, distortion-free representation of the Earth's surface—has the greatest utility of any visual aid in geography. It is the only map of the world that shows the true size and shape of all land and water areas, as well as the true distances and geographical relationships between them. As a model of the rotating Earth, the globe can be used to illustrate illumination from the sun, the relationship of time and longitude, and related concepts.

Although mounting a world map onto a sphere does have special advantages, it also creates some unique problems that usually make flat maps more practical. Only part of the world can be seen at one time, for example. And whatever its size, a globe takes up more space than a flat map of equal scale, is not easily portable, and contains insufficient detail.

Perhaps the greatest disadvantage of globes is their greater cost compared to maps of similar scale. Like any material printed on a flat surface, maps can be produced cheaply in large quantities. Unfortunately, a satisfactory spherical printing press has yet to be invented, so globe maps are also printed on a flat surface and then transformed into a hemisphere by one of four manufacturing processes.

How globes are made. For centuries, globes were made by printing the world map onto 30-degree-wide *gores*, which were cut and pasted onto a wooden sphere by hand. In the Replogle and Cram globe factories, paper gores are still applied by hand, but the wooden sphere has been replaced by plastic.

This handmade process proved too slow to satisfy the public's growing demand for globes. By the middle of the twentieth century, machine-made globes were being mass-produced by a method in which northern and southern polar projections were printed directly onto sheet aluminum and stamped into hemispheres with a hydraulic press. Susceptibility to dents and map stretching during the hemisphere stamping process increases with globe size, however, and these globes could not be larger than twelve inches in diameter.

In the early 1960s, a new type of globe made from chipboard was introduced and has since become the most common type in current use. The maps are printed as interrupted polar projections resembling a propeller with twelve blades, referred to in the business as "rosettes." Each map is glued to chipboard, die-cut into the rosette shape, then glued to another rosette-shaped piece of chipboard, with seams overlapping, before the hydraulic press forms it all into a hemisphere.

One recent development in globe manufacture was the introduction of plastic, raised relief globes. Using a procedure similar to that of metal globes, the polar projections are printed onto sheet plastic, then formed using a vacuum process into their hemispheric shape. This process creates more accurate relief than is possible on chipboard globes. As with metal globes, the maps printed on plastic are drawn with some deliberate distortion, which occurs when the hemispheres are formed. Place-names near the Equator still appear vertically stretched, however. The northern and southern hemispheres of plastic, chipboard, and metal globes are matched at the International Date Line or the island of Sulawesi when they are joined together. A narrow strip of tape is applied over the Equator to cover any gaps and to give a better appearance before the mounting and base are attached.

Types of globes. Terrestrial globes can be classified into three basic groups by type of coloring and information contained: political globes, physical globes, and political-physical combination globes.

The political globe is characterized by multicolored political units and solid blue oceans. There is quite a variety in the amount of political information different manufacturers include on their globes. Some political globes show national units only. Other globe makers add multicolored U.S. state units, and on some models Canada's provinces are also shown in different colors. Still other models show only provincial boundaries of non-North American countries. Names stretched across the length of bodies of water, deserts, and mountain ranges are typically the only evidence of the physical Earth on political globes, although some models also show ocean currents, steamship routes, and one type of relief portrayal.

The physical globe is primarily a representation of the world's relief features. The traditional method of showing relief is by tints, with green for lowlands and lighter green, yellow, and brown for higher elevations. The use of hypsometric tints has recently been subject to the criticism that they do not give a realistic image of the planet's surface. Perhaps as a response to this, some manufacturers have produced "ecoregion" globes that use various shades of green, yellow, and brown to portray forests, grasslands, deserts, and other natural regions on land, and shades of blue to portray the ocean floor. Raised and shaped relief are used extensively on physical globes. Some even feature the ocean floor in indented relief. Almost all physical globes show place-names of physical features and selected cities, and some also include spot heights, ocean currents, and political unit boundaries and names.

The third type of globe is the political-physical combination. It is similar to the political globe in that political units or boundaries are multicolored, but it also contains features found on a physical globe, such as raised and shaded relief, bathymetry of the ocean floor, and spot heights.

"Two-way illuminated" political-physical globes, available from some manufacturers, feature political cartography when not illuminated. When the light is turned on, the ocean floor is revealed in shaded relief, for example, or eco-region cartography. These globes can be considered two globes in one, unlike older illuminated globes, in which light is used for merely decorative purposes.

Special and extraterrestrial globes. Other types of globes include:

■ Outline or project globes, showing only the shapes or outlines of continents on a smooth plastic or slated surface, are designed to be marked with pens or chalk to show various global concepts.
■ Political globes with either French or Spanish text. Globes with text in other foreign languages can be obtained from European globe companies.

■ Globes of celestial bodies other than the Earth, including the moon, Mars, and the solar system. Most are produced from NASA photographs. Celestial globes are available in two versions. One type has yellow stars and planets printed on an opaque blue sphere with lines connecting stars in constellations or the outlines of the characters these constellations represent. The other is a clear plastic sphere with the stars and planets printed on the inside surface and a small Earth model mounted in the center.

While thousands of globes exist, only a handful are readily available from globe manufacturers. Most map libraries have several terrestrial—and sometimes extraterrestrial—globes for study; the Library of Congress' map division has 400 globes on hand.

Globe prices range from under $10 to well over $1,000, depending on size, quality of artwork, and such extras as floor stands, illumination, and raised relief.

There are only a few globe manufacturers, including most of the major map publishers. All companies have free color brochures available upon request.

George F. Cram Company Inc. (P.O. Box 426, Indianapolis, IN 46206; 317-635-5564) manufactures 28 different globes, from a series of nine-inch "budget-priced" globes ($17.95 to $18.95) to 16", illuminated "decorative floor models" ($365 to $425); the highest-priced model is described as "finished in a distressed maple mounted in the gold vein die cast full meridian." A *Globe Activity Handbook* comes with all 12" and 16" models.

Hammond Inc. (515 Valley Street, Maplewood, NJ 07040; 201-763-6000) produces nine 12" globes and one 7¾" globe (there is also a 6" globe bank for $8) ranging from $11 to $75. Hammond's illuminated Scan globes come in two styles: on one, the globe shows a physical map when turned off and a political map when turned on; the other has the same configuration, but when turned on also reveals a relief map superimposed over the political map, including the contour of the ocean floor.

Hearne Brothers (24632 Gibson, Warren, MI 48098; 800-521-0300, 313-755-3700 in Ala. and

Mich.) distributes Replogle globes, manufacturer of more than forty globe models, ranging from a tiny $7.95, 5" "Escort" model to a giant, 32" illuminated floor model, a copy of which is in the White House; it sells for $3,500, plus shipping.

Modern Educational Systems (524 East Jackson Street, Goshen, IN 46526; 800-431-5929) produces eleven globe models for classroom use, ranging from $15 for a 9" globe mounted on plastic to $131 for any of three 16" models on casters.

National Geographic Society (17th and M Streets NW, Washington, DC 20036; 202-921-1200) sells two physical and three political 12" and 16" globes, ranging from $35 to $99.

Nystrom (3333 Elston Avenue, Chicago, IL 60618; 800-621-8086) produces seven 12" and 16" globes, including two raised-relief models, in a variety of mountings; Nystrom has one model with French text, another with Spanish. Made of vinyl, they are designed to be touched and are advertised as "guaranteed unbreakable." Models range from $26.95 to $995. Another Nystrom product is "Form-a-Globe," designed for classroom use, a build-it-yourself paper globe demonstrates how maps and globes differ from and are related to each other. A set of thirty "Form-a-Globes" is $16.

Panoramic Studios (2243 West Allegheny Avenue, Philadelphia, PA 19132; 215-228-2113) manufactures large, intricate globes used by many news organizations, as well as in classrooms and boardrooms. Panoramic's globes and globe prod-

ucts include their seven 23" "Earth Curved Relief Maps" (which resemble slices of their 30" globe) priced at $25 each, and their 30" relief globe that retails for $1,600 and is a popular geographic tool for teachers of the blind.

Rand McNally (P.O. Box 7600, Chicago, IL 60680; 800-323-1887, 312-673-9100 in Ill.) produces 28 terrestrial globes and one celestial model, ranging in price from $16.95 to $800. The terrestrial globes are divided into four series: Political, featuring country boundaries in contrasting colors; International, showing political boundaries in ribbons of color and underwater topography in shades of blue; Antique, combining old world styling with current political information; and World Portrait, showing the earth as seen from space, with natural vegetation and underwater topography. One of its newest products is the "Sesame Street World Globe" ($29.95), a beginner's globe featuring Ernie, Burt, Big Bird, and others. Rand McNally also distributes ten globe models made by Denoyer-Geppert.

Replogle Globes Inc. (2801 South 25th Street, Broadview, IL 60153; 312-343-0900) produces a variety of 12", 16", 20", and 32" globes in both blue ocean and antique styles, including several illuminated models. Their newest globe, the $100 "Weather Watch," is a 16" model with a specially designed base that can aid in tracking global weather. Other popular models include the 16" non-illuminated "Commander," an antique-style floor model that retails for $75, and the 16" "Lafayette," an illuminated globe that comes with a hardwood base and is priced at $475.

Map Aids

Having a map is a good first step toward finding your way, but sometimes even the best map isn't quite enough. Here are some accessories that may help you plot your route or reach your destination. Many of these (or similar) products are readily available in map, travel, and camping supply stores; or you may contact the manufacturer directly. Prices shown are suggested retail prices; many retailers and mail-order houses discount these items. Be aware that there may be shipping and handling charges added for mail orders.

Magnifiers. These come in several shapes, sizes, and materials, depending on whether they will be used in a library or must be sufficiently compact to fit in a pocket or knapsack.

■ **Royal Robbins** (1314 Caldwell Ave., Modesto, CA 95350; 800-344-7277; in Calif., 800-336-8661) sells a Double Lens Pocket magnifier ($3.95) with two 5x lenses; used together, they magnify 10x.

■ **Newcastle Publishing Company** (P.O. Box 7589, Van Nuys, CA 91409; 213-873-3191) sells the Itoya "pocketlens," a thin, plastic magnifier that comes in two sizes: business card ($1.25) and 3" by 5" ($3.49).

■ **Tasco Sales Inc.** (P.O. Box 520080, Miami, FL 33152; 305-591-3670) carries a full line of magnifiers, including a series of "Lite-Up" illuminated models that range from $4.95 to $15.95. Tasco also carries several sizes of pocket loupes, compact powerful fold-out magnifiers designed to slip into a pocket or purse. Price range is $4.95 to $29.95.

■ **Bausch & Lomb** (P.O. Box 478, Rochester, NY 14692; 800-828-1430, 716-338-6000, in N.Y.) manufactures a wide line of magnifiers, some with built-in lights, called "minilights." Prices range from about $10 to $25.

Map cases. A good map gets a lot of use—and abuse. It gets folded and refolded, usually not back to its original form. Used on a hike or a boat, it gets dirty or wet. Map cases provide protection, letting you study the map while it remains safe and dry. There are several varieties of map cases; not all are watertight, for example.

■ **The Outsiders** (Box 262, North Salt Lake, UT 84054; 801-292-7354) manufactures clear "Show-It" map cases, available in many stores for about $4.

■ **Jandd's Mountaineering** (P.O. Box 8369, Calabassas, CA 91302; 818-715-0017) manufactures "Topolite" cylindrical map cases made of ripstop nylon, designed specifically for fifteen-minute and seven-and-a-half-minute topographic maps, both $4.95.

■ **Royal Robbins** (1314 Coldwell Avenue, Modesto, CA 95350; 800-344-7277, 800-336-8861 in Calif.) distributes "Omniseal" waterproof map and document holders, punched for tying in place. Price is $1.95 for a enough Omniseal to hold a standard topographic map, $2.65 to hold an 11" × 13" nautical chart.

Map preservers. One alternative to a map case is map preserver—basically, a liquid or spray applied to maps that renders it waterproof.

■ **Martensen Co.** (P.O. Box 261, Williamsburg, VA 23187; 804-220-2828) manufactures "Stormproof," a clear penetrating liquid treatment that impregnates paper maps. Available in in many map and camping stores in 8 oz. ($5.50) and 16 oz. ($8.50) sizes. An 8 oz. can will treat about a dozen topographic maps or four large nautical charts.

■ **Adventure 16** (4620 Alvarado Canyon Road, San Diego, CA 92120; 800-854-2672, 800-854-0222 in Calif.) distributes two products: "Map Life," a map treatment liquid that also permits writing on a map with a grease pencil, and a similar product, "Map Shield." Both retail for around $4.

Map measurers. These help you obtain accurate measurements of distance from maps, whether measuring hikes, highways, or the high seas. Most models measure both miles and kilometers; some also measure nautical miles.

■ **Precise International** (3 Chestnut Street, Suffern, NY 10901; 800-431-2996, 914-357-6200 in N.Y.) sells "Pathfinder," a topographic map measurer that converts maps into miles using 1:24,000, 1:31,680, and 1:62,500 scales; and

"Roadrunner," similar to Pathfinder, which is better suited for road trips, but which also measures in nautical miles. Both are $9.95.

■ **Johnson Camping** (P.O. Box 966, Binghamton, NY 13902; 607-723-7546) sells "Silva Map Measure Type 40," calibrated to read topo maps in scales of 1:24,000, 1:62,500, and 1:250,000 ($14.35).

Compasses. When hiking, a compass can help you orient yourself with landmarks on a map, keeping you on track. Compasses are sold by dozens of companies, including several listed above. While there are a seemingly endless number of compass "bells and whistles"—sizes, mountings, magnifiers, wrist attachments, luminescence, mirrors, and on and on—almost any compass will do. To function properly, it need only be capable of pointing toward Magnetic North and have some direction and degree markings around its perimeter.

Relief Maps

With the combined advantages of three dimensions and vivid color, relief maps are widely used as teaching aids and decorative items. For students, relief maps provide a graphic tool that brings our multidimensional world to life. There are two types of relief maps: *visual relief* maps are flat maps colored and shaded to provide a three-dimensional look. *Raised relief* maps actually are three-dimensional, with raised mountains and flat valleys. Some map makers use other terms—"environmental relief," for example—but virtually all fall into one of these two categories.

Relief map materials typically range from rubber to plastic to vinyl. There is little consensus as to which material is optimal; vacuum-formed plastic tends to permit greater map detail while rubber and vinyl are more durable.

The following companies produce or sell a variety of relief maps and have catalogs with details and ordering information available upon request.

Hearne Brothers (24632 Gibson, Warren, MI 48098; 800-521-0300, 313-755-3700 in Ala. and Mich.) distributes Geo-Institute, a German manufacturer of raised relief large-scale maps made of durable rubber, including a seven-and-a-half-foot by five-foot world map ($340); and visual relief maps from Esselte, a 160-year-old Swedish map maker, in which the Earth's geographical environments—deserts, mountains, forests, and so on—are color-coded. Esselte calls them "environmental relief" maps.

Hubbard (P.O. Box 104, Northbrook, IL 60062; 800-323-8368, 312-272-7810, in Ill.) produces more than 200 raised relief maps of the country's mountainous areas—everything west of the Rocky Mountains and portions of the eastern U.S., from Alabama to Maine. Hubbard's maps are not as colorful as other companies', but include high-quality detail. Maps vary in size, but are generally 21″ × 21″ and represent approximately 110 × 70 miles. Prices are $14.95 unframed and $34.95 framed in solid wood with a walnut stain finish. Also available is a U.S. (35″ × 22″) and a world (39″ × 21″) map. Both are $15.95 unframed, $39.95 framed.

Kistler Graphics Inc. (4000 Dahlia Street, Box 5467, Denver, CO 80217; 303-399-2581) produces a series of raised relief maps printed on vinyl. Included are one world map (34″ × 22″, $15); three U.S. maps (26″ × 17″, $12.95; 34″ × 22″, $15; 42″ × 28″, $42); maps for thirteen western states, Death Valley, Grand Canyon, Rocky Mountain National Park, Los Angeles, and San Francisco (all roughly 17″ × 22″, $10.95 to $16).

Rand McNally (P.O. Box 7600, Chicago, IL 60680; 800-323-1887, 312-673-9100 in Ill.) produces several visual relief maps, under both the Rand McNally and Denoyer-Geppert product lines, including: visual relief state wall maps for 15 states and British Columbia (41″ × 54″ to 64″ × 44″; $69 to $96) on spring roller mountings; visual relief country and continent maps (54″ × 44″ to 83″ × 76″; $72 to $153) on spring roller mountings; and 12″ ($60) and 16″ ($84) visual relief globes.

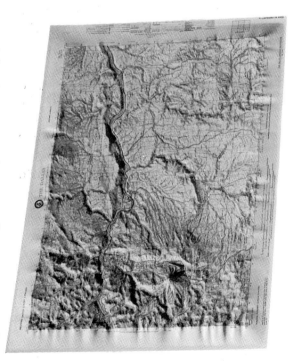

Relief map of The Dalles, on the Oregon-Washington border. Courtesy Hubbard.

APPENDIXES

Federal Map Agencies

The following is a quick reference for obtaining information and ordering maps from the federal government. Various postage rates apply to mail and phone orders.

When writing or calling for information, be as specific as possible about the type, scale, location, quality, and quantity of map you are seeking.

Agricultural Stabilization and Conservation Service

2222 West, 2300 South, P.O. Box 30010, Salt Lake City, UT 84130; 801-524-5856.

The U.S. Department of Agriculture's ASCS distributes aerial photographs produced by it and other branches of the USDA. Payment should be in the form of a money order or check, drawn from a U.S. or Canadian bank in U.S. dollars, made payable to "ASCS."

ASCS's Aerial Photography Field Office will provide free "photoindexes" of specific areas they have available in aerial photographic form. Photoindexes of Forest Service and Soil Conservation Service aerial photographs, as well as those by the ASCS, are available. A price list, order form, and descriptive pamphlet, "ASCS Aerial Photography," will be sent upon request.

Army Corps of Engineers

Public Affairs, Army Corps of Engineers, Department of the Army, Department of Defense, 20 Massachusetts Avenue NW, Room 8137, Washington, DC 20314; 202-272-0011.

The Army Corps of Engineers produces and distributes maps of federal water recreation lands within its regional districts. Write to the district nearest the area for which you need maps. Some maps are free, while others are offered for a minimal fee. For a listing of Corps of Engineers districts and publications, write the Office of Public Affairs at the above address.

Bureau of the Census

Data User Services Division, Customer Services (Publications), Bureau of the Census, Washington, DC 20233; 301-763-4100.

The Customer Services branch will accept Visa, MasterCard, personal checks, and money orders made payable to the "Superintendent of Documents" for Census publications. "Special Maps of the United States, GE-70 Series," "Urban Atlas Tract Data," "SMSA," "Congressional District Atlas," and other order forms describing available maps or series are free upon request.

Certain Census map products are available from the Government Printing Office (Superintendent of Documents, U.S. Government Printing Office, Washington, DC 20402; 202-783-3238), rather than from the Bureau of the Census. These include the state and county subdivision maps, and the *Congressional District Atlas*. The free GPO subject index "Maps and Atlases" describes the Census products available from GPO.

Bureau of Land Management

USGS is distributor for Bureau of Land Management maps. To order BLM map products, write to U.S. Geological Survey (Map Distribution, Federal Center, Building 41, Box 25286, Denver, CO 80225; 303-236-7477).

Information and price lists of BLM maps can be obtained through the USGS or from the National Cartographic Information Center, 507 National Center, 12201 Sunrise Valley Drive, Reston, VA 22092; 703-860-6045 and affiliated offices (see NCIC listing for addresses).

Central Intelligence Agency

CIA maps are available from several sources. The National Technical Information Service distributes most CIA maps published after January 1, 1980. Orders should be directed to NTIS (U.S. Department of Commerce, 5285 Port Royal Road, Springfield, VA 22161; 703-487-4650). Use the

NTIS document number (PB number) when ordering. NTIS accepts personal checks and money orders drawn on U.S. or Canadian banks and made payable to "NTIS."

The Government Printing Office (Superintendent of Documents, Government Printing Office, Washington, DC 20402; 202-783-3238) is distributor for several CIA maps and all of its atlases. The available maps and atlases are listed in the free GPO subject index "Maps and Atlases."

Maps and other CIA publications produced before 1980 are available from the Library of Congress (Photoduplications Service, Washington, DC 20504; 202-287-5650). Staff in the Library's Geography and Map Division can help locate the CIA maps in its collection.

A free catalog listing CIA maps and where to obtain them, "CIA Maps and Publications Released to the Public," is available from the Central Intelligence Agency (Public Affairs Office, Washington, DC 20505; 703-351-2053).

Defense Mapping Agency

DMA Office of Distribution Services, ATTN: DDCP, Washington, DC 20315; 202-227-2495.

The Defense Mapping Agency is the central map producing branch of the Department of Defense. Products may be purchased with a check or money order in U.S. dollars, drawn from a U.S. or Canadian bank and made payable to "Treasurer of the United States."

Catalogs of DMA products are available from the Office of Distribution Services or authorized DMA map dealers for $2.25 each. The "Department of Defense/Defense Mapping Agency Catalog of Maps, Charts and Related Products" is divided into four parts: "Part I, Aerospace Products," "Part II, Hydrographic Products," "Part III, Topographic Products," and "Part IV, World—Small- and Medium-Scale Maps." The catalogs are further subdivided by world region, so when ordering or inquiring about available maps, be sure to specify the country or continent in which you are interested. The "Annual Price List" can be obtained for $1 from the DMA and authorized dealers. The catalogs and price list include listings of authorized DMA map dealers.

EROS Data Center

User Services Section, EROS Data Center, U.S. Geological Survey, Sioux Falls, SD 57198; 605-594-6151.

EROS is the clearinghouse for aerial photographs and satellite and space imagery created by the federal government. EROS (like all USGS branches) accepts checks or money orders in U.S. dollars made payable to the "Department of the Interior/USGS," for the exact amount of the order. Order forms for products can be obtained from either EROS or from the National Cartographic Information Center (507 National Center, 12201 Sunrise Valley Drive, Reston, VA 22092; 703-860-6045) and affiliated offices (see NCIC listing for addresses).

Order forms are available for "Aerial Mapping Photography," "NASA Aircraft Photography," "Inquiry for Geographic Search for Aircraft Data," "NHAP: National High Altitude Photography Program," and "Land Satellite Images." EROS will supply price lists upon request and USGS produces a series of free pamphlets that explain products and ordering procedures. Pamphlet titles include "How to Order Landsat Images," "Looking for an Old Aerial Photograph," "EROS: A Space Program for Earth Resources," "The Aerial Photography Summary Record System," and "How to Obtain Aerial Photographs."

Federal Energy Regulatory Commission

Office of Public Affairs, Federal Energy Regulatory Commission, 825 North Capital Street NE, Washington, DC 20426; 202-357-8300.

FERC produces a series of energy maps relating to hydroelectric power, pipelines, and natural and synthetic fuels. A listing of available maps is free upon request. Some of the maps are distributed by the GPO, and these are listed in the free subject index, "Maps and Atlases," available at most GPO bookstores.

Fish and Wildlife Service

Division of Realty, Fish and Wildlife Service, Washington, DC 20240; 202-343-5634.

The Fish and Wildlife Service provides free maps and brochures for its protected lands. There is no catalog, but the maps can be obtained either at the sites themselves or from the Division of Realty. Address lists of FWS hatcheries can be obtained free from the Division of Hatcheries, and lists of refuges can be obtained free from the Division of Refuges, both located at the above address.

Forest Service

Office of Public Affairs, Forest Service, Room 3008 South Building, Washington, DC 20250; 202-447-6661.

There are maps available for each of the U.S. Forest Service's 122 National Forests. They are available either at the forests' visitors centers or directly from the Forest Service. Most maps cost less than $2 and may be purchased with checks or money order drawn on U.S. dollars and made payable to "USFS." An address list of National Forests will be sent free upon request.

Government Printing Office

Superintendent of Documents, U.S. Government Printing Office, Washington, DC 20402; 202-783-3238.

GPO accepts Choice, Visa, MasterCard, and money orders or personal checks in U.S. dollars drawn on U.S. and Canadian banks and made payable to the "Superintendent of Documents." There are more than a hundred free subject indexes available at most GPO stores, listing products by category, including "Maps and Atlases"; other subject indexes cover areas such as "Farms and Farming," "Oceanography," and "Public and Private Utilities." A free catalog of "U.S. Government Books" lists numerous GPO books, including atlases and other map-filled volumes. Although most GPO bookstores do not carry the full catalog of available maps, most have certain Census Bureau and CIA maps in stock. There are GPO bookstores around the country:

Alabama:
Birmingham GPO Bookstore, 9220-B Parkway East, Birmingham, AL 35206; 205-254-1056.

California:
Los Angeles GPO Bookstore, ARCO Plaza, 505 South Flower Street, Los Angeles, CA 90071; 213-688-5841; **San Francisco GPO Bookstore,** Federal Office Building, 450 Golden Gate Avenue, San Francisco, CA 94102; 415-556-0642.

Colorado:
Denver GPO Bookstore, Federal Office Building, 1961 Stout Street, Denver CO 80294; 303-837-3964; **Pueblo GPO Bookstore,** Majestic Building, 720 North Main Street, Pueblo, CO 80113; 303-544-3142.

District of Columbia:
Commerce Department GPO Bookstore, 14th and E Streets, NW, Washington, DC 20230; 202-377-3527; **Health and Human Services Department GPO Bookstore,** 330 Independence Avenue, SW, Washington, DC 20201; 202-472-7478; **Main GPO Bookstore,** 710 North Capitol Street, Washington, DC 20402; 202-275-2091; **Pentagon GPO Bookstore,** Main Concourse, South End, Washington, DC 20310; 202-557-1821; **State Department GPO Bookstore,** 21st and C Streets, NW, Washington, DC 20520; 202-632-1437.

Florida:
Jacksonville GPO Bookstore, Federal Office Building, 400 West Bay Street, Jacksonville, FL 32202; 904-791-3801.

Georgia:
Atlanta GPO Bookstore, Federal Office Building, 275 Peachtree Street, NE, Atlanta, GA 30303; 404-221-6947.

Illinois:
Chicago GPO Bookstore, Everett McKinley Dirksen Building, 219 South Dearborn Street, Chicago, IL 60604; 312-353-5133.

Maryland:
Retail Sales Branch, 8660 Cherry Lane, Laurel, MD 20810; 202-953-7974.

Massachusetts:
Boston GPO Bookstore, Kennedy Federal Building, Sudbury Street, Boston, MA 02203; 617-223-6071.

Michigan:
Detroit GPO Bookstore, McNamara Federal Building, 477 Michigan Avenue, Detroit, MI 48226; 313-226-7816.

Missouri:
Kansas City GPO Bookstore, Room 144, Federal Building, 601 East 12th Street, Kansas City, MO 64106; 816-374-2160.

New York:
New York GPO Bookstore, 26 Federal Plaza, New York, NY 10278; 212-264-3825.

Ohio:
Cleveland GPO Bookstore, Federal Office Building, 1240 East Ninth Street, Cleveland, OH 44199; 216-522-4922; **Columbus GPO Bookstore,** Federal Office Building, 200 North High Street, Columbus, OH 43215; 614-469-6956.

Pennsylvania:
Philadelphia GPO Bookstore, Federal Office Building, 600 Arch Street, Philadelphia, PA 19106; 215-597-0677; **Pittsburgh GPO Bookstore,** Federal Office Building, 1000 Liberty Avenue, Pittsburgh, PA 15222; 412-644-2721.

Texas:
Dallas GPO Bookstore, Federal Building—U.S. Courthouse, 1100 Commerce Street, Dallas, TX 75242; 214-767-0076; **Houston GPO Bookstore,** 45 College Center, 9319 Gulf Freeway, Houston, TX 77017; 713-226-5453.

Washington:
Seattle GPO Bookstore, Federal Office Building, 915 Second Avenue, Seattle, WA 98174; 206-442-4270.

Wisconsin:
Milwaukee GPO Bookstore, Federal Office Building, 517 East Wisconsin Avenue, Milwaukee, WI 53202; 414-291-1304.

International Boundary Commission, U.S. and Canada

425 I Street NW, Room 150, Washington, DC 20001; 202-632-8058.

IBC sells maps of the U.S.-Canadian borders for $3 each. A listing that details available maps will be sent upon request.

International Boundary Commission, U.S. and Mexico

The Commons, Building C, Suite 310, 4171 North Mesa, El Paso, TX 79902; 915-541-7300.

The International Boundary and Water Commission produces several maps of the region in and around the United States-Mexico border. Map prices vary, and a listing of maps available to the public will be sent upon request.

Library of Congress

Geography and Map Division, Library of Congress, Washington, DC 20540; 202-287-4177.

The Geography and Map Division's Reading Room (located in the James Madison Memorial Building, Room LM B01, 101 Independence Avenue SE, Washington, DC 20540) is open to the general public. Maps may not be taken from the room, but reproduction services are available. Two free pamphlets, available in the Reading Room or through the mail, "Geography and Map Division, The Library of Congress," and "Publications of the Geography and Map Division," provide information about the division, its services, and products.

Price and reproduction information can be obtained from the Library's Photoduplication Service (202-287-5650) at the above address.

National Aeronautic and Space Administration

NASA aircraft photography is available from the EROS Data Center (User Services Section, U.S. Geological Survey, Sioux Falls, SD 57198; 605-594-6511). NASA space imagery is distributed through Bara Photographic Inc. (P.O. Box 486, Bladensburg, MD 20710; 301-332-7900).

A price list and information on available NASA space imagery can be obtained from NASA's Audiovisual Department (National Aeronautics & Space Administration, Room 6035, 400 Maryland Avenue SW, Washington, DC 20546; 202-453-1000).

National Archives Cartographic and Architectural Branch

U.S. General Services Administration, Washington, DC 20408; 703-756-6700.

You must have a researcher's card to use the Archives, which can be obtained at the front desk of the Archives map headquarters (located at 841 S. Pickett Street, Alexandria, VA 22304) to use the reading room of the Archives Cartographic and Architectural collection. A price list for reproduction services is available upon request, or can be quoted over the telephone. (Photocopy facilities are located on the premises, but higher quality reproduction work is sent to an outside service.) It helps to know the file number of the maps you need reproduced, but the staff can sometimes help locate this information. Free inventories and catalogs of various parts of the Archives collection are listed in the free pamphlet "Cartographic and Architectural Branch," available both at the branch location and from the above mailing address. Among the inventories available are "Cartographic Records of the Bureau of the Census," "Cartographic Records of the Forest Service," and Cartographic Records of the United States Marine Corps."

National Cartographic Information Center

507 National Center, 12201 Sunrise Valley Drive, Reston, VA 22092; 703-860-6045.

NCIC and its affiliates are the best single source for information on maps produced or distributed by the federal government. In addition to answering general and technical questions on cartography, geography, geodesy, and remote sensing, NCIC gathers, organizes, and distributes maps, charts, aerial photographs, digital map data, geodetic control data, geographic data, and satellite products. Most sell maps over the counter as well as accepting mail orders. Although it is a part of the USGS, the staff of NCIC can help track down maps from the government's other mapping branches as well. A free booklet, "Popular Publications of the USGS," lists many of the free pamphlets and flyers produced by USGS and available from NCIC.

NCIC *Regional Centers*

Rocky Mountain Mapping Center—NCIC, USGS, Mail Stop 504, Box 25046, Federal Center, Denver, CO 80225; 303-236-5829.

Mid-Continent Mapping Center—NCIC, USGS,

1400 Independence Road, Rolla, MO 65401; 314-341-0851.

Western Mapping Center—NCIC, USGS, 345 Middlefield Road, Menlo Park, CA 94125; 415-323-8111, ext. 2427.

National Space Technology Laboratories—NCIC, USGS, Building 3101, NSTL Station, MS 39529; 601-688-3544.

Alaska Office—NCIC, UGSG, Room 110, 4230 University Drive, Anchorage, AK 99508; 907-271-4148.

Tennessee Valley Authority—NCIC, 200 Haney Building, 311 Broad Street, Chattanooga, TN 37401; 615-751-6277.

NCIC *State Affiliates*

Alabama:
Geological Survey of Alabama, P.O. Drawer O, University, AL 35486; 205-349-2852.

Arizona:
Arizona State Land Department, Information Resources Division, 1624 West Adams, Room 302, Phoenix, AZ 85007; 602-255-4061.

Arkansas:
Arkansas Geological Commission, Vardelle Parham Geology Center, 3815 West Roosevelt Road, Little Rock, AR 72204; 501-371-1488.

Connecticut:
National Resource Center, Department of Environmental Protection, State Office Building, Room 553, 165 Capitol Avenue, Hartford, CT 06106; 203-566-3540.

Delaware:
Delaware Geological Survey, University of Delaware, 101 Penny Hall, Newark, DE 19711; 302-738-2833.

Georgia:
Office of Research and Evaluation, Department of Community Affairs, 40 Marietta Street, NW, 8th Floor, Atlanta, GA 30303; 404-656-2900.

Hawaii:
Department of Planning and Economic Development, Kamamalu Building, 250 South King Street, Honolulu, HI 96813; 808-548-3047.

Idaho:
Idaho State Historical Library, 325 West State, Boise, ID 83702; 208-334-3356.

Illinois:
University of Illinois at Urbana-Champaign, Map and Geography Library, 1407 West Gregory Drive, Urbana, IL 61801; 217-333-0827.

Kentucky:
Kentucky Geological Survey, 311 Breckinridge Hall, University of Kentucky, Lexington, KY 40506; 606-257-3196.

Louisiana:
Office of Public Works, Department of Transportation and Development, P.O. Box 44155 Capitol Station, Baton Rouge, LA 70804; 504-342-7580.

Maryland:
Maryland Geological Survey, The Rotunda, Suite 440, 711 West 40th Street, Baltimore, MD 21211; 301-338-7212.

Massachusetts:
University of Massachusetts, Remote Sensing Center, Hasbrouck Hall, Room 320, Amherst, MA 01003; 413-545-2510.

Michigan:
Division of Land Resource Programs, Michigan Department of Natural Resources, Steven T. Mason Building, Box 30028, Lansing, MI 48909; 517-373-3328.

Minnesota:
Minnesota State Planning Agency, Land Management Information Center, Metro Square Building, Room LL65; Seventh and Robert Streets, St. Paul, MN 55101; 612-297-2490.

Mississippi:
Regional Planning Branch, Mississippi Research and Development Center, P.O. Drawer 2470, Jackson, MS 39205; 601-982-6606.

Missouri:
Missouri Department of Natural Resources, Division of Geology and Land Survey, P.O. Box 250, Rolla, MO 65401; 314-364-1752.

Montana:
Montana Bureau of Mines and Geology, Montana Tech, Main Hall, Room 200, Butte, MT 59701; 406-496-4167.

Nebraska:
Conservation and Survey Division, University of Nebraska, Lincoln, NE 68508; 402-472-3471.

Nevada:
Nevada Bureau of Mines and Geology, University of Nevada, Reno, NV 89557; 702-784-6691.

New Jersey:
Department of Environmental Protection, New Jersey Geological Survey, CN-029, Trenton, NJ 08625; 609-292-2576.

New Mexico:
University of New Mexico, Technology Applications Center, 2500 Central Avenue, SE, Albuquerque, NM 87131; 505-277-3622.

New York:
Map Information Unit, Department of Transportation, State Campus, 1220 Washington Avenue, Albany, NY 12232; 518-457-3555.

North Carolina:
Geological Survey Section, Division of Land Resources, DNRCD, P.O. Box 27687, Raleigh, NC 27611; 919-733-2423.

North Dakota:
North Dakota State Water Commission, State Office Building, 209 East Boulevard, Bismark, ND 58501; 701-224-2750.

Oregon:
Oregon State Library, Public Services, Salem, OR 97310; 503-378-4502.

Pennsylvania:
Department of Environmental Resources, Bureau of Topographic and Geologic Survey, P.O. Box 2357, Harrisburg, PA 17120; 717-787-2169.

Rhode Island:
Sea Grant Depository, Pell Marine Science Library, University of Rhode Island, Narragansett, RI 02882; 401-792-6277.

South Carolina:
South Carolina Land Resources Conservation Commission, 2221 Devine Street, Suite 222, Columbia, SC 29205; 803-758-2823.

Tennessee:
Tennessee Division of Geology, 701 Broadway, Nashville, TN 37203; 615-742-6696.

Texas:
Texas Natural Resources Information System, P.O. Box 13087, Austin, TX 78711; 512-475-3321.

Utah:
Utah Geological and Mineral Survey, 606 Black Hawk Way, Research Park, Salt Lake City, UT 84108; 801-581-6831.

Virginia:
Department of Conservation and Economic Development, Division of Mineral Resources, Natural Resources Building, Box 3667, Charlottesville, VA 22903; 804-293-5121.

Washington:
Washington State Library, Information Services Division, Olympia, WA 98504; 206-753-4027.

West Virginia:
West Virginia Geological and Economic Survey, Cartographic Center, P.O. Box 897, Morgantown, WV 26505; 304-594-2331.

Wisconsin:
State Cartographer's Office, 144 Science Hall, 550 North Park Street, Madison, WI 53706; 608-262-3065.

Wyoming:
State Engineer, Barrett Building, Cheyenne, WY 82002; 307-777-7354.

National Climatic Data Center

Federal Building, Asheville, NC 28801; 704-259-0682.

The National Climatic Data Center, part of the National Oceanic and Atmospheric Administration, has an Historical Climatology Series that includes several long-term weather records, maps, and atlases. A free catalog of the series, as well as a price list, are available upon request. Payment can be made with American Express, Visa, and MasterCard, or check or money order drawn on U.S. funds and made payable to "Commerce-NOAA-NCDC."

National Ocean Service

Distribution Branch, (N/CG33), National Ocean Service, Riverdale, MD 20737; 301-436-8726.

NOS, a branch of the National Oceanic and Atmospheric Administration, distributes nautical and aeronautical charts of the U.S. created by NOAA and the Defense Mapping Agency. The products may be purchased with Visa and MasterCard or with a check or money order made payable to "NOS, Department of Commerce, N/CG33." Five catalogs of available nautical charts and tables—"Atlantic and Gulf Coasts," Pacific

Coast," "Alaska," "Great Lakes and Adjacent Waterways," and "Bathymetric Maps and Special Purpose Charts"—are free upon request, as is the "Catalog of Aeronautical Charts and Related Publications."

Maps and charts can also be purchased from three NOS services offices:

National Ocean Service, 439 W. York Street, Norfolk, VA 23510; 804-441-6616.

National Ocean Service, 1801 Fairview Avenue East, Seattle, WA 98102; 206-442-7657

Chart Sales & Geodetic Control, Federal Building and Courthouse, 701 C Street, Box 38, Anchorage, AK 99513; 907-271-5040.

National Ocean Service maps can also be obtained at hundreds of authorized dealers around the country (most are map, sports equipment, boating and tackle, and aviation equipment stores). The dealers are listed in the free catalogs.

Nautical and aeronautical maps of foreign countries are distributed through the Defense Mapping Agency.

National Park Service

Office of Public Affairs, National Park Service, Room 3043, Washington, DC 20240; 202-343-7394

The Park Service supplies the visitor information centers of its national parks, forests, seashores, and historical sites with maps and information folders that are free to the public. The maps and folders can also be obtained through the Office of Public Inquiries. The Government Printing Office is the distributor for Park Service publications, including booklets or studies of parks and historic sites, many of which also contain maps and guides.

Tennessee Valley Authority

Mapping Services Branch, Map Sales, 400 West Summit Hill Drive (WPA3), Knoxville, TN 37902; 615-632-2717.

TVA produces a wide variety of maps related to its region. Maps may be purchased with a check or money order in U.S. dollars, drawn on a U.S. or

Canadian account, and made payable to the "Tennessee Valley Authority."

A "Catalog of Selected Maps and Data Available," as well as indexes of TVA nautical and topographic maps, will be sent free upon request.

More information on TVA mapping services can be obtained from the Mapping Services Branch (Map Information and Records Unit, 200 Haney Building, Chattanooga, TN 37401; 615-751-6277).

U.S. Geological Survey

Map Distribution, Federal Center, Building 41, Box 25286, Denver, CO 80225; 303-236-7477.

USGS accepts money orders and personal checks made payable to the "Department of the Interior/ USGS." State-by-state indexes of topographic, geologic, and general maps, as well as listings of maps by category (land use, national atlas, etc.); indexes by map scale; price lists; and order forms are available free upon request from either the map distribution center, or from regional Public Information Offices:

USGS Public Inquiries Office, 4230 University Drive, Room 101, Anchorage, AK 99501; 907-561-5555.

USGS Public Inquiries Office, Building 3, Room 122, Mail Stop 533, 345 Middlefield Road, Menlo Park, CA 94025; 415-323-8111, ext. 2817.

USGS Public Inquiries Office, 169 Federal Build-ing, 1961 Stout Street, Denver, CO 80294; 303-844-4169.

USGS Public Inquiries Office, 1-C-45 Federal Building, 1100 Commerce Street, Dallas, TX 75242; 214-767-0198.

USGS Public Inquiries Office, 8105 Federal Building, 125 South State Street, Salt Lake City, UT 84138; 801-524-5652.

USGS Public Inquiries Office, 503 National Center, Room 1-C-402, 12201 Sunrise Valley Drive, Reston, VA 22092; 703-860-6167

Information, indexes, and free pamphlets produced by USGS are also available from the National Cartographic Information Center (507 National Center, 12201 Sunrise Valley Drive, Reston, VA 22092; 703-860-6045) and its affiliated offices. EROS Data Center is the USGS distributor of Landsat images and aerial photographs and photomaps. Hundreds of map and travel stores, as well as state offices, are authorized dealers of USGS products. Names and addresses of USGS map dealers are listed on the state indexes already mentioned. The maps may also be purchased over the counter at the USGS's Reston, Virginia, location.

Alaska residents may purchase geologic, hydrologic, and topographic maps of Alaska from the Alaska Distribution Section, USGS, New Federal Building, Box 12, 101 Twelfth Avenue, Fairbanks, AK 99701; 907-456-7535.

Appendix B

State Map Agencies

Alabama:
Archives: Archives and History, 624 Washington Avenue, Montgomery, AL 36130; 205-261-4361; **Aviation:** Department of Aeronautics, 817 South Court Street, Montgomery, AL 36130; 205-261-4480; **Fish and Game:** Department of Conservation, Division of State Parks, 64 North Union Street, Montgomery, AL 36130; 205-261-3444; **Geology:** Geological Survey, P.O. Drawer 0, University, AL 35486; 205-349-2852; **Highways:** Highway Department, Bureau of Planning & Programming, Room 313, 11 South Union Street, Montgomery, AL 36130; 205-832-6128; **Historic Preservation:** Historical Commission, 725 Monroe Street, Montgomery, AL 36130; 205-261-3190; **Tourism:** Bureau of Publicity & Information, Room 403, State Highway Building, Montgomery, AL 36130; 205-832-5510, 800-633-5761.

Alaska:
Archives: Department of Administration, Pouch C, State Office Building, Juneau, AK 99811; 907-465-2275; **Aviation:** Division of Aviation, Department of Public Works, Pouch 6900, Anchorage, AK 99502; 907-243-1111; **Fish and Game:** Department of Fish and Game, P.O. Box 3-2000, Juneau, AK 99802; 907-465-4100; **Geology:** Division of Geological and Geophysical Surveys, 3001 Porcupine Dr., Anchorage, AK 99510; 907-274-9681; **Highways:** Department of Highways, P.O. Box 1467, Juneau, AK 99802; 907-364-2121; **Historic Preservation:** Historical Commission, Old City Hall, Suite 207, 524 West 4th Avenue, Anchorage, AK 99501; 907-274-6222; **Natural Resources:** Department of Natural Resources, Pouch M, Juneau, AK 99811; 907-465-2400; **Tourism:** Division of Tourism, Department of Commerce and Economic Development, Pouch E, Juneau, AK 99811; 907-465-2010.

Arizona:
Archives: Department of Library, Archives and Public Records, State Capitol, 1700 West Washington, Phoenix, AZ 85007; 602-255-4035; **Eco-nomic Development:** Office of Economic Planning and Development, Room 505, 1700 West Washington, Phoenix, AZ 85007; 602-255-5371; **Fish and Game:** Department of Fish and Game, P.O. Box 9099, Phoenix, AZ 85068; 602-942-3000; **Highways:** Department of Transportation, Room 118, 206 South 17th Avenue, Phoenix, AZ 85007; 501-255-7011; **Historic Preservation:** State Parks Board, 1688 West Adams, Room 106, Phoenix, AZ 85007; 602-255-4174; **Mining:** Bureau of Mines, 845 North Park Avenue, Tucson, AZ 85719; 602-884-2733; **Tourism:** State Office of Tourism, 1480 East Bethany Home Road, Phoenix, AZ 85014; 602-255-3618.

Arkansas:
Archives: Natural and Cultural Heritage Department, 200 Heritage Center, 225 East Markham, Little Rock, AR 72201; 501-371-2539; **Aviation:** Division of Aeronautics, Adams Field-Old Terminal Building, Little Rock, AR 72202; 501-376-6781; **Fish and Game:** Game and Fish Commission, 2 Natural Resources Drive, Little Rock, AR 72205; 501-223-6305; **Geology:** Geological Commission, 3815 West Roosevelt Road, Little Rock, AR 72204, 501-371-1488; **Highways:** Department of Highways and Transportation, P.O. Box 2261, Little Rock, AR 72203; 501-569-2211; **Historic Preservation:** Department of Natural and Cultural Heritage, 200 Heritage Center, 225 East Markham, Little Rock, AR 72201; 501-371-2763; **Tourism:** Department of Parks and Recreation, Capitol Mall, Little Rock, AR 72201; 501-371-1087.

California:
Archives: Secretary of State, 1230 J Street, Sacramento, CA 95814; 916-445-4293; **Aviation:** Division of Aeronautics, Department of Transportation, 1120 N Street, Sacramento, CA 95814; 916-322-2090; **Fish and Game:** Office of Fish and Game, 1416 9th Street, Sacramento, CA 95814; 916-445-3535; **Geology:** Office of Conservation, 1416 9th Street, Sacramento, CA 95814; 916-445-1923; **Highways:** Department of Trans-

portation, 1120 N Street, Sacramento, CA 95814; 916-445-2201; **Natural Resources:** Department of Conservation, 1416 9th Street, Sacramento, CA 95814; 916-322-1080; **Water:** California Department of Water Conservation, Map Information Office, Division of Planning, P.O. Box 388, Sacramento, CA 95802; 916-445-9259.

Colorado:
Archives: Department of Administration, 1525 Sherman Street, Denver, CO 80203; 303-866-2055; **Fish and Game:** Department of Natural Resources, 6060 Broadway, Denver, CO 80216; 303-297-1192; **Geology:** Geological Survey, Department of Natural Resources, Room 715, 1313 Sherman Street, Denver, CO 80203; 303-866-2611; **Highways:** Mapping Unit, Planning & Research Division, Department of Highways, 4201 East Arkansas Avenue, Denver, CO 80222; 303-757-9261; **Historic Preservation:** Department of Higher Education, Colorado Heritage Center, 1300 Broadway, Denver, CO 80203; 303-866-2136; **Parks:** Department of Natural Resources, 1313 Sherman Street, Denver, CO 80203; 303-866-3437; **Planning:** Office of the State Cartographer, Division of Planning, Room 520, State Capitol Building, Denver, CO 80203; 303-866-3386; **Tourism:** Department of Local Affairs, 1313 Sherman Street, Denver, CO 80203; 303-866-2205.

Connecticut:
Archives: State Library, 231 Capitol Avenue, Hartford, CT 06106; 203-566-4770; **Aviation:** Department of Transportation, Bureau of Aeronautics, Brainard Airport, Hartford, CT 06114; 203-566-4417; **Geology:** Geological & Natural History Survey, Department of Environmental Protection, Capitol Building, Hartford, CT 06106; 203-566-3540; **Highways:** Department of Transportation, 24 Wolcott Hill Road, Wethersfield, CT 06109; 203-566-3477; **Historic Preservation:** Historical Commission, 59 South Prospect Street, Hartford, CT 06106; 203-566-3005; **Natural Resources:** Department of Environmental Protection, Natural Resources Center, Room 561, State Office Building, Hartford, CT 06115; 203-566-2110; **Tourism:** Department of Economic Development, 210 Washington Street, Hartford, CT 06106; 203-566-2496.

Delaware:
Archives: Historical and Cultural Affairs, P.O. Box 1401, Hall of Records, Dover, DE 19903; 302-736-5315; **Aviation:** Department of Transportation, P.O. Box 778, Dover, DE 19903; 302-736-4593; **Fish and Game:** Department of Natural Resources, 89 Kings Highway, P.O. Box 1401, Dover, DE 19903; 736-5295; **Geology:** Geological Survey, University of Delaware, 101 Penny Hall, Newark, DE 19711; 302-738-2833; **Highways:** Department of Transportation, P.O. Box 778, Dover, DE 19901; 302-678-4301; **Historic Preservation:** Department of State, P.O. Box 1401, Hall of Records, Dover, DE 19903; 302-736-5313; **Parks:** Department of Natural Resources, 89 Kings Highway, P.O. Box 1401, Dover, DE 19903; 736-4401.

District of Columbia:
Archives: Commission on the Arts and Humanities, 1111 E Street NW, Washington, DC 20004; 202-724-5613; **Historic Preservation:** Historic Preservation Office, 614 H Street NW, Washington, DC; 202-673-7665; **Parks:** Department of Recreation, 3149 16th Street NW, Washington, DC 20010; 202-673-7665; **Transportation and Tourism:** D.C. Map Information Center, 1400 Pennsylvania Avenue NW, Washington, DC 20004; 202-789-7000.

Florida:
Archives: Division of Archives, History, and Records Management, Gray Building, Room 303, Tallahassee, FL 32301; 904-488-1480; **Aviation:** Department of Transportation, Hayden Burns Building, 605 Suwannee Street, Tallahassee, FL 32304; 904-488-8444; **Fish and Game:** Game and Fresh Water Fish Commission, 620 South Meridian Street, Tallahassee, FL 32301; 904-488-2975; **Geology:** Department of Natural Resources, Bureau of Geology, 903 West Tennessee Street, Tallahassee, FL 32304; 904-488-4191; **Highways:** Department of Transportation, Hayden Burns Building, 605 Suwannee Street, Tallahassee, FL 32304; 904-488-6721; **Historic Preservation:** Division of Archives, History, and Records Management, Gray Building, Room 303, Tallahassee, FL 32301; 904-488-1480; **Parks:** Department of Natural Resources, Division of Recreation & Parks, 3900 Commonwealth Blvd., Tallahassee, FL 32303; 904-488-6131; **Tourism:** Division of Tourism, Department of Commerce, Collins Building, Suite 510C, Tallahassee, FL 32301; 904-488-5606.

Georgia:
Archives: Archives and History Department, 330 Capitol Avenue SE, Atlanta, GA 30334; 404-656-2359; **Economic Development:** Department of Industry & Trade, P.O. Box 1776, Atlanta, GA 30301, 404-656-3545; **Fish and Game:** Department of Natural Resources, 270 Washington Street SW, Atlanta, GA 30334; 404-656-3523; **Geology:** Department of Natural Resources, 270 Washington Street SW, Atlanta, GA 30334; 404-656-3214; **Highways:** Department of Transportation, Division of Programming & Planning, 2 Capitol Square SW, Atlanta, GA 30334; 404-656-5206; **Historic Preservation:** Department of Natural Resources, 270 Washington Street SW, Atlanta, GA 30334; 404-656-3500; **Natural Resources:** Department of Natural Resources, 270 Washington Street SW, Atlanta, GA 30334; 404-656-2754; **Parks:** Department of Natural Resources, 270 Washington Street SW, Atlanta, GA 30334; 404-656-2754; **Tourism:** Department of Industry and Trade, 1400 North Omni International, P.O. Box 1776, Atlanta, GA 30301; 404-656-3553.

Hawaii:
Archives: Archives, Iolani Palace Grounds, Honolulu, HI 96813; 808-548-2355; **Aviation:** Division of Airports, Honolulu International Airport, Honolulu, HI 96819; 808-548-4711; **Fish and Game:** Department of Land and Natural Resources, P.O. Box 621, Honolulu, HI 96809; 808-548-4000; **Geology:** Office of Water and Land Development, Box 373, Honolulu, HI 96809; 808-548-7643; **Highways:** Hawaii Department of Transportation, 869 Punchbowl Street, Honolulu, HI 96813; **Historic Preservation:** Department of Land and Natural Resources, P.O. Box 621, Honolulu, HI 96809; 808-548-6408; **Natural Resources:** Department of Land and Natural Resources, P.O. Box 621, Honolulu, HI 96809; 808-548-6550; **Parks:** Department of Land and Natural Resources, P.O. Box 621, Honolulu, HI 96809; 808-548-2536; **Tourism:** Hawaii Visitors Bureau, 2270 Kalakaua Avenue, Suite 801, Honolulu, HI 96815; 808-923-1811.

Idaho:
Archives: Archives, 325 West State Street, Boise, ID 83702; 208-334-3356; **Aviation:** Department of Transportation, 3311 West State Street, P.O. Box 7129, Boise, ID 83707; 208-334-3183; **Fish and**

Game: Department of Fish and Game, P.O. Box 25, 600 South Walnut, Boise, ID 83707; 208-334-5159; **Geology:** Department of Lands, University of Idaho, Moscow, ID 83720; 208-885-7991; **Historic Preservation:** State Department of Education, 610 North Julia Davis Drive, Boise, ID 83706; 208-334-2120; **Parks:** Department of Parks and Recreation, State House Mail, 2177 Warm Springs Avenue, Boise, ID 83720; 208-334-2154; **Tourism:** Division of Tourism and Industrial Development, Room 108, State Capitol Building, Boise, ID 83720; 208-334-3416.

Illinois:
Archives: Secretary of State, State House, Room 213, Springfield, IL 62756; 217-782-4682; **Aviation:** Department of Transportation, 1 Langhorn Bond Drive, Capitol Airport, Springfield, IL 62706; 217-753-4400; **Fish and Game:** Department of Conservation, 600 North Grand Avenue West, Springfield, IL 62706; 217-782-6424; **Geology:** Illinois State Geological Survey, Natural Resources Building, Urbana, IL 61801; 217-344-1481; **Historic Preservation:** Department of Conservation, Lincoln Towers, Suite 100, Springfield, IL 62706; 217-782-6302; **Parks:** Department of Conservation, Lincoln Towers, Suite 100, Springfield, IL 62706; 217-782-6302; **Tourism:** Department of Commerce and Community Affairs, 310 South Michigan Avenue, Chicago, IL 60604; 312-793-4732.

Indiana:
Archives: State Library, 140 North Senate Avenue, Indianapolis, IN 46206; 317-232-3737; **Aviation:** Department of Transportation, 143 West Market Street, Suite 300, Indianapolis, IN 46204; 317-232-1470; **Geology:** Publications Section, Geological Survey, 611 North Walnut Grove, Bloomington, IN 47401; 812-335-2862; **Fish and Game:** Department of Natural Resources, State Office Building, Indianapolis, IN 46204; 317-232-4080; **Highways:** State Highway Commission, State Office Building, 100 North Senate Avenue, Indianapolis, IN 46204; 317-232-5526; **Historic Preservation:** Historical Bureau, 140 North Senate Avenue, Room 408, Indianapolis, IN 46204; 317-232-2537; **Parks:** Division of State Parks, Department of Natural Resources, State Office Building, 100 North Senate Avenue, Indianapolis, IN 46204; 317-232-4125;

Tourism: Department of Commerce, 1 North Capitol, Indianapolis, IN 46204; 317-232-8870.

Iowa:
Archives and **Historic Preservation:** Historical Department, East 12th Street and Grand, Des Moines, IA 50319; 515-281-5113; **Aviation:** Department of Transportation, Aeronautics Building, Des Moines, IA 50319; 515-281-4289; **Fish and Game:** Conservation Commission, Wallace State Office Building, Des Moines, IA 50319; 515-281-5154; **Geology:** Geological Survey, 123 North Capitol Street, Iowa City, IA 52242; 319-338-1267; **Natural Resources:** Conservation Commission, Wallace State Office Building, Des Moines, IA 50319; 515-281-5385; **Parks:** Conservation Commission, Wallace State Office Building, Des Moines, IA 50319; 515-281-5886; **Tourism:** Travel Development Division, Development Commission, 250, Jewett Building, Des Moines, IA 50309; 515-281-3100.

Kansas:
Archives: State Historical Society, 120 West 10th, Memorial Building, Topeka, KS 66612; 913-296-4792; **Aviation:** Department of Transportation, State Office Building, Topeka, KS 66603; 913-296-2553; **Fish and Game:** Fish and Game Commission, Route 2, Box 54A, Pratt, KS 67124; 316-672-5911; **Geology:** Geological Survey, 1930 Constant Avenue, University of Kansas, Lawrence, KS 66044; 913-864-3965; **Parks and Recreation:** Parks and Resources Authority, P.O. Box 977, 503 Kansas Avenue, Topeka, KS 66603; 913-296-2281; **Tourism:** Tourism Division, Department of Economic Development, 400 West 8th Street, 5th Floor, Topeka, KS 66683; 913-296-2009.

Kentucky:
Archives: Department of Libraries and Archives, Department 537, Frankfort, KY 40602; 502-564-7433; **Aviation:** Kentucky Division of Aeronautics, 419 Ann Street, Frankfort, KY 40506; 502-564-4480; **Fish and Game:** Tourism Cabinet, Capitol Plaza Tower, 24th Floor, Frankfort, KY 40601; 502-564-3400; **Geology:** Geological Survey, University of Kentucky, 307 Mineral Industries Building, 120 Graham Avenue, Lexington, KY 40506; 606-258-5863; **Highways:** Department of Transportation, State Office Building, Frankfort, KY 40601; 502-564-4890; **Historic Preservation:** Historical Soci-

ety, Old Capitol Annex, Department H, Frankfort, KY 40602; 502-564-3016; **Tourism:** Tourism Cabinet, Capitol Plaza Tower, 24th Floor, Frankfort, KY 40601; 502-564-4930.

Louisiana:
Archives: Department of State, P.O. Box 94125, Baton Rouge, LA 70803; 504-342-1206; **Aviation:** Department of Transportation and Development, Office of Aviation, P.O. Box 94245, Baton Rouge, LA 70803; 504-925-7730; **Fish and Game:** Department of Wildlife and Fisheries, P.O. Box 15570, Baton Rouge, LA 70895; 504-925-3625; **Geology:** Geological Survey, Box G. University Station, Baton Rouge, LA 70893; 504-342-6754; **Historic Preservation:** Department of Culture, Recreation and Tourism, P.O. Box 44247, Baton Rouge, LA 70804; 504-342-6682; **Natural Resources:** Department of Natural Resources, P.O. Box 44396, Baton Rouge, LA 70803; 504-342-4500; **Tourism:** Department of Culture, Recreation and Tourism, P.O. Box 44291, Baton Rouge, LA 70804; 504-925-3853.

Maine:
Archives: Secretary of State, Statehouse, Room 223, Station 29, Augusta, ME 04333; 207-289-2451; **Aviation:** Bureau of Aeronautics, Department of Transportation, State House, Station 16, Augusta, ME 04333; 207-289-3185; **Fish and Game:** Department of Inland Fisheries and Wildlife, 284 State Street, Station 41, Augusta, ME 04333; 207-289-3371; **Geology:** Geological Survey, Department of Conservation, Station 22, ME 04333; 207-289-2801; **Highways:** Department of Transportation, Transportation Building, Augusta, ME 04333; 207-289-2551; **Historic Preservation:** Department of Educational and Cultural Services, State House Complex, Station 23, Augusta, ME 04333; 207-289-2132; **Natural Resources:** Department of Environmental Protection, State House, Station 17, Augusta, ME 04333; 207-289-2811; **Parks:** Department of Conservation, Station 22, Augusta, ME 04333; 207-289-3821; **Tourism:** Office of the Governor, State Development Office, State House, Station 1, Augusta, ME 04333; 207-289-2656.

Maryland:
Archives: General Services, 301 West Preston Street, Room 1401, Baltimore, MD 21201; 301-

383-2779; **Aviation:** State Aviation Administration, P.O. Box 8766, Baltimore-Washington International Airport, Baltimore, MD 21240; 301-859-7060; **Fish and Game:** Department of Natural Resources, Tawes State Office Building, Annapolis, MD 21401; 301-269-3776; **Geology:** Geological Survey, 711 West 40th Street, Suite 440, Baltimore, MD 21211; 301-338-7068; **Highways:** Department of Transportation, P.O. Box 8755, Baltimore, MD 21218; 301-859-7397; **Historic Preservation:** Department of Economic and Community Development, 45 Calvert Street, Annapolis, MD 21401; 301-269-2851; **Natural Resources:** Forest Service, Department of Natural Resources, Tawes State Office Building, Annapolis, MD 21401; 301-269-3041; **Parks:** Park Service, Tawes State Office Building, Annapolis, MD 21401; 301-269-3761; **Tourism:** Department of Economic and Community Development, 45 Calvert Street, Annapolis, MD 21401; 301-269-2686.

Massachusetts:
Aviation: Department of Transportation and Construction, 10 Park Plaza, Boston, MA 02108; 617-973-7000; **Archives:** Secretary of the Commonwealth, State House, Room 50, Boston, MA 02133; 617-727-2816; **Fish and Game:** Office of Environmental Management, 100 Cambridge Street, Boston, MA 02202; 617-727-3180; **Geology:** State Geologist, Department of Public Works, Room 805, 100 Nashua Street, Boston, MA 02114; 617-727-4796; **Historic Preservation:** Historical Commission, 294 Washington Street, Boston, MA 02108; 617-727-8470; **Natural Resources:** Department of Environmental Management, 100 Cambridge Street, Boston, MA 02202; 617-727-3163; **Parks:** Department of Environmental Management, Division of Forests and Parks, 100 Cambridge Street, Boston, MA 02202; 617-727-3155; **Tourism:** Department of Commerce and Development, 100 Cambridge Street, Boston, MA 02202; 617-727-3218.

Michigan:
Archives and **Historic Preservation:** State Department, Treasury Building, 1st Floor, Lansing, MI 48909; 517-373-6362; **Aviation:** Department of Transportation, Box 30050, Lansing, MI 48909; 517-373-1834; **Fish and Game:** Department of Natural Resources, Box 30028, Lansing, MI 48909;

517-373-3375; **Geology:** Department of Natural Resources, Box 30028, Lansing, MI 48909; 517-373-8014; **Highways:** Department of State Highways and Transportation, State Highways Building, 425 West Ottawa, P.O. Box 30050; Lansing, MI 48909; 517-373-2114; **Parks:** Department of Natural Resources, Parks Division, P.O. Box 30028, Lansing, MI 48909; 517-373-1270; **Tourism:** Travel Bureau, Department of Commerce, P.O. Box 30226, Lansing, MI 48909; 517-373-0670 or 800-248-5456.

Minnesota:
Archives: Historical Society Research Center, 1500 Mississippi Street, St. Paul, MN 44101; 612-296-6980; **Aviation:** Aeronautics Division, Department of Transportation, Room 417, Transportation Building, John Ireland Boulevard, St. Paul, MN 55155; 612-296-8046; **Fish and Game:** Department of Natural Resources, 658 Cedar Street, 3rd Floor, St. Paul, MN 55155; 612-296-3344; **Geology:** Geological Survey, 2642 University Avenue, St. Paul, MN 55114; 612-373-3372; **Highways:** Department of Transportation; Transportation Building, St. Paul, MN 55155; 612-296-3131; **Historic Preservation:** Historical Society, Historical Building, 690 Cedar Street, St. Paul, MN 55101; 612-296-2747; **Natural Resources:** Department of Natural Resources, 658 Cedar Street, 3rd Floor, St. Paul, MN 55155; 612-296-2549; **Parks:** State Parks and Recreation Division, Department of Natural Resources, 444 Lafayette Road, 2nd Floor, St. Paul, MN 55101; 612-296-2270; **Tourism:** Department of Energy and Economic Development, 980 American Center Building, 150 East Kellogg Boulevard, St. Paul, MN 55101; 612-296-2755.

Mississippi:
Archives: Department of Archives and History, P.O. Box 571, Jackson, MS 39205; 601-359-1424; **Aviation:** Aeronautics Commission, 400 Robert E. Lee Building, P.O. Box 5, Jackson, MS 39205; 601-359-1270; **Fish and Game:** Department of Wildlife Conservation, P.O. Box 451, Jackson, MS 39205; 601-961-5311; **Geology:** Department of Natural Resources, P.O. Box 5348, Jackson, MS 39216; 601-354-6228; **Highways:** State Highway Department, Woolfolk State Office Building, P.O. Box 1850, Jackson, MS 39205, 601-354-7142; **Historic Preservation:** Department of Archives and History,

P.O. Box 571, Jackson, MS 39205; 601-359-1424; **Natural Resources:** Department of Natural Resources, P.O. Box 20305, Jackson, MS 39209; 601-961-5000; **Parks:** Bureau of Recreation and Parks, P.O. Box 10600, Jackson, MS 39209; 601-961-5240; **Tourism:** Tourism and Public Affairs, Agricultural and Industrial Board, P.O. Box 849, Jackson, MS 39205; 601-359-3418.

Missouri:
Archives: Secretary of State, P.O. Box 778, Jefferson City, MO 65102; 314-751-3319; **Aviation:** Aviation Division, Department of Transportation, P.O. Box 1250, Jefferson City, MO 65101; **Fish and Game:** Department of Conservation, 2901 North Ten Mile Drive, P.O. Box 180, Jefferson City, MO 65102; 314-751-4115; **Geology:** Division of Geology and Land Survey, Department of Natural Resources, P.O. Box 250, Rolla, MO 65401; 314-364-1752; **Highways:** Department of Highways and Transportation, Capitol and Jefferson Streets, Jefferson City, MO 65102; 314-751-4622; **Natural Resources:** Department of Natural Resources, 1915 Southridge Plaza, Jefferson City, MO 65102; 314-751-4422; **Parks:** Department of Natural Resources, 1915 Southridge Plaza, Jefferson City, MO 65102; 314-751-2479; **Tourism:** Division of Tourism, 301 West High Street, Jefferson City, MO 65102; 314-751-4133.

Montana:
Archives: Secretary of State, State Capitol, Room 225, Helena, MT 59620; 406-444-2034; **Aviation:** Aeronautics Division, Department of Commerce, 2630 Airport Road, Helena, MT 59604; 406-444-2506; **Fish and Game:** Department of Fish, Wildlife and Parks, 1420 East 6th Avenue, Helena, MT 59620; 406-444-3186; **Geology:** Board of Oil and Gas, 2535 St. John Avenue, Billings, MT 59102; 406-656-0040; **Highways:** Information Unit, Department of Highways, 2701 Prospect, Helena, MT 59620; 406-444-6200; **Historic Preservation:** Historical Society, 225 North Roberts, Helena, MT 59620; 406-444-2694; **Natural Resources:** Department of Natural Resources and Conservation, 1520 East 6th Avenue, Helena, MT 59620; 406-444-6699; **Parks:** Department of Fish, Wildlife, and Parks, Forest Capitol Station, Helena, MT 59620; 406-444-3750; **Tourism:** Travel Promotion Unit, Department of Highways, 1424 9th Avenue, Helena, MT 59620; 406-444-2654.

Nebraska:
Archives: Historical Society, 1500 R Street, Lincoln, NE 68509; 402-471-2186; **Aviation:** Department of Aeronautics, P.O. Box 82088, Lincoln, NE 69501; 402-471-2371; **Fish and Game:** Game and Parks Commission, P.O. Box 30370, 2200 North 33rd, Lincoln, NE 68503; 402-464-0641; **Geology:** Geological Survey, Conservation and Survey Division, 113 Nebraska Hall, University of Nebraska, Lincoln, NE 68588; 402-471-3471; **Highways:** Department of Roads, P.O. Box 94759, Lincoln, NE 68509; 402-471-6012; **Historic Preservation:** Historical Society, 1500 R Street, Lincoln, NE 68509; 402-471-4745; **Parks:** Game and Parks Commission, P.O. Box 30370, 2200 North 33rd, Lincoln, NE 68503; 402-464-0641; **Tourism:** Travel and Tourism Division, Department of Economic Development, P.O. Box 94666, Lincoln, NE 68509; 402-471-3794.

Nevada:
Archives: Division of Archives and Records, Capitol Complex, Carson City, NV 89710; 702-885-5210; **Fish and Game:** Department of Wildlife, P.O. Box 10678, Reno, NV 89520; 702-789-0500; **Geology:** Department of Minerals, 400 West King Street, Suite 106, Carson City, NV 89710; 702-885-5050; **Highways:** Department of Highways, 1263 South Stewart Street, Carson City, NV 89712; 702-887-5400; **Historic Preservation:** Conservation and Natural Resources Department, 201 South Fall Street, Carson City, NV 89710; 702-885-5138; **Natural Resources:** Conservation and Natural Resources Department, 201 South Fall Street, Carson City, NV 89710; 702-885-4360; **Tourism:** Travel and Tourism Division, Department of Economic Development, Capitol Complex, Carson City, NV 98710; 702-885-4322, 800-992-0900.

New Hampshire:
Archives: Secretary of State, State House, Room 204, Concord, NH 03301; 603-271-2236; **Aviation:** Aeronautics Commission, Concord Airport, Concord, NH 03301; 603-271-2551; **Fish and Game:** Department of Fish and Game, 34 Bridge Street, Concord, NH 03301; 603-271-3512; **Geology:** Department of Resources and Economic Development, Office of State Geologist, 117 James Hall, University of New Hampshire, Durham, NH 03824; 603-862-1216; **Highways:** Department of Public

Works and Highways, John O. Morton Building, 85 Loudon Road, Concord, NH 03301; 603-271-3734; **Historic Preservation:** Department of Resources and Economic Development, 105 Loudon Road, P.O. Box 856, Concord, NH 03301; 603-271-3483; **Natural Resources:** Department of Resources and Economic Development, 105 Loudon Road, P.O. Box 856, Concord, NH 03301; 603-271-2411; **Parks:** Department of Resources and Economic Development, 105 Loudon Road, P.O. Box 856, Concord, NH 03301; 603-271-3254; **Tourism:** Office of Vacation Travel, P.O. Box 856, State House Annex, Concord, NH 03301; 603-271-2666.

New Jersey:
Archives: 2300 Stuyvesant Avenue, CN 300, Trenton, NJ 08625; 609-633-7373; **Aviation:** Department of Transportation, 1035 Parkway Avenue, Trenton, NJ 08625; 609-292-3020; **Fish and Game:** Department of Environmental Protection, Labor and Industry Building, Room 802, CN 402, Trenton, NJ 08625; 609-292-9410; **Geology:** Bureau of Geology and Topography, Map and Publication Sales Office, P.O. Box 2809, Trenton, NJ 08625; 609-292-2578; **Highways:** Department of Transportation, 1035 Parkway Avenue, Trenton, NJ 08625; 609-292-3535; **Historic Preservation:** Historical Commission, 113 West State Street, CN 305, Trenton, NJ 08625; 609-292-6062; **Parks:** Department of Environmental Protection, Labor and Industry Building, Room 802, CN 402, Trenton, NJ 08625; 609-292-2733; **Tourism:** Department of Commerce and Economic Development, 1 West State Street, Trenton, NJ 08625; 609-292-2496.

New Mexico:
Archives: Records and Archives Center, 404 Montezuma Avenue, Santa Fe, NM 87503; 505-827-8860; **Aviation:** Department of Aviation, P.O. Box 1028, PERA Building, Santa Fe, NM 87503; 505-827-4590; **Fish and Game:** Department of Natural Resources, Villagra Building, Santa Fe, NM 87503; 505-827-7899; **Geology:** Energy and Minerals Department, 525 Camino de los Marquez, Santa Fe, NM 87503; 505-827-5970; **Highways:** Department of Transportation, P.O. Box 1028, PERA Building, Santa Fe, NM 87503; 505-827-4651; **Natural Resources:** Department of Natural Resources, Villagra Building, Santa Fe, NM 87503; 505-827-7835; **Parks:** Department of Natural Resources,

Villagra Building, Santa Fe, NM 87503; 505-827-7465; **Tourism:** Economic Development and Tourism Department, Bataan Memorial Building, Santa Fe, NM 87503; 505-827-6238.

New York:
Aviation: Department of Transportation, State Campus, 1220 Washington Avenue, Albany, NY 12232; 518-457-4422; **Fish and Game:** Department of Environmental Conservation, 50 Wolf Road, Albany, NY 12232; 518-457-5690; **Geology:** State Geological Survey, State Science Service, Cultural Education Center, Rm 3140, Albany, NY 12230; 518-457-7480; **Highways:** Map Information Unit (NCIC State Affiliate), Department of Transportation, State Campus, 1220 Washington Avenue, Albany, NY 12232; 518-457-3555; **Historic Preservation:** Office of Historic Preservation, Agency Building No. 1, Empire State Plaza, Albany, NY 12238; 518-474-0468; **Natural Resources:** Department of Environmental Conservation, 50 Wolf Road, Albany, NY 12232; 518-457-6934; **Parks:** Office of Parks and Recreation, Agency Building No. 1, Empire State Plaza, Albany, NY 12238; 518-474-0439; **Tourism:** Travel Bureau, Department of Commerce, 99 Washington Avenue, Albany, NY 12245; 518-473-0715.

North Carolina:
Archives: Department of Cultural Resources, 109 East Jones Street, Raleigh, NC 27611; 919-733-7305; **Aviation:** Division of Aeronautics, Department of Transportation, P.O. Box 25201, Raleigh, NC 27611; 919-733-2491; **Fish and Game:** Department of Natural Resources and Community Development, 512 North Salisbury Street, Raleigh, NC 27611; 919-733-4984; **Geology:** Department of Natural Resources and Community Development, 512 North Salisbury Street, Raleigh, NC 27611; 919-733-3833; **Highways:** Department of Transportation, P.O. Box 25201, Raleigh, NC 27611; 919-733-2520; **Historic Preservation:** Department of Cultural Resources, 109 East Jones Street, Raleigh, NC 27611; 919-733-4763; **Natural Resources:** Department of Natural Resources and Community Development, 512 North Salisbury Street, Raleigh, NC 27611; 919-733-4984; **Parks:** Department of Natural Resources and Community Development, 512 North Salisbury Street, Raleigh, NC 27611; 919-733-4181; **Tourism:**

Department of Commerce, 430 North Salisbury Street, Raleigh, NC 27611; 919-733-4171.

North Dakota:
Archives and **Historic Preservation:** Historical Society, North Dakota Heritage Center, Bismarck, ND 58505; 701-224-2667; **Aviation:** Aeronautics Commission, P.O. Box 5020, Bismarck, ND 58502; 701-224-2748; **Fish and Game:** Department of Fish and Game, 2121 Lovett Avenue, Bismarck, ND 58505; 701-224-2180; **Geology:** Geological Survey, University Station, Grand Forks, ND 58201; 701-777-2231; **Highways:** Highway Department, State Highway Building, Capitol Grounds, Bismarck, ND 58505; 701-224-2525; **Parks:** Department of Parks and Recreation, 1424 West Century Avenue, Bismarck, ND 58501; 701-224-4887; **Tourism:** Economic Development Commission, Liberty Building, Bismarck, ND 58505; 701-224-2527.

Ohio:
Archives and **Historic Preservation:** Historical Society, 1985 Velma Avenue, Columbus, OH 43211; 614-466-1500; **Aviation:** Department of Transportation, 25 South Front Street, Columbus, OH 43215; 614-466-7120; **Fish and Game:** Department of Natural Resources, Fountain Square, Columbus, OH 43224; 614-265-6305; **Geology:** Department of Natural Resources, Division of Geologic Survey, Fountain Square, Building B, Columbus, OH 43224; 614-265-6605; **Highways:** Department of Transportation, Room B100, 25 South Front Street, Columbus, OH 43215; 614-466-2335; **Natural Resources:** Department of Natural Resources, Fountain Square, Columbus, OH 43224; 614-265-6877; **Parks:** Division of Parks, Department of Natural Resources, Fountain Square, Columbus, OH 43224; 614-265-6561; **Tourism:** Department of Development, 30 East Broad Street, P.O. Box 1001, Columbus, OH 43216; 614-466-8844.

Oklahoma:
Archives: Archives and Records Commission, State Capitol Building, Suite 118, Oklahoma City, OK 73105; 405-521-2502; **Aviation:** Aeronautics Commission, 200 N.E. 21st, Oklahoma City, OK 73105; 405-521-2377; **Fish and Game:** Department of Wildlife Conservation, P.O. Box 53465, Oklahoma City, OK 73152; 405-521-3851; **High-**

ways: Department of Transportation, 200 N.E. 21st Street, Oklahoma City, OK 73105; 405-521-2631; **Historic Preservation:** Historical Society, 2100 North Lincoln Boulevard, Oklahoma City, OK 73105; 405-521-2491; **Parks:** Department of Tourism and Recreation, 500 Will Rogers Building, Oklahoma City, OK 73105; 405-521-2413; **Tourism:** Department of Tourism and Recreation, 500 Will Rogers Building, Oklahoma City, OK 73105; 405-521-2413.

Oregon:
Archives: Archives, 1005 Broadway NE, Salem, OR 97310; 503-378-4241; **Aviation:** Aeronautics Division, 3040 25th Street SE, Salem, OR 97310; 503-378-4880; **Fish and Game:** Department of Fish and Wildlife, 506 SW Mill Street, P.O. Box 3503, Portland, OR 97208; 503-229-5406; **Geology:** Department of Geology and Mineral Industries, 1005 State Office Building, Portland, OR 97201; 503-229-5580; **Highways:** Department of Transportation, 135 Transportation Building, Salem, OR 97310; 503-378-6388; **Natural Resources:** Office of the Governor, State Capitol Building, Salem, OR 97310; 503-378-3981; **Parks:** Department of Parks and Recreation, 525 Trade Street SE, Salem, OR 97310; 503-378-5019; **Tourism:** Travel Information Council, 7420 SW Hunziker Road, Plaza 217E, Tigard, OR 97223; 503-229-5275.

Pennsylvania:
Archives: Historical and Museum Commission, P.O. Box 1026, Harrisburg, PA 17108; 717-787-3051; **Aviation:** Bureau of Aviation, Department of Transportation, Capitol City Airport, New Cumberland, PA 17070; 717-787-5574; **Fish and Game:** Game Commission, 8000 Dairy Street, P.O. Box 1567, Harrisburg, PA 17105; 717-787-3633; **Geology:** Department of Environmental Resources, Bureau of Topographic and Geological Survey, 913 Executive House, 101 South 2nd Street, Harrisburg, PA 17120; 717-787-2169; **Highways:** Department of Transportation, Room 912, Transportation and Safety Building, Commonwealth and Forester Street, Harrisburg, PA 17120; 717-787-5574; **Historic Preservation:** Historical and Museum Commission, P.O. Box 1026, Harrisburg, PA 17108; 717-787-2891; **Natural Resources:** Department of Environmental Resources, P.O. Box 2063, Harrisburg, PA 17120;

717-787-2814; **Tourism:** Bureau of Travel Development, Room 206, Department of Commerce, Forum Building, Harrisburg, PA 17120; 717-787-5453.

Puerto Rico:
Tourism: Puerto Rico Department of Transportation and Public Works, Minillas Governmental Center, Box 8218, G.P.O. San Juan, Puerto Rico 00910; 809-726-4270.

Rhode Island:
Archives: Secretary of State, State House, Room 218, Providence, RI 02903; 401-277-2353; **Aviation:** Department of Transportation, Green Airport, Warwick, RI 02886; 401-737-4000; **Fish and Game:** Department of Environmental Management, 83 Park Street, Providence, RI 02903; 401-789-3094; **Geology:** Department of Environmental Management, 75 Davis Street, Providence, RI 02908; 401-277-6820; **Highways:** Department of Transportation, State Office Building, Smith St., Providence, RI 02903; 401-277-2481; **Historic Preservation:** Historical Preservation Commission, 150 Benefit Street, Providence, RI 02903; 401-277-2678; **Natural Resources:** Department of Environmental Management, 83 Park Street, Providence, RI 02903; 401-277-2771; **Parks:** Department of Environmental Management, 83 Park Street, Providence, RI 02903; 401-277-2635; **Tourism:** Tourist Promotion Division, Department of Economic Development, 7 Jackson Walkway, Providence, RI 02903; 401-277-2601, 800-556-2484 (Northeastern U.S.).

South Carolina:
Archives and **Historic Preservation:** Department of Archives and History, 1430 Senate Street, P.O. Box 11669, Columbia, SC 29211; 803-758-5816; **Aviation:** Aeronautics Commission, Columbia Metropolitan Airport, Box 1769, Columbia, SC 29202; 803-758-2766; **Fish and Game:** Department of Wildlife and Marine Resources, P.O. Box 167, Columbia, SC 29202; 803-758-0007; **Geology:** Research and Statistical Services, 337 Dennis Building, 1000 Assembly Street, Columbia, SC 29201; 803-758-6431; **Highways:** Department of Highways and Public Transportation, State Highway Building, P.O. Box 191, Columbia, SC 29202; 803-758-2716; **Natural Resources:** Land Resources Conservation Commission, 2221 Devine Street, Columbia, SC 29205; 803-758-2823; **Parks:** Department of Parks, Recreation and Tourism, 1205 Pendleton Street, Columbia, SC 29201; 803-758-7507; **Tourism:** Department of Parks, Recreation and Tourism, 1205 Pendleton Street, Columbia, SC 29201; 803-758-2536.

South Dakota:
Archives: Historical Resource Center, 500 East Capitol Avenue, Pierre, SD 57501; 605-773-3615; **Fish and Game:** Department of Game, Fish, and Parks, 445 East Capitol Avenue, Pierre, SD 57501; 605-773-3387; **Geology:** Geological Survey, Science Center, University of South Dakota, Vermillion, SD 57069; 605-677-5227; **Highways:** Department of Transportation, State Highway Building, Pierre, SD 57501; 605-773-3265; **Historic Preservation:** Education and Cultural Affairs Department, 700 North Illinois, Pierre, SD 57501; 605-773-3458; **Natural Resources:** Department of Water and Natural Resources, 523 East Capitol Avenue, Pierre, SD 57501; 605-773-3151; **Parks:** Department of Game, Fish, and Parks, 445 East Capitol Avenue, Pierre, SD 57501; 605-773-3391; **Tourism:** Department of State Development, P.O. Box 6000, Capitol Lake Plaza, Pierre, SD 57501; 605-773-3331.

Tennessee:
Archives: Library and Archives, 403 7th Avenue North, Nashville, TN 37219; 615-741-2451; **Aviation:** Department of Transportation, James K. Polk Building, Suite 700, Nashville, TN 37219; 615-741-3227; **Fish and Game:** Wildlife Resources Agency, P.O. Box 40727, Melrose Station, Nashville, TN 37204; 615-360-0552; **Geology:** Department of Conservation, Division of Geology, 701 Broadway, Nashville, TN 37203; 615-742-6691; **Highways:** Department of Transportation, 807 Highway Building, Nashville, TN 37219; 615-741-8481; **Historic Preservation:** Department of Conservation, 701 Broadway, Nashville, TN 37203; 615-742-6719; **Natural Resources:** Department of Conservation, 701 Broadway, Nashville, TN 37203; 615-742-6749; **Parks:** Division of State Parks, Department of Conservation, 701 Broadway, Nashville, TN 37203; 615-742-6656; **Tourism:** Department of Tourist Development, P.O. Box 23170, Nashville, TN 37223; 615-741-1904.

Texas:
Archives: Library and Archives Commission, P.O. Box 12927, Capitol Station, Austin, TX 78711; 512-475-2445; **Aviation:** Aeronautics Commission, P.O. Box 12607, Capitol Station, Austin, TX 78711; 512-475-9262; **Fish and Game:** Department of Parks and Wildlife, 4200 Smith School Road, Austin, TX 78744; 512-479-4866; **Geology:** Bureau of Economic Geology, University of Texas at Austin, University Station, Box X, Austin, TX 78712; 512-471-1534; **Highways:** Travel and Information Division, Department of Highways and Public Transportation, 11th and Brazos Streets, Austin, TX 78701; 512-475-2877; **Historic Preservation:** Historical Commission, P.O. Box 12276, Austin, TX 78711; 512-475-3092; **Parks:** Department of Parks and Wildlife, 4200 Smith School Road, Austin, TX 78744; 512-479-4866; **Tourism:** Tourist Development Agency, P.O. Box 12008, Capitol Station, Austin, TX 78711; 512-475-4326.

Utah:
Archives: Administrative Services, State Office Building, Room 2100, Salt Lake City, UT 84114; 801-533-5250; **Aviation:** Transportation Commission, 4501 South 2700 West Street, Salt Lake City, UT 84119; 801-533-5057; **Fish and Game:** Division of Wildlife Resources, 1596 West North Temple, Salt Lake City, UT 84116; 801-533-9333; **Geology:** Geological and Mineral Survey, Department of Natural Resources, 606 Black Hawk Way, Salt Lake City, UT 84108; 801-581-6831; **Highways:** Department of Transportation, 612 State Office Building, Salt Lake City, UT 84114; 801-965-4113; **Historic Preservation:** Community and Economic Development, 300 Rio Grande, Salt Lake City, UT 84101; 801-533-5755; **Natural Resources:** Department of Natural Resources and Energy, 1636 West North Temple, Salt Lake City, UT 84116; 801-533-5356; **Parks:** Department of Natural Resources and Energy, 1636 West North Temple, Salt Lake City, UT 84116; 801-533-6011; **Tourism:** Travel Council, Council Hall, Capitol Hill, Salt Lake City, UT 84114; 801-533-5681.

Vermont:
Archives: Secretary of State, State Office Building, Montpelier, VT 05602; 802-828-3395; **Aviation:** Department of Aeronautics, State Administration Building, 133 State Street, Montpelier, VT 05602;

802-828-2657; **Fish and Game:** Department of Fish and Wildlife, 79 River Street, Heritage II Building, Montpelier, VT 05602; 802-828-3371; **Geology:** Office of State Geologist, Environment Conservation Agency, 79 River Street, Heritage I and II Buildings, Montpelier, VT 05602; 802-828-3180; **Highways:** Agency of Transportation, Planning Division, 133 State Street, Montpelier, VT 05602; 802-828-2657; **Historic Preservation:** Agency of Development and Community Affairs, 109 State Street, Montpelier, VT 05602; 802-828-3211; **Natural Resources:** Environmental Conservation Agency, 79 River Street, Heritage II Building, Montpelier, VT 05602; 802-828-3130; **Parks:** Department of Forests, Parks, and Recreation, Montpelier, VT 05602; 79 River Street, Heritage II Building, Montpelier, VT 05602; 802-828-3375; **Tourism:** Travel Division, Agency and Development and Community Affairs, 109 State Street, Montpelier, VT 05602; 802-828-3211.

Virginia:
Archives: State Library, Library Building, Richmond, VA 23219; 804-786-5579; **Aviation:** Department of Aviation, P.O. Box 7716, Richmond, VA 23231; 804-786-6284; **Fish and Game:** Game and Inland Fisheries Commission, 4010 West Broad Street, Richmond, VA 23220; 804-257-1000; **Geology:** Division of Mineral Resources, P.O. Box 3667, Charlottesville, VA 22903; 804-293-5121; **Highways:** Department of Highways and Transportation, 1401 East Broad Street, Richmond, VA 23219; 804-786-2051; **Historic Preservation:** Historic Landmarks Commission, 221 Governor Street, Richmond, VA 23219; 804-786-3143; **Natural Resources:** Department of Conservation and Economic Development, 1100 Washington Building, Richmond, VA 23219; 804-786-2121; **Parks:** Division of Parks and Recreation, 1201 Washington Building, Richmond, VA 23219; 804-786-2132; **Tourism:** State Travel Service, 9th Street Office Building, 5th Floor, Richmond, VA 23219; 804-786-2701.

Washington:
Archives: Secretary of State, Legislative Building, Olympia, WA 98504; 206-753-5485; **Aviation:** Department of Transportation, 8600 Perimeter Road, Boeing Field, Seattle, WA 98108; 206-764-4131; **Fish and Game:** Game Department, 406 General

Administration Building, Olympia, WA 98504; 206-753-5710; **Geology:** Department of Natural Resources, Public Lands Building, Olympia, WA 98504; 206-459-6372; **Highways:** Department of Transportation, Transportation Building, Olympia, WA 98504; 206-753-6054; **Historic Preservation:** Archaeology and Historic Preservation, 111 West 21st Street, Olympia, WA 98504; 206-754-1625; **Natural Resources:** Department of Natural Resources, Public Lands Building, Olympia, WA 98504; 206-753-5317; **Parks:** Parks and Recreation Commission, 7150 Clearwater Lane, Olympia, WA 98504; 206-753-5757; **Tourism:** Department of Commerce and Economic Development, 101 General Administration Building, Olympia, WA 98504; 206-753-5600.

West Virginia:
Archives and **Historic Preservation:** Department of Culture and History, Cultural Center, Capitol Complex, Charleston, WV 25403; 304-348-0230; **Aviation:** Department of Finance and Administration, State Capitol, Building 1, Room E117, Charleston, WV 25405; 304-348-3355; **Fish and Game:** Department of Natural Resources, 1800 Washington Street East, Charleston, WV 25305; 304-348-2771; **Geology:** Geological and Economic Survey, P.O. Box 879, Morgantown, WV 26507; 304-594-2331; **Highways:** Department of Highways, 1900 Washington Street East, Charleston, WV 25403; 304-348-3259; **Natural Resources:** Department of Natural Resources, 1800 Washington Street East, Charleston, WV 25305; 304-348-2754; **Parks:** Division of Parks and Recreation, Room 311, Department of Natural Resources, 1800 Washington Street East, Charleston, WV 25305; 304-348-2764; **Tourism:** Office of Economic and

Community Development, 1900 Washington Street East, Charleston, WV 25305; 304-348-2286.

Wisconsin:
Aviation: Division of Aeronautics, P.O. Box 7914, Madison, WI 53707; 608-266-1113; **Fish and Game:** Department of Natural Resources, P.O. Box 7921, 101 South Webster Street, Madison, WI 53707; 608-266-2193; **Geology:** Geological and Natural History Survey, University of Wisconsin, 1815 University Avenue, Madison, WI 53706; 608-262-1705; **Highways:** Department of Transportation, State Office Building, 4802 Sheboygan Avenue, Madison, WI 54702; 608-266-1113; **Historic Preservation:** Historical Society, 816 State Street, Madison, WI 53706; 608-262-3266; **Natural Resources:** Department of Natural Resources, P.O. Box 7921, 101 South Webster Street, Madison, WI 53707; 608-266-2185; **Tourism:** Department of Development, P.O. Box 7970, Madison, WI 53707; 608-267-9551.

Wyoming:
Archives and **Historic Preservation:** Archives, Museums, and Historical Department, Barrett Building, Cheyenne, WY 82002; 807-777-7519; **Aviation:** Aeronautics Commission, 200 East 8th Avenue, Cheyenne, WY 82002; 807-777-7481; **Fish and Game:** Department of Fish and Game, 5400 Bishop Boulevard, Cheyenne, WY 82002; 807-777-7631; **Geology:** Geological Survey, P.O. Box 3008, University Station, Laramie, WY 82071; 307-742-2054; **Parks:** Recreation Commission, Herschler Building, Cheyenne, WY 82002; 807-777-7695; **Tourism:** Travel Commission, I-25 at Etchepare Circle, Cheyenne, WY 82002; 307-777-7777.

International Map Agencies

Afghanistan:
Cartographic and Cadastral Survey Institute, Institute of Cartography, Kabul.

Albania:
Ministry of Industry and Mining, Tirane.

Algeria:
Ecole Nationale de Sciences Geodesiques, B.P. 13, Arzew; **Institute National de Cartographic,** 123 rue de Tripoli, B.P. 32 Jisseom-Dey, Algiers; **Institute des Sciences de la Terre,** Universite des Sciences et de la Technologie Houari Boumediene, B.P. 9, Dar Al Beida-Alger.

Angola:
Direccao de Servicos de Geologia e Minas, Caixa Postal 1260-C, Luanda.

Argentina:
Instituto Geografico Militar, Avenida Cabildo 301 (1426), 1426 Buenos Aires.

Australia:
Bureau of Mineral Resources, Geology, and Geophysics, P.O. Box 378; Canberra, City, A.C.T. 2601; **Department of Resources and Energy,** Box 858, Canberra, City, A.C.T. 2601.

Austria:
Bundesamt fur Eich-und Vermessungwesen, Gruppe Landesaufnahme, Krotenthallergasse 3, A-1080 Vienna; **Bundesamt Fur Eich-und Vermessungswesen,** Gruppe Kataster, Grundlagenvermessung, Staatsgrenzen, Fasangartengasse 101, A-1130 Vienna; **Bundesministerium fue Handel,** Gewerbe und Industrie, Stubenring 1, A-1011 Vienna; **Osterreichische Kommission fur die Internationale Erdmessung,** Technische Universitat Wien, Gusshausstrasse 27-29, A-1040 Vienna; **Austrian National Tourist Office,** 20th Floor, 500 Fifth Avenue, New York, NY 10010; 212-944-6880.

Bahamas:
Director of Lands and Surveys, P.O. Box N-592, Nassau; **Bahamas Tourist Office,** Suite 510, 1730 Rhode Island Avenue, NW, Washington, DC 20036.

Bangladesh:
Land Records and Survey Department, Tejgaon Industrial Area, Dhaka; **Survey of Bangladesh,** Tejgaon Industrial Area, Dhaka.

Barbados:
Barbados Board of Tourism, 800 Second Avenue, New York, NY 10017; 212-986-6516.

Belgium:
Institut Geographique National, 13 Abbaye de la Cambre, 1050 Brussels; **Ministere des Travaux Publiques,** Service de Topographie et de Photogrammetrie, 155 Rue de La Loi, 1040 Brussels; **Belgian National Tourist Office,** 745 Fifth Avenue, New York, NY 10151; 212-758-8130.

Bermuda:
Bermuda Department of Tourism, 6th Floor, 630 Fifth Avenue, New York, NY 10111-0068; 212-397-7700.

Bhutan:
Department of Trade and Industries, Thimbu.

Bolivia:
Centro de Investigacion y Applicacion de Sensores Remotes, Federico Zuazo, Esq. Reyes Ortiz, Casilla de Correo 2729, La Paz; **Instituto Geografico Militar,** Avenida Saavedra, Cuartel Miraflores, La Paz; **Servicio Geologico de Bolivia,** Federico Zuazo, Esq. Reyes Ortiz, Casilla de Correo 2729, La Paz; **Servicio de Hidrografia Naval,** Avenida Argentina 2057, Cassilla de Correo 3052, La Paz.

Botswana:
Department of Surveys and Lands, Ministry of Local Government and Lands, Private Bag 37, Gaborone; **Geological Survey Department,** Ministry of Mineral Resources and Water Affairs, Private Bag 14, Lobatse.

Brazil:
Diretoria de Geodesia e Cartografia, Instituto Brasileiro de Geografia e Estatistica (IBGE), Avenida Brasil, 15015, 21241 Rio de Janeiro, RJ; **Diretoria do Servico Geografico do Exercito,** SMU-QG Ex., Bloco F, 2 (degrees) Pav., 70630 Bra-

silia, D.F.; **Instituto de Pesquisas Espaciaais,** Caixa Postal 515, 12200 Sao Jose dos Campos, Sao Paulo, SP; **Projeto RADAM,** Av. Antonio Carlos Magalhaes, 1131, Edf. marechal Ademar de Queiroz, 4 (degrees) Andar, 40000 Salvador, BA; Brazilian Tourist Authority, 60 East 42nd Street, New York, NY 10165; 212-286-9600.

Brunei:
Survey Department of Brunei, Bandar Seri Begawan.

Bulgaria:
Academy of Sciences, Central Laboratory for Geodesy, 1, 7 Noemvri Street, Sofia 1000.

Burma:
Central Research Organization, Kanbe Road, Yankin P.O., Rangoon; **Survey Department,** Ministry of Agriculture and Forestry, Thirimingala Lana, Kaba Aye Pagoda Road, Rangoon.

Cameroon:
Centre Geographique National, B.P. 157, Ave. Monseigneur Vogt, Yaoundem; **Institut des Recherches Agricoles et Forestieres,** B.P. 2123, Younde; **Institut de Recherches Geologiques et Minieres,** B.P. 4110, Yaounde.

Canada:
Alberta Energy and Natural Resources, Renewable Resources Technical Division, Natural Resources Building, 109 Street & 99 Avenue, Edmonton, Alberta T5K 2E1; 403-427-7417; **Geological Survey of Canada,** 601 Booth Street, Ottawa, Ontario K1A 0E8; 613-994-5325; **Public Archives of Canada,** National Map Collection, 395 Wellington Street, Ottawa, Ontario K1A 0N3; 613-992-0468; **Soil Research Institute,** Cartographic Section, Central Experimental Farm, Ottawa, Ontario; 613-994-9447.

Central African Republic:
High Commission for Scientific and Technological Research, Bangui; **Office de la Recherche Scientifique et Technique,** Outre-mer, Centre de Bangui, B.P. 893, Bangui; **Ministry of Public Works and Town Development,** Bangui.

Ceylon:
Ceylon Tourist Board, Suite 714, 609 Fifth Avenue, New York, NY 10017; 212-935-0369.

Chad:
Direction du Genie Rural, B.P. 47, N'Djamena;

Direction des Mines et Petrole, B.P. 816, N'Djamena.

Chile:
Instituto Geografico Militar, Nueva Santa Isabel 1640, Santiago; **Servicio Aerofotogrametrico,** Fuerz Aerea de Chile, Casilla 67, Correo Los Cerrillos, Santiago.

China:
Remote Sensing Application, Beijing; **National Bureau of Surveying and Cartography,** Beijing; **Surveying,** Wuhan.

Colombia:
Centro Interamericano de Fotointerpretacion, Carrera 30 # 47A-57, Bogota, D.E.; **Direcion Marutima y Portuaria-Armada Nacional,** Ministerio de Defensa Nacional, CAN, Bogota, D.E.; **Instituto Geografico Agustin Codazzi,** Carrera 30 # 48-51, Apartado Aereo 6721, Bogota, D.E.

Congo:
Cadastre du Congo, B.P. 544, Brazzaville; Institut Geographique, B.P. 125, Brazzaville; Service **Topographique et du Cadastre,** Agence de Brazzaville, B.P. 125, Route du Djove, Brazzaville.

Cook Islands:
Department of Survey and Physical Planning, Secretary of Survey and Physical Planning, Raratonga.

Costa Rica:
Instituto Geografico Nacional, Apartado 2272 1000 San Jose.

Curacao:
Curacao Tourist Board, Suite 311, 400 Madison Avenue, New York, NY 10017; 212-751-8266.

Cyprus:
Department of Lands and Surveys, Ministry of the Interior, Nicosia.

Czechoslovakia:
Geodeticka a Kartograficka Sprava, [Geodetic and Cartographic Administration], Arbesovo nam. 4, Praha 5 - Smichov; **Vojensky zemepisny ustav,** [Military Geographical Institute], Rooseveltova 23, 150 01 Praha 6.

Denmark:
Geodetic Institute, Rigsdagsgaarden 7, DK-1218 Copenhagen K; **Ministry for Greenland,** Oils and

Minerals Department, Hausergade 3, DK-1128 Copenhagen K; **Danish Tourist Board,** 655 Third Avenue, New York, NY 10017; 212-949-2333.

Dominican Republic:
Instituto Geografico Universitario, Facultad de Ciencias, Universidad Autonoma de Santo Domingo.

Ecuador:
Instituto Geografico Militar, Apartado 2435, Quito.

Egypt:
Aerial Survey of Egypt, 308 El-Haram Street, Giza, Cairo; **Egyptian Remote Sensing Center,** 101 Kasr El Aini Street, Cairo; **Survey of Egypt,** Sharia El Misaha, Giza, Cairo.

El Salvador:
Instituto Geografico Nacional, Ingeniero Pablo Arnoldo Guzman, Ministerio de Obras Publicas, Avenida Juan Bertis No. 79, San Salvador; **Ministerio de Agricultura y Ganaderia,** Boulevard Los Heroes y 21 Calle Poniente, San Salvador; **Ministerio de Obras Publicas,** Palacio Nacional, San Salvador; **Servicio Hidrologico,** Direccion General de Riego y Drenaje, Ministerio de Agricultura y Ganaderia, Nueva San Salvador.

Ethiopia:
Cartography Unit, UNECA, Africa Hall, P.O. Box 3001, Addis Ababa; **Ethiopian Mapping Agency,** P.O. Box 597, Addis Ababa; **Natural Resources Division,** UNECA, Africa Hall, P.O. Box 3001, Addis Ababa.

Fiji:
Department of Lands and Survey, Ministry of Lands, Local Government and Housing, P.O. Box 2222, Government Building, Suva; **Mineral Resources Division,** Ministry of Energy and Mineral Resources, Private Mail Bag, G.P.O., Suva.

Finland:
Geodeettinen Laitos, [Geodetic Institute], Ilmalankatu 1 A, 00240 Helsinki 24; **Maanmittaushallitus,** [National Board of Survey], PL 84, 00521 Helsinki 52; **Maanmittaushallituken Karttapaino,** [National Board of Survey, Publication Division], PL 85, 00521 Helsinki 52; Finland National Tourist Office, 655 Third Avenue, New York, NY 10017; 212-949-2333.

France:
Centre d'Etude et de Realisations Cartographiques et Geographiques, 191, rue St. Jacques, 75114 Paris; **Laboratoire d'Information et de Documentation en Geographie,** 191, rue St. Jacques, 75114 Paris; **Institut Geographique National,** 136 bis, rue de Grenelle, 75700 Paris; French Government Tourist Office, 610 Fifth Avenue, New York, NY 10020; 212-757-1125.

Gabon:
Bureau de Recherches Geologiques et Minieres, B.P. 175, Libreville.

Gambia:
Survey Department, Half Die, Banjul.

Ghana:
Buildings and Roads Research Institute, Council of Scientific and Industrial Research, P.O. Box 40, University Post Office, Kumasi; **Ghana Geographical Association,** University of Ghana, Legon.

Greece:
Hellenic Army Geographic Service, 3 Evelpidon Street, GR-113 62 Athens; **Greek National Tourist Organization,** 645 Fifth Avenue, New York, NY 10022; 212-421-5777.

Guatemala:
Instituto Geografico Militar, Avenida de las Americas 5-76, Zona 13.

Guinea:
Ministry of Mines and Geology, B.P. 295, Conakry.

Guinea-Bissau:
Ministry of Natural Resources, Caixa Postal 399, Bissau.

Guyana:
Lands and Surveys Department, Ministry of Agriculture, Upper Hadfield Street, Georgetown.

Haiti:
Service de Geodesie et de Cartographie, Boulevard Harry Truman, Cite de l'Exposition, Port-au-Prince; **Haitian Government Tourist Bureau,** 2311 Massachusetts Avenue, NW, Washington, DC 20045; 202-328-1888, 202-328-4090.

Honduras:
Direccion General de Minas e Hidrocarbouros, Ministerio de Recursos Naturales, Boulevard Cen-

tro America, Tegucigalpa, D.C.; **Instituto Geografico Nacional,** Apartado Postal 758, Barrio La Balsa, Comayaguela, D.C.; Oficina Nacional de Programa Catastral, Edificio Didemo, 4 Piso, Tegucigalpa, D.C.

Hong Kong:
Hong Kong Tourist Association, Suite 200, 1000 Connecticut Avenue, NW, Washington, DC 20036; 202-833-9393.

Hungary:
Magyar Tudomanyos Akademia, Geodeziai es Geofizkai Kutato Intezet, [Research Institute for Geodesy and Geophysics], H-9400 Sopron, Muzeum u. 6; **MEM Orszagos Foldugyi es Terkepeszeti Hivatal,** [National Cadaster and Cartography Bureau], H-1055 Budapest, V., Kossuth Lajos ter 11.

Iceland:
Iceland Geodetic Survey, Laugavegi 178, 105; **Icelandic National Tourist Board,** 655 Third Avenue, New York, NY 10017; 212-949-2333.

India:
Geodetic and Geophysical Surveys, Survey of India, Dehra Dun 248001; **Indian Photo-Interpretation Institute,** 4, Kalidas Road, P.B. No. 235, Dehra Dun, Uttar Pradesh; **National Remote Sensing Agency,** Department of Science and Technology, No. 4 Sardar Patel Road, Secunderabad 500003, Andhra Pradesh; **Survey of India,** Surveyor General Office, P.O. Box 37, Dehra Dun 248001; **India Government Tourist Board,** 30 Rockefeller Plaza, New York, NY 10112; 212-586-4901.

Indonesia:
Badan Koordinasi Survai Dan Pemetaan Nasional [National Coordinating Body for Survey and Mapping], Jalan Raya Jakarta km 46, Cibinong, Bogor; **Department Pertambangan Dan Energi** [Ministry of Mines and Energy], Jalan Merdeka Selatan 18, Jakarta Pusat, Jakarta; **Direktorat Sumber Daya Mineral** [Directorate of Mineral Resources], Jalan Diponegoro 57, Bandung; **Direktorat Tata Guna Tanah** [Directorate of Land Use], Ministry of Internal Affairs, Jalan Sisingamangaraja 2, Jakarta Selatan, Kebayoran, Jakarta; **Jawatan Pemotretan Udara** [Aerial Mapping Service], Komplek Lapangan Udara Halim Perdanadusuma, Jakarta; **Jawatan Topografi Angkatan Darat** [Army Topographic Service],

Jalan Gunung Sahari 90, Jakarta; **Pusat Survai dan Pemetaan A.B.R.J.** [Armed Forces Surveys and Mapping Agency], Jalan Dr. Wahidin I/11, Jakarta Pusat, Jakarta.

Iran:
National Cartographic Center, P.O. Box 1844, Mahrabad, Tehran; **National Geographic Organization,** Tehran.

Iraq:
Directorate General of Geological Survey and Mineral Investigation, State Organization for Minerals, P.O. Box 986, Alwiyah, Baghdad; **State Establishement for Oil and Gas Exploration,** Iraqi National Oil Company, P.O. Box 476, Khullani Square, Baghdad; **State Establishment for Studies and Design,** Iraq State Organization for Dams, P.O. Box 11001, Karadah, Baghdad; **State Establishment for Surveying,** Ministry of Irrigation, P.O. Box 5813, Gailani Square, Baghdad; **State Organization for Groundwater Investment,** P.O. Box 3231, Waziriyah, Baghdad.

Ireland:
Ordinance Survey, Phoenix Park, Dublin 8; **Irish Tourist Board,** 590 Fifth Avenue, New York, NY 10036; 212-869-5500, Action Line for Travel agents, 800-223-6470; **Irish Tourist Board,** Suite 524, 900 17th Street, NW, Washington, DC 20006; 202-293-0317.

Israel:
Department of Surveys, Ministry of Labor, P.O. Box 14171, 1 Rehov Lincoln, Tel Avi; **Earth-Science Research Administration,** Ministry of Energy and Infrastructure, P.O. Box 1442, Jerusalem.

Italy:
Istituto Geografico Militare, Via Cesare Battisti 10, 50122 Firenze.

Ivory Coast:
Institut Geographique de Cote d'Ivoire, Ministere des Travaus Publics et des Transports, 01 BP 3862, Abidjan 01; **Societe pour le Development Minier de la Cote d'Ivoire,** B.P. 2816, Abidjan.

Jamaica:
Survey Department, P.O. Box 493, Kingston.

Japan:
Geographical Survey Institute, Ministry of Con-

struction, 1, Kitasato, Yatabe-cho, Tsukuba-gun, Ibaraki-ken 305.

Jordan:
Department of Lands and Surveys, Ministry of Finance, P.O. Box 70, Amman; **Jordan National Geographic Center,** P.O. Box 20214, Amman; **Natural Resources Authority,** P.O. Box 7, 39, or 2220, Amman.

Kenya:
Survey of Kenya, P.O. Box 30046, Nairobi.

Kuwait:
Director of Building and Survey Department, Kuwait Municipality, P.O. Box 10, Safat.

Laos:
Service Geographique Nationale, Office of the Council of Ministers, B.P. 167, Vientiane.

Lesotho:
Department of Lands, Surveys and Physical Planning, Ministry of Interior, Chieftainship Affairs and Social Welfare, P.O. Box 174, Maseru 100, Lesotho.

Liberia:
Liberian Cartographic Service, Ministry of Lands, Mines and Energy, P.O. Box 9024, Monrovia; **Ministry of Lands, Mines and Energy,** Capitol Hill, P.O. Box 9204, Monrovia.

Libya:
Department of Surveying Secretariat of Planning, P.O. Box 600, Tripoli; **Geological Department,** Faculty of Science, Al-Fateh University, P.O. Box 398, Tripoli; **Planning Division,** Secretariat of Agrarian Reform and Land Reclamation, P.O. Box 190, Tripoli.

Liechtenstein:
Landesbauamt des Furstentums Liechtenstein, Stadte 49, 9490 Vaduz; **Landwirtschaftamt** [Agricultural Office], Stadtle 49, 9490 Vaduz.

Luxembourg:
Administration du Cadastre et de la Topographic, 54 Avenue Gaston Diderich.

Madagascar:
Institut National de Geodesie et de Cartographic, 3 Lalana J.H. Ravelomanantsoa, B.P. 323, Andohalo, Antananarivo; **Ministere de l'Industrie, de l'Energie at de Mines,** B.P. 280, Antananarivo.

Malawi:
Survey Department, Ministry of Natural Resources, P.O. Box 349, Blantyre.

Malaysia:
Directorate of National Mapping, Banguanan Ukor, 4th Floor, Jalan Gurney, Kuala Lumpur.

Mali:
Institut National de Topographie, B.P. 240, Bamako.

Malta:
Information Division, Augerge de Castille, Valletta.

Mauritania:
Service Topographique et Cartographique, B.P. 237, Nouakchott.

Mauritius:
Departmento Geografico Militar, Servicio Cartografico, Secretaria de la Defensa Nacional, Lomas de Sotelo, Mexico 8, D.F.

Mongolia:
Institute of Geography and Permafrost Studies, Academy of Sciences, Ulan Bator.

Morocco:
Direction de la Recherche Agronomique, Service Cartographique des Sols et de l'Erosion, Avenue de la Victoire, B.P. 415, Rabat; **Ministere de l'Agriculture et de la Reforme Agraire,** Quartier Administratif, Rabat.

Mozambique:
Direccao Nacional de Geografia e Cadastro [National Directorate for Geography and Mapping], Avenida Josina Machel, 589/Maputo, P.O. Box 288, Maputo; **Secretariado de Estado do Carvao e Hidrocarbonetos** [State Secretariat for Coal and Hydrocarbons], Avenida Samora Machel, 39, P.O. Box 2904, Maputo.

Namibia:
The Surveyor General, P/B 13182 Kaiser Street, Windhoek.

Nepal:
Survey Department, Ministry of Land Reform, Dilli Bazar, Kathmandu.

Netherlands:
Dienst van het Kadaster, Waltersingel 1, 7314 NK Apeldoorn; **Topografische Dienst,** Westvest 9, 2611 AX Delft.

New Caledonia:
Service Topographique, Territorial Administration Center, Avenue Paul Doumer, Noumea Nouvelle.

New Zealand:
Surveyor General, Head Office, Department of Lands and Survey, Private Bag, Charles Ferguson Building, Wellington.

Nicaragua:
Instituto Geografico Nacional, Ministerio de Fomento y Obras Publicas, Apartado Postal 2120, Managua.

Nigeria:
Cartographic Section, Geological Survey Department, P.M.B. 2007, Kaduna South, Kaduna State; **Direction du Service Topographique et du Cadastre,** Ministere des Finances, B.P. 250, Niamey; **Surveys Division,** Federal Ministry of Works, Igbosere Road at Okjesuna Street, Lagos.

North Korea:
Geology and Geography Research Institute, Academy of Sciences, Mammoon-dong, Central District, P'yongyang.

Norway:
Continental Shelf Institute, Hakon Magnussonsgt 1B, Postboks 1883, 7001 Trondheim; **Norsk Polarinstitutt,** [Norwegian Institute for Polar Affairs], Rolfstangveien 12, Postboks 158, 1330 Oslo Lufthavn.

Oman:
Ministry of Defense, P.O. Box 113, Muscat.

Pakistan:
Survey of Pakistan Shahrah-i-Muhammad Raza Shah Pehlavi, Post Box 10, Rawalpindi.

Panama:
Instituto Geografico Nacional, Apartado Postal 5267, Zona 5.

Papua New Guinea:
Department of Natural Resources, Papua.

Paraguay:
Instituto Geografico Militar, Avenida Artigas Casi Peru, Asuncion.

Peru:
Direccion de Hidrografia y Navegacion de la Marina, Calle Saenz Pena No. 590, La Punta (CAllao), Casilla Postal #80, Callao, Lima; **Instituto**

Geografico Militar, Av. Andres Aramburu 1198, Apartado 2038, Lima; **Instituto Geologico Minero y Metalurgico,** Pablo Bermudez 211, Apartado 889, Lima; **Oficina Nacional de Evaluacion de Recursos Naturales,** Calle 17 #355, Urb. El. Palomar, San Isidro, Lima; **Servicio Aerofotografico Nacional,** Base Aerea "Las Palmas," Barranco, Lima.

Philippines:
Bureau of Coast and Geodetic Survey, 421 Barraca Street, Binondo, Manila 2807.

Poland:
Glowny Urzad Geodezji i Kartografii, [Coordinative and Administrative Body], ul. Jasna 2/4, 00-013 Warszawa; **Instytut Geodezji i Kartografii,** ul. Jasna 2/4, 00-013 Warszawa; **Instytut Geografii i Przestrzennego Zagospodarowania PAN,** ul. Krakowskie Przedmiescie 30, 00-325 Warszawa; **Instytut Geologiczny,** ul. Rakowiecka 4, 00-975 Warszawa.

Portugal:
Instituto Geografico e Cadastral, Ministerio das Finances e do Plano, Praca da Estrela, 1200 Lisboa.

Qatar:
Department of Petroleum Affairs, Ministry of Finance and Petroleum, P.O. Box 83, Doha; **Industrial Development Technical Center,** P.O. Box 2599, Doha.

Romania:
Institutul de Geografie si Geologie, Str. Dimitrie Racovita no. 9, Bucharest.

Rwanda:
Ministere des Ressources Naturelles, B.P. 413, Kigali.

Saudi Arabia:
Ministry of Petroleum and Mineral Resources, Aerial Survey Department, P.O. Box 247, Riyadh.

Senegal:
Institut Geographique National, 7, rue Mermoz, B.P. 4016, Dakar; **Service Geographique du Senegal,** 14, rue Victor Hugo, B.P. 740, Dakar.

Sierra Leone:
Surveys and Land Division, Ministry of Lands and Mines, and Labor, New England, Freetown.

Singapore:
Head Mapping Unit, Ministry of Defense, Dover Road Camp I, Dover Crescent, 0513; **Land Surveyors Board,** Ministry of Law, 3rd Floor, National Development Building, Maxwell Road, 0106.

Somalia:
Survey and Mapping Department, Ministry of Defense, P.O. Box 24, Mogadishu.

South Africa:
Director of Surveys and Mapping, Private Bag, Mowbray, Cape Town, 7700.

South Korea:
Hydrographic Office, Ministry of Transportation, 355, Chungrim-dong, Chung-Gu, Seoul; **Korea Institute of Energy and Resources,** 219-5, Garibong-dong, Guro-Gu, Seoul; **Korean Society of Geodesy,** Photogrammetry and Cartography, 18, Kyonam-dong, Jongro-Gu, Seoul.

Spain:
Direccion General del Instituto Geografico Nacional, General Ibanez Ibero, 3, Madrid 3; **Real Sociedad Geografica,** Valverde 22, Madrid 13.

Sri Lanka:
Surveyor-General's Office, Kirula Road, Colombo 5.

Sudan:
Ministry of Internal Affairs, Survey Department, P.O. Box 306, Khartoum.

Surinam:
Centraal Bureau Luchtkaartering, P.O. Box 971, Dr. Sophie Redmondstraat 131, Paramaribo.

Swaziland:
Department of Surveys, Ministry of Works, Power and Communications, P.O. Box 58, Mbabane.

Sweden:
Statens Lantmateriverk, [The National Landsurvey of Sweden] S-801 12 Gavle.

Switzerland:
Bundesamt fur Landestopographie, [Federal office for Topographical Survey], Seftigenstrasse 264, CH-3084 Wabern.

Syria:
National Remote Sensing Center, Ministry of Electricity, Sultan Salim St., Damascus; **Service Geographique de l'Armee,** Ministry of Defense, P.O. Box 3094, Damascus.

Taiwan:
Agriculture and Forestry Aerial Survey Team, Taiwan Provincial Forestry Bureau, 101-1, Ho Ping West Road, Section 2, Taipei; **Central Geological Survey,** P.O. Box 968, Taipei; **Combined Service Forces,** Ministry of National Defense, Chieh Shou Hall, Chungking South Road, Taipei.

Tanzania:
Mapping Production, Ministry of Lands, Housing and Urban Development, P.O. Box 9301, Dar es Salaam; **Survey and Mapping Division,** Ministry of Lands, Housing and Urban Development, P.O. Box 9201, Dar es Salaam.

Thailand:
Energy Investigation Division, National Energy Administration, Ministry of Science, Technology and Energy, Kasatsuk Bridge, Bangkok 10500; **Geological Survey Division,** Department of Mineral Resources, Rama VI Road, Bangkok 10600; **National Energy Administration,** Ministry of Science, Technology and Energy, Kasatsuk Bridge, Bangkok 10500; **National Research Council of Thailand,** Ministry of Science, Technology and Energy, 196 Paholyothin Road, Bangkok 10900; **Remote Sensing Division,** National Research Council of Thailand, Ministry of Science, Technology and Energy, 196 Paholyothin Road, Bangkok 10900; **Royal Thai Survey Department,** Supreme Command Headquarters, Ministry of Defense, Rachinee Road, Bangkok 10200; **Topographical Survey Division,** Royal Irrigation Department, Ministry of Agriculture and Cooperatives, Tivanondh Road, Amphoe Pakkred, Nonthaburi 11120.

Togo:
Service Topographique, Ministrere des Mines, de l'Energie, des Ressources Hydrauliques et des Travaux Publics, B.P. 500, Lome.

Trinidad and Tobago:
Lands and Surveys Department, Mapping and Control Section, 2b, Richmond Street, Port-of-Spain.

Turkey:
General Directorate of Turkish Mapping Service, Ministry of Defense, Cebecci-Ankara.

Uganda:
Department of Lands and Surveys, P.O. Box 7061, Kampala.

United Kingdom:
Directorate of Military Survey, Ministry of Defense, Elmwood Avenue, Feltham, Middlesex TW13 7AE; **Directorate of Overseas Surveys,** Foreign and Commonwealth Office, Kingston Road, Tolworth, Surbiton, Surrey KT5 9NS; **Ordnance Survey,** Ramsey Road, Maybush, Southampton S09 4DH; **British Tourist Authority,** 3rd Floor, 40 W. 57th Street, New York, NY 10019; 212-581-4708.

Union of Soviet Socialist Republics:
Main Administration for Geodesy and Cartography, Applied Geodesy SRI, Novosibirsk, NII Prikladnoy Geodezii.

Upper Volta:
Direction du Cadastre et Topographie, Service Topographique, Ministere des Finances et du Commerce, B.P. 7054, Ouagadougou.

Uruguay:
Direccion de Topografia, Ministerio de Transporte and Obras Publicas, Rincon 561 2d Piso, Montevideo; **Servicio Geografico Militar,** Avenida 8 de Octubre 3255, Montevideo; **Servicio de Hidrografia de la Marina,** Capurpo 980, Montevideo.

Venezuela:
Direccion de Cartografia Nacional, Edificio Camejo, Piso 2, Ofic. 230, Centro Simon Bolivar, Caracas.

Vietnam:
Service Geographique Nationale, Ministere de la Defense Nationale, Dalat.

West Germany:
Arbeitsgemeinshaft der Vermessungsverwaltungen der Laender der Bundesrepublik Deutschland, Warmbuechenkamp 2, 3000 Hannover 1; **Bundesminister der Verteidigung,** Streitkraefteamt, Militaerisches Geowesen, Theaterplatz 10-18, 5300 Bonn 2; **Institut fur Angewandte Geodaesie,** Richard-Strauss-Allee 11, 6000 Frankfurt am Main 70; **German National Tourist Office,** 33rd Floor, 747 Third Avenue, New York, NY 10017; 212-308-3300.

Western Samoa:
Lands and Survey Department, Main Beach Road, Apia.

Yemen: Ministry of Public Works, Khormaksar, Aden.

Yugoslavia:
Institut za kartografiju, |Institute for Cartography|, 39, Bulevar Vojvode Misica, 11000 Belgrade; **Federal Administration for International Scientific, Educational, Cultural and Technical Cooperation,** 29, Kosancicev venac, 11000 Belgrade.

Zaire:
Institut Geographique du Zaire, 106 Blvd du 30 Juin, B.P. 3086, Kinshasa.

Zambia:
Survey Department, Ministry of Lands and Natural Resources, Mulungushi House, P.O. Box 50397, Lusaka.

Zimbabwe:
Department of the Surveyor General, Ministry of Lands, Resettlement, and Rural Development, P.O. Box 8099, Causeway, Harare.

Appendix D

Selected Map Libraries

The following are substantial map libraries and collections in the United States and Canada:

United States:

Alabama:
Auburn University, Special Collections Department, Auburn, AL 36830; 205-826-4500; **Birmingham Public Library,** Rucker Agee Cartographic Collection, 2020 7th Ave., North Birmingham, AL 35202; 205-254-2534; **University of Alabama,** Department of Geology and Geography, P.O. Box 1945, University, AL 35486; 205-348-5095.

Alaska:
Alaska Division of State Libraries and Museums, Alaska Historical Library, Pouch 5, Juneau, AK 99811; 907-465-2925; **U.S. Fish and Wildlife Service,** Bureau of Commercial Fisheries, Fisheries Research Library, Box 155, Auke Bay, AK 99821; 907-789-7321, ext. 125.

Arizona:
Arizona Historical Society, Research Library, Map Section, East Second Street, Tucson, AZ 85710; 602-882-5774; **University of Arizona,** Library, Map Collection, Tucson, AZ 85721; 602-884-2596.

Arkansas:
University of Arkansas, Department of Geology, Fayetteville, AR 72701; 501-575-3355; **University of Arkansas,** Mullins Library, Reference Department and Special Collections, Fayetteville, AR 72701; 501-575-4101.

California:
Berkeley Public Library, Berkeley, CA 94701; 415-843-0800; **California State University,** Library, Collection for the History of Cartography, P.O. Box 4150, Fullerton, CA 92634; 714-870-3444; **California State University,** Library, Government Publications and Maps, Chico, CA 95929; 916-895-6802; **University of California,** General Library, Map Room, Berkeley, CA 94720; 415-642-4940; **Whittier College,** Department of Geology, Fairchild Aerial Photograph Collection, Whittier, CA 90608; 213-693-0771.

Colorado:
Marathon Oil Company, Research Center Library, Littleton, CO 80120; 303-794-2601; **U.S. Geological Survey,** Library, Stop 914, Box 25046, Denver Federal Center, Denver, CO 80225; 303-234-4133; **University of Colorado,** Map Library, Guggenheim Building, Boulder, CO 80302; 303-492-7578.

Connecticut:
Yale University, Library, Map Collection, Box 1630A Yale Station, New Haven, CT 06520; 203-436-8638.

Delaware:
University of Delaware, Morris Library, Map Library, Newark, DE 19711; 302-738-2238.

District of Columbia:
National Capital Planning Commission, Office of Graphic Services, 1325 G Street, NW, Washington, DC 20576; 202-382-1895; **National Geographic Society,** Map Library, 17th and M Streets, NW, Washington, DC 20036; 202-296-7500; **Pan American Union,** Columbus Memorial Library, Washington, DC 20006; 202-381-8254; **Defense Mapping Agency Nautical Chart Library,** Washington, DC 20390; 202-763-1216; **Defense Mapping Agency Topographic Center,** Information Resources Division, 6500 Brooks Lane, Washington, DC 20315; 202-227-2036; **Department of the Navy,** Library, Building 220, Washington Yard, Washington, DC 20374; 202-433-4131; **Federal Highway Administration,** Cartographic Section, Washington, DC 20590; **Library of Congress,** Geography and Map Division, Washington, D.C. 20540; 202-287-6277; **National Archives and Records Service,** Cartographic Archives Division, 8th and Pennsylvania Avenue, NW, Washington, DC 20408; 202-962-3181; **U.S. Postal Service,** Library, 475 L'Enfant Plaza West, Washington, DC 20260; 202-245-4023.

Florida:
Florida State University, Strozier Library, Map Section, Tallahassee, FL; 904-644-3764; **University of Florida,** University Library, Map Library, Gainesville, FL 32611; 904-392-0803.

Georgia:
Georgia Historical Society, 501 Whitaker Street, Savannah, GA 31401; 912-944-2128; **University of Georgia,** Library, Science Library, Map Collection, Athens, GA 404-542-4535

Hawaii:
Bernice P. Bishop Museum, Pacific Scientific Information Center, P.O. Box 6037, Honolulu, HI 96818; 808-847-3511; **University of Hawaii,** Library, Map Collection, 2550 The Mall, Honolulu, HI 96822; 808-948-8263.

Idaho:
Boise State University, Library Map Section, 1910 College Blvd., Boise, ID 83725; 208-385-3958.

Illinois:
Illinois Historical Survey Library, 1a University Library, University of Illinois, Urbana, IL 61801; 217-333-1777; **Rand McNally,** Map Library, P.O. Box 7600, Chicago, IL 60680; 312-673-9100, ext. 516; **Southern Illinois University,** Morris Library, Science Division, Map Library, Carbondale, IL 62901; 618-453-2700.

Indiana:
Indiana Historical Society Library, 140 North Senate Avenue, Indianapolis, IN 46204; 317-633-4976; **Indiana State University,** Department of Geography-Geology, Departmental Library, Terre Haute, IN 47809; **Indiana University,** Department of Geology and Indiana Geological Survey, Geology Library, 1005 East 10th Street, Bloomington, IN 47401; 812-337-7170.

Iowa:
Iowa State University, Library, Map Room, Ames, IA 50010; 515-294-3956; **University of Iowa,** Libraries, Map Collection, Harlan, IA 52242; 319-353-4467.

Kansas:
Kansas State Historical Society, 120 W. 10th, Topeka, KS 66612; 913-296-3251; **University of Kansas,** Map Library, Room 110 Kenneth Spencer Research Library, Lawrence, KS 66045; 913-864-4420.

Kentucky:
University of Kentucky, Geology Library, 100 Bowmann Hall, Lexington, KY 40506; 606-258-5730; **University of Kentucky,** King Library Map Department, Lexington, KY 40506; 606-257-2660.

Louisiana:
Louisiana State University, Department of Archives and Manuscripts, Baton Rouge, LA 70803; 504-388-2240; **Louisiana State University,** School of Geoscience Map Library, Baton Rouge, LA 70803; 504-388-5318.

Maine:
Colby College, Geology Department, Map Collection, Waterville, ME 04901; 207-873-1131, ext. 241; **Maine Historical Society,** 485 Congress Street, Portland, ME 04111; 207-774-1822.

Maryland:
Johns Hopkins University, Eisenhower Library, Audio-Visual and Map Room, Baltimore, MD 21218; 301-366-3300, ext. 842; **National Oceanic and Atmospheric Administration,** Atmospheric Sciences Library, Room 806, 8060 13th Street, Silver Spring, MD 20910; 301-427-7800; **National Ocean Survey,** Map Library, 6001 Executive Blvd., Rockville, MD 20852; 301-496-8031; **University of Maryland,** McKeldin Library, Documents/Map Room, College Park, MD 20742; 301-454-3020

Massachusetts:
Clark University, Graduate School of Geography, Guy H. Burnham Map and Aerial Photograph Library, Woods Hole, MA 01610; 617-793-7322; **Harvard University,** Department of Geological Sciences, Map Room, 24 Oxford Street, Cambridge, MA 02138; 617-868-7600, ext. 2029; **Massachusetts Institute of Technology,** Boston Stein Club Map Room, Room 14S-100, Cambridge, MA 02139; 617-253-5685; **University of Massachusetts,** Morrill Library, Map Room, Amherst, MA 01002; 413-545-2733; **Woods Hole Oceanographic Institution,** Chart and Map Reference Library, Woods Hole, MA 02543; 617-548-1400, ext. 471.

Michigan:
Eastern Michigan University, Center of Educational Resources, Map Library, Ypsilanti, MI 48197; 313-487-3191; **Northern Michigan University,** Geography Department, Map Library, Marquette; MI 49855; 906-227-2500; **University of Michigan,** Harlan Hatcher Graduate Library, Map

Room, Room 825, Ann Arbor, MI 48104; 313-764-0407.

Minnesota:
Carleton College, Department of Geology, Map Library, Northfield, MN 55057; 507-645-4431, ext. 424; **Mankato State College,** Memorial Library, Map Room, Mankato, MN 56001; 507-389-1913; **University of Minnesota,** Geology Library, Map Room, 204 Pillsbury Hall, Minneapolis, MN 55455; 612-373-4062.

Mississippi:
Mississippi Geological Survey, Library, Jackson, MS; 601-354-6228; **University of Mississippi,** Library, Documents Department, University, MS 38677; 601-232-7091.

Missouri:
Kansas City Public Library, Business and Technical Department, Map Room, 311 East 12th Street, Kansas City, MO 64106; 816-221-2685; **Defense Mapping Agency,** Aerospace Center (Attn: RDSL), St. Louis Air Force Station, Kansas City, MO 63118; 314-268-4841; **Washington University,** Earth and Planetary Sciences Library, Kansas City, MO 63130; 314-863-0100.

Montana:
Montana State University, Department of Earth Sciences, University Map Library, Bozeman, MT 59715; 406-994-3331; **University of Montana,** Library, Documents Division, Missoula, MT 59801; 406-243-6700.

Nebraska:
University of Nebraska, Geology Library, Lincoln, NE 68508; 402-472-2653; **University of Nebraska,** Map Library, 016 Avery Hall, Lincoln, NE 68508; 402-472-2865

Nevada:
Nevada Historical Society, Box 1129, Reno, NV 89504; 702-784-6397; **University of Nevada, Reno,** Library, Reno, NV 89507; 702-784-6596.

New Hampshire:
Dartmouth College, Library, Map Room, Hanover, NH 03755; 603-646-2579; **Keene State College,** Map Library, Keene, NH 04341; 603-352-1909, ext. 236.

New Jersey:
General Drafting Co. Inc., Library, Canfield Road, Convent Station, 07961; 201-538-7600, ext. 56;

Princeton University, Library, Map Division, Princeton, NJ 08540; 609-452-3214; **Rutgers University,** Alexander Library, Reference Department, Government Publications Unit, New Brunswick, NJ 08901; 201-932-7526.

New Mexico:
New Mexico Institute of Mining and Technology, Serials Department, Martin Speare Memorial Library, Socorro, NM 87801; 505-835-5416; **University of New Mexico,** Zimmerman Library, Special Collections Department, Map Collection, Albuquerque, NM 87131; 505-277-4800.

New York:
Colgate University, Geography Department, Hamilton, NY 13346; 315-824-4042; **Engineering Societies Library,** 345 East 47th Street, NY, NY 10017; 212-752-6800; **New York Public Library,** Map Division, Fifth Avenue and 42nd Street, NY, NY 10018; 212-790-6286; **New York Department of Transportation,** Map Information Unit, State Campus, Building 4, Room 105, Albany, NY 12232; 518-457-4755; **State University of New York at Binghamton,** Science Library, Map Room, Binghamton, NY 13901; 607-798-2219; **United Nations,** Dag Hammarskjold Library, Map Collection Unit, New York, NY 10017; 212-PL4-1234, ext. 834; **U.S. Military Academy,** Department of Earth, Space and Graphic Sciences, Map Library, West Point, NY 10996; 914-938-2302.

North Carolina:
Appalachian State University, Geography Department, Map Library, Boone, NC 28608; 704-262-3000; **University of North Carolina,** Library, Maps Collection, Chapel Hill, NC 27514; 919-933-3028

North Dakota:
Minot State College, Science Division, Map Library, Minot, ND 58701; 701-838-6101, ext. 271; **North Dakota State University,** Library, Fargo, ND 58102; 701-237-8876.

Ohio:
Kent State University, Map Library, Kent OH 44242; 216-672-2243; **Ohio State University,** Map Library, Room 428 Main Library, 1858 Neil Avenue, Columbus, OH 43210; 614-422-2393; **Ohio University,** Alden Library, Athens, OH 45701; 614-594-7275

Oklahoma:
Oklahoma State University, Library, Map Collection, Stillwater, OK 74074; 405-372-6211, ext. 6136; **University of Oklahoma,** Bizzel Memorial Library, Map Library, 401 West Brooks Street, Norman, OK 73069; 405-325-3141.

Oregon:
Oregon State University, William Jasper Kerr Library, Corvallis, OR 97331; 503-754-2971.

Pennsylvania:
Free Library of Philadelphia, Map Collection, Logan Square, Philadelphia, PA 19107; 215-686-4622; **Pennsylvania Historical and Museum Commission,** Bureau of Archives and History, Division of Archives and Manuscripts, Harrisburg, PA 17120; 717-787-3023; **Temple University,** Samuel Paley Library, Map Room, Philadelphia, PA 19122; 215-787-8212; **University of Pennsylvania,** Geology Map Library, Hayden Hall, Philadelphia, PA 19174; 215-243-5630

Puerto Rico:
University of Puerto Rico, General Library, Documents and Maps Room, Rio Piedras, PR 00931.

Rhode Island:
Brown University, Library Documents Division, Providence, RI 02912; 401-863-2517.

South Carolina:
Department of Archives and History, P.O. Box 11669, Capitol Station, Columbia, SC 29211; 803-758-5816; **University of South Carolina,** Department of Geography, Geography Map Depository, Columbia, SC 29208; 803-777-2802.

South Dakota:
Historical Resource Center, Memorial Building, Pierre, SD 57501; 605-224-3615.

Tennessee:
Tennessee Valley Authority, Maps and Surveys Branch, Map Information and Record Unit, 100 Haney Building, Chattanooga, TN 37401; 615-755-2122; **Tennessee Valley Authority,** Maps and Engineering Records, 416 Union Avenue, Knoxville, TN 37902; 615-522-7181; **University of Tennessee,** Department of Geography, Map Library, Knoxville, TN 37916; 615-974-2418

Texas:
Southern Methodist University, Science Library, Edwin J. Foscue Map Library, Dallas, TX 75275;

214-692-2285; **Texas A & M University,** Sterling C. Evans Library, Map Room, College Station, TX 77843; 713-845-1451.

Utah:
Brigham Young University, Lee Library, Documents and Maps Sections, Provo, UT 84602; 801-347-1211.

Vermont:
Middlebury College, Map Library, 410 Warner Science Hall, Middlebury, VT 05753; 802-366-4051; **University of Vermont,** Guy W. Bailey Library, Map Room, Burlington, VT 05401; 802-656-2020.

Virgin Islands:
St. Thomas Public Library, P.O. Box 390, Charlotte Amalie, St. Thomas, VI 00801; 774-0630.

Virginia:
American Automobile Association Library, 8111 Gatehouse Road, Falls Church, VA 22042; 703-222-6466; **U.S. Geological Survey,** Library, Reston, VA 22092; 703-680-6679; **University of Virginia,** Alderman Library, Public Documents Section, Map Collection Center, Charlottesville, VA 22901; 703-924-3133.

Washington:
University of Washington, Library, Map Center, Seattle, WA 98105; 206-543-5244; **Western Washington State College,** Map Library, Bellingham, WA 98225; 206-676-3272.

West Virginia:
Department of Archives and History, Room E-400, Capitol Building, Charleston, WV 25305; 304-348-2277; **Geological and Economic Survey,** Library, Morgantown, WV 26506; 304-296-4461.

Wisconsin:
University of Wisconsin, Map and Air Photo Library, 384 Science Hall, Madison, WI 53706; 608-262-1471; **University of Wisconsin-Milwaukee,** Map and Air Photo Library, 385 Sabin Hall, 3407 North Downer Avenue, Milwaukee, WI 53201; 414-963-4871; **University of Wisconsin-Eau Claire,** Simpson Geographic Research Center, Geography Department, Eau Claire, WI 54701; 715-836-3362.

Wyoming:
University of Wyoming, Coe Library, Documents Division, Box 3334, University Station, Laramie, WY 82071; 307-766-2174; **State Engineers Office,**

State Office Building, Cheyenne, WY 82001; 307-777-7354.

Canada

Alberta:

Alberta Energy and Natural Resources, Renewable Resources Technical Division, Map & Photo Library, Room 325, Natural Resources Building, 109 Street & 99 Avenue, Edmonton, Alberta T5K 2E1; 403-427-7417; **University of Calgary Library,** Maps Library, Calgary, Alberta T2N 1N4; 403-284-5969.

British Columbia:

Simon Fraser University, Library, Social Sciences Division, Map Collection, Burnaby, BC V5A 1S6; 604-291-4656; **University of British Columbia,** Library, Map Division, 2075 Wesbrook Place, Vancouver, BC V6T 1W5; 604-228-2231; **University of Victoria,** McPherson Library, Circulation Division, University Map Collection, Room 142, Cornett Building, Vancouver, BC V8W 2Y2; 604-477-6911.

Manitoba:

University of Manitoba, Reference Services Department, Map and Atlas Collection, Winnipeg, Manitoba R3T 2N2; 204-474-9844.

New Brunswick:

University of New Brunswick, Harriet Irving Library, Map Room, Fredericton, New Brunswick E3B 5H5; 506-453-4752.

Newfoundland:

Memorial University of Newfoundland, Department of Geography, Map Collection, St. John's, Newfoundland A1C 5S7; 709-753-1200 ext. 3448.

Nova Scotia:

Dalhousie University, Library, MacDonald Science Library, Map Collection, Halifax, Nova Scotia; 902-424-3747.

Ontario:

Carleton University, Geography Department, Map Library, Ottawa K1S 5B6; 613-231-4392; **Geological Survey of Canada,** Library, 601 Booth Street, Ottawa, Ontario K1A 0E8; 613-994-5325; **McMaster University,** Map Library, Room 137, BSB, Hamilton, Ontario L8S 4K1; 416-525-9140; **Public Archives of Canada,** National Map Collection, 395 Wellington Street, Ottawa, Ontario K1A 0N3; 613-992-0468; **Queen's University,** Geological Sciences Library, Kingston, Ontario K7L 3N6; 613-547-2653; **Soil Research Institute,** Cartographic Map Reference Library, Cartographic Section, Central Experimental Farm, Ottawa, Ontario; 613-994-9447; **University of Guelph,** McLaughlin Library, Humanities and Social Sciences Division, Map Collection, Guelph, Ontario N1G 2W1; 519-824-3150; **University of Western Ontario,** Department of Geography, Map Library, London, Ontario; 519-679-3424; **Metropolitan Toronto Central Library,** History Section, Map Room, 214 College Street, Toronto, Ontario M5T 1R3; 416-924-9511 ext. 40; **University of Toronto,** John P. Roberts Library, Map Library, 130 St. George Street, Toronto, Ontario M5S 1A1; 416-928-3372; **University of Waterloo,** Environmental Studies Library, Waterloo, Ontario N2L 3G1; 519-885-1211.

Quebec:

Ecole Polytechnique, La Bibliotheque, C.P. 6079 Succursale "A," Montreal, Quebec H3C 3A7; 514-344-4847; **McGill University,** Department of Geography, University Map Collection, P.O. Box 6070, Station "A," Montreal, Quebec H3C 3G1; 514-392-5492; **Universite du Quebec,** La Cartotheque, 300 Avenue des Ursulines, Rimouski, Quebec G5L 3A1; 418-724-1669.

Saskatchewan:

University of Regina, Division of Social Sciences, Map Library, Regina, Saskatchewan S4S 0A2; 301-584-4401.

Appendix E

Selected Map Stores

The list of map stores is constantly growing. The International Map Dealers Association, a trade association for retail map dealers, distributors, and manufacturers of maps and related products, can provide names and addresses of map dealers in your area. IMDA is located at 105 E. Court St., P.O. Box 1789, Kankakee, IL 60901; 815-939-3509.

Alabama:
Maps Unlimited, 7766 Airport Blvd., Mobile, AL 36606; **Nautical Publications,** 2625 Highland Ave. South, Birmingham, AL 35205; **Re-Print Corporation,** 2025 First Ave. North, Birmingham, AL 35203.

Arizona:
Arizona Adventures, 2716 E. Bell Rd., Phoenix, AZ 85004; **Arizona Hiking Shack,** 11645 N. Cave Creek Rd., Phoenix, AZ 85020; **Desert Mountain Sports,** 4506 N. 16th St., Phoenix, AZ 85016; **Earth Tracks,** 3644 E. McDowell Rd., Phoenix, AZ 85008; **Places & People,** 2623 N. Campbell Ave., Tucson, AZ 85719; **Valle Verde Topo Map Sales,** 71 W. Duval Mine Rd., Green Valley, AZ 85614; **Wide World of Maps,** 2626 W. Indian School Rd., Phoenix, AZ 85018; 1526 N. Scottsdale Rd., Tempe, AZ 85281; 1440 S. Country Club Dr., Mesa, AZ 85202.

Arkansas:
AAA Map Company, 6917 Geyer Spring Rd., 7N, Little Rock, AR 72209; **Shepherd's Inc.,** 603 W. Markham St., Little Rock, AR 72205.

California:
A-1 Map Center, 5511 33rd Ave., Sacramento, CA 92501; **Backpacker Shop,** 832 N. Indian Hill Blvd., Claremont, CA 91711; **Bay Marine,** 600 E. Franklin St., Monterey, CA 93940; **Bookends Bookstore,** 1014 Coombs St., Napa, CA 94559; 201 W. Napa St. #18, Sonoma, CA 95476; **Charter Maps,** 2730 N. Main St., Santa Ana, CA 92703; **Compass Maps,** 1172 Kansas Ave., Modesto, CA

95352; **Dictate & Duplicate,** 43 W. Calle Laureles, Santa Barbara, CA 93105; **Global Graphics,** 2004 Harkness St., Manhattan Beach, CA 90266; **Global Map Store,** 735 Fulton St., Fresno, CA 93726; **Map Center,** 2440 Bancroft, Berkeley, CA 94704; **Map Centre,** 2611 University Ave., San Diego, CA 92104; **Map Store,** 1634 Westwood Blvd., Los Angeles, CA 90049; **Maps Etc.,** 21919 Sherman Way, Canoga Park, CA 91303; **Mountain Man Sports,** 217 Main St., Chico, CA 95926; **Nature Store,** 1887 Solano Ave., Berkeley, CA 94703; **Pacific Map Co. Inc.,** 17000 S. Vermont Ave., Gardens, CA 90247; **Pacific Travelers Supply,** 529 State St., Santa Barbara, CA 93101; **Pack-n-Travel,** 3416 Via Oporto #102, Newport Beach, CA 92663; **Progressive Map Store,** 401 N. Fresno St., Fresno, CA 93721; **Rand McNally Map Store,** 595 Market St., San Francisco, CA 94105; **Renie's California Map Center,** 1626 W. 7th St., Los Angeles, CA 90049; **Sequoia Natural History Association,** Sequoia & Kings Canyon National Parks, Three Rivers, CA 93271; **Sports Ltd. of Long Beach,** 1628 Long Beach Blvd., Long Beach, CA 90801; **Thomas Brothers Maps,** 550 Jackson St., San Francisco, CA 94104; **Thomas Brothers Maps,** 17731 Cowan, Los Angeles, CA 92714; **Thomas Brothers Maps and Books,** 603 W. 7th St., Los Angeles, CA 90017; **Travel Centers of the World,** P.O. Box 1673, Hollywood, CA 90078; **Trail Company,** 5064 Katella Ave., Los Alamitos, CA 90720; **Travel Market,** 130 Pacific Ave. Mall, San Francisco, CA 94111; **Valley Map Center,** 12926 Saticoy St., N. Hollywood, CA 91604; **Westwide Maps Company,** 114 W. Third St., Los Angeles, CA 90013; **World Journeys,** 971-C Lomas Santa Fe Dr., Solana Beach, CA 92075.

Colorado:
Crossroads Map Co., 2717 E. Louisiana Ave., Denver, CO 80210; **Hotchkiss Inc.,** 1222 Glenarm Place, Denver, CO 80205; **Learning Materials Center,** El Paso Community College, Colorado Springs, CO 80907; **Mountain Maps,** 147 W. 3rd St., Salida, CO 81201; **Park County Historical Society,** Interpretive Association, Fairplay, CO 80440; **Pierson Graphics,** 620 13th St., Denver, CO 80216; **Wilderness Society,** 4260 E. Evans Ave., Denver, CO 80220; **YMCA of the Rockies,** Association Camp, CO 80511.

Connecticut:
Huntington's Book Stores, 65 Asylum, Hartford, CT 06105; **Map House,** 1520 Rhey Ave., Wallingford, CT 06492; **Whitlock's Inc.,** 17 Broadway, New Haven, CT 06511.

Delaware:
Explorers, Ltd., 2107 Grant Ave., Wilmington, DE 19899; **First State Map Co.,** 12 Mary Ella Dr., Wilmington, DE 19805; **Newark Newsstand,** 70 E. Main St., Newark, DE 19711; **Ninth Street Book Shop,** 110 W. 9th St., Wilmington, DE 19801.

District of Columbia:
Hudson Trail Outfitters, 4437 Wisconsin Ave. NW, Washington, DC 20015; 529 14th St. NW, Washington, DC 20045; **Lloyd Books,** 3145 Dumbarton St. NW, Washington, DC 20007; **The Map Store, Inc.,** 1636 Eye St. NW, Washington, DC 20006; **National Geographic Bookstore,** 17th and M Sts. NW, Washington, DC 20036.

Florida:
Central Florida Map Company, 2216 Vincent Rd., Orlando, FL 32817; **Champion Map Corp.,** 200 Fentress Blvd., Daytona Beach, FL 32014; **Map and Globe Store,** 1120 E. Colonial Dr., Orlando, FL 32807; **Map World,** 2220 4th St. N., St. Petersburg, FL 33713.

Georgia:
Borders Book Shop, 3655 Roswell Rd. NE, Atlanta, GA 30342; **Lattitudes,** 2246 Perimeter Mall, P.O. Box 467518, Atlanta, GA 30346; **Oxford Book Store,** 2345 Peachtree Rd. NE, Atlanta, GA 30305.

Hawaii:
Pacific Map Center, 647 Auahi St., Honolulu, HI 96813; **Whole Earth Bookstore & Wilderness Shop,** 2743 S. King St., Honolulu, HI 96815.

Idaho:
Hunt Enterprises, 6208 Cassia St., Boise, ID 83709; **Sawtooth Mountaineering,** 5200 Fairview Ave., Boise, ID 83704; **Western Auto Association Store,** 358 Yellowstone, Pocatello, ID 83201.

Illinois:
Rand McNally Map Store, 23 E. Madison St., Chicago, IL 60602; **Sidwell Company,** 28 W. 240 North Avenue, W. Chicago, IL 60185; **Suburban Map Store,** 910 Riverside Dr., Unit 2, Elmhurst, IL 60126; **Top of the World Store,** 111 W. Washington, Urbana, IL 60187.

Indiana:
George F. Cram Co. Inc., 301 S. LaSalle, P.O. Box 426, Indianapolis, IN 46201; **Map World,** 645 Eastern Blvd., Clarksville, IN 47130; **Odyssey Map Store,** 222 E. Market St., Indianapolis, IN 46204; **Print Graphics,** 2505 E. 52nd, Indianapolis, IN 46205; **Riegel's Inc.,** 624 S. Calhoun St., Ft. Wayne, IN 46802.

Iowa:
Haunted Bookshop, 227 S. Johnson St., Iowa City, IA 52240; **Oak Ridge Sports Inc.,** 117 W. 11th St., Dubuque, IA 52001; **Robert's Maps,** 811 Locust St., Des Moines, IA 50309; **Travel Genie,** 113 Colorado Ave., Ames, IA 50010; **University Bookstore,** Iowa State University, Ames, IA 50010.

Kansas:
Forsyth Travel Library, 9154 W. 57th St., Shawnee Mission, KS 66201; **McCleod's Inc.,** 2226 E. Douglas St., Wichita, KS 67203; **Rector's Bookstore,** 206 E. Douglas Ave., Wichita, KS 67202; **Sportsmen's Maps Headquarters,** 333 E. English St., Wichita, KS 67202; **Superior School Supply Center,** 241 N. Hydraulic, Wichita, KS 67214; **Trail-Phernalia Shop,** 2018 S. Ridgewood, Wichita, KS 67203.

Kentucky:
La Belle Gallery, 741 E. Chestnut, Louisville, KY

40202; **Owl and Pussycat,** 314 S. Ashland Ave., Lexington, KY 40502.

Louisiana:
Beaucoup Books, 5418 Magazine, New Orleans, LA 70130; **Carol's Map Place,** 832 Boston St. #3, Covington, LA 70433; **Globe Map Company,** 206 Milam St., Shreveport, LA 71102; **McCurnin Nautical Charts,** 2318 Woodlawn Ave., Metairie, LA 70001; **New Orleans Map Company,** 3130 Paris Ave., New Orleans, LA 70123; **Passport Map and Globe,** 3601 Johnston St., Lafayette, LA 70501; **Photomaps, Inc.,** 412 O'Keefe Ave., New Orleans, LA 70130.

Maine:
Books-N-Things, Oxford Plaza, Oxford, ME 04270; **DeLorme Mapping Co.,** P.O. Box 298, Freeport, ME 04032; **Kennebec Books,** 82 Western Ave., Augusta, ME 04330; **Macbeans of Brunswick,** Inc., 134 Maine St., Brunswick, ME 04011; **Maine Graphics,** 55 1/2 Main St., Lincoln, ME 04240.

Maryland:
Bookstall, 9927-B Falls Rd., Potomac, MD 20854; **Greetings and Readings,** 809 Taylor Ave., Towson, MD 21204; **Hudson Trail Outfitters,** 10560 Metropolitan Ave., Kensington, MD 20895; Annapolis Mall #86, Annapolis, MD 21401; 701 Russell Ave., Gaithersburg, MD 20877; 118 Shawan Rd., Cockeysville, MD 21031; **Travel Books Unlimited,** 4931 Cordell Ave., Bethesda, MD 20814.

Massachusetts:
Eastern Mountain Sports, 189 Linden St., Wellesley, MA 02181; **Globe Corner Bookstore,** 1 School St., Boston, MA 02108; **Grey Lady of the Sea Company,** Old South West, Nantucket, MA 02554; **Harvard Square Map Company,** 40 Brattle St., Cambridge, MA 02138; **Map Grotto,** 31 Homestead Circle, Hamilton, MA 01936.

Michigan:
Michigan United Conservation Clubs, 2101 Wood St., Lansing, MI 48912; **Universal Map Enterprises,** 1606 E. Michigan, Lansing, MI 48912.

Minnesota:
Books Abroad, 25 University Ave. SE, Minneapolis, MN 55414; **Hudson Map Company,** 2510 Nicollet Ave., Minneapolis, MN 55404; **Map Store,** 348 N. Robert, St. Paul, MN 55101; 120 S. 6th St., Minneapolis, MN 55402.

Mississippi:
George's Map Service, 564 Dryden Ave., Jackson, MS 39209.

Missouri:
Map and Travel Store, 3161 Fee Fee Rd., Bridgeton, MO 63044; **Wilderness, Inc.,** 911 E. Broadway, Columbia, MO 65201.

Montana:
Trail Head, 501 S. Higgins, Missoula, MT 59801; **Yellowstone Nordic,** 30 Madison, W. Yellowstone, MT 59578.

Nebraska:
Stephenson School Supply Co., 1112 O St., Lincoln, NE 68508.

New Hampshire:
Goodman's, 383 Chestnut St., Manchester, NH 03101; **Wilderness Trails, Inc.,** Pettee Brook Lane, Durham, NH 03824.

New Jersey:
Geostat Map Center, Greentree Square Center, 910 N. Route 73, Marlton, NJ 08053; Calder Shopping Center, Route 210 and 202, Morris Plains, NJ 07950; Route 206 and 518, Skillman, NJ 08558; **Geographia Map Company,** 317 St. Paul's Ave., Jersey City, NJ 07306; **Geographic Aids,** 28 Arthur Terrace (6EO), Hackettstown, NJ 07840; **Geographics Inc.,** 208 Glenridge Ave., Montclair, NJ 07042; **International Map Company,** 595 Broad Ave., Ridgefield, NJ 07657; **McCarthy Map Company,** 86 Park St., Montclair, NJ 07042.

New Mexico:
Base Camp, 121 West San Francisco Street, Santa Fe, NM 87501; **Burnt Horses Book Store,** 307 Johnson Street, Santa Fe, NM 87501; **Holman's,** 401 Wyoming Blvd. NE, Albuquerque, NM 87123; **Page One,** 11200 Montgomery Blvd. NE, Albuquerque, NM 87111; **Wilderness Society,** Catwalk Road, Glenwood, NM 88030.

New York:
Broadway Ltd. Antique Co., 2768 Broadway, New York, NY 10025; **Complete Traveler Bookstore,** 199 Madison Ave., New York, NY 10016; **Geographia Map Company,** P.O. Box 688, Times Square Station, New York, NY 10036; **Hagstrom Map & Travel Center,** 57 W. 43rd St., New York, NY 10036; **Historic Urban Plans,** Box 276, Ithaca, NY 14850; **Marshall Penn-York Co.,** 538 Eric Blvd. West, Syracuse, NY 13204; **Rand McNally Map Store,** 666 W. Third Ave., New York, NY 10017; **Sanborn Map Co.,** 629 Fifth St., Pelham, NY 10801.

North Carolina:
Geoscience Resources, 2990 Anthony Rd., P.O. Box 2096, Burlington, NC 27216; **Treasure Hutch,** 5800 Yadkinville Highway, Pfafftown, NC 27040.

North Dakota:
Book Fair, 212 DeMers Ave., Grand Forks, ND 58201; **Tel-E-Key,** Highway 2, Grand Forks, ND 58201.

Ohio:
Duttenhofer's Map Store, 210 W. McMillan, Cincinnati, OH 45219; **Leo's Book Shop,** 330 N. Superior, Toledo, OH 43604; **Ohio Canoe Adventures, Inc.,** Backpackers Shop, 5128 Colorado Ave., Sheffield Lake, OH 44054; **Wilderness Trace, Inc.,** 1295 Bethel Rd., Columbus, OH 43215.

Oklahoma:
Mosher-Adam Maps, 400 SW 25th St., Oklahoma City, OK 73109; **Topographic Mapping Co.,** 6709 N. Classen, Oklahoma City, OK 73116.

Oregon:
Book Mark, 856 Olive St., Eugene, OR 97401; **Powell's Books,** 1005 W. Burnside St., Portland OR 97209.

Pennsylvania:
Biking & Hiking, 5144 Peach St., Erie, PA 16509; **Book Swap,** 316 Horsham Rd., Horshan, PA 19044; **Alan Bradd Book Stores,** Cheltenham Shopping Center, Cheltenham, PA 19012; **Franklin Maps,** 333 S. Henderson, King of Prussia, PA 19406; **Geostat Map Center,** 125 S. 18th St., Philadelphia, PA 19103; **Pathfinder,** 1104 Carlisle Rd., Camp Hill, PA 17011; **Alfred B. Patton,** Swamp Rd. and Center, Doylestown, PA 18901; **Pilot House Inc.,** 1820 Callowhill St., Philadelphia, PA 19130; **Travel Bound Bookstore,** 2020 Smallman St., Pittsburgh PA 15222; **J.R. Weldin Company,** 415 Wood St., Pittsburgh, PA 15222.

Rhode Island:
Base Camp, 401 Kingstown Rd., Wakefield, RI 02880; **The Map Center, Inc.,** 204 Broad St., Providence, RI 02903; **Outdoorsman,** 753 Oaklawn Ave., Cranston, RI 02910.

South Carolina:
Capitol Map Supplies, 107 Charleston Highway, W. Columbia, SC 29169; **Luden Marine Supplies,** Concord at Charlotte Sts., Charlestown, SC 29401; **Map Shop,** 5-B Coffee St., Greenville, SC 29602.

Tennessee:
Footsloggers, 2220 N. Roan St., Johnson City, TN 37601; **Real Bicycle Shop,** 2001 Highland Ave., Knoxville, TN 37920.

Texas:
Allstate Map Makers, 1201 Henderson, Ft. Worth, TX 76102; **Ferguson's Map,** 175 E. Houston St., San Antonio, TX 78205; **Key Maps Inc.,** 1411 W. Alabama St., Houston, TX 77066; **Mapsco,** 5308 Maple Ave., Dallas, TX 75235; 13536 Preston Rd., Dallas, TX 75240; **One Map Place,** 11351 Harry Hines Blvd, Dallas, TX 75229; **Southwest Map,** 12215 Coit Rd., Dallas, TX 75251; **Southwest Map Drafting,** 3225 Forest Lane, Garland, TX 75042; **Venture Map & Globe,** 2130 Highland Mall, Austin, TX 78752.

Utah:
Map World, 6526 S. State, Salt Lake City, UT 84107.

Vermont:
Lost Mountain Bookshop, 6 Main St., Randolph, VT 05060.

Virginia:
Hudson Trail Outfitters, 9683 Lee Highway, Fairfax, VA 22030; **Mapcom Systems Inc.,** 6947 Hull St., Richmond, VA 23224; **Ober United Travel**

Center, 2836 Duke St., Alexandria, VA 22304.

Washington:
Arnold Map Service, 119 W. 24th St., Vancouver, WA 98660; **Metsker Map of Tacoma,** 4020 S. Steel St., Suite 107, Tacoma, WA 98409; **Pacific Northwest National Parks Association,** Mount Rainer Branch, Longmier, WA 98397; **Pioneer Maps,** 14125 NE 20th St., Bellevue, WA 98007; **Shorey Bookstore,** 110 Union St., Seattle, WA 98101.

West Virginia:
Appalachian Trail Conference, P.O. Box 236, Harper's Ferry, WV 25425; **H.T. Hall Company,** 3622 MacCorkle Avenue SE, Charleston, WV 25304; **Mountaineer Adventures,** U.S. Route 60, Falls View, WV 25411.

Wisconsin:
Clarkson Map Company, 1225 Delanglade,

Kaukauna, WI 54130; **Green Bay Map Company,** 1303 S. Webster Ave., Green Bay, WI 54301; **Milwaukee Map Service, Inc.,** 4519 W. North Ave., Milwaukee, WI 53208.

Wyoming:
Mountain Sports, 543 S. Center St., Casper, WY 82601; **Teton Mountaineering,** 86 E. Broadway, Jackson, WY 83001; **Wilderness Institute,** P.O. Box 1843, Jackson, WY 83001.

Canada:
Canada Map Company, 211 Yonge St., Toronto, Ontario, M5B 1M4; **International Book Distributors,** P.O. Box 2290, Vancouver, British Columbia V6B 3W5; **Perly's Maps,** 31 Portland St., Toronto, Ontario, M5V 2V9; **Oxford Book Shop,** 740 Richmond St., London, Ontario, N6A 1L6; **Ulysses Books and Map Distribution,** 1208 St-Denis, Montreal, Quebec, H2X 3J5.

Selected Map Terms

aeronautical chart—a map showing recognizable features as seen from the air, required for air navigation or planning around airports.

base map—a map used in the construction of other maps. The term formerly referred to what are now called "outline maps." Base maps also are known as "mother maps."

bathymetric map—a map delineating the shape of the bottom of a body of water by the use of depth contours, called "isobaths."

bench mark—a relatively permanent object, natural or artificial, bearing a marked point whose exact elevation is known. It may appear as an official government seal embedded in rock or soil.

boundary monument—any object placed on or near a boundary line to preserve and identify its location.

cadastral map—a map showing the boundaries of subdivisions of land, often including the bearings and lengths of the boundaries and the areas of individual tracts, for purposes of describing and recording ownership. It also may show culture, drainage, and other features relating to land use and value.

cartography—the art and science of making maps and charts. The term may comprise all the steps needed to produce a map: planning, aerial photography, field surveys, photogrammetry, editing, color separation, and printing. Map makers, however, tend to limit use of the term to map-finishing operations, in which the master manuscript is edited and color separations prepared for printing.

chart—any map used for nautical or aeronautical purposes, although the term is sometimes applied to describe other special-purpose maps.

contour—an imaginary line on the ground, all points of which are at the same elevation. The difference between two adjacent contour lines is known as the "contour interval."

coordinates—two-dimensional linear or angular quantities that designate the position a point occupies on a map.

cultural features—any man-made objects that are under, on, or above the ground, including roads, trails, buildings, canals, sewer systems, and boundary lines. In a broader sense, the term also applies to all names, identification, and legends on a map.

diazo process—a rapid method of copying documents in which the image is developed by exposure to ammonia, used in some types of map reproduction.

feature separation—the process of preparing a separate drawing, engraving, or negative for selected types of data in preparation of a map or chart.

flood plain—the belt of low, flat ground bordering a stream that is flooded when runoff exceeds the capacity of the stream channel.

geodesy—the science concerned with the measurement and mathematical description of the size and shape of the Earth and its gravitational field. The term also refers to large-scale, extended surveys used to determine positions and elevations of points, in which the size and shape of the Earth must be taken into account.

grid—a network of uniformly spaced parallel lines intersecting at right angles. When superimposed on a map, it usually carries the name of the projection used for the map—the "universal transverse Mercator grid," for example. The numbers and letters used to describe specific points on the grid are known as "grid coordinates."

ground survey—a survey made at ground level, as distinguished from an aerial survey taken from above ground.

hachure—a series of lines used on a map to indicate the general direction and steepness of slopes. The lines are short, heavy, and close together for steep slopes; longer, lighter, and more widely spaced for gentle slopes.

hydrology—the scientific study of the Earth's waters, especially in relation to the effects of precipitation and evaporation on the character of ground water.

imagery—visible representation of objects as detected by cameras or other sensing devices. Recording may be on photographic film or on magnetic tape for subsequent conversion and display on a computer screen.

isobath—the contour lines designating the bottom of a body of water on a bathymetric map.

latitude—the angular distance north or south from the Equator, measured in degrees, minutes, and seconds. Latitudes are sometimes called "parallels."

legend—an explanation of symbols and other information shown on a map, usually appearing as a list or table in the map's margin.

longitude—the angular distance east or west of the Greenwich meridian, measured in degrees, minutes, and seconds.

map projection—an orderly, mathematical system of parallels and meridians used to prepare a map. Several different projections are used in cartography, with the Mercator projection being most common.

mean sea level—the arithmetic mean of hourly water levels observed over a specific nineteen-year cycle. Shorter series are specified in the name—"monthly mean sea level," for example.

meridian -- a great circle passing through the geographical poles and any given point on the Earth's surface. All points on a given meridian have the same longitude.

mosaic—an assembly of aerial photographs whose edges usually have been matched to the imagery on adjoining photographs to form a continuous representation of a portion of the Earth's surface.

mother map—another name for a "base map."

multispectral scanner (MSS)—a device for sensing radiant energy of the electromagnetic spectrum used in satellite imagery.

neatline—the line that bounds the body of a map, separating it from the margin.

offshore—a comparatively flat zone of variable width that extends from the outer margin of a shoreline to the edge of the continental shelf.

orthophotograph—a photograph having the properties of an orthographic projection, derived from a conventional photo through a means that removes image displacements caused by camera tilt and terrain. An orthophotograhic map is a map produced by assembling orthophotographs at a uniform scale.

orthophotoquad—an orthophotographic map with contours and cartographic treatment.

outline map—a simple map with a single line showing only the political divisions of a continent, state, or smaller region. Also refers to what is now called a "base map."

photogrammetry—the science or art of obtaining reliable measurements or information from photographs or other sensing systems.

photomap—an aerial photograph over which additional cartographic data have been placed.

planimetric map -- a map that represents only the horizontal positions for features represented, distinguished from a topographic map by the omission of relief in measurable form.

plat—a diagram drawn to scale showing all essential data pertaining to the boundaries and subdivisions of a tract of land as determined by a survey or protraction.

prime meridian—the meridian of zero degrees, used as the origin for measurements of longitude. The meridian of Greenwich, England, is the internationally accepted prime meridian on most maps and charts, although other local or national prime meridians are sometimes used.

projection—see *map projection*.

quadrangle—a four-sided area, bounded by parallels of latitude and meridians of longitude, used as an area unit in mapping. The dimensions of a quadrangle (or "quad") need not be the same in both directions.

reconnaissance map—a map not based on rigid trigonometric surveys, but possessing detailed data, generally made from rapid surveys.

relief map—any map that is, or appears to be, three-dimensional. "Relief" refers to elevations and depressions of the land or sea bottom.

satellite imagery—see *imagery*.

scale—the relationship between a distance on a map, chart, or photograph and the corresponding distance on the Earth.

section—a unit of subdivision of a township; normally a quadrangle one mile square.

series—a group of maps produced simultaneously and designed in accordance with the same general specifications.

survey—an orderly process of determining data relating to any physical or chemical characteristics of the Earth.

thematic map—any map designed to provide information on a single topic, such as population, rainfall, or geology.

topography—the configuration of the land surface or sea bottom.

Credits

Page 4:
Permission for reproduction granted by Rockford Map Publishers, Inc.

Page 11:
Copyright © 1983 by Jesse Levine. Reprinted with permission of Laguna Sales, Inc.

Page 12:
Mercator and Peters Projection maps from *The New Cartography*, Friendship Press, New York, copyright © 1983. Used by permission.

Page 21:
Courtesy University of Minnesota, Department of Soil Science.

Page 23:
Reprinted with permission of Historic Urban Plans.

Page 27:
Reprinted with permission of the Metropolitan Washington Council of Governments, 1875 Eye Street, Washington, D.C. 20006.

Page 28:
Reprinted with permission of BikeCentennial, the Bicycle Travel Association.

Page 33:
Copyright © 1986 American Map Corporation. Reprinted with permission.

Page 35:
Reprinted with permission of the American Map Corporation.

Page 37:
Copyright © 1982 by Rand McNally & Company. Reprinted with permission.

Page 47:
Map courtesy of Dr. Karl Koenig, reproduced with permission of Basin Street Press.

Page 50:
Reproduced with permission of Sanborn Map Company.

Page 63:
Courtesy of Hansen Planetarium Publications and Marriott Library Special Collections.

Page 65:
© 1986 CNES, Courtesy SPOT Image Corporation.

Page 66:
Courtesy of Rowe and Field, Inc., 1624 S. Kentucky Ave., Evansville, Indiana 47714. Copyright © 1985.

Page 85:
Courtesy Mount Vernon Ladies' Association of the Union.

Page 89:
Reprinted with permission from Rand McNally & Company *Historical Atlas of the World*, copyright © 1965.

Page 90-91:
Copyright © 1985, Native American Science Education Association. Reproduced with permission.

Page 95:
Permission for reproduction granted by Rockford Map Publishers, Inc.

Page 103:
Reproduced with permission of Rand McNally & Company.

Page 121:
Reprinted with the permission of the Florida Trail Association, Inc.

Page 122:
Reprinted with permission of Pittmon Map Company, 930 S.E. Sandy Blvd. Portland, OR 97214; 503-232-1161.

Page 128:
Courtesy, Idaho Department of Transportation.

Page 138-139
By Tomas Filsinger. Copyright © 1981. Used with permission of Celestial Arts, P.O. Box 7327, Berkeley, CA 94707.

Page 163:
Reprinted with permission of Rand McNally & Company.

Page 193:
Reprinted with permission of Questionnaire Service Company.

Pages 194 and 195:
These maps reproduced with the permission of Strategic Locations Planning, Inc.

Page 196-197:
Much of this information was excerpted from "Globes: A Librarian's Guide to Selection and Purchase," by James Coombs, from the March 1981 issue of the *Wilson Library Bulletin*. Reprinted with permission.

Page 201:
Photograph courtesy of Hubbard Scientific, Northbrook, Illinois.

INDEX